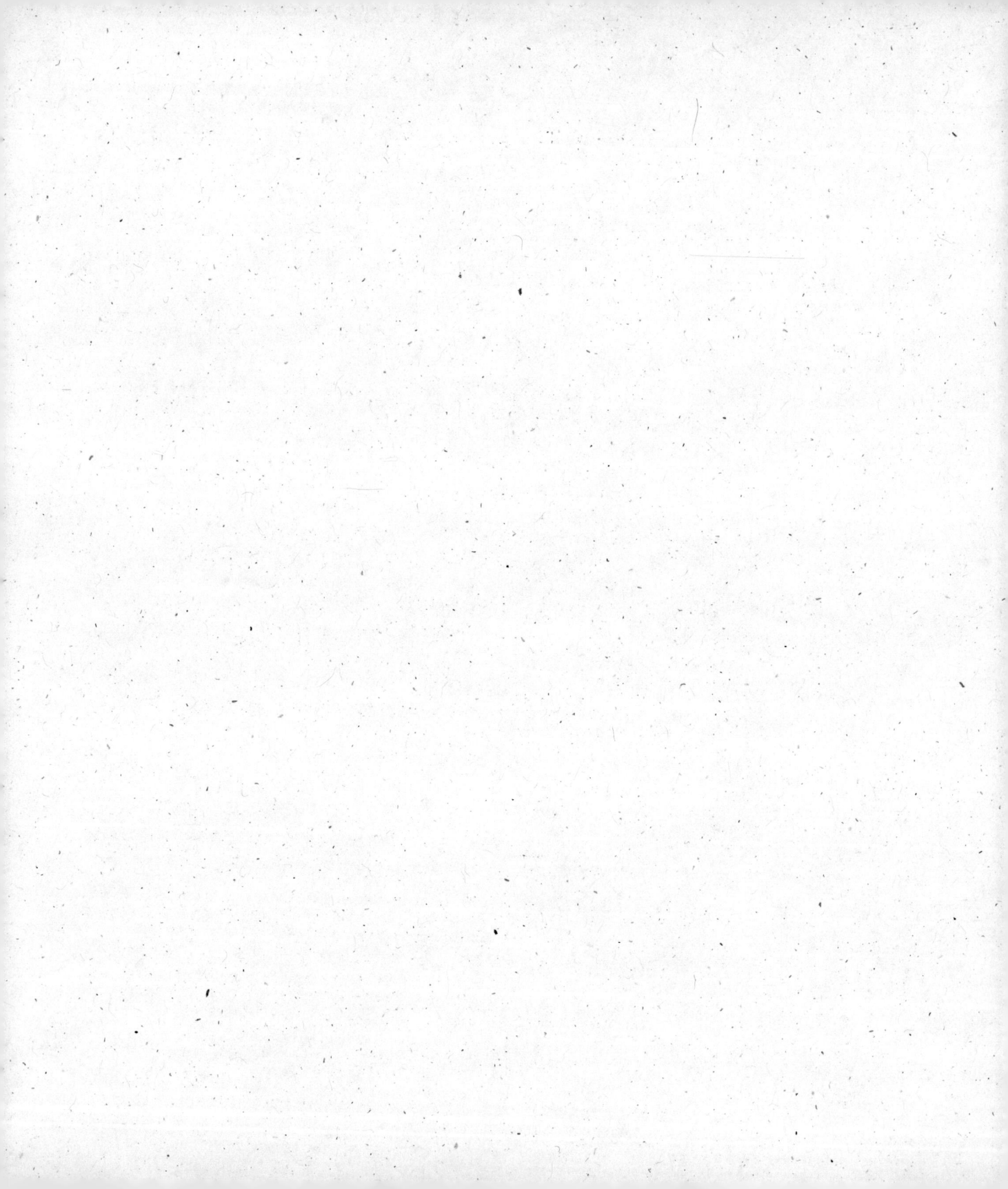

THE LARGEST ART

THE LARGEST ART

A MEASURED MANIFESTO
FOR A
PLURAL URBANISM

BRENT D. RYAN

The MIT Press   Cambridge, Massachusetts   London, England

This book was set in Adobe Garamond and Neue Haas Grotesk by the MIT Press. Printed and bound in Canada.

Library of Congress Cataloging-in-Publication Data

Names: Ryan, Brent D., 1969- author.
Title: The largest art : a measured manifesto for a plural urbanism / Brent D. Ryan.
Description: Cambridge, MA : The MIT Press, 2017. | Includes bibliographical references and index.
Identifiers: LCCN 2017017108 | ISBN 9780262036672 (hardcover : alk. paper)
Subjects: LCSH: City planning--Philosophy.
Classification: LCC NA9031 .R93 2017 | DDC 711/.4--dc23 LC record available at https://lccn.loc
    .gov/2017017108

10   9   8   7   6   5   4   3   2   1

To John Louis Ryan and Isidro Bello Verdeal
Inspirations in family, work, and life

Contents

Preface

Midway through architecture school, I first heard the term "urban design." I found the idea amusing: could one really design a city? My fellow students and I found the design of buildings to be challenging enough; designing a city seemed impossible, never mind unlikely. Gradually I warmed to the idea. At New York City's Department of City Planning, myself and my colleagues, architects all, sketched design concepts and wrote zoning regulations for growing areas of the city, mostly in Manhattan where developers sought to build more than was currently permitted. Our urban design was slow and halting; regulations took years to be enacted and we urban designers could not oblige building construction—that had to wait for market interest. Participating in New York's incremental urban design, watching its cityscape slowly respond, was a different creative satisfaction than my schoolmates possessed. As architects they could design smaller spaces where every detail reflected their hand. My urban design hand was spread widely over the cityscape, but its imprint was fainter.

When I departed New York to become involved in urban design education, I saw a different side of the discipline. As in architecture school, urban design students represented their ideas through plans, sections, and perspectives. Gazing one day at a plan for a hilltop complex with hundreds of new housing units in dozens of buildings, I was struck both by the drawing's seeming completeness and by my realization that the project, if constructed, would take years if not decades to complete. Although my students saw and represented urban design as scaled-up architecture, I knew it to be a gradual enterprise, constructed by many and built over time. Why did we design such projects as pop-up cities—ready to build, complete in and of themselves, and immune from the realities that afflicted real urban design? Maybe it was because we knew nothing else, no other means of design.

What was urban design? Was it the gradual, incremental aesthetic enterprise of my time in New York, or was it the large, ready-to-build project of our urban design studios? My colleagues, experienced and talented as they were, either did not know or could not articulate the difference. All knew that cities were constructed over time and that urban design took time as well (of course) but nevertheless, we continued teaching and producing ready-to-build models. Urban design, it seemed, was a paradoxical field whose practitioners and scholars seemed uninterested in its paradoxes. We taught urban design as a larger version of architecture, but it functioned this way only rarely in practice, where it was a slower, piecemeal art. We felt urban design to be both a formal and a social enterprise but these latter ideals contributed little to the three-dimensional schemes that constituted the discipline's visual language.

History and theory offered only intermittent assistance in resolving these paradoxes. Urban design histories were mostly turgid affairs: long, beautifully illustrated lists of cities that culminated somewhere in the twentieth century. Urban design theory consisted either of best practices—anodyne but attractive to many students—or of tracts of political economy or even philosophy that came from outside the discipline and rarely ventured far within. Most interesting by far were urban design manifestos, each purportedly a radically new take and disdaining, even attacking others. It seemed that nearly all such manifestos had been written by architects except for one, *Good City Form*, written by city planner Kevin Lynch.

Lynch was himself paradoxical; extremely well known, he remained an outlier in urban design's intellectual universe. He did not self-identify as an architect, yet all aspiring urban designers knew his first book *The Image of the City*, and he garnered no disrespect from architects. Lynch wrote about history, but his books were not histories. Nor were they best practices; except for *Image*, they were difficult to apply in classroom or studio settings. Lynch's work puzzled me mightily; well known as it was, it had failed over several decades to stimulate significant later work, either by theorists or practitioners. I found much of interest in Lynch's work, yet his observations on urban design seemed under-recognized today: contemporary discussions of "urbanism" oscillated between different visions, none of which referred to Lynch's work, almost as if his ideas had never been.

I felt differently. Lynch's thoughts mirrored my own convictions from my New York work, and they seemed more apt than ever. I knew that urban design had unique qualities—this art's vast scale, length of time for construction, and dependence on multiple builders differed radically from those of architecture. And the public was a living, active agent, enmeshed in urban design as inhabitant, shaper, and designer. Urbanism was always public.

Treating urban design as a problem that could only be solved by architectural methods explained architects' dominance in the studio, as well as the predominance of architectural thinking in much contemporary urban design dialogue. How limiting this was for urban design! Whereas urban design was nearly limitless in its qualities, architecture required a single site, often a single client, and a single form completely rendered and constructed. No wonder that urban design mimicked architecture's qualities: instead of urban design having its own inherent qualities recognized and expressed, the larger art was being shaped by its smaller sibling.

I have seen many urban design problems that architects could never solve; places that needed a design vision to save them from unintended, unshaped growth, places with multiple municipalities and thousands of inhabitants. I saw cities where thoughtless developers constructed towers wherever they wished, damaging cityscapes while citizens endured speeding cars and crumbling parks. I saw places that needed to shape their directionless growth, where inhabitants lived in shacks while shopping malls rose behind their houses and where traffic choked every road. These were not architectural problems to be solved by a single building complex, no matter how vast. Nor were these planning problems either; aesthetic visions could not come from land use plans or participatory processes. These places needed urban design, but they needed urban design of a foundationally different kind than that offered by schools, scholars, and studios.

I thought there was a lot still to say about urban design. Urban design was a distinct and unusual art; one that was needed everywhere, one whose presence was often faint, and one that was incompletely understood. Urban design needed a new manifesto that would declare it for what it really was, and that would distinguish it once and for all from the other building arts: architecture, landscape, sculpture, and land art.

I would structure this manifesto by reaffirming and describing urban design's plural qualities. Unlike other building arts, urban design was *plural* first and foremost. Why pluralism? The term was widespread in studies of politics and society; I borrowed it for its broad meaning of multiplicity or manyness. Urban design was plural in scale, time, property, agency, and form; these qualities distinguished it from its sister building arts, and it was these qualities that enabled it to be the largest of all arts.

The Largest Art is a declaration of independence for urban design, a descriptive theory explaining the many qualities that distinguish urban design, or urbanism, from its sister building arts, particularly architecture. Throughout the book, I use the two terms urbanism and urban design interchangeably; many would view the term urbanism as broader and more encompassing than urban design, but this larger term is also consistent with this book's broader understanding of urban design as a plural art. The book is not a history; there are no lists of designed cities, nor canonical urban design projects. Nor is it a compendium of best practices, a guidebook for professionals. Instead this book is a measured manifesto, a declaration of urban design's plural qualities that is intended for scholars, students, and devotees of urban design. Projects, designers, cities, and history are to be found in this book, but only as supportive elements of theory, the concept of *plural urbanism*. *The Largest Art* is the product of my twenty-plus-year encounter with urban design; it constitutes my understanding and aspirations for urban design. I hope that the book's readers will find it to be rewarding and compelling.

Chapter 1, "Unitary Architecture, Plural Cities," presents urban design's current "dead end(s)," as framed by critic Michael Sorkin, as a false alarm. Instead, the chapter explains that urban design has never been fully understood as the plural art it actually is; beginning with early twentieth-century modernist schemes, through modernism's midcentury crisis, to the "dead end(s)" of today, urban design has wandered stylistically while remaining confined to what I call its unitary conceptions, stemming from monumental architecture such as Versailles. I highlight an alternative concept of the discipline that was cut off at midcentury, when architects stylistically imitated Cedric Price's radical architectural proposal for an unfinished "Fun Palace," while ignoring its deeper lessons for a balance between designer and public. I conclude the chapter by defining the qualities of and differences between unitary and plural urban design, or urbanism.

Chapter 2, "Five Dimensions of Plural Urbanism," by far the longest chapter in the book, is a descriptive theory of urban design's plural qualities. Plural scale explains how urban design has the widest scalar range of any of the building arts (i.e., architecture, landscape, sculpture, and land art), ranging from the space beyond a building to the scale of a metropolitan region, or even larger. Through scale, urban design becomes the largest of the building arts. Plural time explores urban design's profound relationship with history, where a design gesture becomes part of a city's life, even after its destruction. Plural property reminds us that urban design has many owners, and that these plural properties make urbanism the most challenging of the building arts. Plural agents describe the many makers of urban design, ranging from the designer to the public. Urbanism is a collective art, yet this very collectivity can diminish urban design's meaning, an existential tension that has stimulated profound urban design thinkers. Lastly, chapter 2 describes urban design's plural form. More than others, this plural art possesses a distributed quality that allows it to exist among diverse elements of the city that are not part of an urban design idea. Together, these definitions of urban design's plural quality secure the plural art's distinction from unitary building arts, particularly architecture, that lack these qualities.

Chapter 3, "Three Pluralist Projects," contextualizes chapter 2 within the setting of three urban design projects constructed at various times and locations during the twentieth century. Each ensemble is linked to well-known designers and artists, and the design of each has been long acclaimed, but none of these projects has been understood and analyzed through the lens of pluralism until now. The first, Constantin Brancusi's sculptural ensemble in Târgu Jiu, Romania, economically shapes an urban axis and a city center through three exquisite Platonic forms: circle, arch, and column. The second, a social housing project at Twin Parks in New York City's Bronx, intersperses late modernist apartment towers between vernacular Bronx tenements to shape a monumental, large-scale composition with both social and formal meaning. The chapter's culmination comes with Jože Plečnik's work in the Slovenian capital Ljubljana, a programmatically, formally, and spatially diverse grouping of projects that range from infrastructure to landscape to private and civic buildings, but that together shape what is the finest built example of plural urban design.

Chapter 4, "Three Plural Urbanists," revisits the thoughts and works of three urban designers from the late years of modernism, from 1960 to the 1980s. Each of these urban designers was also considered an urban planner, which is an interesting commentary on their devotion to the city as a plural space. These three urban designers knew that urbanism was not simply large-scale architecture. Each of them understood urban design's plural qualities, wrote about these qualities, and incorporated their understandings into their built work, though none did so to their full satisfaction. Before entering into decades of professional practice, David Crane published a series of articles in the early 1960s on a concept he called the "capital web." Edmund Bacon is well known as Philadelphia's chief planner for almost twenty years, but he was also a scholar whose 1967 book *Design of Cities* emphasized a conceptual tool called the "movement system." Kevin Lynch, familiar from this preface, both wrote and practiced much, and his ideas of "city design" come closest to this book's theory of plural urbanism, though Lynch's thought eventually veered into other directions. Understanding these designers' ideas contextualizes this book's theory of plural urbanism within a trajectory of modernist urban design thought whose innovative qualities were never fully understood.

Chapter 5, "Designing Pluralist Urbanism," takes the reader from existing projects and designers into three scenarios for imaginary places, fantasies of plural urbanism in locations that have many connections to reality but that do not fully exist. Each is borrowed from personal experience, and the design ideas—founded in precepts of plural urbanism explored in the previous three chapters—are mine, though the delightful illustrations come from my collaborative discussions with a talented former student, now an architect in Texas. These three scenarios remind us that a variety of locations exist that might benefit from plural urban design, and that the creative potential of plural urbanism is as vast as that of any other creative discipline. Like any of the building arts, plural urban design will stem from the qualities of a place and from a designer's (or designers') inspiration, but these scenarios also show that urban design's plural qualities of scale, time, property, agency, and form are what transform these diverse environments into something special: the largest art.

Chapter 6, "Principles and Potentials of Plural Urbanism," concludes this book by outlining three signal considerations that every urban designer must acknowledge: eternal change, inevitable incompletion, and flexible fidelity. Cities are entities whose inhabitation by thousands or millions of autonomous actors make them as ceaselessly active and motile as an anthill. By becoming part of the plural cityscape, any urban design project will itself change perpetually as it is added to, subtracted from, or otherwise altered. Generating art whose aesthetic qualities can survive perpetual change is a challenge for plural urbanists. Incompletion is embarrassing and dysfunctional in architecture, but it is inevitable in urban design, where projects take decades, styles change, and political regimes shift support with comparative rapidity. Unlike unitary urban design, plural urbanism need not be complete to succeed, for this largest of the arts can never be complete. Similarly, fidelity of a finished work to a designer's intention is the hallmark of every art from sculpture to landscape, and diminution of that intention is correspondingly a diminution of that art's value. Plural urbanism, in contrast, must be content with more flexible fidelity, because it is too large to be effectively controlled by a single actor and because its many other plural qualities preclude a high degree of control. Urban designers must create a design that can survive enactment by others with less capability or even commitment. These three principles need be appreciated and accentuated through great creativity, and the book closes by calling for creativity from all quarters to continue the enterprise of plural urbanism, the largest art.

inefficient street networks, cluttered shops and packed streets, and straggling peripheral areas all were replaced by consciously designed, identical structures.

Cities in 1922 (and today) grew in a disorganized, seemingly uncontrolled manner, but Le Corbusier's Ville Contemporaine defeated disorganization: it was complete in and of itself, with all human needs seemingly being met in a single design. This vision, unlike any existing city of the time, may seem totalitarian and even terrifying today, but in their era Le Corbusier's ideas provided a tempting vision of a world where architect-engineers had wholesale control over the form of the built environment. This vision of the totipotent architect-engineer would deeply influence the formal academic programs in urban design, including that of Harvard, that would appear forty years after Corbusier's urban vision was first proposed.

Influenced by the chaotic quality of existing cities and by the temptation of total design that could remake these cities, modernist urban design remained throughout the twentieth century committed not to reforming existing cities but to replacing them. Other modernist urban design projects such as Ludwig Hilberseimer's *Großstadtarchitektur* (1927)[11] only reinforced Le Corbusier's propositions.

Following the Second World War, a second generation of modernist urban designers—including Josep Lluís Sert, dean of Harvard's Graduate School of Design—retained the fundamentally radical philosophy of Le Corbusier's 1922 vision of the totally designed city, although they introduced additional refinements such as variations of building type and open space. Sert's 1960 Peabody Terrace housing in Cambridge, Massachusetts, was a graduate housing development that described in miniature a comprehensive formal vision for a city shaped by clearly defined open spaces and diverse building dimensions. Such refined modernist urban design was a refreshing alternative to monotonous, poorly built speculative urban neighborhoods, but even second-generation modernist urbanism rejected contemporary cities as often as it reformed them. Le Corbusier's own Unité d'Habitation, designed in the late 1940s as an urban neighborhood contained within a single, mixed-use building, did not replace the city, but simply rejected it entirely. The building was autonomous, standing apart from the city in a forested landscape. Where there once were city streets, the Unité instead provided traditional neighborhood features like shops and schools inside its concrete structure.

Modernism's avant-garde urban design was both promising and demanding. Where existing cities were monotonous, poorly built, and seemingly out of control, modernism promised to entirely reorganize urban functions within a wholly new, full designed setting. But modernism was also demanding; in order to achieve this new

1.2   Josep Lluís Sert's 1960 Peabody Terrace in Cambridge, Massachusetts, was a large-scale
housing development that was also a small-scale realization of an ideal vision of the city.

1.3 Le Corbusier's postwar Unité d'Habitation combined traditional functions of the city such as housing, retail, and social services within the form of a single building, implying that the city itself was unnecessary.

1.4 Jane Jacobs was the most vocal and most eloquent critic of the modernist urbanism embodied by Le Corbusier and Josep Lluís Sert. Jacobs advocated the complete cessation of large-scale urban design in cities.

order, the entire past must be abandoned. Modernist fundamentalism, so strong in its commitment to the future but so unable to accommodate the past, contained within it the seeds of the critique that would ultimately lead to the ideology's abandonment. Faced with modernism, an ideal that sought to destroy the existing city, doubters reacted equally strongly *against* it, generating a counterreaction called postmodernism, which would prove to be just as radical and intolerant as modernism had been.

The Counterreaction: Postmodernism

Given modernist urban design's vision of a "total city" with little connection to the past, it was little surprise that any reaction against modernism would look not forward, but backward, to the design of existing cities. In this sense the reaction to modernism shared some aspects of previous antitechnology movements, like the Luddites, that had also looked back to preindustrial agricultural society.[12] The postmodern counterreaction to modernism feared technology too, in the form of hygienic towers that had begun to replace the existing city, and it too would look back to a preindustrial past.

The first spokesperson for the counterreaction to modernist urbanism in the United States was the author and activist Jane Jacobs. Appearing to her sexist foes as a stay-at-home housewife,[13] Jacobs was in reality a highly erudite reporter-*cum*-public intellectual who placed modernist urbanism directly in her sights in her now-canonical book *The Death and Life of Great American Cities* (1961). Jacobs's attack was conceptually elegant: Where modernist urbanism claimed progress—new housing, efficient cities, improved economies, and enhanced quality of life—Jacobs saw the opposite—inefficient, inhumane, economically damaging, and above all, antihuman places. Her critique was astute and well timed, finding fertile ground in skeptics of modernism across North America and Europe who had had enough of poorly designed modernist projects that had too often replaced what were in retrospect attractive older neighborhoods.

Yet Jane Jacobs was no urban designer herself. Her book disowned the Corbusian public housing towers and highway ramps overrunning Manhattan, but as an alternative to these modernist interventions Jacobs suggested only the common city street, using her own Hudson Street in Greenwich Village as an example. Today, sympathetic critics continue to seek an alternative urban design ideology to modernism in Jacobs's work, but there is little to find.[14] Straightforward but sparse maxims for good neighborhoods ("small blocks," "old buildings," etc.) aptly describe Greenwich Village, but these qualities are difficult to generate de novo, and they simply do not exist in many contemporary urban neighborhoods. In this sense, Jacobs was herself a bit of a Luddite, disliking the looming future and thereby turning back to admire the past.

Yet much of Jacobs's critique was no doubt correct, as Sorkin, certainly no fan of postmodernism, admitted in "The End(s) of Urban Design." Modernist urban design had wrought much destruction, and modernist city districts were often stunningly monotonous. These modernist flaws argued in Jacobs's favor. Her critique of modernism was also more sophisticated than a simple dislike of high-rise, abstract buildings. Jacobs saw cities as the built products of complex interactions between social and economic forces. No matter how artful their design, large clusters of identical buildings could not replace such interactions. Jacobs described instead the city as an entity that was growing, changing, alive, and animated by myriad human interactions. She was convinced that urban design should be not just the definer of human interaction, but also the product of it. This was the opposite of modernism. "[Modernism] is the substitution of art for life," she warned, and "[such a] substitution is art-killing as well as life-killing."[15]

Whatever modernism's flaws, practicing urban designers could not elude their professional responsibilities: buildings still needed to be designed and built, as did university campuses, airports, subdivisions, and much more. Abandoning modernist urban design philosophies, as Jacobs proposed, could not be enough; alternative philosophies were required. Postmodern urban design provided this alternative by projecting the design of future cities as a variation on the design of historic ones, a philosophy that was called neotraditionalism.

Neotraditionalism was not new. Historic revivalism had characterized many urban design projects of the 1920s, whether in Europe, in places such as Amsterdam South or Welwyn Garden City, or in the United States, as at Mariemont, Ohio. The rebirth of neotraditionalism in the 1970s could draw upon genuine premodern cities such as Annapolis, Maryland, or the older districts of Philadelphia, as well as upon the urban design projects of the early twentieth century that predated the growth of modernism. The "new neotraditionalism's" most vocal and prolific promoters in the United States would be the husband-wife team of Andrés Duany and Elizabeth Plater-Zyberk (DPZ). Their urban design work in the late 1970s and early 1980s merged a critique of modernism together with a revivalism similar to the 1920s to form the kernel of an urban design movement called new urbanism (New Urbanism to its promoters) that would grow to great prominence in the 1990s.

Duany Plater-Zyberk's first constructed urban project, a design for the resort town of Seaside, Florida, was extremely influential. Much of what DPZ designed after

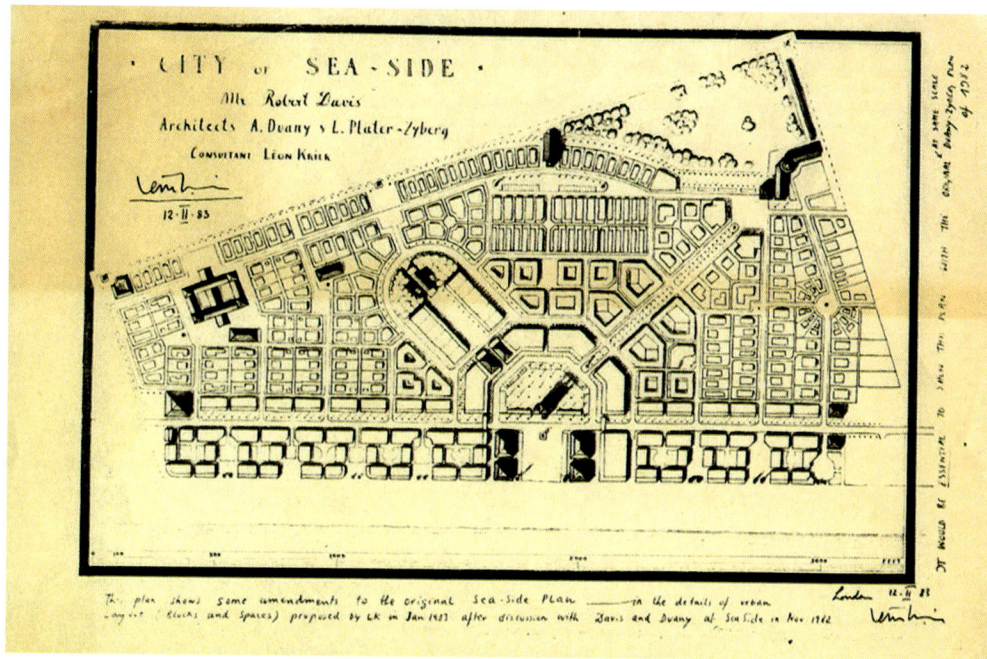

1.5 By 1980, modernist urbanism's disrepute was complete as Florida architects Andrés Duany and Elizabeth Plater-Zyberk proposed a suburban version of a neotraditionalist city in Seaside, Florida.

1980 was based on the design principles first explored in Seaside, and the town also had many other imitators, all of whom admired its design of dense housing, quiet, pedestrian-oriented streets, varied neighborhood parks, broad public beachfront, and clearly defined neighborhoods. Once constructed, Seaside was so idyllic that it even ended up as the setting for a fictional, all-encompassing reality TV show in the 1998 movie *The Truman Show*.

Seaside's neighborly qualities may have seemed a little unreal, but they were a charming alternative to the straggling suburban landscape of Florida, where strip shopping centers and gated communities dominated the landscape. In America, many consumers and developers swiftly realized that Seaside presented a new kind of design philosophy—one that looked old, but that was brand new, providing modern conveniences together with seemingly old-fashioned values such as walkability and sociability. Real estate values in Seaside and other new urbanist towns escalated, and neotraditionalist urban design's credibility increased by leaps and bounds.

New urbanist literature was filled with promises of diversity, choices, and difference, but ultimately postmodern urban design shared much of the fundamentalism of its predecessor. Where modernism rejected the flawed charm of the existing city, neo-traditionalism in turn rejected the pragmatic reality of highways, industrial parks, even of skyscrapers. New urbanist settlements like Seaside were admittedly charming and tranquil, but at a larger scale the ideology's rejection of most of the components of contemporary cities—the same components that had been fetishized by Le Corbusier in his Ville Contemporaine—simply disowned the reality of much of twenty-first-century life. Truck stops and football stadiums may have been ugly intrusions into the city, but they were here to stay, even if new urbanism provided them little space.

It was new urbanism's very unreality that made Michael Sorkin so despise it in "The End(s) of Urban Design." Modernism had been brutal, but at least it was honest; Sorkin saw postmodern urban design as a bourgeois charade, an excuse for global capitalism that he called "Starbucks urbanism." Much of Sorkin's language was unfair; new urbanism was not responsible for social inequality, and modernism had been just as accepting of global capitalism in its time. But Sorkin's identification of postmodernism as being as intolerant as modernism and more artificial to boot was on target, a frustrating truth for those who had hoped for a better future after modernism. The flaws of postmodernism showed it as an end of urban design, not a beginning.

The 1980s brought another urban design alternative, one that avoided the historicism of postmodernism while recapturing much of modernism's future-oriented spirit. This was the ideal that Sorkin and others referred to as posturbanism, and what Rem Koolhaas, the third philosophy's primary promoter, called "bigness."

Posturbanism or Bigness: The City within a Building

Le Corbusier's Unité d'Habitation, his 1948 building in Marseille that neatly combined over three hundred apartments with shops and community facilities in a single slablike concrete structure, was hardly the first large building to incorporate such a mix of public and private spaces. Increasing programmatic and formal complexity had marked urban architecture since the late nineteenth century when skyscrapers first began to appear.[16] By the 1930s, New York City skyscrapers such as Rockefeller Center and the New York Athletic Club stacked facilities as diverse as swimming pools, shops, restaurants, offices, and hotel rooms within a single building, thanks to the structural

1.6 Koolhaas and Zenghelis's Hotel Sphinx project of 1975–1976, sited in Times Square, reflected and consumed that lively place. The hotel's bewildering variety of programs and activities was a polemical mirror of the variety of the city outside its doors.

flexibility of steel and to the intense consumer demand provided by dense urban populations.

The formal complexity of large buildings was the foundation of a new urban design ideology promoted by Dutch architect Rem Koolhaas through a series of theoretical projects in the mid-1970s and subsequently in constructed projects in later decades. Koolhaas's ideas, developed through the work of his aptly named firm OMA (Office for Metropolitan Architecture) and through a series of short but provocative manifestos, were oppositional to those of postmodernist urban designers. Where new urbanists wanted to rebuild historic cities, or at least to build new ones that resembled the old, Koolhaas expanded the idea of the large building into an ideology of urban design that he called bigness, and that others would later call posturbanism.[17] Koolhaas expounded upon these ideals in several essays ("Bigness," "What Ever Happened to Urbanism?," "Junkspace," "Atlanta," and others).[18]

Koolhaas's essays had a consistent argument. The contemporary city was not a historic space for the urban designer to restore or replicate, but was rather a lightly or entirely undesigned space that was increasingly beyond the control of the urban designer. As Koolhaas saw it, there was not much of a role for urban design at all in today's cities, except for those qualities of the city that architects could recreate within very large buildings. Koolhaas explained this approach in "Bigness, or the Problem of Large," where he wrote that "bigness [e.g., the large building] no longer needs the city; it competes with the city; it represents the city; it preempts the city, or better still, it *is* the city." And where Jane Jacobs and new urbanists based their urban design ideals on context, and even fetishized that context as the source for future design, Koolhaas was equally emphatic in the opposite direction: "[Bigness's] subtext is *fuck* context."[19]

To Koolhaas, an architect interested in urban design was wasting their time trying to design cities; such work belonged to engineers, developers, and regulators, none of whom cared much about design. "Architecture as we know it is in difficulty," Koolhaas said in "Bigness," "but … a strategic position is regained through retreat and concentration, yielding the rest of a concentrated territory to enemy forces."[20] This provocative, quasi-militaristic language warned would-be urbanists to abandon the street, to retreat into the building.

Bigness was a compelling polemical argument. Since urban space was evidently undesignable, the urban designer—an architect above all—should not bother with urban design at all. For evidence, one need only look at the city of Atlanta, Georgia, where Koolhaas said that "the [zoning] regulations are so weak that the exception is the

1.7 What Rem Koolhaas called "bigness...architecture that preempts the city" was realized in his firm's massive, object-like China Central Television headquarters completed in 2012 in Beijing.

◄ **1.8** Wholly designed city districts often seem to lack the humanity and comfort provided in older cities. Ex-Soviet city districts, such as this 1970s-era neighborhood in Kherson, Ukraine, are particularly cheerless.

◄ **1.9** Even the finest neotraditional districts, such as Berlage's Amsterdam South, feel somewhat artificial, an environment where every conceivable variable has been designed to be harmonious. Is such complete harmony really possible, or desirable?

▲ **1.10** In contrast to the dullness of designed settlements, places undesigned except by their inhabitants such as Comuna 13 in Medellín, Colombia, might be dirty, even dangerous; but they are never uninteresting.

illegal businesses persist. And undesigned, disordered city districts are abundant, just as Rem Koolhaas noted in his manifesto on bigness. It was these same places that Jane Jacobs both perceived and preferred to the arid, overdesigned spaces of modernist urban design.

But not all modernism was quite as arid as Jacobs claimed. In particular, a seminal 1961 project—proposed for London but never constructed—promised an entirely different relationship between the "order" of the designer and the "disorder" of the public. In 1961 London architect Cedric Price, a recent graduate little known at the time, was commissioned by theater director Joan Littlewood to design a building that Price called a "Fun Palace." The Fun Palace was to be a new kind of theater, with structured and unstructured activities where people would "dance, talk, or be lifted up ... sit out over space with a drink ... start a riot or begin a painting—or just lie back and stare at the sky."[26] The mix of sybaritic and ludic imagery was provocative and refreshing after a grim decade of postwar life, in which London life had not been particularly fun. Nor did many modernist urban projects of the time include populist ideas like entertainment and freedom within their design purview.

On one level, the Fun Palace was just that—entertainment. But on a deeper level, the Fun Palace spoke to an essential quality of the city as a place for excitement, adventure, fun, and danger. Architecturally, it was quite modest: a simple structural framework of trusses animated by temporary, festive accoutrements like signage and lighting, and by the varied, constant human activities occurring within. Quick and inexpensive to construct (or take down), the Fun Palace's attraction lay not in its expensive, center-city location—it was located in a marginal industrial valley instead—but in its offerings of fun and freedom. Similar desires for fun and freedom had drawn people to marginal districts of the city since time immemorial.

The Fun Palace could not be called a typical modernist building of the time, nor was it neotraditional in any way. In common with many modernist buildings, its low-cost, minimalist aesthetic alluded to factory designs focusing on structural clarity and with little or no ornament. These same qualities had inspired important modernist projects like Walter Gropius's Fagus Factory of 1913. But uniquely, the Fun Palace took this industrial aesthetic and animated it with cultural activity and urban life, allowing its own users to modify the appearance and program of the structure. This malleability permitted freedom of expression, excitement, even mystery and danger—qualities that Jane Jacobs was simultaneously observing in Greenwich Village in the early 1960s. Price's Fun Palace showed that modernist abstraction and city liveliness could coexist

1.11 Cedric Price's 1961 Fun Palace incorporated the freedom and openness of undesigned city space into the framework of a building. Architecture merged with urbanism, but at the cost of formal control over building form.

rather than oppose or cancel each other out. By integrating modernist aesthetics with the seeming disorder of city life, the Fun Palace refuted Jacobs's accusations of modernist sterility at the same time as it refuted the neotraditionalism that would come to shape postmodern urban design. In the Fun Palace, contemporary architectural design and user input were very far from incompatible.

As a framework or latticework whose program and infill were left to its users in the same manner as a set builder annotated stage interiors, the Fun Palace was only partially designed by "master" architect Cedric Price; the rest was left to the public. This constituted a substantial retreat from the traditional, highly determinative notion of architecture as a discipline where the designer could and should order every aspect of space. Famous examples of modernist housing such as Mies van der Rohe's 860 and 880 Lake Shore Drive in Chicago permitted little or no alteration, or even personal expression, by users. Windows in Mies's apartment buildings even opened inward, leaving the exterior facade unaltered. The Fun Palace emulated the abstract, simple structural expression of

1.12 Mies van der Rohe's splendid, minimalist steel towers on Chicago's Lake Shore Drive famously embodied structural expression, but the only exterior expression permitted to the buildings' users was the position of their white window shades.

Mies's buildings, but it used the simplicity of its design to permit greater user expression, instead of repressing it. Price offered architecture the opportunity to encompass city life and city freedom within the building, as long as architects were willing to relinquish total control over the building's form and appearance.

Even though it was a building, not a city district, the Fun Palace provides many lessons for the discipline of urban design. First of all, it permitted people to have fun and enjoy themselves, allowing a number of ludic or heterotopic experiences city-dwellers might otherwise experience only in an older city district, such as London's Piccadilly Circus. The Fun Palace, in other words, provided the activities of a busy urban entertainment district within itself, incorporating urban life within architecture. Such an ability to internalize urban functions within a building had previously appeared in Le Corbusier's Unité d'Habitation, and this potential would later inspire Rem Koolhaas's concept of bigness as well. But unlike the Unité or Koolhaas's buildings, which strictly defined the user experience, the Fun Palace diminished the importance of its own architecture by permitting users the opportunity to reshape the building's design.

Where modernist urban design sometimes restricted even the presence of shopping and signage as an imposition on the overall design, the Fun Palace mocked modernist rigidity by indicating that buildings could be as flexible as their users wished them to be. Nor was the Fun Palace in line with Jane Jacobs's mantra to stop big projects, listen to citizens, and design small-scale; it was itself a big project that was also a profound manifesto for dialogue between large- and small-scale components: the structural framework provided by the architect, and the activities created by users. This manifesto saw the built environment's form changing over time in response to multiple inputs, for user activities and interventions were always changing, and saw these multiple inputs coming both from designers and from the public.

None of these qualities were signal features of modernism or neotraditionalism; Le Corbusier or DPZ may have favored different urban design aesthetics, but neither advocated relaxation of the designer's control. Seaside was typical: to restrict the suburban features that disfigured other towns in Florida, DPZ created strict design controls governing everything from roadway material (crushed pink coral) to acceptable paint colors on houses (pastels). Neotraditionalism abandoned modernism's abstract aesthetic, but left the orthodoxy of designer control firmly intact.

The aesthetic debate that pitched Rem Koolhaas against Andrés Duany and that animated Michael Sorkin's proclamation of urban design's "end(s)" centered around an either-or approach: either the machinelike, abstract aesthetic of modernism, or

the humane, village-like, familiar aesthetic of neotraditionalism. This debate focused on urban design's formal, stylistic quality, but left the possibility of the shift, even the reduction of design control, proposed by the Fun Palace unexamined.

The Fun Palace was a building that meshed the ideas of a single designer with the multiple ideas of the building's many users. We can therefore understand this building as having both *unitary* qualities (a single designer, a single structure) and *plural* qualities (multiple users, multiple design interventions by those users). The Fun Palace was both a unitary and a plural structure. Its unitary qualities lay in the elements provided by the architect: the building's structural framework, its site, its overall program, even the designer's decision to relinquish control of much of the design to the public. Many of these qualities are typical of architecture, and of typical urban design as well, as we will see. But it was the Fun Palace's plural qualities that made it unique. The Fun Palace was to be used by a number of different people, and it was open to architectural annotation by those same people. As a result, the Fun Palace could have no single form, no single designer, no single user. Rather, it was ever-changing with regard to both its design and its inhabitants.

The analogy of the Fun Palace to a city, and to the design of the city, should be obvious. Cities, too, can be designed by a single individual, but they are inhabited by thousands or millions of people, each of whom may participate in building a small part of that city. Cities, too, may not have a single form, single designer, or single user. The city is a plural entity par excellence, and the space of the city is not the unitary space of a typical building, but a plural space. In that respect urban design, while it is a building art like architecture and landscape architecture, is also a plural art, one that possesses many plural qualities.

Toward Plural Urbanism: Unitary and Plural Space

Much as Savannah, Georgia, had been almost three hundred years earlier, the DPZ-designed town of Seaside, Florida, was constructed on what had formerly been a forest. Landowner and developer Robert Davis had inherited a large tract of land from his family's forestry company and, sensing a change in the economic weather, had elected to promote a resort development on his formerly rural land.[27] Urban designers Duany Plater-Zyberk were presented a nearly blank slate, at least in terms of human construction: Seaside's site held little more than forest and a state highway, albeit a forest governed by countywide zoning regulations, as Duany still points out.[28]

◄ **1.13**   The 1972 Centre Pompidou in Paris was a facade of the Fun Palace, mimicking the latter's technological and formal expressiveness, but without permitting actual alteration by building users. Urban life was instead confined to the Pompidou's exterior plaza.

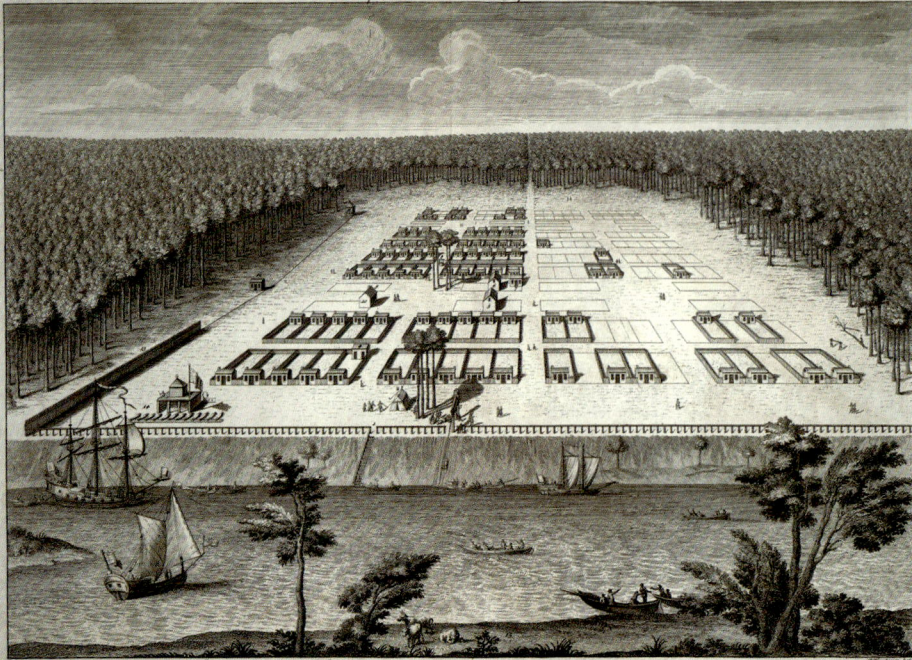

A View of Savanah as it stood the 29 of March 1734

To the Honble the Trustees for establishing the Colony of Georgia in America
This View of the Town of Savanah is humbly dedicated by their Honours
Obliged and most Obedient Servant.
VUE de Savanah dans la Georgie   Peter Gordon.

Before the construction of Seaside resulted in the subdivision of its site into multiple parcels comprising the town, Seaside was a *unitary* site, a single plot of land with a single owner. Just as Seaside was first a unitary site, so too was the site of Brasília, the modernist capital city constructed by presidential fiat in Brazil's empty center beginning in 1956. So was Chandigarh, the new capital of Punjab designed by Le Corbusier and others in the 1950s. The list of unitary sites goes on: their role in urban design history is very great because the process of subdivision of a single parcel of land is a common means of preparing it for development and human settlement.

Urban design does not require subdivision, however: many urban design projects occur on unsubdivided, or unitary, sites. College campuses are unitary sites, owned by the single entity of the university. Hospital campuses, large tracts of government-owned land such as military bases and national parks, even the National Mall in the center of Washington, DC, are all unitary sites, and so are quasi-private or fully private facilities such as airports, factories, corporate headquarters, and gated residential communities, where even the roads may be private. Central London is surprisingly a small grouping of unitary sites because much of Westminster and Bloomsbury were once feudal estates. Its land is today held by its original owners even though it is occupied by thousands of different buildings.

Unitary sites may not always have been unitary. Occasionally, areas of land that were previously subdivided can be reconverted into larger unitary sites. A developer may acquire several older buildings to build one or more new structures, such as in Rockefeller Center in Midtown Manhattan. Reconversions to unitary sites may be very large in scale. Central Park in Manhattan comprised hundreds of smaller parcels of land in the 1850s, but Olmsted and Vaux's design for a single large rectangle of open space required the acquisition and combination of these parcels. And unitary space and plural space are not always compatible; when Central Park was constructed, many low-income squatters, with uncertain or insecure land title, were evicted and their modest homes demolished.[29]

Modernist urban design projects, with their rank upon rank of ordered skyscrapers, required the greatest reconversion of plural to unitary parcels yet seen. One can only imagine how many smaller parcels Le Corbusier's Plan Voisin in central Paris, or Ludwig Hilberseimer's proposals for Chicago, would have required in order to be constructed.[30] The modernist-inspired towers of public housing and miles of urban

◄ **1.14**   When British colonists carved Savannah, Georgia, out of the primordial forest beginning in 1733, they transformed what we can understand as a unitary site into plural space, owned and controlled by many different individuals.

◄ **1.15**   Many canonical urban design projects, such as the city of Brasilia, also began their lives as a unitary site, in this case on the vast Brazilian *planalto*. The design and subdivision of unitary parcels constitutes a major area of work for urban designers.

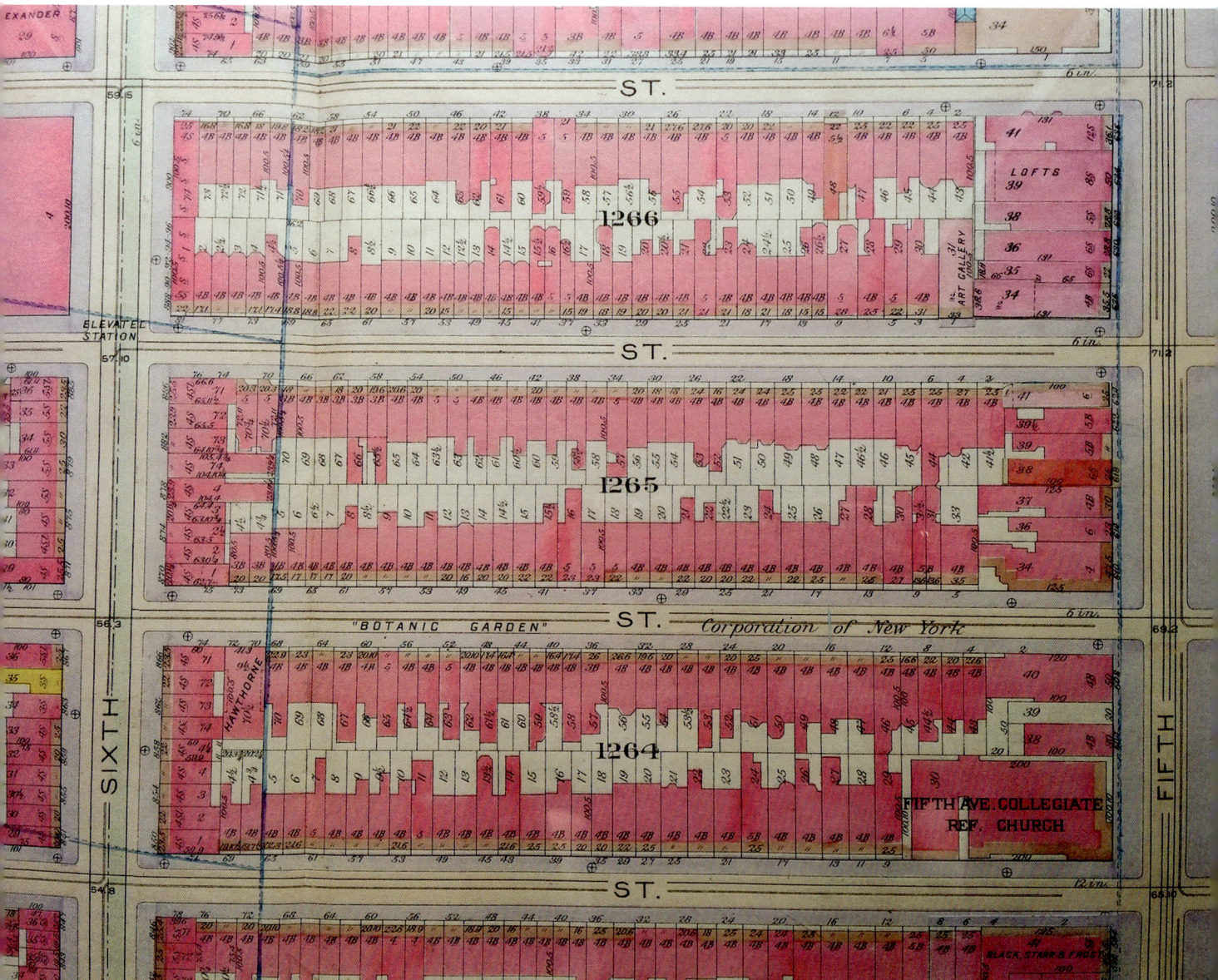

1.16 Plural space can be reconverted to unitary space, but such action requires great amounts of money and often power. Rockefeller Center is one such reconversion; its developers purchased and combined over one hundred parcels to provide its site in Midtown Manhattan, shown here in a 1915 map. The RCA Building is now located on the block numbered 1265.

interstate highways constructed in American cities between 1930 and 1970 were almost all built on large unitary parcels reconverted from many smaller ones.

Whether subdivided, unsubdivided, or reconverted, unitary sites would seem to be the foundation of urban design. Urban design texts are filled with projects or proposals built on one of the three types of unitary sites, and most paradigmatic urban design projects, whether built or unbuilt, occupy unitary sites.[31] A few examples from New York City alone demonstrate this point. Central Park, the Freedom Tower (and the preceding World Trade Center twin towers), the United Nations, Hudson Yards, and the Bronx's Co-op City are all unitary sites. This close association of unitary sites with urban design often leads one to see the two as equivalent. Urban design texts certainly seem to think so, rarely noting the parallel of urban design projects and unitary sites.

Unitary sites offer urban designers with a high degree of design control. Despite the presence of existing buildings, large-scale property owners such as universities or airport authorities can generally demolish, replace, and redesign areas of campus at will; one such structure, extant for over sixty years, was demolished outside my office window during the writing of this book, with little input from abutting office users. And formerly subdivided unitary sites can effectively obliterate their past. New York's public housing complexes, for example, show little of their former histories. Unitary urban design's high level of design control is attractive for urban designers, and the dominance of unitary design is continually reinforced by the publication of paradigmatic urban design projects constructed on unitary sites. Without being aware of it, urban designers and unitary sites have a close, almost codependent relationship.

Unitary sites enable urban designers with a high level of design control, but this control is not infinite. Seaside's architects shaped the overall form of the town, but they did not design every individual building within it, and Seaside's seemingly unitary site was still divided by a preexisting state highway and governed by existing county codes and regulations. A college campus or an airport is a single large parcel, but these parcels always contain existing buildings, not all of which can be removed. Even a reconverted unitary site might have elements remaining from its plural past. Central Park seems completely unitary, but it still contains a preexisting building (the Arsenal), while another piece of infrastructure (the old Croton Aqueduct) was not removed until 1930.[32] Not every unitary site can provide total design freedom.

In their dependence on unitary sites, the ideological differences that divided modernists from neotraditionalists disappear. Just as neotraditional Seaside occupied a unitary site, so too did the modernist City for Three Million, the Plan Voisin, and the

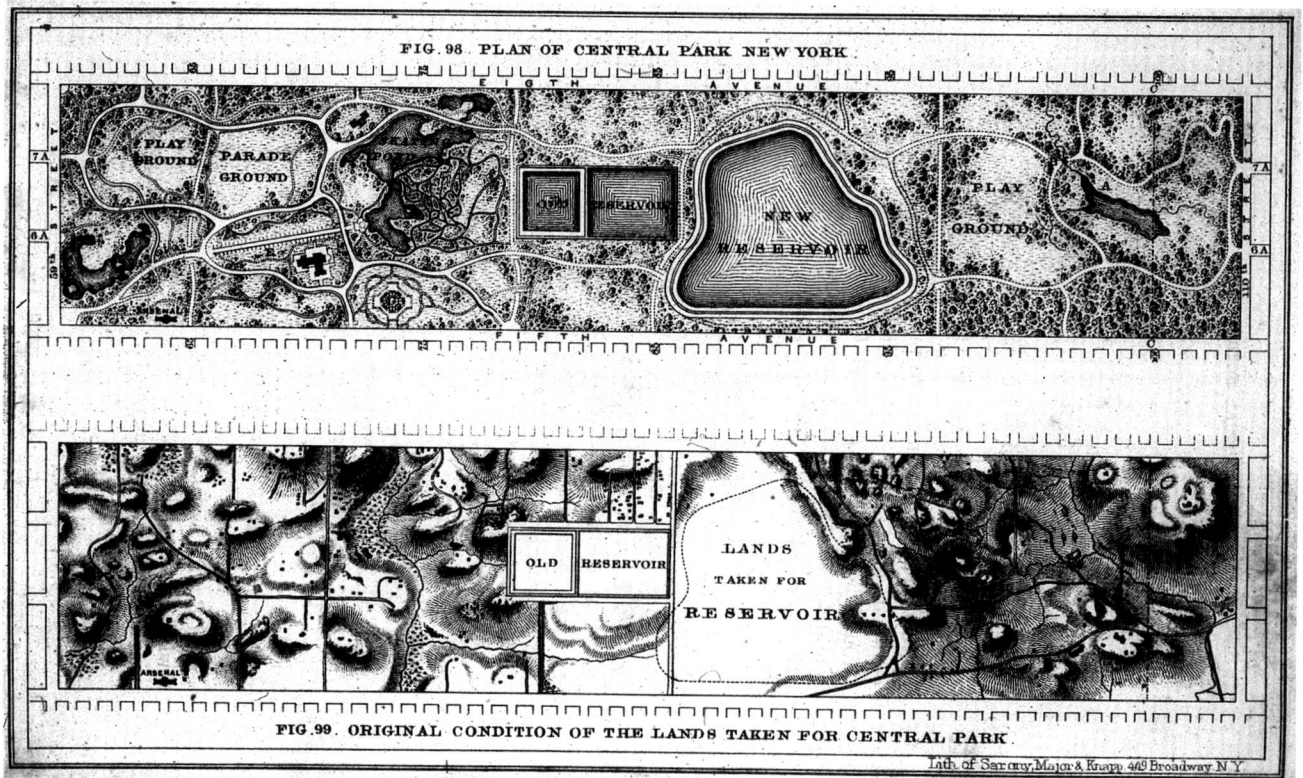

FIG. 98. PLAN OF CENTRAL PARK NEW YORK.

FIG. 99. ORIGINAL CONDITION OF THE LANDS TAKEN FOR CENTRAL PARK.

1.17 The pluralist past of many reconverted unitary sites often remains visible. Even Central Park contained preexisting buildings and infrastructure that were permitted to remain or that could not be removed.

1.18 Unitary sites often resemble plural city spaces, but this is an illusion. This district of Boston resembling a city center is controlled by about ten hospitals and educational institutions; it is a collection of large unitary sites.

constructed cities of Brasília and Chandigarh. Modernist housing developments such as Mies van der Rohe and Ludwig Hilberseimer's Lafayette Park in Detroit were assembled into unitary sites from thousands of individual parcels before being subdivided again, just like the art deco Rockefeller Center. The modernist public housing constructed in the postwar United States were replaced by new-urbanist-inspired housing in the 1990s, but the latter developments, different in many ways, retained their unitary status. Every new airport designed in China during the past twenty years, and every new urbanist development built in the United States during the same time, was designed as a unitary site. In fact, there is no one-to-one relationship between unitary sites and any particular urban design ideology; all ideologies have taken advantage of the opportunities and freedom for design that unitary sites provide.

Thus far, all is clear. Unitary sites are common, urban designers possess numerous (and competing) aesthetic ideals for designing them, and the great majority of well-known urban design projects reinforces urban design's unitary quality. But if this is the case, why did Rem Koolhaas label urban design a "failed fantasy," proclaiming "what ever happened to urbanism?" If unitary sites are so abundant and urban design strategies for them are so successful, why did Koolhaas call for architects to "retreat from contested territory" into the interior world of "big" buildings?

Answering this puzzle takes us further into the realm of the city's plural quality, and into the plural nature of urban space and therefore of urban design. Bigness recommended "retreat" not from unitary sites but from plural ones: from the part of the city that is not unitary but plural. Cities, of course, are not unitary; each comprises tens or hundreds of thousands of individual parcels, each owned by an individual entity. A city will contain many unitary sites, including the aforementioned campuses, parks, and other large properties, but cities themselves are not single parcels, and they most certainly do not have a single owner.

It is precisely this quality of city space from which Koolhaas recommended "retreat." Bigness was necessary for Koolhaas because the plural quality of urban space was not available for design control at the level possible in a unitary site. By "retreating" to the large building, designers thereby "cede" the uncontrollable thousands, even millions, of individual parcels that compose the rest of the city. Plural space, for Koolhaas, was uncontrollable space for designers. Indeed, each of the design paradigms in Koolhaas's 1975 "retroactive manifesto" *Delirious New York* is unitary: Rockefeller Center, Luna Park (an amusement park on Coney Island), the United Nations. Given the high level of design control possible on unitary sites, Koolhaas's conclusion that

1.19 Other unitary sites more directly reflect their singular function and nature. Pei Cobb Freed's Dallas-Fort Worth International Airport presents an interesting formal contrast with the plural suburbia that surrounds it.

urbanism's future lies in large buildings constructed on unitary sites should not be wholly unexpected.

But Koolhaas's understanding of urbanism, however expansive and ambitious it may seem, is limited. In one sense bigness's decrying of plural space is correct: the difficulty of imposing a design idea on multiple parcels is great. Certainly the hundreds of towers popping up in global cities such as New York, Shanghai, or São Paulo, or the thousands of dwellings proliferating on the hillsides of Latin American cities, seem to defy any larger-scale spatial order. Lacking the overall structure of a city plan like that of Brasília, or strict design codes like those of Seaside, these global cities are seemingly chaotic, the result of their thousands of different builders' individual whims.

Retreat, like that recommended by Koolhaas, has its advantages, allowing consolidation, perhaps recovery. But retreat also has costs; it leaves territory open to other parties and to other ideas. In recommending "abandonment"[33] of the urban territory to developers, politicians, bureaucratic planners, and citizens, Koolhaas neglected the possibility that other, later urban designers might not find this plural urban territory to be beyond the reach of urban design. Perhaps these later urban designers might see some design potential in the city, even if the city could never be designed in the same manner as a unitary site.[34]

But the eyes of urban designers today do not seem fixed on the plural space of the city. Instead, urban designers are focused on traditional unitary sites like campuses or subdivisions or on large buildings, realizations of Koolhaas's bigness. Many contemporary urban design offices and urban design academic programs, particularly those well known for "projective" (i.e., innovative) urban design ideas rather than protective, contextual standards, deal mostly with unitary sites or with large buildings, sometimes even treating the city's plural sites as a large unitary site in the same manner as Le Corbusier's Plan Voisin.[35] The continuing temptation to treat the city as a unitary site is not difficult to imagine. Not only are abundant historical precedents from modernism available, but contemporary architectural rhetoric, from Koolhaas to critics like Pier Vittorio Aureli or Charles Waldheim,[36] also reinforces such treatment. In the realm of construction, many developing countries, notably China but also many others, have replaced small-scale urban fabrics with unitary projects just as New York and other US cities did fifty years ago during the heyday of modernist urban design. Unitary urban design seems far from dead.

But let us imagine another, greater possibility. What if, instead of abandoning the plural city, urban design engaged with it? What if innovative urban design thinking transcended unitary ideals like bigness or neotraditionalism? What if urban designers were not concerned just with airports, college campuses, and residential subdivisions, but felt free to reimagine the form of city blocks, city districts, even the city itself, each entity containing hundreds, thousands, or even millions of parcels? What if urban design did not seek to reduce cities to the simplicity of a unitary site, but instead took the city's plural quality as a basis for a *plural urbanism*?

Those designers interested in the potential for a plural urban design would discover some important things. Koolhaas was right: the design of cities is still very much an open question. Outside of historical city centers such as those of Paris or Savannah, Georgia, a typical city has comparatively little evident urban design. Myriad building and zoning codes may govern São Paulo, Manhattan, and Shanghai, but those codes have little perceptible aesthetic effect. One cannot blame only reductive codes or those who administer them for the resulting lack of urban design in the contemporary city; one must blame urban designers themselves, for failing to understand and engage with the plural city.

This book seeks to remedy that situation by broadening the art of urban design beyond its current status as too closely related to, even a subsidiary of, the building art of architecture. Architects can design buildings and many unitary sites, but the urban design skill required to shape plural sites is very different. Such plural urbanism is not an expanded version of architecture, nor can architectural strategies shape it. Instead, plural urbanism requires the incorporation of many principles that are unknown or foreign to architecture and to unitary urban design: principles that will be fully explored over the course of the succeeding chapters. Of course, plural urbanism does not stand apart from other building arts; it is comprised of them. Urban design contains architecture, as well as landscape, sculpture, and other building arts. But plural urban design is an *independent* art, one that possesses its own qualities, its own formal strategies, and its own ideals. By studying plural urbanism's particular dimensions, as we will do in the next chapter, we will come to understand plural urban design as the largest art, with qualities that are all its own.

Five Dimensions of Plural Urbanism

Introduction

Despite the preponderance of thinking and practice that shows urban design as a unitary art, urban design reveals its plural dimensions in several respects. This chapter explores five dimensions of plural urban design: scale, time, property, agency, and form. Collectively, these dimensions demonstrate that urban design is a plural art different both in kind and degree from its sister building arts: architecture, landscape, sculpture, and land art. Each of urban design's five dimensions may exist individually, but only plural urban design possesses each of these dimensions. And, while these dimensions distance plural design to some extent from unitary arts like architecture, plural urbanism welcomes these dimensions. Pluralism enhances rather than reduces urban design.

The first dimension of plural urban design is that of *scale*. Urban design's scalar reach is broad indeed. The dimension of scale is featured in everything from a pocket park or a single parcel of land on a city street, to larger sites such as a city district and beyond to the size of a metropolitan region. Urban design is the only building art with such a great scalar range; no other building art even approaches it. And, as scale increases, so do the additional plural dimensions of urbanism.

The most mysterious and difficult to understand plural dimension of urban design is the element of *time*. Plural time is ineluctably linked to the scale of urban design, which in turn is linked to the limits of human beings' capacity to build. For even a small urban design ensemble is constituted of a combination of structures, spaces, and properties. Small ensembles may take only forty years to build, but larger urban design ensembles may take hundreds or thousands of years, and must take into account the existing cityscape. In ancient cities such as Barcelona, urban design ensembles are shaped by structures and spaces dating from the Middle Ages to the late twentieth century. Urban design is not simply an arrangement of elements in space, but also a shifting arrangement of elements over time.

The third dimension is *property*. As urbanism increases in scale, so does the likelihood that the site of an urban design project will spill over the boundaries of individual properties or parcels. Every structure in a city sits on a separate parcel of land that is defined by law; many cities are composed of little more than endlessly subdivided parcels divided by streets. Urban design is the only building art that can encompass multiple parcels having multiple owners. This is true whether an urban design concept is as simple as consistent building heights or is much more complex. Confronting and transcending the pluralism of property is a major challenge for plural urbanism.

Plural *agency* is the fourth dimension of plural urbanism, for cities are inhabited by people, and urban design is by nature a public art. Its accessibility, openness, and public use distinguish urban design from other building arts, which may be entirely private. Urban design's public is a plural entity made up of observers, users, and contributors to urban design. No single individual can build a large-scale urban design; the number of required actors may number in the thousands or more, and their plural methods make urban design an art shaped collectively, which again differs from building arts that are shaped by a more or less unitary agent.

Any large-scale urban design idea, divided among different properties with different actors, will possess the fifth and final dimension of plural urbanism, plural *form*. While a very small urban design ensemble may have only two or three constituent elements, a larger ensemble may have dozens. And urban design, unique among the building arts, need not possess unitary form to exist; an urban design concept can be diffuse, scattered, or fragmented without losing its coherence. In fact, in a plural environment the dimension of plural form is not only a necessity, but also an asset that incorporates other elements of the city into plural urban design.

The Dimension of Scale

Scale has a range of meanings. As used by architects scale often conveys the relationship between a certain representation of a structure and the structure itself. Geographers share this definition, referring by a map's scale to the proportional relationship between a map and a real space. Scale may also refer to the relationship between an element of real space, such as the human figure, and other elements in that space. In all cases, spatial scale implies a set of relationships, either between an abstracted representation and a true one, or between one spatial element and another. Space is not the only domain in which scale operates. Temporal scales relate spans such as human life to other, larger timespans, such as a century or more. In both space and time, enlargements of scale tend to push scale to, or beyond, limits of human perception: those too far beyond our own closely defined scales of space and time tend to be less comprehensible and less meaningful.

Consistency of spatial scale is a hallmark of many arts, perhaps due to the material limits or structural characteristics of an artwork. Stone, for example, requires reinforcement to reach great spans or heights. A painting canvas can only be so large before it transcends the spatial confines of any room or the structural limits of canvas. Other scales of art may be tied to an artist's capacity; a painting or sculpture's scale, for example, may be constrained by the amount of time an artist has available. Michelangelo took four years to paint the ceiling of the Sistine Chapel, and his envisioned sculptural ensemble for the tomb of Julius II would have taken even longer. Ultimately, the scale of the human body shapes the scale of creation, display, and form of most art, whether it directly refers to the human body or not.

It follows that architecture is also consistent with the scale of the human body. Architecture's scale obliges strictly defined lower limits with less strictly defined upper limits. No building could be much smaller than Le Corbusier's summer Cabanon on the shores of Roquebrune-Cap-Martin in France. At only slightly more than thirteen square meters, this tiny building, sometimes called "micro-architecture,"[1] is at or very near the smallest scale possible for a habitable structure, at least by contemporary standards. In contrast, upper levels of architectural scale are shaped both by material potentials and the technological and programmatic needs driving the creation of the space. Architecture's scalar explosion occurred in concert with the equally explosive technological capacity of the mid-twentieth century. Some of the largest interior spaces in the world, such as Skidmore, Owings and Merrill's United Airlines Maintenance Hangar (constructed in 1958) and Max Urbahn's 526-foot-tall Vehicle Assembly Building (VAB) for NASA (built between 1962 and 1966), were designed to enclose two of the largest machines of that time, the Douglas DC-8 jet and Atlas rockets.

While architecture may yet attain larger (or perhaps smaller) scales than NASA's VAB or Le Corbusier's Cabanon, its scalar reach pales in comparison to the parallel and

2.1 Architecture's scalar range is not infinite. Le Corbusier's Cabanon at Roquebrune-Cap-Martin is about as small as habitable structures can be.

2.2 The increasing scale of twentieth-century transport technology necessitated ever-larger structures, leading to the construction of the largest building of its time, NASA's Vehicle Assembly Building at Cape Canaveral.

much greater scalar range of urban design. More than any other art, urban design possesses great plasticity of scale. In contrast to painting, sculpture, and even architecture, there is no typical scale of urban design: the scale of urban design shifts when the work's scope is extended or contracted.[2]

In other words, urban design lacks strictly defined upper and lower limits of scale. At its smallest scales, urban design dissolves into the cityscape's constituent components—streets, buildings, open space, and infrastructure; at its largest scales, urban design can merge almost imperceptibly into the natural and man-made landscape, into what Germans call more precisely *Landschaft*, the made landscape. Between these lower and upper scalar limits, urbanism ranges from the scale of the smallest spaces within a city to the scale of a city itself, and ultimately to scales larger than the city such as a metropolitan region or even a cluster of designed metropolises.

There is, of course, much overlap between urbanism and other arts within this scalar range, and some architecture, landscape architecture, and land art is as large as or even larger than small-scale urban design. One might first characterize Central Park, for instance, as a work of landscape architecture, but one might also characterize the park's engagement and interaction with the city fabric as a larger work of urban design, perhaps the finest that New York City possesses. It would be equally hard to categorize the low-density, designed town of Columbia, Maryland, developed by James Rouse in the 1960s and 1970s, as solely a work of urban design or of landscape architecture; it doubtless is both. Nor is a large-scale building such as L'Illa Diagonal in Barcelona, designed by architect Rafael Moneo and urbanist Manuel de Solà-Morales, merely a work of large architecture. All these works are unarguably urban design, even as they are also works of landscape or architecture. Urban design is so closely bound to its sibling arts that fixed definitions of what is or is not urban design may be both impossible and unnecessary. Perhaps what is or is not urban design may even be as much in the eye of the beholder as in any strict definition of form, process, or aesthetic.

Urbanism is also, inescapably, a public art, just as cities are public entities. Urban design's public nature often distinguishes it from aesthetic enterprises of similar scales. One ought not consider a large work of land art such as Walter De Maria's *Lightning Field* to be urban design: located in western New Mexico, the site is indeed large, one mile by one kilometer in size, but the work is open to the public only by appointment for short visits. On the other hand, a smaller designed residential neighborhood such as Ladd's Addition in Portland, Oregon, only half a mile on each side,[3] is a work of urban design. Ladd's Addition is not only located in a city and mostly residential, but its streets are fully open to the public.

The smallest scale of urban design is the sort sociologist William H. Whyte describes as a *small urban space*.[4] One such space is Paley Park, or Samuel Paley Plaza, in New York City. Paley Park is minute, a pocket park of less than 0.1 acre (0.04 ha) located midblock on Manhattan's 53rd Street, on the site of a demolished building. Built on donated private land in the 1960s and still privately owned and managed, the elegantly simple park is little more than a paved space and grid of trees interspersed with tables and seating. Bounding the space on three sides and screening much of the cityscape beyond are ivied walls and a waterfall running along the rear wall of the park. In his book *City: Rediscovering the Center*, Whyte noted that Paley Park was "a delight to passersby as well as sitters" owing to its small scale and its openness to the street, which makes it, according to Whyte, "hard to tell where [the street] ends and [the park] begins." Paley Park was "the best of examples. The sidewalk in front of it is an integral part of the park. ... Passersby use Paley too. About half will turn their heads and look

2.3 Other arts besides urban design can be very large in scale, but they differ in that they may have little or no public component. Walter De Maria's *Lightning Field* is a work of land art that is open only for short visits.

in. … The sight of the park, the knowledge that it is there, becomes part of the image we have of a much wider area."[5] Paley Park, tiny as it is, is a work of urban design; it is a piece of cityscape that provides a new aesthetic to a formerly anonymous city block.

As urban design increases in scale, it increases in complexity. *Large urban spaces* are common elements of urban design. One such, larger than Paley Park, is the plaza of Mies van der Rohe's Seagram building. This is a privately owned public square surrounded by spatially related structures and larger urban spaces: the Seagram building and its plaza, the much older Racquet and Tennis Club across the street, and Park Avenue. The careful alignment of the Seagram building with the Club, combined with the transparent, public entrance of the Seagram building and the much-praised sunny plaza, make each element critical in establishing Seagram's plaza as a work of urban design. Here, every element—architecture, open space, streets—contributes to the function and aesthetic of the space.

Urban design's multiscalarity is well illustrated by the public square adjacent to Barcelona's Mercat de Santa Caterina. The Mercat (market), renovated by architect Enric Miralles in the 1990s, is itself programmatically complex, with additional components that include social housing. It is also part of a larger urban design ensemble comprising the market square as well as an adjacent larger plaza to the west, fronted by the city's medieval cathedral.[6] This urban design ensemble of Mercat, plaza, and cathedral—larger and much more diverse in age, program, and architectural composition than Seagram's austere plaza—is, like Seagram, made up of a related ensemble of spatial elements. While the Mercat's urban design ensemble is merely one plaza in a city with many fine public squares, these Barcelona spaces demonstrate how urbanism's constituent elements increase in number as scale increases. Even at the relatively small scale of the Mercat de Santa Caterina ensemble, it is difficult to determine exactly how many elements belong to it, but the number is certainly many more than at the Seagram Plaza.

As urban design increases in scale, it takes on a fractal quality, where numerous small ensembles make up bigger ensembles that are in turn part of even larger ensembles. In Barcelona, the Mercat de Santa Caterina's public space seamlessly merges into a larger space at the intersection of Via Laietana and the cathedral plaza. The plaza is itself composed of several smaller spaces, including the Placita de la Seu directly in front of the cathedral, and the adjacent Plaça Nova. This plaza sequence is just one episode of urban design among many that link Barcelona's old city to the harborfront and to the Ensanche grid to the north. Adding to this complexity is the presence of multiple eras of construction in the Barcelona plaza sequence. This temporal complexity introduces

2.4 The Seagram Building's plaza is a small-scale work of urban design that engages the public of the plaza, the facing Racquet and Tennis Club, and Park Avenue, which is itself a larger-scaled work of urbanism.

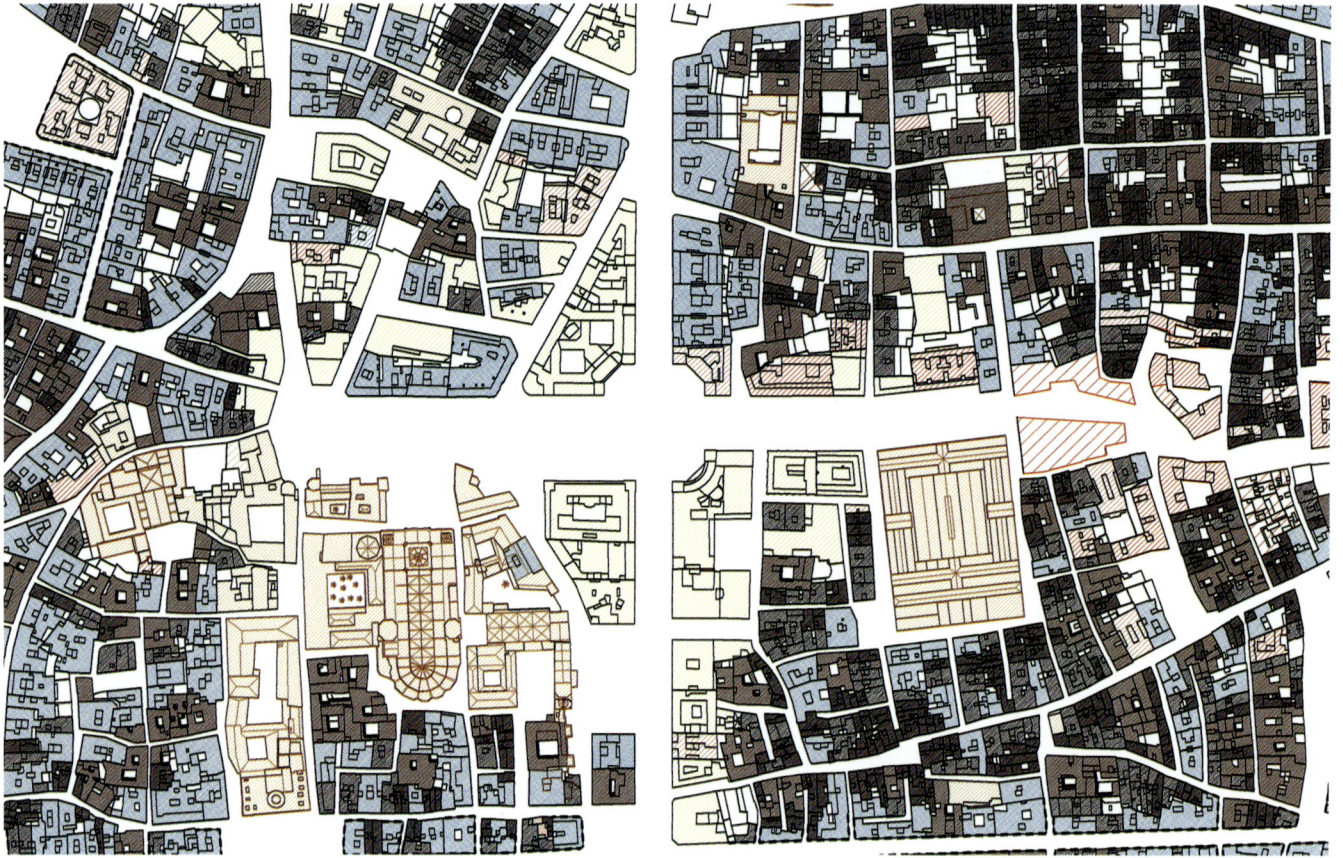

2.5 Urban design has a fractal quality, with elements of different scales nested within and flowing into each other, as in Barcelona's cathedral plaza, shown here extending horizontally from left to right in this drawing by Joan Busquets.

another element of pluralism in urban design, that of time. Time's presence in urban design has been remarked upon by many scholars,[7] and we will explore it in the next section of this chapter.

Urban design's fundamentally multiscalar, fractal quality was noted in Philadelphia planning director Edmund Bacon's *Design of Cities*.[8] Bacon called this multiscalarity a quality of "interlocking" in which "buildings reach out across space to other buildings, each one firmly implanted in the space in which it is located and creating interrelations in between."[9] Bacon's own work ultimately brought such an interlocking order to his home city of Philadelphia, as we will see in chapter 4.

As urban design increases in scale, its fractal quality is accompanied by diversifications in its nature and function. While public squares only rarely attain great scale, *streets* are common large-scale elements of urban design. All cities have streets, but not all streets are works of urban design; most are functional thoroughfares with little aesthetic character.[10] Some urban streets, however, rank among the most notable works of urbanism. Urban designer Allan Jacobs praised "great streets," stating that streets that had been "put together well, artfully" were "joyful … entertaining … places to act and to dream."[11] Jacobs cited the Boulevard St. Michel in Paris and the Ramblas in Barcelona as streets whose careful design was supported by the surrounding urban fabrics.

Streets such as New York's Park Avenue or Avenue Foch in Paris are exemplary works of urban design. For almost two miles between 59th and 96th Street, Park Avenue boasts consistently scaled thirteen- to seventeen-story buildings. All are luxury apartment buildings facing a roadway with a central mall of plantings. In Paris, eight-story apartment houses consistently line Avenue Foch, a very wide street connecting the Bois de Boulogne with the Place de l'Étoile (Place Charles de Gaulle) and the Arc de Triomphe. Given their larger scale, urban streets possess an even greater pluralism of constituent elements than do public squares. Avenue Foch is bounded by some twenty-six separate city blocks, each comprising several buildings and each contributing to the street's urban design.

Both Avenue Foch and Park Avenue are also fractal, partaking of both smaller- and larger-scale urban design elements. South of 59th Street, Park Avenue gives way to an office district and then to the Grand Central Station neighborhood that was once called "Terminal City," while Avenue Foch is one element of Paris's carefully designed 16th and 17th arrondissements (city districts). Such *city districts* are perhaps the most typically understood scale of urban design. Paris has twenty such arrondissements, each marking a distinct effort and era of urban design.

2.6 Park Avenue is just one of many streets in the Manhattan grid, but its consistently scaled buildings and distinct structure make it a large-scaled work of urban design within the city.

Because they are widespread, city districts are the urban design scale most often featured in compendia of contemporary urbanism. In Joan Busquets and Felipe Correa's *Cities, X Lines*, for example, three of the ten "lines" (i.e., "tactical maneuvers," "piecemeal aggregations," and "traditional views") are city districts.[12] And like other scales of urban design, city districts have flexible borders: in both Paris and Barcelona, city districts are part of larger urban design elements. As city districts increase in scale they become what we might call *macrodistricts*. The west side of Paris is one such macrodistrict, in which smaller-scale districts such as the Place de l'Étoile, surrounding the Arc de Triomphe, are connected to other squares by boulevards such as Avenue Foch. This west side macrodistrict comprises an unusually consistent city fabric of eight-story buildings, and it comprises a substantial portion of historic Paris.

The Ensanche or "expansion" of Barcelona (Eixample in Catalan) is a signal example of a macrodistrict, one that also includes a great deal of the city's center.

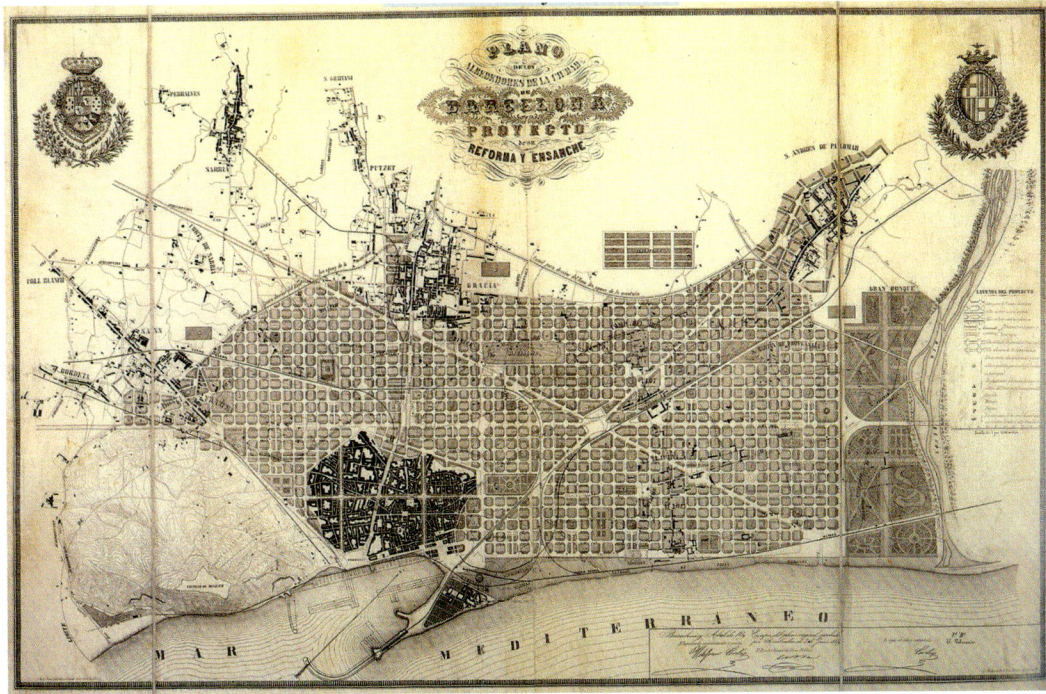

2.7 Barcelona's Ensanche, or Eixample, proposed by Indefons Cerdà in an 1859 competition, is a wondrous work of urban design at the city district scale, and it has become the heart of the city.

Designed by engineer Ildefons Cerdà in 1859, the Ensanche, organized as a grid with chamfered (cut-off) block corners, is unusual among European cities, few of which possess grids. Even in Spain, where many cities possess *ensanche* districts, the great scale of Barcelona's Ensanche makes the city unique. Initially designed as an expansion of the city,[13] the Ensanche eventually came to constitute much of the business and touristic center of Barcelona. Today, tourists stroll the Ensanche's wide Passeig de Gràcia boulevard with much of the city's commercial office fabric, a great deal of its high-priced residential real estate, and abundant shopping nearby.

Few cities have had the will or ability to create and sustain such large-scaled designed city districts with consistent aesthetic intention and clarity. The 16th arrondissement and the Barcelona Ensanche, with their strict building controls and carefully defined boulevards, are exceptions in a world of less carefully designed cities. Yet there are urban design scales still larger than these macrodistricts. Cities themselves may constitute very large-scale works of urban design—and the urban scale seems to be the largest that urban designers have yet been able to conceive, at least as a fully realized work of design.[14] Though designed cities are rare, many were created during the twentieth century.

The archetype of a large-scale, completely designed city is Brasília, the new-built capital of Brazil. This city was designed and constructed in the incredibly short time of four years between 1956 and 1960 as part of a fast-track campaign by the country's president Juscelino Kubitschek.[15] Brasília is highly unusual, even unique, in being designed *and constructed*, from its street pattern to its urban fabric to the *superquadra* apartment blocks, all in a manner embodying the distinct vision of its designers, architect-planner Lúcio Costa and architect Oscar Niemeyer.

Built rapidly to the highest standards of the modernist design paradigm dominant at the time, Brasília is a tempting vision for architect-urbanists eager to engage in the design of such large-scale built environments. Brasília seems to urge the creation of equivalently compelling spatial propositions, formulated at the scale of the city. Such a fully designed city offers the architect-urbanist the opportunity to design and shape at every scale, from an individual housing block up to a city's street pattern, even to the scale of a regional plan. Little wonder that the Brasília project, particularly as its modernist aesthetic has returned to fashion, is highly regarded by urban designers today.[16] But Brasília's promise of a wholly designed city is a chimera; cities can never be large works of architecture, and such thinking ignores the numerous plural dimensions of urban design that we explore in this chapter.

Brasília represents the largest scale of urban design that has been proposed and constructed at a "complete" level of detail, but an even larger scale can be aesthetically shaped by human action: the city region. Few such regional-scale designs exist at any level of completion, because both the motivation and the capacity to enact design on such a massive scale are rare. Most regional-scale propositions, in fact, have a touch of utopia about them, including the well-known examples of Ebenezer Howard's Garden City from the 1890s and Burnham and Bennett's *Plan of Chicago* of 1909.

The most notable built example of design at the scale of a city region is London's Green Belt. Urban designer Patrick Abercrombie first proposed the idea in the Greater London Plan of 1944. Conceived not as a program for construction but as a restriction on urban growth, the Green Belt mostly banned development in a ring around the metropolis, except where Abercrombie designated satellite cities for London's expansion.[17] Much of the plan's motivation was social and economic, but its

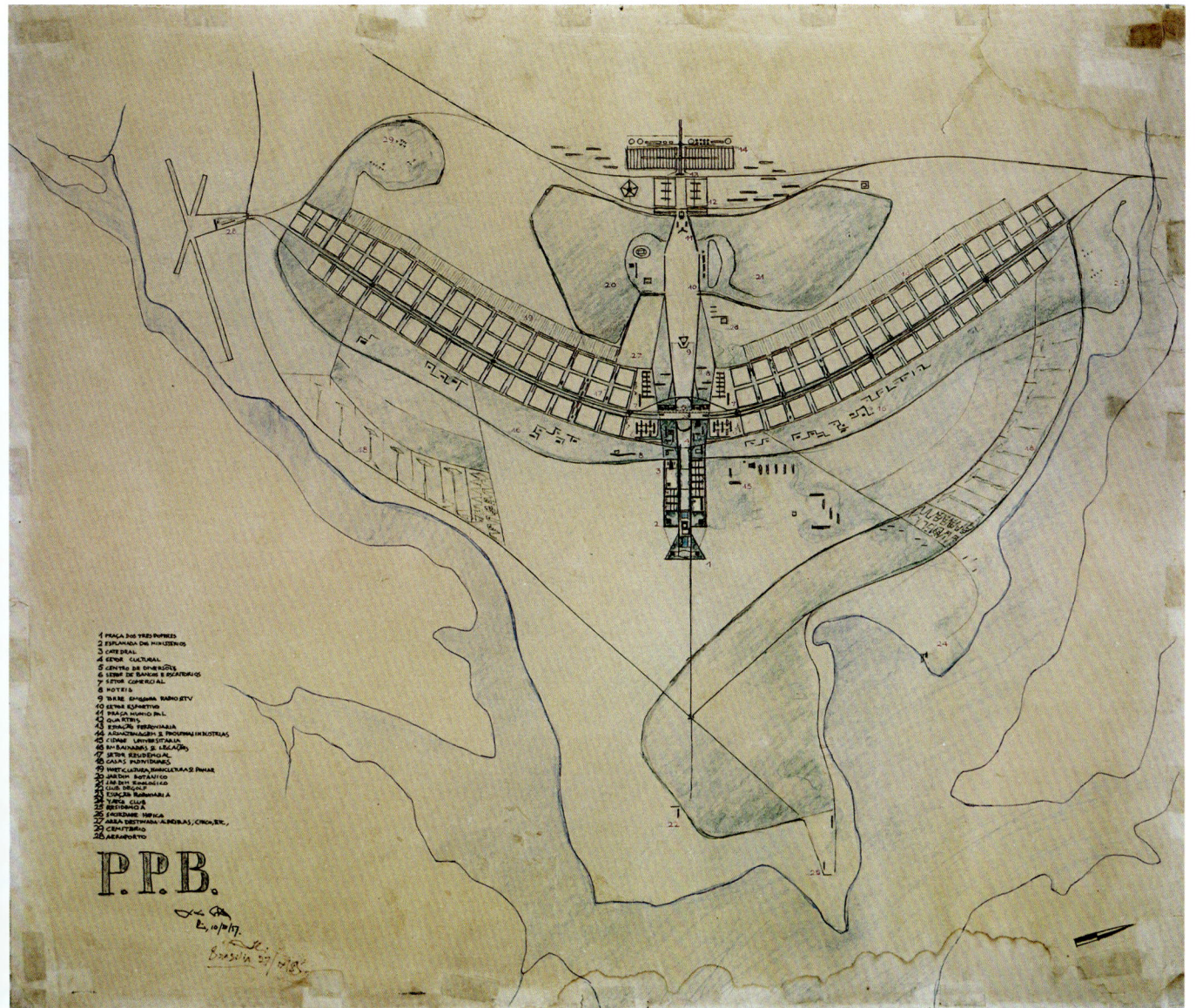

2.8 The plan of Brasília, proposed in 1956, is a tempting paradigm of a completely designed city. But its fixed form, resembling a large-scaled work of architecture, ignores urbanism's numerous plural qualities and has led to the plan's marginalization.

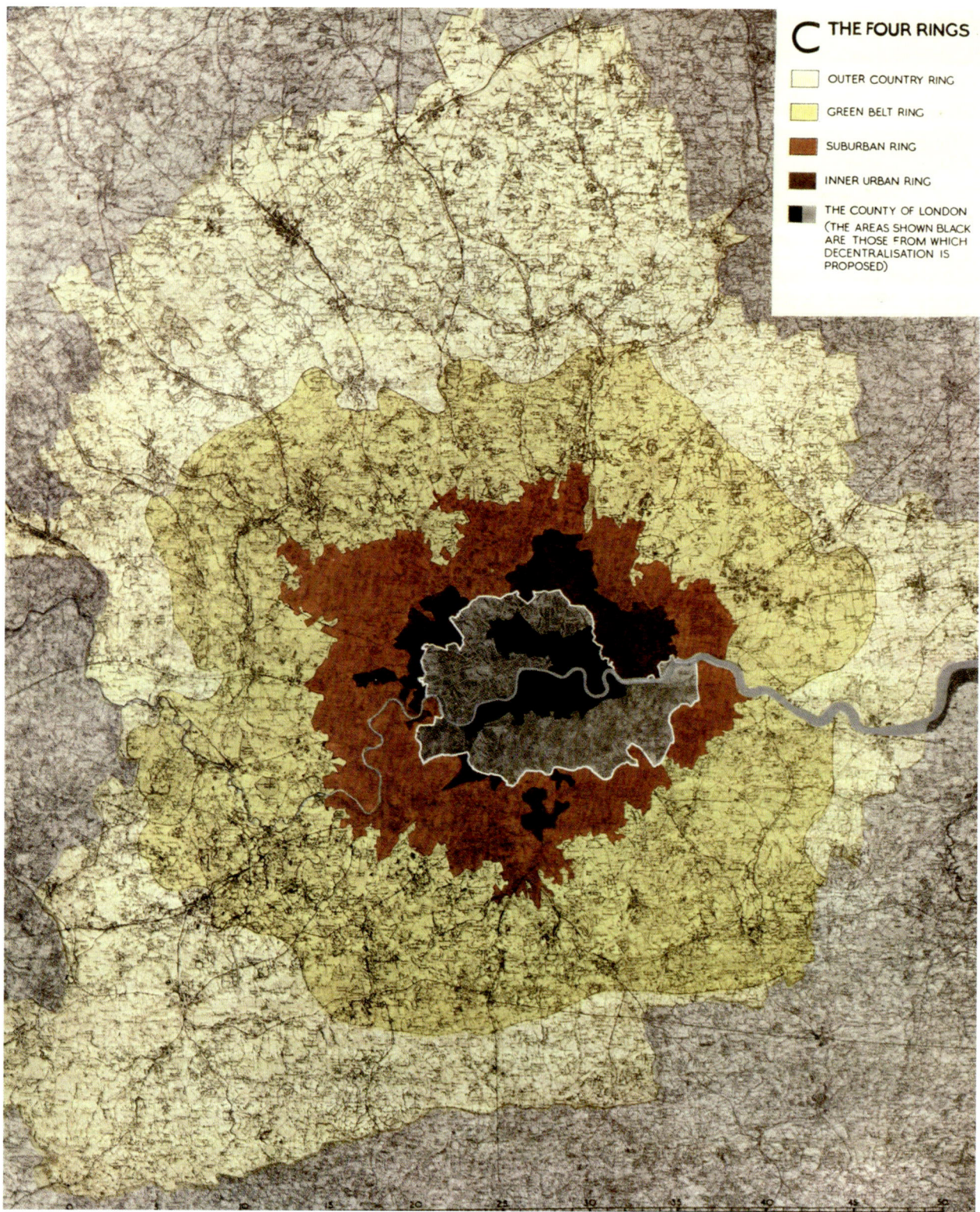

central concept was clearly aesthetic: one study stated that the plan's "concrete, single vision of the desired end form of the city" lay "firmly within the tradition of architect plans" of the early and mid-twentieth century: a concept whose origin lay in Howard's Garden City Plan.[18] Once enacted, London's Green Belt succeeded, as no urban design idea had before it, in governing the form of a gigantic metropolis. Of course, the Green Belt was in a sense a *negative* form of urban design; it was conservative rather than projective, recommending few new settlement areas within the Belt, just preservation of those that already existed.

Abercrombie's plan, backed by the Town and Country Planning Act of 1947, succeeded in ways that its framers never imagined. Only twenty-five years later planning scholar Peter Hall and his colleagues argued not only that London's countryside had been protected, just as the Green Belt plan had envisioned, but that the plan had unexpectedly caused regional property price inflation, suppression of architectural experimentation with housing types, reduction of living choices for poor Londoners, and an unequal privileging of the small portion of society able to afford houses in protected areas. London's very large-scale urban design was a significant spatial achievement that was also an object lesson in unintended consequences. Shaping space at such a large scale, particularly through the rigidity of a "concrete, single vision of [a] desired end form" for a dynamic global metropolis, adversely impacted the societies and economies constrained by that single vision. Today, in no small part due to the Green Belt, London's property prices are among the highest in the world.[19]

The scalar reach of urban design is broad. But another plural dimension of urbanism is even greater: that of time. Not only does construction of urban design's multiple elements (buildings, open spaces, infrastructure, etc.) take time, but as urban design increases in scale, so do the myriad ways in which time influences urbanism. The plural dimensions of scale and time are closely interwoven.

The Dimension of Time

Time's place in urban design is almost always underestimated. This may be because time's role in urban design is difficult to perceive and, therefore, to appreciate. Understanding urban design as an art inescapably influenced by time does not necessarily mesh well with typical conceptions of urban design as large-scale, static compositions

◄ **2.9** London's Green Belt, designed by Patrick Abercrombie and implemented beginning in 1947, is perhaps the largest spatial concept to have been consistently imposed on a city region, with consequences that have become ever more problematic as London has grown economically.

of buildings and spaces. Yet urban design has a relationship to time that is very much its own. The art of urban design is both temporally demanding, because urbanism takes time to be constructed, and temporally durable, because urban design persists for unusually long spans of time. Applied to urban design, the ancient aphorism *ars longa, vita brevis* (life is short, the art long) finds true justification.

One aspect of temporal pluralism—the presence of multiple eras of time within urban design—is well understood and well accepted. Most urban designers readily acknowledge the importance of elements from the past, and many are generous in incorporating such elements into design schemes. Some urban designers even view the past's presence as a necessary component of good urbanism. In this sense, time is a friend. But urban designers are less forgiving of the amount of time required for urban design's construction, because time can also be an enemy. Too much time for construction increases the likelihood that a design will not be completed, and longer spans of time can change the social mores and aesthetic values that generated design schemes conceived in previous eras, leading to incompleteness. But incompleteness can be a virtue, a requirement for future development and change, reconsideration, and perhaps improvement of urban design, and we will see in chapter 6 that incompleteness is an inescapable and fundamental element of plural urbanism.

Histories of urban form[20] conventionally begin at or before the dawn of recorded human history, in the Bronze Age before the invention of writing, when cities such as Çatalhüyük (in today's Turkey) were founded. The subsequent urban history is quite familiar, advancing in time from early designed cities such as Miletus (Turkey), Xi'an (China), and Teotihuacán (Mexico) into the classical era with Rome and Roman colonies such as Timgad (Algeria). Whether or not cities like Çatalhüyük were designed (as we currently understand the term) is unresolved. If they were indeed designed, then the field of urban design would be accordingly ancient;[21] but as we saw in chapter 1, other scholars see urban design as a distinct discipline emerging only in the 1950s, with the initiation of formal training in the art.[22] Whatever the discipline's formal longevity, cities clearly have a long history, and many contain abundant physical traces of the past. These traces mesh consciously or unconsciously with elements of other eras in what British urbanist Colin Rowe called "bricolage" or accidental collage.[23]

The presence of past buildings or settlement patterns in the present day provides cities with a sense of time that sociologist Sharon Zukin called *kairos*, "a sense of the past that intrudes into the present."[24] Colin Rowe found *kairos* in contemporary Rome, and *kairos* is equally strong in cities such as Jerusalem, Istanbul, Cuzco, and

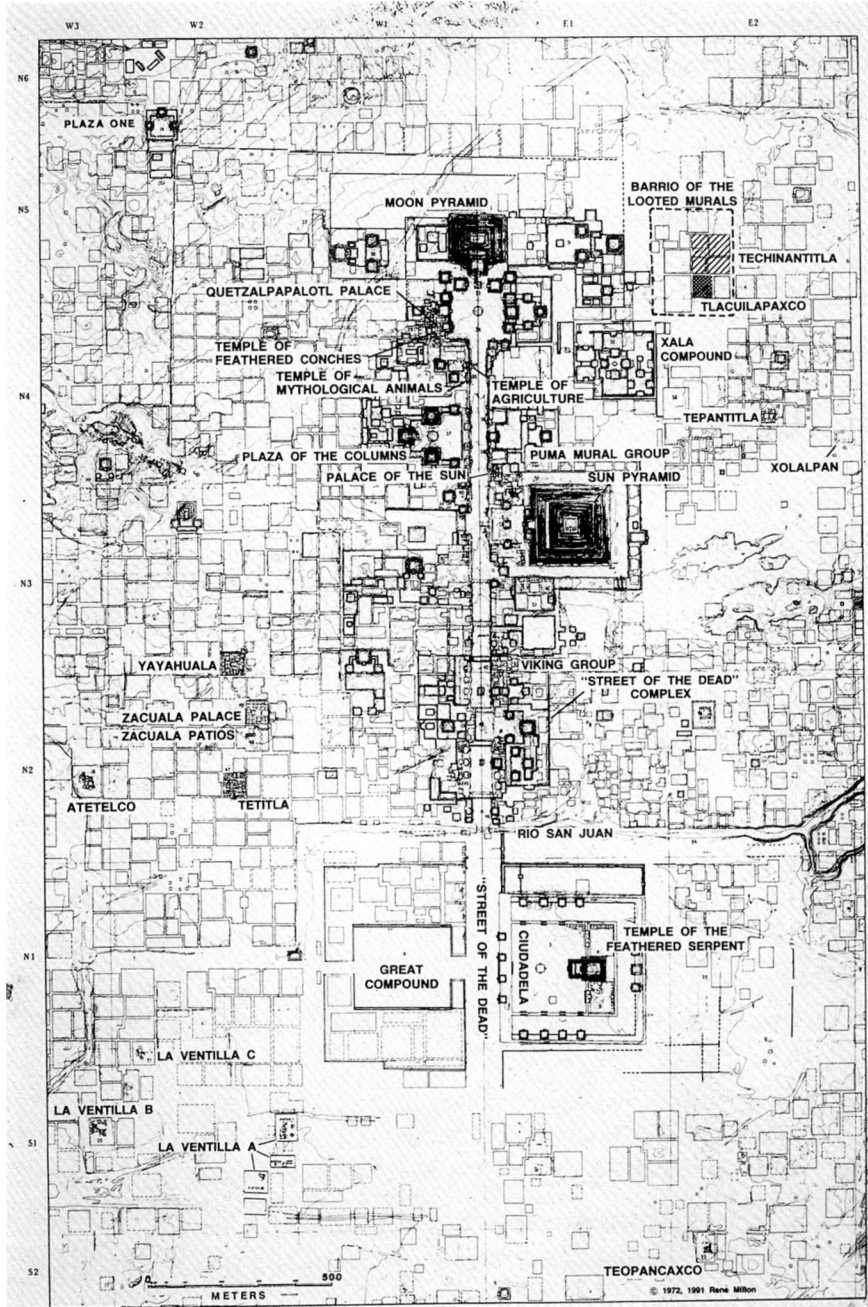

2.10 Cities have had intentional form for thousands of years, across a range of civilizations ranging from Europe to the Middle East to East Asia to the Americas, as shown here in the plan of Teotihuacán in central Mexico.

others with substantial elements remaining from past eras. *Kairos* is correspondingly weak in newer cities, whether cities like Dallas in developed countries or any of the hundreds of peripheral settlements that have sprung up in recent decades in developing nations.

Yet Zukin also found *kairos* where one might not necessarily expect it. Within its all-encompassing grid, New York City possesses *kairos* in pieces of its urban pattern that predate the grid—think Broadway or Greenwich Village—and in the numerous activities found on its side streets. Zukin, a resident of Manhattan's East Village, feels *kairos* quite strongly there, on streets where ethnic businesses have somehow resisted rampant gentrification and preserved a lower-income past that is still within living memory.[25] Not far away, Jane Jacobs once felt a similar quality in the West Village, one that she translated into a "need for old buildings."[26] Jacobs was fond of old buildings' practical ability to host eccentric businesses, house elderly and low-income people, and provide an economic and social complexity absent in large-scale building projects. Today, Jacobs's modest West Village is itself history, yet one recent writer found a sense of *kairos* still present near her former home on Hudson Street, faint recollections of the nearly vanished working-class neighborhood of Jacobs's time.[27]

Noting the past's presence in cities does not mean that cities are historic artifacts frozen in time. For the most part cities are the opposite, temporally dynamic entities that can change at rates from gradual and calm to frantic. In a nation whose economy is growing rapidly, cities will change at rates that defy easy comprehension, what Jane Jacobs called "explosive urban growth."[28] Many a nineteenth-century observer, from Dickens to Engels, was bewildered and troubled by Britain's explosive urban growth, and London's Green Belt was one long-delayed reaction. Following World War II, a similarly rapid rate of change in American cities brought on by government-sponsored urban renewal spurred Jacobs's criticisms of "cataclysmic" transformations[29] as well as urban designer Kevin Lynch's proposals for moderating rates of urban change.[30] In recent years, China's rapid destruction of older districts and construction of new city districts has been equally astonishing.

Kairos, it would seem, is quite resilient, and time's traces are difficult to eradicate from the city entirely. Irrespective of whatever economic benefit or aesthetic pleasure time's patina may provide the city, the past subsists whether urban designers wish it or not. Time's presence in urban design takes multiple forms: urban design as *artifact*, as *palimpsest*, and as *patchwork*.

Artifact

Urban design is inevitably an artifact of the time when it was designed and constructed. Once built, a work of urban design will age and become a part of the life of its surroundings. Just as a book, a painting, or even a city plan becomes a part of the stream of time, so urbanism reflects time's passage in its aesthetic and age.[31] Time's passage inevitably dates any work of urbanism, allowing us to read in its architecture, street patterns, and land uses its era of construction, and the astute observer can always find clues to the date of these eras.[32] The artifactual imprint of time on urban design, in which urbanism ages just as does monumental architecture, is the simplest way in which to understand time's relationship to urban design.

Historic preservationists treat scales of urban design in much the same way as they do individual works of architecture. To the preservationist, urban design is an artifact, so although historic districts are sometimes larger than individual buildings, change within them is forbidden just as it is in a historic building. Alterations and demolitions are not permitted in historic districts, and new structures, if any, must conform to the historic aesthetic of the area. In this way places like Paris's Place des Vosges, a sixteenth-century square that once embodied the latest principles in open space design, are restored to reflect their original era of construction. At Place des Vosges, an urban space has become a single artifact.

It is hard to argue against the transformation or preservation of some cities—old Vienna, Paris, Saint Petersburg—as large-scale monuments. But preservation in this way also seems to reflect an unrealistic desire to stop the passage of time entirely. Beyond a certain scale, change in a city fabric is inevitable, and it becomes impossible to treat a temporally dynamic city as a static, unitary object. Unitary space can perhaps be preserved as an artifact, but plural space can never be. Just where the scalar boundary between unitary or plural time should lie remains a matter of dispute and an issue that we will revisit later in this section.

Palimpsest

A new work of architecture may be relatively free of the past, particularly if a building is located in a newly created setting. But in cities, time is omnipresent. Traces of the past are visible, for example, in many New York City neighborhoods. Take the succession of extremely tall and narrow (for their day) office buildings that line lower Broadway east of Greenwich Village. Constructed during the early twentieth century in an era of rapid

2.11 A work of urban design, once complete, enters into the stream of time and will eventually become an artifact of the era in which it was constructed. Paris's Place des Vosges is an intact artifact of the early seventeenth century.

growth, the mini-towers' street frontages and building depths reflect the precise dimensions of row houses that once occupied the site, just as the towers' building heights reflect the early twentieth century's elevators, structural steel, and pressures of market demand. A few blocks away, two surviving row houses (now historic monuments) show the original architecture that formed this parcel pattern. Tokyo, a massive city originally composed of tiny houses, is also such a palimpsest.

Property, we will see in later in this chapter, is perhaps the most immutable presence of a city's past. Were Manhattan to be entirely redeveloped with new structures, its street grid and property boundaries, most dating from the early nineteenth century, would continue to shape development. In Lower Manhattan, a recent high-rise at 351–355 Bowery near Broadway's early twentieth-century mini-towers adjoins two early nineteenth-century buildings. The two older buildings' combined width equals that of the new tower, showing the new structure's parcel to be the combination of two older lots. Because of property history, every city is an inevitable palimpsest of decisions affecting construction and landownership that sometimes date back hundreds of years.

The presence of the past may be more direct than the existence of property lines. Old buildings often remain as a barrier, or sometimes an inspiration, to urban design. Old buildings may be simply labeled "context," but context is in fact extremely diverse, and urban designers treat context in many different ways. Scale will influence urbanism's engagement with context: an urban designer may be unable or unwilling to respect small context, or conversely, an urban design must forcibly respect large context. China's small-scale *hutong* dwellings, for example, were obliterated in droves to make way for recent development in Beijing; but Rome's Coliseum is too big and significant to ignore. Just as there is no single urban context, there is no single way for urban design to confront or engage the past. What is certain, at least in cities, is that context will exist in some form, even if only as an invisible property boundary.

Just as nineteenth-century buildings are commonly understood as context, contemporary works of urban design will in time become a piece of city fabric with which future urban design efforts will have to contend. This palimpsest quality of the urban fabric asks that urban designers accept their work's eventual subsuming within the stream of time and past construction. Modernist urban design, which once attempted to negate or override the stream of time within the city, is today itself historic: Le Corbusier's famed houses at Pessac are just another part of the historic city, made as ordinary as their inhabitants may wish, just like any house in Levittown.[33] Under ordinary circumstances, any given urban design effort never represents the end of history.

2.12 The past is always present in cities, but this past can take many forms, ranging from the survival of old buildings to the persistence of lot lines. The New Museum's site combines three smaller former building parcels.

Patchwork

Like the goddess Athena, springing forth fully grown and fully armed from Zeus's head, some urban design efforts are created complete, a piece of city fabric that needs no further annotation by later designers. Le Corbusier's capitol complex at Chandigarh, for example, was designed and constructed as a single architectural ensemble in which time's inevitable passage seems to have had little role. The capitol composition was temporally static: monumental, unchanging, seemingly permanent. Chandigarh's capitol complex was designed, like a building, to be constructed in its entirety and to then remain so for eternity. Perhaps thinking of monumental compositions such as the Acropolis, Le Corbusier projected for his Chandigarh capitol complex an atmosphere of solidity and permanence in materials, language, and spatial arrangement.

But Le Corbusier failed to reckon with three aspects of urban design's temporal pluralism. First, the capitol complex was never completed. Its centerpiece, the governor's palace, remained unbuilt, depriving the ensemble of an important visual focal point. Second, the judicial bureaucracy ensconced in the sculptural High Court soon required more space, necessitating the construction of additional buildings behind. Le Corbusier either never foresaw or remained uninterested in the reality that the capitol complex would require additions, leaving his less capable successors with the disadvantage of a complex whose form was complete and did not easily permit expansion.[34]

The third and perhaps most serious shortcoming of temporal pluralism in the Chandigarh capitol's urban design has to do with its relationship to the rest of the city, to the city's own temporal instability. Le Corbusier placed the capitol complex at the edge of Chandigarh, in scenic juxtaposition to the Himalayan foothills behind. This setting offers a stark, powerful contrast between built and natural form in a manner reminiscent of ancient Greek cities such as Priene or Delphi. When the capitol is not in use, its monumental, somewhat mournful buildings do attain a sublime conjunction with its grand surrounding landscape, doubtless just as Le Corbusier envisioned. But Chandigarh itself is not a ruin: it is a rapidly growing city. Adding to the problem of informal settlements that have bedeviled the city in general is the location of such settlements. Today the city has spread to behind the capitol complex itself, interrupting the ideal conjoining of monument and mountain that Le Corbusier had created. Envisioning a city as an architectural object, Le Corbusier designed a work of urbanism that could not encompass the effects of time.[35] A profound but ultimately static monumental city was trumped by India's dynamic urban reality in more ways than one.

2.13 Le Corbusier's capitol complex at Chandigarh was designed to be eternal, but both the complex and the city around it have continued to evolve.

Is Chandigarh's evident flight from its designer's intentions a failure of the city's planning bureaucracy to enforce and preserve Le Corbusier's vision? Or does this departure simply reflect the practical, welcome reality of a growing city? Tension between urban design and city growth repeatedly confronts the urban designer. Again and again, urban design shows itself to be the most fluid of design creations, endlessly appended onto, selectively demolished, reused, repurposed, and replaced. Far from being a final and complete composition, urban design is much more a patchwork, a perennially changing series of physical maneuvers, influenced by the past but not always overtly constrained by it.

Urban designers are not entirely to blame for the tension that exists between the practical reality of growing (and shrinking) cities and the ideal of monumental stability driving urban design schemes like Chandigarh. Urban design training derives primarily from architectural tradition, producing (at best) visually, formally, and functionally exemplary projects in a manner similar to architectural design. It is of little surprise that urban design proposals are static. But whereas architecture is unitary, urban design is plural, and it therefore relates to time differently than does architecture. Reconceiving urban design as a temporally dynamic entity requires both a reconceptualization and a separation from architectural paradigms that have shaped the discipline. We will explore this necessary reconception of urban design further in chapter 6.

Scale and Time

Urban design's relationship to time is also a function of scale. Small-scale urban design, such as Paley Park, can easily resist the passage of time in the same manner as a monument or building by behaving as an artifact. But small-scale urban design is also vulnerable; just as a building can be demolished with relative ease, so may one obliterate a small-scale work of urbanism.[36] As small-scale urbanism is paradoxically both easier to preserve and easier to destroy, so large-scale urban design is also both resistant and susceptible to time's passage. The large number of buildings, infrastructural elements, open spaces, and so on in a large-scale ensemble makes it more difficult to remove all of them: even Boston's comprehensively eradicated Scollay Square faintly remains in the infrastructure lines shaped by vanished streets. As scale increases, the likelihood that any single given parcel within an ensemble will experience change becomes ever higher. Urban streets, for example, cannot remain completely immune to time's passage. Both Park Avenue and Avenue Foch were constructed during times of great economic

2.14 Works of urban design are difficult to eradicate because of their scale. Even the comprehensively eradicated Scollay Square in Boston remains in the form of subsurface transit lines.

expansion: the former during the prosperous 1920s and the latter during Paris's famous fin de siècle. Each street's urban fabric is accordingly consistent, even homogeneous, but each also manifests temporal pluralism. Neither street was completely built out during their period of greatest growth and both, therefore, are dotted with aesthetically inconsistent buildings from later decades.

The larger a work of urban design, the greater the difficulty of resisting time's influence. Barcelona's Ensanche is a very large city district, with over 750 blocks in Cerdà's original scheme,[37] and a seemingly homogeneous, historical character that draws legions of tourists today. This character, however, is illusory; only the central Ensanche was developed before 1950, while much of the rest was either vacant or dotted with low-rise industry.[38] The Ensanche was so ambitious in scale that it has taken a long time to build it out. Today, over one hundred and fifty years after the Ensanche was proposed, outlying parcels in it are still being redeveloped for larger residential and office buildings.

Barcelona's Ensanche will never be complete, even if each of its blocks is occupied with the maximum permitted amount of building space. Since its parcels are perpetually, incrementally replaced according to the demands of their many different owners, the Ensanche cannot be finalized: nor can any work of plural urban design. At the same time, the physical form of the Ensanche is impressively resilient: the grid's property structure, street pattern, high number of architecturally consistent buildings, and restrictive building regulations all drive the conservation of the district's essential physical qualities and form. The result is the dynamic stability, simultaneously permanent yet ever changing, of this grand ensemble of plural urbanism.

Just as time wreaks inevitable change upon urban design, so too does time impede the realization of urbanism through the span of years required to construct any substantial project. A large building may be constructed within the space of one to two years, but urban design projects are likely to take much longer, and the risk of incompletion or abandonment of any scheme grows greater the larger-scaled an urban design project is.

The talented Spanish urbanist Manuel de Solà-Morales was well aware of the tension between urban scale and incompletion. According to his colleague Marcel Smets,[39] Solà-Morales believed in limiting urban design to the "intermediate scale" in order to avoid "adopting grand or lengthy schemes that exceed the client's capacity for implementation." Solà-Morales saw this scalar restriction, excluding urban design larger than a small district, as yielding projects "big enough to aggregate the interrelated components and give way to a coherent urban fragment, yet small enough to get achieved in a foreseeable time period."[40]

2.15 Only under great political and economic pressure can the growth of a city be stopped, or even influenced. Twentieth-century Communist revolutions in cities such as Shanghai changed societies drastically, but halted physical change. This still from Michelangelo Antonioni's 1972 *Cina* shows a city unchanged from 1949.

In this way Solà-Morales, acting as a unitary rather than a plural urbanist, sought to defy urbanism's inherent temporal pluralism by conserving in scale. Solà-Morales applied to urban design the same design resolution, formal quality, and completion that he had achieved in smaller architectural work. These scalar limits permitted him to succeed where Le Corbusier at Chandigarh had failed, achieving both a high level of formal control and discrete, well-resolved, and completed projects.

Solà-Morales's numerous works bear out the logic of his scalar approach. Projects such as the Stationsplein in Leuven, Belgium, an integrated infrastructure and public space project constructed between 1992 and 2000, or the seaside Passeio Atlantico at Porto constructed from 1999 to 2002, are ideal works of district-scale unitary urban design.[41] Functionally exemplary, formally compelling, and generous in their public realm benefits and enhancement, they are wholly consistent with Solà-Morales's

2.16 Manuel de Solà-Morales, Spain's most accomplished urban designer, consciously limited projects like his Moll de la Fusta promenade in Barcelona to the "intermediate scale" because he was concerned about seeing his work achieved during a reasonable timeframe.

understanding of urban design as a generous contribution to a city's built environment. These projects may also represent just about the largest scale at which urban design can remain unitary and resist the plural dimension of time.

Does Solà-Morales's "intermediate scale" mean that larger-scale urban design should be avoided, to resist the corroding effects of time? Or might urban design accommodate temporal pluralism apart from attempting to evade it? Solà-Morales's exemplary work provides guidance to architects wishing to build at a scale larger than that of the individual building, but it provides little help to plural urbanists interested in conceiving aesthetic ideas for the city that transcend the scale of the urban project: in other words, in an urban design that can accept the dimension of plural time.

Whatever aesthetic can be achieved at a scale larger than that of Solà-Morales's "urban fragments," it will have to differ in ways that urban designers have only begun to explore. Before we answer the question of what urban design aesthetic might encompass scalar and temporal pluralism, we will consider three additional dimensions of plural urbanism, including that of property.

The Dimension of Property

Sometimes, urban design is simply a tool in the service of property speculators. In a capitalist economy, cities are comprised of pieces of property; in order for a city to exist, property must come into existence as well. Urban design cannot exist without the existence of property, and property's creation often spurs that of urban design as well. One of the more dramatic examples of urban design's close link to property occurred in the early history of the US state of Oklahoma. In 1889, one of the American frontier's final "empty quarters" was opened for settlement, leading to a land rush into the former Indian Territory that historian John Reps called "overnight" urbanization, or instant colonization.[42] On April 23 of that year, the almost 2,950 square miles of unassigned land in central Indian Territory were opened to settlement.[43] At the firing of a gun at noon, around 50,000 would-be settlers rushed on horseback, carriage, and foot onto the unassigned land to stake their claim on the so-called virgin soil. But this soil was not quite virgin: apart from it being already inhabited, several railroads ran through it, and hundreds if not thousands of squatters had also illegally earlier moved onto the land to secure what they perceived as prime sites. Additionally, small-scale sidings already existed every ten or so miles along the train track, providing nascent town sites, and the land had already been surveyed: Reps reports that the unassigned land was divided into the quarter-mile-square "sections" of America's Public Land Survey System, the same grid that had shaped settlement patterns west of the thirteen original British colonies.[44] Claimants of Indian Territory's "virgin land," in other words, would settle territory according to already-determined frameworks of infrastructure and survey. All that remained was for these claimants to stake and legalize their claim.

Several cities were founded on April 23 along Santa Fe railroad stops in what would become Oklahoma Territory. Initially it was far from clear which small town would become the dominant metropolis, for nineteenth-century American urbanization was a speculative enterprise. In that era, the Midwest and West were littered with towns such as Central City (Pennsylvania, Kentucky, Nebraska, Iowa, and Colorado) and Metropolis (Illinois) that optimistically projected further growth but were soon disappointed. The ambitiously labeled "Oklahoma City" founded on April 23 was different

2.17 Oklahoma City, together with many others in the former Indian Territory, was founded on April 23, 1889. The city began to exist when its new property owners rode into the Territory on horseback or on trains, then staked out street grids and private parcels on the virgin prairie.

from other would-be metropolises in the former Indian Territory. Lucky or perhaps strategic, this place was designated state capital in 1908 and has grown steadily to a metropolitan population of 1.3 million today.

The founding of Oklahoma City and its peers in the 1889 land rush was based on a single principle of democratically distributed, privately held land. Far from religious cosmology or autocratic mandate, this practical principle alone shaped nineteenth-century American cities. Oklahoma Territory did not even have formal governance until a year after the land rush.[45] Such as it was, urban design in the Oklahoma Territory had nothing to do with state grandeur, and everything to do with generating a framework for claiming and distributing private property as quickly, efficiently, and equitably as possible. The aim of all was to satisfy and ultimately legalize the holdings of hundreds of claimants who on April 23 had literally sat down on the prairie where Oklahoma City would soon be. The sitters were waiting for surveyors to certify that the land on which they sat was no longer simply a piece of prairie but an urban parcel in their undisputed possession.

John Reps, longtime Cornell professor of planning history, is a chronicler of American urbanization whose two major books on the topic total almost 1,500 pages. Each features hundreds of reproductions of lithographs showing new American cities of the eighteenth and nineteenth centuries soon after their founding. American urban design history is conventionally depicted as a story of utopian exemplars with unique town designs,[46] and Reps's chronicles are no exception to this rule. Each exemplar, from New Haven, Connecticut, to Savannah, Georgia, from Philadelphia, Pennsylvania, to Annapolis, Maryland, from Santa Fe, New Mexico, to New Orleans, Louisiana, has a plan that speaks to its founders' cultural practices, intellectual aspirations, or idealistic longings. There is little doubt that Reps's catalogs of innovative examples had a pedagogical purpose, indicating that creative urban design is both possible and desirable. If the founder of, say, Savannah could be so creative, could not similarly intentioned urban designers do the same today?[47]

But to understand Reps only through exemplars limits our understanding. Just as provocative as stellar urbanism like that of Savannah or New Haven is the overwhelming homogeneity of America's nineteenth-century cities. Hundreds of cities such as Chicago, Atlanta, Kansas City, Denver, Phoenix, Dallas, Portland (Oregon), San Francisco, and many others were parceled into private properties at their foundation in the same manner as Oklahoma City, into homogeneous building lots set within uniform grids of rectangular or square blocks. America's monotonous cities carpet the continent's striking

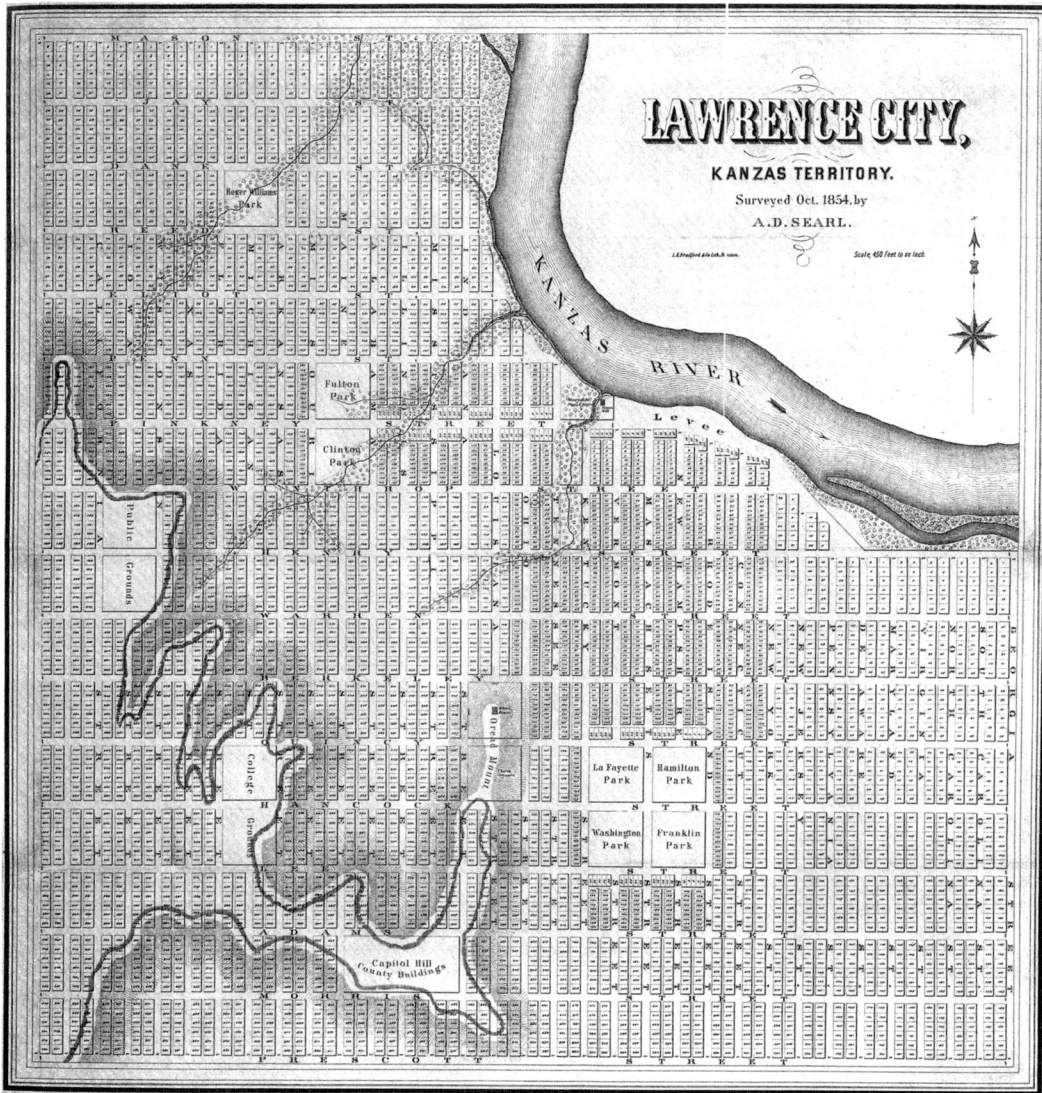

2.18 The prolific city-founding of the nineteenth-century United States was based on the primacy and equality of private property. The resulting cities are dull speculative grids with little open space and few monumental features.

landscape but make little accommodation to terrain: San Francisco is perhaps the most striking example of this insouciance. Nor do these homogeneously platted cities provide space for monumental buildings, possess intentional scenic vistas, or provide hierarchy of streets, neighborhoods, or public spaces beyond a wide "Main Street." Designed to maximize and democratize landownership, America's city grids represent the democracy and the pluralism of property in its purest form. They are the physical manifestation of a society where none of its many landowners should have financial advantage over any other, and where each piece of land has apparently as much access, and as much importance, as any other. American urbanism is founded not just on private property's existence but on celebrating the pluralism of property ownership, and thereby of economic opportunity, in its urban design. Understanding the prominence of plural property allows us to understand why these gridded and homogeneous cities were intentionally designed to be drab. A lack of distinction among different properties was precisely what the founders of Oklahoma City and those of thousands of other American settlements envisioned.

Reps decried the bland urban design of American nineteenth-century cities with their accentuation of plural property, but an earlier observer with different principles in mind celebrated the very same quality. Alexis de Tocqueville, that astute French chronicler of politics and society, visited the United States in the early 1830s. He found a society that had been independent for only fifty-five years but that had fully formed social values, structures, and politics that were distinct from those of continental Europe. As Tocqueville traveled around the young nation, recording his impressions in his landmark *Democracy in America* (1835–1840), he was struck above all by the pervasive nature of American democracy, and by the strong faith, again contrasting with Europe, that Americans held in their political system. Democracy, he observed, had been part of America since the seventeenth century: "The population of New England grew rapidly, and while the hierarchy of ranks still classed men despotically in the mother country, the colony more and more offered the new spectacle of a society homogeneous in all its parts. Democracy such as antiquity had not dared to dream of sprang fully-grown and fully armed from the midst of the old feudal society."[48]

Although city form was certainly not Tocqueville's chief interest, his observations of the American landscape insightfully and presciently distinguished America's republican, democratic urbanism from that of the European monarchies. Property was paramount: "in America there are no proletarians. Each one, having a particular good to defend, recognizes the right of property in principle. ... The government of democracy makes the idea of political rights descend to the least of its citizens, as the division of goods puts the idea of the right of property in general within reach of all men."[49] Tocqueville was also struck by America's antimonumental tendencies, the result of its people's interest in private property, individual liberty, and self-improvement. Cities were accordingly drab: Tocqueville observed that "democracy not only brings men to make a multitude of minute works [individual houses]; it also brings them to raise a few very great monuments [important buildings]. But between these two extremes there is nothing."[50] In a nation where all were focused on enriching themselves, there was little need for collective monuments, nor much need for a collective celebration of society through the design of cities—Paris being an example that must have been uppermost in Tocqueville's mind. America's seemingly modest assemblages of individual properties in anonymous, homogeneous city grids inhabited by individualist citizens constituted a democratic version of collective celebration that France manifested in palaces, grand avenues, and Paris itself.

Tocqueville's readers were not architects or engineers, and there is little indication that he intended his remarks for such a professional audience. But his words perfectly illuminate the motives that continue to shape urbanism in North America. Oklahoma City was a city in the same sense that Paris and London were: each had a population, economy, buildings, government, and the like. To its inhabitants, though, Oklahoma City meant very different things than these European cities did to their inhabitants. In 1889 Oklahoma City had little cultural importance or political history; it lacked the national stature of Paris, and it lacked the monumentally inclined, hegemonic government that had shaped that city as well. In contrast, Oklahoma City was designed to facilitate property ownership, and in doing so to further the prosperity of as many people as possible in the United States' democratic tradition. Tocqueville did not fail to note that prosperity—or the pursuit of happiness, in Jefferson's words—was a significant contributor to the continued success of American democracy, just as it remains today. One could therefore see American urbanism (despite occasional utopian experiments in novel city form) as the product of a longstanding belief in plural, democratic property ownership, and crucial to the maintenance of democracy that constitutes the United States.

Besides representing an epitome of plural property's role in urban design, the story of Oklahoma City's founding illustrates a challenge for urban design in places where plural property is a paramount social value. Apart from a large interstate highway, downtown Oklahoma City's most distinguishing formal features are three conflicting street grids. The creation of these grids was closely linked to the town's founding in 1889.

According to Reps, the first claimants arriving at the nascent Oklahoma City site in the early afternoon of April 23, 1889, found "Sooners," settlers who had gotten there earlier, already there.[51] Whether these were corrupt government officials or unscrupulous settlers who had hidden on the land prior to its legal opening is unclear, but the Sooners had already established a land company to survey the city site, laying out blocks parallel to the existing Santa Fe railroad tracks. The newly arrived claimants in turn established a rival land company, which then laid out its own blocks parallel to the Public Land Survey previously mentioned.[52] Reps notes that the two companies' parallel land surveys failed to align. On Saturday April 27, just four days after the city was founded and before a local government had even been elected, representatives of the two companies agreed to reconcile their conflicting city grids by creating larger, irregular "gore" blocks at the mismatch. But the block sizes of the two surveys was different, so the north-south streets of Oklahoma City could not be fully aligned. To make matters worse, a *third* survey grid created by another competing land company also failed to align with either of its neighbors, creating two street mismatches and block size changes in the city's downtown. This misaligned street grid, shaped by competing land companies and resolved by late-night compromises, shapes Oklahoma City's downtown block pattern to this day.

Oklahoma City's mismatched urban design is an amusing story today, but across nineteenth-century America the personal fortunes and life chances of thousands of individuals hinged upon the rapid and durable survey of land into city blocks and private parcels. Any violation or obliteration of any one of those parcels, no matter how erroneously or unscrupulously surveyed, put at potential risk *every* private parcel, and therefore the life chance of every landowner. The reconciliation of Oklahoma City's poorly aligned city grids was a necessary and logical action that had nothing to do with aesthetics and everything to do with the primacy of property in urban design. The same process of city-building shaped most of the city-founding efforts conducted across the American continent. Little wonder nineteenth-century American cities looked mostly alike.

It does not take much expansion of the mindset that shaped these western cities to see why contemporary American homeowners, each committed to the maintenance and value of their home and motivated by concern for their personal fortunes and life chances, would resist surrendering their property for any purpose.[53] Thus Tocqueville found that democracy, far from making Americans risk-takers and revolutionaries, generated instead tranquility and a sense of calm among the populace. Americans, convinced that democracy was their best chance for maximizing their fortune, resisted

2.19 Oklahoma City's competing street grids reflected different land companies' flawed survey techniques. To preserve the sanctity of private property, the grids were clumsily reconciled four days after the city's founding. The street mismatches persist to this day.

social or political changes that might endanger that chance, just as they generated dull urban designs that showed only the dominant role of plural property. Coming from early nineteenth-century monarchist Europe, where revolution and monumental city-building were the order of the day, Tocqueville was stunned. "Not only do men of democracies not naturally desire revolutions, but they fear them. There is no revolution that does not more or less threaten acquired property."[54]

Nineteenth-century America's mundane urban design raises the question of how the social and economic benefits of plural property might be reconciled with the aesthetic aims of urban design. We will leave this dilemma unanswered—for now. Instead, we will briefly examine another national setting where plural property was mostly absent, where large landowners monopolized a few large parcels of land, and where the suppression of pluralism provided a fertile environment for urban design. Where America provides a natural experiment that is shaped by plural property, Russia provides an opposite but equally enlightening natural experiment where private property has historically been a privilege of few or none.

The Russian Antithesis

In his *Letters from Russia*, Tocqueville's contemporary and fellow Frenchman Astolphe de Custine chronicled his 1839 trip to Russia. Unlike Tocqueville's depiction of America, however, Custine was hardly complimentary of his subject. And unsurprisingly, his work was suppressed by the czarist government of the time. Custine is far less read today, yet his insights into Russian society have quite as much currency as Tocqueville's do for America. They provide an insightful understanding of Russian society, politics, and city building in what was and remains the most spacious nation in the world, one that has historically held individual rights and private property in low regard. Just as Tocqueville found that democratic America's plural property had impeded monumental cities, Custine found that a nation with large properties and powerful entities was rich territory for dramatic urbanism.

Tocqueville was thrilled by America, but Custine's reading of Russia was harsh. There, he found a feudal society with little or no prospect of political, social, or economic reform, and ruled by an absolute monarch. This combination of European grandeur and feudal servitude struck Custine as particularly repugnant: "The empire of Russia is a country whose inhabitants are the most miserable on earth, because they suffer at one and the same time the evils of barbarism and of civilization."[55] Where

Tocqueville had found an elected president in America, Custine found all Russians, rich and poor alike, bound to Czar Nicholas I: "The emperor is the god, the life, the passion, of this unhappy people. ... Every man takes his position [in Russian society] according to the favor of the prince."[56] Until the 1860s, Czarist Russia's peasantry was bound to the estates of the aristocracy; it was the largest sector of the Russian population, and Russia's agriculture dominated the economy of the country. Custine was shocked to see "this class of men, who live in the possession of no acknowledged rights, and who yet form the nation. Deprived of everything by law, they are still not so much degraded morally as they are socially."[57] But Russia's absolute power was not entirely negative: it had created a great city.

Custine was impressed by the illogical yet magnificent existence of Saint Petersburg: "What a tremendous power is that which can thus cause a metropolis to spring up in the wilderness, and which, with one word, can restore to solitude all that it has taken!"[58] Russia's planned imperial capital had been spectacularly and savagely constructed by the command of Czar Peter the Great beginning in 1703. Custine was simultaneously awestruck by Saint Petersburg's beauty and shocked by the arbitrary cruelty that had created a city in such inhospitable territory. "St. Petersburg, in all its magnificence and immensity, is a trophy raised by Russians to the greatness of the future. Never ... has the faith of a people in its own destinies raised up from the earth a greater wonder than St. Petersburg. ... Yet it may not be forgotten that one hundred thousand men, victims of obedience, were lost in converting the pestilential swamp into a capital!"[59] The city, directly inspired by Versailles, had outdone its French model spectacularly. Where Louis XIV had merely constructed a palace and grounds, Peter had constructed a city that was itself a sort of gigantic palace. Saint Petersburg's city plan directly reflects Czarist power: all streets radiate outward from the Admiralty, headquarters of Peter the Great's new Russian navy, and the adjoining Winter Palace, home of 5,000 staff in Custine's time. Like much that Custine found in Russia, Saint Petersburg's grandeur was splendid even as it was a monument to cruelty, power, and oppression.

Russia's tendency toward grandiose urbanization would assume even greater ascendance after the Russian Empire transitioned to Communism after 1917. The Russian Revolution produced a Communist government that progressively abolished private enterprise as well as profiteering or capitalism during the 1920s. Property ownership, already the privilege of relatively few in Czarist Russia, shifted from being a source of wealth to being forbidden over the course of ten years. This shift disadvantaged proportionally few urban Russians: historian Timothy Colton notes that in 1912 fewer

2.20 The grandiose, incomparably magnificent cityscape of Saint Petersburg required the despotic power of Czar Peter the Great and the deaths of many serfs to come into being. For better or worse, urban design generally thrives in undemocratic settings.

than 5 percent of Muscovites owned the house they lived in.[60] Most of the city's housing was apartment houses held by wealthy, often absentee landlords—those paradigmatic "parasitic profiteers," as Lenin called them—whom Communism demonized, despised, and ultimately destroyed. Confiscating Moscow's rentier property was relatively easy. As the city's population grew over the course of the 1920s and as the government seized more and more private properties, Moscow became a city with almost no private property at all.[61] By 1930 most bourgeois or aristocratic landowners had fled or were imprisoned, their properties allotted to peasants, to factory employees, or to factories themselves. Increasingly, Muscovites lived in structures owned and operated by their work enterprises. The plural property of Oklahoma City in 1889 was nowhere to be seen in Communist Moscow.

By the 1930s, Stalin's consolidation of power and the gradual recovery of the Communist economy placed the Soviet Union in a position to restart the enterprise of large-scale urbanism. With Stalin in charge, Moscow could be dramatically reshaped: site acquisition was hardly a problem. Colton details how the dictator, with a flick of the wrist, could designate that a monument be moved, a square widened, even a massive building such as the Cathedral of Christ the Redeemer demolished.[62] With private property "long ago liquidated," as Stalin's minion Lazar Kaganovich said in 1934,[63] the Soviets had a free hand with which to reshape Moscow. Urban designers had never had so much institutional power or so much personal vulnerability: just as Stalin's hand demolished a building and widened city squares, it could demolish the career of an architect or planner in a moment.[64]

Moscow's master plan of 1935 is a convincing demonstration of urbanism without plural property. The plan, authored by a group of architects, was unquestionably dramatic, proposing 15 million square meters of new housing, a 10-kilometer green belt, 530 new schools, the enlargement of Red Square, and the rebuilding of dozens of other squares and monumental avenues, together with several major highway projects. The plan's ideas were intentionally retrograde; the innovative constructivism of the 1920s had already retreated, and sympathetic European architects such as Ernst May and Hannes Meyer had left by the early 1930s, frustrated with Stalin's lack of interest in their talents. The 1935 plan's grandiose squares, public buildings, and boulevards were more consistent with Peter the Great's time than they were with 1920s-style modernism.

Although most of the 1935 Moscow plan did not come to pass, Stalin built much during his nearly twenty remaining years in power. In the early 1950s his architects added seven skyscraper complexes to Moscow together with dozens of apartment houses for the Party elite, providing a Soviet equivalent to the skylines of capitalist cities. These structures did not solve Moscow's housing needs, but they did glorify and palliate the needs of the Soviet elite.[65] Throughout Soviet times right up to 1989, the location of new buildings and construction of new city districts was the least of an urban designer's problems. Instead, designers called upon the Soviet state's "firm hand, solid apparatus, and unshakable discipline."[66] Private land and therefore plural property did not exist, removing one of the principal dimensions of urban design.

Today, private property ownership is again widespread in Russia, but the state's power with respect to urban development sometimes seems scarcely diminished from

СХЕМА ПЛАНИРОВКИ МОСКВЫ

МОССОВЕТ
ОТДЕЛ ПЛАНИРОВКИ
1935 г.

▲ **2.21** Moscow's Master Plan of 1935 was mostly unbuilt, but not because the Soviet government lacked the power to implement it. The absence of private property rights made Russian cities rich territories for urban design.

▶ **2.22** The recent expansion of Moscow by presidential fiat in order to provide space for new government facilities reflects Russia's traditional relationship between state power, lack of individual rights, and urban design.

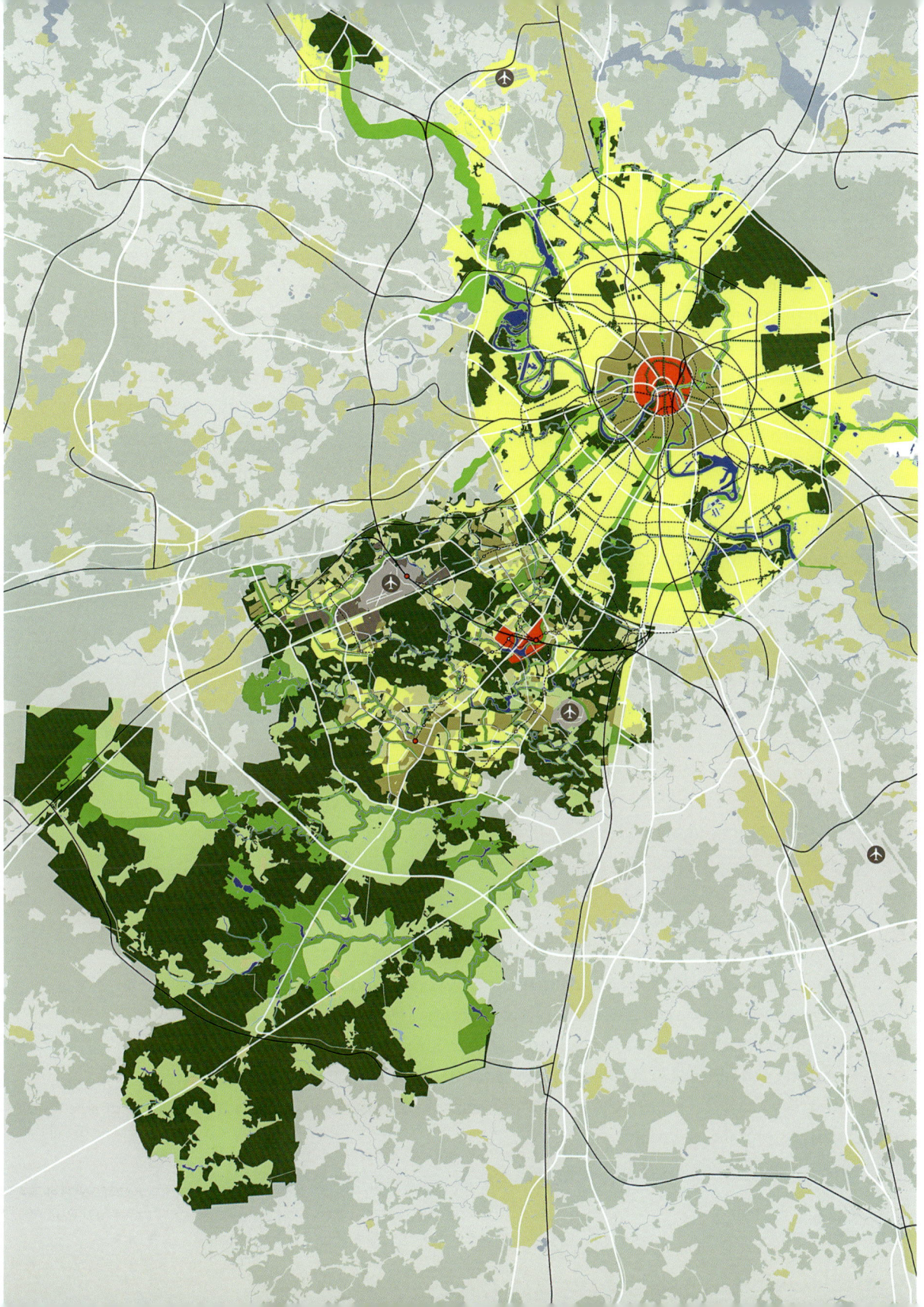

Soviet times. Moscow is currently in the midst of a scheme to extend the city to the southwest. The idea is promoted by President Vladimir Putin, who claims that "the city is suffocating"[67] and that expansion would permit the modernization of government facilities and the alleviation, or at least decentralization, of traffic problems. The plan is imperial in scope: Moscow's area would be more than doubled, and the annexed land would include many parcels owned by powerful entities whose profits will doubtless skyrocket as their land becomes Moscow's new Central Business District.[68] The expansion plan's architectural competition in 2012 short-listed several foreign firms, with the winning design, by "Capital Cities Planning Group," delivering the same grandiose vistas and shining skyscrapers that fill other post-Soviet republics such as Azerbaijan, Kazakhstan, and Turkmenistan. It seems little coincidence that the southwesterly expansion also encompasses land that was valued in Soviet times: Stalin located his "nearer dacha," where he spent almost every night, near this area.[69] In today's Russia just as in the past, state power is used to generate grandiose urban vistas but also to enhance governmental capacity and to enrich landowners close to power. Custine would have found all of this quite familiar.

The existence of plural property does not guarantee democracy, nor vice versa. Nevertheless, it seems societies in which property ownership is highly decentralized, with a wide distribution of different owners, are likely to be places where any urban design effort that might disadvantage a large number of property owners will be likely to encounter resistance. Plural property is a necessary component of plural urbanism, but plural property also makes the enterprise of urban design more challenging. Unitary urban designers need to suppress plural property through parcel assemblage, condemnation, or other means, but plural urbanism needs to fully accommodate it. How it might do so is something we will explore in the following chapters.

The Dimension of Agents

Cities are constructed by a multiplicity of agents, ranging from developers to everyday citizens. The plural agents constructing the city stand in contradistinction to the large-scale aesthetic order of unitary urban design. How does urban design accommodate these plural agents? How can an aesthetic ideal exist amid the clamoring voices of a city's thousands or millions of inhabitants? Serious discussion of this dilemma is rare, but any assessment of urban design's pluralism must confront this most visible of design's plural dimensions.

The city of Barcelona provides a whimsical example of the dialogue between plural agents and aesthetic order. On a block of the Passeig de Gràcia within the Ensanche of central Barcelona are four buildings known poetically as La Manzana de la Discordia, or the Apple (or City Block) of Discord.[70] Today, crowds of tourists are attracted by one "slice" of the apple, Casa Batlló. This is a house exuberantly reconstructed between 1904 and 1906 by Antoni Gaudí and recently opened to visitors. Casa Batlló, together with two adjoining houses constructed in the same exuberant Art Nouveau style, provide the origin of the moniker Apple of Discord. Each of the buildings comprising the Manzana is exuberant in its own right, and they obviously compete with each other. Which of us, the houses seem to ask, is the finest?

The Apple of Discord is faintly preposterous, and tourists today may find this exuberant competition, between fin-de-siecle architects designing outrageous buildings to outshine their colleagues, all a bit silly. Yet the Apple has a more rueful meaning if one sees it as a metaphor for architectural competition within cities. This Barcelona block's architectural discord of form, material, and message mirrors most cities' discordant form. It even mirrors the superficial competition within suburbs where homeowners, at a pettier scale than the Manzana, create analogous beauty contests by painting their homes a different color, adding an enclosed porch, or just parking a bigger car in the driveway. In every case, the architect's or homeowner's exercise in discord is an attempt to set themselves apart from the rest in status, taste, or income.

The Apple of Discord also stands in slightly embarrassing contrast to the Ensanche grid that surrounds it. The Ensanche is an ordered, harmonious urban environment whose urban fabric was seemingly designed by a single hand. The Ensanche's harmony is atributable to its consistency of materials, with warm Catalonia limestone and brick predominating; its form, with buildings of eight or so stories; its street activity, with cafés on the corners and along the major streets; and its mixed uses, with commerce below and mostly apartments above. Severally and together, the Ensanche shows a high level of unified intention and construction. It is a song of urban harmony that shows how multiple actors (developers, architects, landowners, and regulators) can collectively generate successful aesthetic ends.

The seductive potential of urban harmony has inspired visitors to cities since urbanization began. Classical thinkers saw harmony as closely tied to the city's unitary appearance. Plato, in his *Laws*, wrote about his ideal city that "care ought to be taken of all the buildings, and the manner of building of each of them, and also of the temples and walls … the whole city [should be] built on the heights in a circle … for the sake of

2.23 Barcelona's Manzana de la Discordia, city block (or apple) of discord, is a quirky, amusing reminder that different actors, with different tastes, collectively construct cities.

purity … the private houses ought to be arranged from the first so that the city may be one wall. … The form of the city being that of a single dwelling will have an agreeable aspect."[71] Throughout the twentieth century, harmonious city districts dominated urban design texts to the extent that one might fairly interpret the discipline's sole purpose as *being* that of generating aesthetically harmonious districts. Certainly urban designers such as Werner Hegemann, Daniel Burnham, Raymond Unwin, H. P. Berlage, Gordon Cullen, Allan Jacobs, and Rob Krier all saw aesthetic harmony as one of urban design's chief goals. Paging through Hegemann's *American Vitruvius*, Cullen's *Townscape*,[72] Jacobs's *Great Streets*,[73] Duany and Plater-Zyberk's *Towns and Town-Making Principles*,[74] and many other urban design texts, one finds that ideal urban designs all feature symmetrical streetscapes, unity of form and proportion, regular civic spaces, and an overall sense of visual calm. All of these felicitous features are also present in Barcelona's Ensanche.

In urban design, this same interest in harmony has motivated more than just paeans to urban order. Harmony of height, material, function, or scale has also shaped the development of building regulations, zoning regulations, historic preservation guidelines, design guidelines, even environmental controls. Where planning guidelines

2.24 Despite occasional discord, Catalonia's consistent material, buildings, and urbanistic traditions generated an extremely harmonious environment in the historic central Ensanche.

pertaining to form are not governed by a sense of efficiency,[75] they are often guided by this drive for harmony. New York City's 1975 "Housing Quality" zoning guidelines, for example, state that "developments which provide continuous street facades and activities are considered more favorably than those which tend to break continuity or have empty spaces on the street."[76] Another urban design text affirms that urban design's goal is to create "coherent and satisfying patterns of development … a cumulative effect … a sum of parts adding up to a greater whole."[77] Without harmonious urban design, the authors warn, the risk is dire: "confusion and chaos … a fractured disjointed world [with] no identifiable center."[78]

The Apple of Discord, nestled amid Barcelona's harmonious Ensanche, is a gentle reminder of harmony's vulnerability. The Apple warns us that urban design is not necessarily consistent with self-interested plural agents, each seeking only to better themselves or just to show off. And indeed the unity of aesthetic spirit animating Barcelona seems sadly lacking in most cities. While Savannah or Annapolis, earlier praised by Reps, provide exceptions, America's landscape provides fertile ground for critics of visual disorder. The 1960s seemed to be a particularly robust era for such critiques. Jeremiads such as Peter Blake's *God's Own Junkyard*[79] and Ian Nairn's *The American Landscape*[80] listed telephone poles, randomly placed houses, and commercial sprawl as some of the many flaws of the American cityscape, most of which these authors saw as caused by rapid suburban growth.

Today we may be hardened to the sight of suburban sprawl, but the spreading informal settlements of the developing world demonstrate a disorder several orders of magnitude greater than America's chaotic suburban landscape. America's disorder is at least legally governed by zoning and thus relatively intentional, but we cannot say the same for developing-world cityscapes. Architectural assessments of informal cities accordingly suffer from an air of frustration and futility: what to do? Elegant staircases inserted into favelas[81] or monumental libraries placed in slums, as in Medellín, Colombia,[82] may work when and if they are constructed, but such seemingly random, incremental interventions do not resolve the visual disorder of the larger, often unattractive urban settings in which they are located.

The disappointing visual reality of most cities, whether in Arizona or Algeria, tells us that Barcelona's visual harmony is an aspiration rarely realized. Urban designers often confront confusion and chaos that is much more serious than a block of the Passeig de Gràcia gently disrupted by whimsical row houses. Visually chaotic, ugly cities are an uncomfortable reality that offer little inspiration for urban design.

But the presence of plural actors is an inescapable reality of the city. Chaos and disorder in cityscapes only exist because cities are designed by nearly innumerable actors. Whether from developers' self-interest, as in America's loud shopping strips, where "just about the *only* factor … is unregulated private profit,"[83] or from desperate residents seeking a foothold in the urban economy of Medellín, contemporary cities suffer from the visual disorder caused by their multiplicity of actors.

2.25 The rapid growth of commercial suburbia in the 1960s generated a series of critiques of America's self-interested businesses and of the discordant environments that resulted.

While serious discussion of plural actors and urban design is rare within the discipline, acceptance or even advocacy of this pluralism is even rarer. But there are notable exceptions. Three important designers, Denise Scott Brown, Rem Koolhaas, and John Habraken, have each accepted the seeming chaos and confusion stemming from plural actors shaping cities, and each has embedded this chaos into a normative position on urbanism. These designers' positions define important possibilities for incorporating plural agents in urban design.

Denise Scott Brown's well-known book *Learning from Las Vegas*—a canonical text for architects interested in the city—was cowritten with her husband Robert Venturi and their partner Steven Izenour, and published in 1972. Less relevant here is the book's principal argument, as stated in its 1977 revision, that architecture is a "system of signs and symbols." Its other, more urbanist argument is that Las Vegas's landscape

2.26 Denise Scott Brown saw Las Vegas as a vernacular realization of modernist design principles, and as a populist environment that deserved serious attention. How urban designers might respond to this environment, however, was a matter that Scott Brown left unresolved.

of commercial sprawl (the Strip) was *not* a despicable mistake in need of visual order, but a popular, even attractive built environment deserving of architectural attention.[84] The Strip's garish casinos and pleasure palace architecture were an irregular, but vibrant landscape that Scott Brown was reluctant to regularize. Scott Brown and her coauthors saw Las Vegas as a lesson, not a warning.

The book reinforced Venturi's earlier argument for a greater "complexity and contradiction" than could be found in high modernist architecture.[85] Yet Las Vegas looked the way it did not because the Strip's designers sought to refute modernist monotony; in fact the Strip's designers may not have been aware of modernist orthodoxy at all. The Strip was simply undesigned, shaped by the vernacular forces of real estate development and the entertainment market. Scott Brown saw this popularization of an originally abstract ideal as inevitable: "[A] motel on a bleak stretch of highway.... alludes to the international stylishness of a Brazilian resort, which, in turn, derives from the

International Style of middle Corbu. This evolution from the high … the middle … to the low … took only 30 years."[86]

Las Vegas was comparatively deregulated, but political libertarianism was not on the authors' minds: their advocacy of chaos, complexity, and contradiction was not an agenda for a deregulated society or for anarchism of whatever stripe. Scott Brown and Venturi's preference was purely formal. They liked the *look* of commercial sprawl, even if it just looked messy. The people building and buying in Las Vegas may not have thought much about the visual consequences of their actions, but Venturi and Scott Brown did, and they liked it.

Ironically, apart from a few community projects of the 1970s, Venturi and Scott Brown built very little at the urban scale. Scott Brown attributes this drought to the poor economics of urban-scale work,[87] but one suspects that she also felt her opportunity for creative work was limited in this arena. As a result, Scott Brown admitted by 1990 that she had "perhaps gone 'back' to architecture."[88] But Venturi and Scott Brown's populist aesthetic would have restricted their ability to carry out urban design in any event. By accepting Las Vegas or any other myriad places constructed by nonprofessionals as "almost all right,"[89] they had essentially declared that their work, at the urban scale at least, was accomplished already. If the populist environments they so admired were currently being constructed, why was the urban designer even needed? Venturi and Scott Brown's architectural work never answered this essential question.

Rem Koolhaas, as we have already seen, emerged out of modernism's ruin in the 1970s, taking the seeming chaos and confusion of the contemporary cityscape not as inspiration for his own work but as a foil against which his own formally and programmatically complex buildings could stand out all the more. As successor to Venturi and Scott Brown's populism, Koolhaas took the position that the city's visual chaos was not something to imitate or to mourn, but simply something to accept and therefore ignore without further turmoil. In arguing that "the generic city" possessed a visual and functional chaos that was impossible for architects to confront or regularize, Koolhaas called for designers to internalize the complexity and visual interest of the city within the space that architects *can* control, that of the building itself. Each of Koolhaas's essays, "Bigness, or the Problem of Large,"[90] "What Ever Happened to Urbanism?,"[91] "Junkspace,"[92] and "The Generic City,"[93] regarded the existing cityscape's visual disorder as antithetical to the enterprise of design.

Like Venturi and Scott Brown, Koolhaas's buildings have consistently aligned with his theoretical approach. But where Venturi and Scott Brown saw the pop qualities of

Las Vegas as something to emulate, Koolhaas goes further. His buildings, too, often display bold graphics and signage in direct allusion to commercial clutter. OMA's building exteriors, such as the McCormick Tribune Campus Center at the Illinois Institute of Technology in Chicago, often advertise interior novelty in a brashly graphic manner reminiscent of Venturi's "duck" trope.[94] But Koolhaas also incorporates elements of the city into his buildings, just as he advocated in "Bigness." Even the comparatively small Rotterdam Kunsthalle, from 1992, incorporates public walkways, dramatic views of the surroundings, adjacent urban spaces, and even a city street into the project. Koolhaas's buildings represent a skepticism and insouciance regarding traditional notions of urban harmony and context. But they also ambitiously absorb urban disorder—or the architect's version of it—into the building itself.

Koolhaas's stand-alone approach to urbanism could be labeled pessimistic, and it certainly offers little solace to regulators seeking to rein in fractious developers in the interest of greater urban order. This is unfortunate, not because planners can or should necessarily adopt Koolhaas's pessimism toward urban order, but because Koolhaas seems to have discovered that city form is not quite as uncontrolled as he once proclaimed. His 2011 exhibit "Cronocaos,"[95] calling for regulation to remove "junkspace" instead of preserving historic districts, would have little meaning if markets and capital actually had free rein to reshape New York City. Contrary to what Koolhaas once boldly claimed of all cities in "Bigness," seemingly unfettered New York City is tightly governed by planning and building controls. "Cronocaos" was stimulated by a paradox: New York City's urban form appears undesigned, but it is in fact tightly controlled: too much so for the tastes of aesthetic libertarians like Koolhaas.

Both Scott Brown and Koolhaas reacted to the disordered cityscapes created by self-interested developers. But the most powerful and active agents in the city's tendency toward visual chaos are not developers but citizens themselves. Koolhaas acknowledged this entropic agent in his study of Lagos, at the time a benighted city of "up to fifteen million people."[96] Koolhaas's photographs of Lagos, taken mostly from the air, convey an urban condition that seems troubling, at least to the Western eye. Koolhaas and his students documented how "agents considered marginal, liminal, informal, or illegal" shaped much of the African city's apparent form.[97] According to Koolhaas, Lagos's own population, together with small-scale business enterprises, operated "in the near-complete absence of those infrastructures, systems, organizations, and amenities" used to shape cities in Europe and North America. Lagos, to Koolhaas, was a city designed by the highly decentralized force of its individual citizens. It was a bottom-up city whose plural

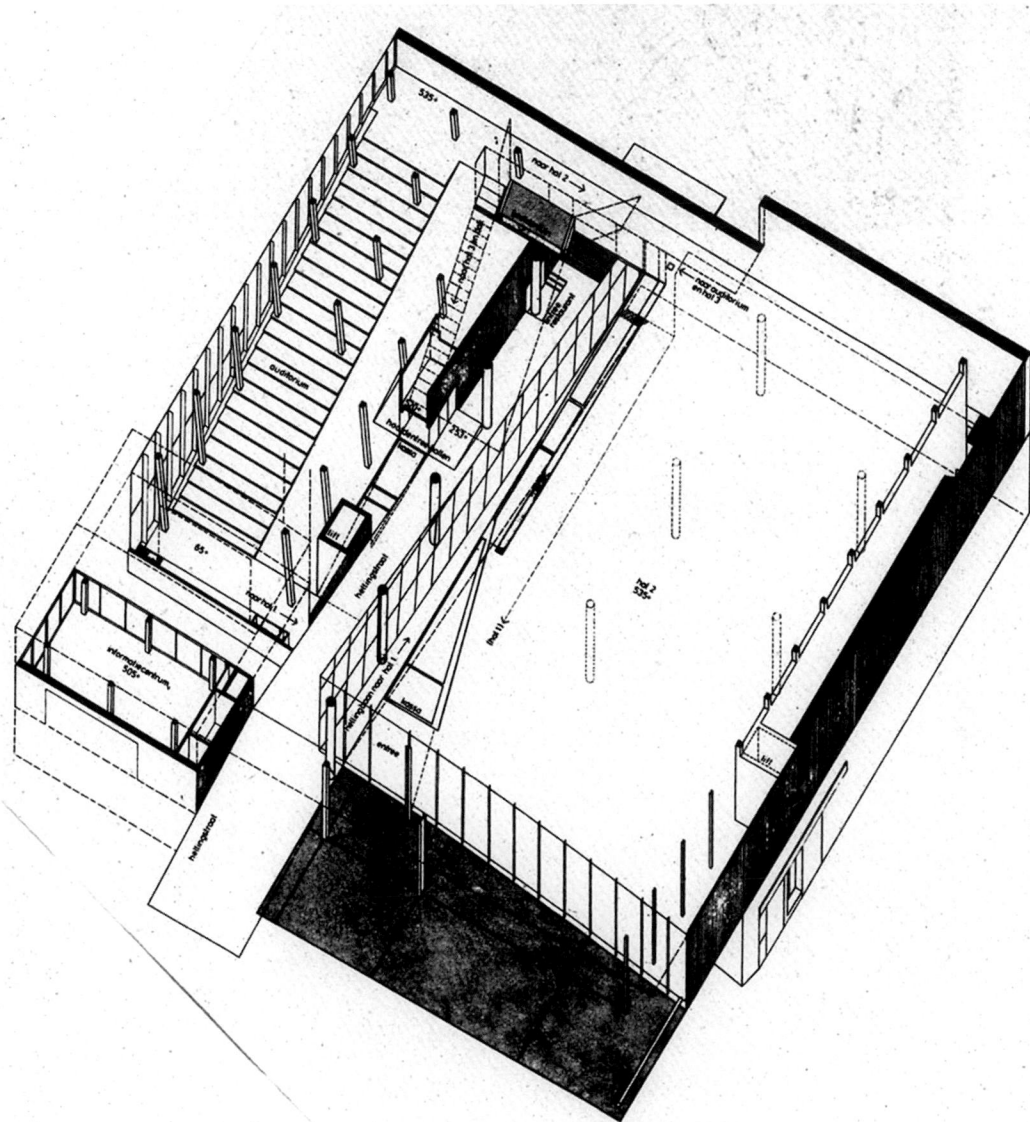

2.27 Rem Koolhaas, as we have already observed, advocated the incorporation of urban elements into architecture and began to do so even in comparatively small buildings such as the Rotterdam Kunsthalle, completed in 1992.

2.28 In the early 2000s Koolhaas became fascinated by the chaotic city of Lagos, Nigeria, where none of the forces that shaped urbanism seemed to operate except for small-scale commercial activity and ever-increasing human settlement. Lagos was a paradigm of disorder, yet it managed to function.

agents had become the city's sole urban designers because conventional institutions such as real estate developers, government planning bureaus, even architects and planners either didn't exist or were unable or too disenfranchised to function. Lagos was an intensely plural city, but one that had, at least for Koolhaas, effectively no urban design at all.

Lagos's chaotic appearance was in part a historical artifact. The city in 2000 was at a particularly dysfunctional point in its history: Nigeria had been under military rule for the past twenty years and the country's kleptocracy had siphoned away most of the country's vast oil wealth, leaving to rot an infrastructural network that had once promised to make Nigeria one of the leading nations of Africa. Scholars also took issue with Koolhaas's work.[98] One accused Koolhaas of "Orientalizing" Lagos in a "journalistic" attempt to demonstrate "what Lagos is not [e.g., a typical Western city] rather than what it is." At the same time, the critic admitted that Lagos did actually have numerous problems: high crime, a lack of legal protection, and a fortified built environment characterized by social mistrust.[99] In other words, much of Lagos's seeming dysfunction was in fact real.

Whatever one's normative position on cities such as Lagos, the role individuals and small-scale institutions play in shaping the built environment in developing cities is substantial indeed. The dilemma of urban design and plural agents remains: can the designer balance the order of urban design with the disorder wrought by plural agents? Should cities such as New York or London give up the ghost, releasing their stringent zoning controls to permit unfettered markets and uncontrolled skylines? Or should cities clamp down further on plural agency, restricting formal experimentation and market freedom to promote the harmony seen in Barcelona or Paris?

A third designer, John Habraken, has centered his life's work around the question of design's intersection with plural agency. Habraken is a Dutch theorist and practitioner who has consistently sought to strengthen the design role of inhabitants of large-scale housing developments and, at the urban scale, to extend the role of small-scale builders within large-scale developments. Habraken's writings, and the projects of his followers at SAR (Foundation for Architectural Research), provide a considered and sympathetic assessment of how the aesthetic harmony sought by urban designers can mesh with the apparent disorder wrought by plural actors.

Habraken's understanding of architecture is not formalist but fundamental; as Ole Bouman of the Netherlands Architecture Institute put it, his work "[attacks] architecture that is about aestheticism as a goal in itself. His architecture is not ... about the facade. It's about the organization of space."[100] Habraken sees the built environment as composed of multiple levels of scale, each of which is subject to control by a different entity. An individual, for example, may only shift furniture within a room but not the room itself, whereas moving interior walls requires a contractor and perhaps an architect. Constructing a house requires building professionals, and the construction of a large-scale area will require participation by the state or local government. Habraken diagrams these levels of control in a series of steps or levels.[101]

Unusually for an architect, Habraken is formally agnostic. What a building or settlement *looks* like is not his stated concern. What he is concerned with is its *function*, particularly with respect to the user's degree of agency, where the agency of space-shapers is maximized. At the architectural scale, this translates to maximizing agency of housing inhabitants, and at the urban scale, to maximizing agency of individual builders or architects. Habraken's normative position comes from his childhood experiences in Indonesia, where he saw vernacular building forms that struck him as harmonious and "well organized."[102] But Habraken's advocacy of small-scale agents is also harmonious with the advocacy position toward neighborhood residents espoused by New Left planners like Paul Davidoff in the 1960s. At that time, both Habraken and New Left planners reacted similarly against the design of large-scale housing developments such as Amsterdam's Bijlmermeer—a modernist housing complex with significant social problems—by recommending a higher level of user participation in the design of such developments.

Like both Scott Brown's and Koolhaas's, Habraken's built work is consistent with his ideological stance. Habraken believes that "users," broadly considered, should control the shaping of the built environment, at least at the level of space in and around the housing unit. Habraken's work, however, maintains two important differences from his colleagues. Scott Brown and Koolhaas both advocate that the architect's design confront populist design, or visual "chaos," an approach that alters the form of a building but preserves the architect's traditional level of control. Habraken instead diminishes the architect's role, providing informal actors, whether house-dwellers or small-scale builders, additional control over a project's design. In SAR's social housing in Papendrecht, Netherlands, for example, house inhabitants could contribute to the design of their own unit by collaborating with the architect in an organized process. The architects also provided large terraces outside dwelling units that inhabitants might plant and decorate as they wished.[103] Today the Papendrecht project has aspects of both garden cottages and pueblo dwellings, the result of its inhabitants' accumulated alterations of the exterior spaces.

2.29 Dutch architect John Habraken and his disciples constructed housing at Papendrecht, the Netherlands, that reflected their desire to permit inhabitants the maximum ability to shape and reshape their environment.

While Habraken differs from Scott Brown and Koolhaas in that he advocates the agency of small-scale actors, he does retain the architect-urbanist's control over scales of design larger than the housing unit itself. At the urban scale, Habraken advocates neither Scott Brown's laissez-faire populism, where Main Street is "almost all right,"[104] nor Koolhaas's "surrender of contested territory"[105] to the tender mercies of an unfettered market. Habraken's normative stance on urban design instead emerges from a scaling up of his approach to architecture. At the building scale, Habraken sees the architect as creating a framework, what Habraken called "supports,"[106] within which building users, primarily inhabitants, can make alterations. The aim of this approach is to mesh expert design (the architect) with user design (the inhabitants). In Habraken and SAR's urban design, agents shift roles, but the dialogue between large-scale control and small-scale improvisation holds. At Habraken's urban scale, the agent providing supports is an urban designer or master planner, while the small-scale actor is not a housing inhabitant but an individual builder or architect designing within the "supports" of the master plan.

Just as he is agnostic on a building's formal appearance, Habraken does not establish a normative stance on urban design; in other words, he does not firmly dictate a neighborhood's design or formal configuration. Instead, Habraken's urban designer generates a loose urban design framework that provides a high degree of freedom for the architects or builders who construct within it. Here the autonomous agent is the architect-builder, not the inhabitant. The desired effect is somewhat akin to Habraken's childhood Indonesia, where harmious vernacular building patterns generated houses that empowered their inhabitants and cityscapes that remained orderly.

Habraken's urban design approach ideally generates an urban design as harmonious as Barcelona or Paris. This approach may be productive and meaningful in the Netherlands, where the liberal state is both strong, able to administer the "support" system of urban design, but also relaxed, willing to relinquish substantial design control to individual builders. Advocating this same mix of control and autonomy is quite a different matter in libertarian places such as the United States, where larger-scale controls (e.g., zoning or other standards) are driven by social or fiscal demands. And this mix is an even more dubious idea in functionally weak states such as Koolhaas's Nigeria. Lagos's users are not autonomous from anything, since the larger-scale supports do not exist.

Habraken's user empowerment made sense as a reaction against master-planning modernists who exerted a high degree of control, perhaps too much, over the design of housing such as Amsterdam's Bijlmermeer. But his activist stance turns out to be surprisingly passive vis-à-vis urban form at scales larger than the housing complex. Habraken's theory prescribes only that urban design decisions permit smaller-scale agents to have autonomy within them. It so happens that the few projects constructed by SAR disciples at a relatively large scale, such as Java-eiland in Amsterdam harbor, are essentially historicist and traditional, fitting cleanly and unobtrusively into their surroundings. But they equally well could have been modernist in form; at least to Habraken, this should not matter.

This is the puzzle of Habraken's user-centered philosophy. At the architectural scale, his philosophy diminishes the master architect's control, but at the urban scale it enhances it, since the urban designer shapes the overall "supports" within which architects design housing. Individual users are left out of Habraken's urban design: Java-eiland's houses do not permit the user alterations that Habraken encouraged in his own housing complexes, because houses are fixed in their design. User annotations are few. So Habraken's ideas, conceived as a reaction to overly rigid housing design, provide laudable agency at the architectural scale, but little formal guidance to urban designers. Nor do his ideas provide accommodation to the individual citizen-builders, who instead fade away to be replaced by individual architects' work. Habraken's urban design philosophy does not truly accommodate plural agents.

It may not be surprising that these three theorist-practitioners of plural actors and urbanism, each cognizant of the potential for design at the urban scale but each practicing mostly at the level of architecture, ultimately shy away from proposing an urban design philosophy that accommodates plural agents within an ordered cityscape. Scott Brown and Venturi are seduced by the exuberance and splendor of popular architecture and cityscape, and wish to leave it alone, or just to emulate it. Koolhaas accepts this populist cityscape as a matter of live and let live: people should do what they want and build what they want, including himself, the architect, who is ideally the most powerful actor. Habraken sympathizes most deeply with the individual agent, incorporating agents' autonomy as a part of architectural design, though he limits this autonomy at the urban scale. Each of these theorist-practitioners shies away from releasing control to plural agents, instead retaining a role for the professional designer. This is reflected in the practice of two of the three; both Scott Brown and Koolhaas, after their early polemical bursts, conducted architectural practices that were substantially conventional in manner. Only Habraken resisted the typical practice model, carrying out much of his research and writing in universities and through the agency of his SAR working group.

At the architectural scale, the boundary between user and designer control is open to some debate and is likely to remain so. A house-dweller's degree of autonomy in architectural design is more or less an ideological position: either one may favor greater autonomy for citizen-builders or one may not. But at the urban scale, admitting the autonomy of individual builders, developers, or other agents in the urban design process is not a choice but a functional necessity. Whatever decisions urban designers may or may not make, cities consist of thousands of individual parcels owned and inhabited by distinctly separate individuals. These users will continue to build; and ad hoc additions to the cityscape are possible, both in places where urban design does and does not exist, because plural actors are the true builders of cities.

Urban design theory and practice are unresolved about the role of plural agents in shaping cities. The acclaimed urban design of Barcelona, Paris, Vienna, and the like implies that "successful" urban design ideally requires substantial control over smaller-scale agents. A corollary of this approach may be found in conventional urban design controls such as Battery Park City's design guidelines specifying everything from building materials to fenestration.[107] Urban designers' attitude toward plural agency is unfriendly: the discipline is based on the imposition of harmony on fractious, uncooperative builders and architects.

Perhaps the urban design profession's focus on increasing regulation is misguided. Instead of trying to transform pluralist space into unitary urban form, urban design might incorporate pluralism into its aesthetic embrace, finding beauty within multiplicity rather than outside of it. To accommodate plural actors, urban design might permit more agency rather than less. Before we examine three pluralist urban design projects that achieve just this, we shall explore the final plural dimension of urban design, that of plural form.

The Dimension of Form

Walking through Paris, even the most uninformed, uninterested observers can sense that they are within an intentionally shaped built environment. Parisian buildings are mostly faced with a pale limestone and have a consistent height of six or so stories; streets are straight and feature generous sidewalks and landscape elements such as trees and seating. Buildings are conventionally sited and scaled adjacent to the street and with heights that are in rough proportion to the width of streets. Pedestrian passage along these streets is often punctuated by arrival in a square or *rond-point* (rotary), from which numerous other streets branch off in different directions. Parisians are fortunate that their city's form, though occasionally monotonous, is pleasingly regular yet still varied enough to be interesting. Even better, Paris's urbanism is extensive; one may walk for many hours within this designed urban environment. Historian Donald Olsen called this city's consistent urban design—consistent in its organization, homogeneity, alignments, and harmony—nothing less than a "work of art."[108] This harmonious urban pattern and architectural fabric together compose the city's urban design.

Pedestrians in Manhattan, however, experience far less intentionality in their built environment. Some areas of the island, such as Fifth Avenue along Central Park or the tenements of Washington Heights, do have a homogeneous building stock and scale, and in some cases this consistent environment has been designated a historic district, as with Fifth Avenue along and below Central Park. But even Fifth Avenue's buildings vary in height, and although the avenue faces Central Park, the street's design is ordinary, little different in design from any other of Manhattan's avenues. Manhattan's street

2.30 Much of Paris can be considered a single work of urban design that is composed of thousands of constituent parts. This consistency of organization and alignment led historian Donald Olsen to label it "a work of art."

pattern is completely regular—much more so than Paris's, in fact—but this regularity is balanced by the grid's dramatically, even chaotically, different scales of buildings and types of activities.

New York's relationship of street and structure is so inconsistent that it inspired Rem Koolhaas and Zoe Zenghelis's 1972 *City of the Captive Globe* project, which portrays a Manhattan grid filled with structures radically diverse in their architectural design. Within this project's Manhattan-like grid, "changes in [an] ideological skyline will be rapid and continuous," with divergent towers of "complete certainty and serenity" clashing with towers of "soft structures of tentative conjectures and hypnotic suggestions."[109] Together with Elia Zenghelis they sited another project, *Hotel Sphinx*, in Times Square (see figure 1.6), combining a space of architectural exuberance with a structure containing an almost infinite building program, a microcosm of the many activities found in New York City.[110]

These two Koolhaas/Zenghelis projects identify and amplify the New York grid's potential to accommodate a wide range of unpredictable, even unimaginable architectural creations. For these architects, New York's grid became a springboard for architectural diversity, a not unrealistic scenario given the grid's ability to accommodate architecture as divergent as the brownstone and the Empire State Building. These New York projects show a street pattern and building form that, far from being in harmony, have little to do with each other.

Paris and New York notwithstanding, let us now imagine pedestrians strolling through a different place, London's Bloomsbury neighborhood. They might lose their way more often than those walking in Paris or New York City, since Bloombury, like the rest of London, has notoriously irregular streets. But whereas New York's building heights nearly obliterate regularity, Bloomsbury's confusing street pattern does not obliterate the district's urban design. In Bloomsbury the pedestrian instead discovers the city's urban design by intervals, time and again coming upon a park or square bounded by brick row houses, each with surprising regularity and delicacy of detail. Leaving such a square, a pedestrian might wander through other streets filled with equally regular row houses, before happening on one of the city's larger, less attractive major streets lined by less regular buildings. Yet beyond this street is likely yet another Bloomsbury district centered around another park or square. London's urbanism is very different from that of Paris or New York, but this urbanism has its own sense of order, where form—row house and park—is plural instead of unitary.

2.31 Central London possesses an urban design composed of related districts of terrace houses and green squares separated by undistinguished commercial thoroughfares. London lacks Paris's overall order, but its fragmented urbanism is not displeasing.

Unlike Paris's symphony of beautiful streets and *ronds-points*, with buildings linked together by broad avenues in a monumental hierarchy, Bloomsbury comprises simple, small clusters of streets, squares, and houses interspersed with districts of no perceptible quality that are organized in no perceptible manner. London has little of Paris's grandeur, but its distinct urban design is not without quality. Architect Steen Eiler Rasmussen, in his 1934 paean to this "unique city," noted Bloomsbury's enclosed nature being "very different than the grand continental square [e.g., of Paris]. ... The English square ... is a restricted whole as complete as the courtyard of a convent. [The squares] form fine geometrical figures. ... They are regular and completely uniform ... and a series of such squares may be linked together in any order."[111]

An astute observer of urban form, Rasmussen was pleased by London's irregularity compared to highly ordered continental cities such as his own Copenhagen. Rasmussen admired London's series of similar but not identical "restricted wholes" of urban design—its squares surrounded by identical houses. Rasmussen admired not only the formal quality of each Bloomsbury "island" but the aggregative effect of these islands as well, even though that aggregation resulted from accidental juxtapositions of aristocratic properties developed over time.

Bloomsbury is characterized by islands of urban design floating within an otherwise undesigned fabric. These islands differ fundamentally from the "subordinate elements in [the] great composition" of Paris. London is comprised of plural form, not the unitary form of Paris's "great composition." Its comparative lack of larger-scale urban design provides greater freedom for the lesser composition of Bloomsbury's archipelago of eighteenth-century neighborhoods, centered around green parks.

Assemblages and Archipelagos

Leaving London, let us imagine another urban neighborhood, one that is comparatively uninteresting but studded every so often with a distinct work of architecture. One such place is Oak Park, Illinois. It is a typical suburb except for its twenty-five structures designed by Frank Lloyd Wright, all within just a few blocks of each other, and all built between 1889 and 1913. Another such place is Paris's more visually impressive 16th arrondissement, where there are three houses by Le Corbusier within a short distance of each other. Our scenario could be anyplace where innovative architecture by a single designer occupies different spaces in the neighborhood fabric, whether this fabric is urban or suburban. We can think of such a grouping as an *architectural assemblage*.

2.32 Frank Lloyd Wright designed twenty-five individual structures, such as the Cheney house shown here, in Oak Park, Illinois between 1889 and 1913, but these structures do not constitute urban design, both because of adventitious siting and because Wright lacked a spatial strategy to relate them.

Collectively, such an assemblage transcends its individual structures, and it will attract attention accordingly, as Frank Lloyd Wright's buildings do in Oak Park.

Could one call the sum total of Wright's or Le Corbusier's architectural assemblages urban design? Not really. In Oak Park, Wright's homes are more or less randomly scattered within the otherwise ordinary village grid; these houses were commissioned separately over a period of years as clients purchased house lots or made renovation decisions.[112] Wright's assemblage, all in a single locale with a single designer, fails to cohere into a spatial relationship for two reasons. First, Wright had very little site control; he could not place his houses in a meaningful relationship to each other even had he wished to, for his clients provided him with the locations, resulting in more or less adventitious sites. Nor did Wright display much interest in urban design, at least not at that point in his career.[113] Wright, in other words, either did not or could not see Oak Park's pluralist canvas as a site for urban design. Instead, working within an urban grid whose monotonous form he likely disdained and with his work surrounded by multiple structures that he did not design, Wright treated Oak Park simply as a neutral canvas for individual works of architecture.

Le Corbusier built much less in Paris than Wright did in Oak Park, but his dramatic projects bear similarly little relationship to the existing city, perhaps because Corbusier was not particularly interested in Paris's "great composition." In contrast to Wright, Le Corbusier made it clear early in his career—with both the City for Three Million and Plan Voisin—that he saw Paris less as a fabric to annotate than a barrier to overcome. Even had he received twenty more villa commissions in the 16th arrondissement, Le Corbusier might not have deemed the design of this district as worthy of consideration.

Neither Wright nor Le Corbusier, despite building within existing urban settings, considered those pluralist fabrics as components of a larger-scale design. Left unrealized in both Oak Park and Paris was the possibility that individual works of architecture could participate in an urban design strategy that was more than just the sum of their parts. Both Oak Park and Paris remained architectural assemblages, and both architects would have to wait until later in their careers to conceive or construct urban design.

The late modern period of the 1960s and 1970s diversified urban design thinking. As modernism matured, new threads of thought entered the discipline. One of these examined urban design as a composition of spatially disparate elements. Two pamphlets most significantly illustrated this way of thinking about urban design: Fumihiko Maki's *Investigations in Collective Form* in 1960 and again in 1964,[114] and Oswald Mathias Ungers's 1977 manifesto *The City in the City: Berlin, a Green Archipelago*.[115]

Maki's *Investigations* was an astute concatenation of urban design thinking up to the current day. Derived from his early experience in the Japanese metabolist movement (a precursor of megastructural thinking),[116] Maki's pamphlet outlined three "structural principles" or "major approaches" in making what he called "collective form," or "groups of buildings and quasi-buildings … that have reasons to be together … not a collection of unrelated, separate buildings."[117] Maki called these three approaches the compositional, the structural, and the sequential. The compositional approach was "commonly accepted and practiced," "a natural extension of the architectural approach" where groups of buildings created a "static," "formal" composition.[118] Maki viewed Brasília, Chandigarh, and Rockefeller Center as being examples of this approach. Though he did not discuss property or other site considerations, we can infer that the compositional approach could only occur on a unitary site. The *compositional* approach, in other words, is one of unitary urban design.

Maki's second, *structural* approach embraced a megastructure concept, or as he described it, "a large frame in which all the functions of a city or part of a city are housed." Maki liked megastructure because it combined the capacities of architecture with those of the city. It was "a kind of master form which can move into ever new states of equilibrium and yet maintain visual consistency and a sense of continuing order in the long run … [in which] the whole maintains its identity and longevity while at the same time being affected by other [events]."[119] We can see here the great attraction of megastructure for architects interested in engaging city activities within the compass of architectural design. Also apparent is the connection to Koolhaas's essay on bigness, which would come thirty years later.

But it is Maki's final, *sequential* approach that was the most revolutionary. He referred to this approach as "group form," and described it as "a system of generative elements in space," where "consistent use of basic materials" was accompanied by "human scale" and "sequential development … a series of buildings or elements without apparent beginning or end … developed over a period of time."[120] Maki defined group form as existing in historic vernacular settlements; his pamphlet includes images of Japanese villages and other vernacular towns in Africa and Greece. Maki was particularly taken with the seeming holistic unity of group form, where open spaces, nature, housing, and topography seemed to merge together into a harmonious and unified whole. But he was uncertain about the potential for group form to be created in the contemporary world, which is not surprising, since architectural thought at the time favored megastructures over vernacular villages.

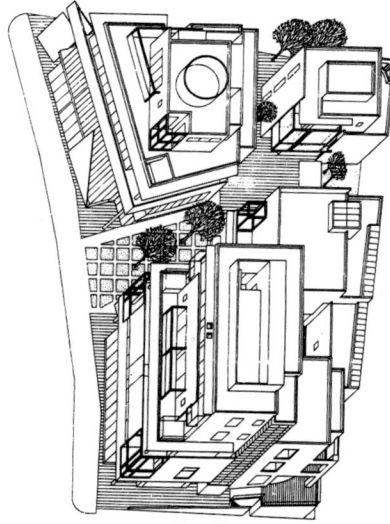

Phase VI
1992

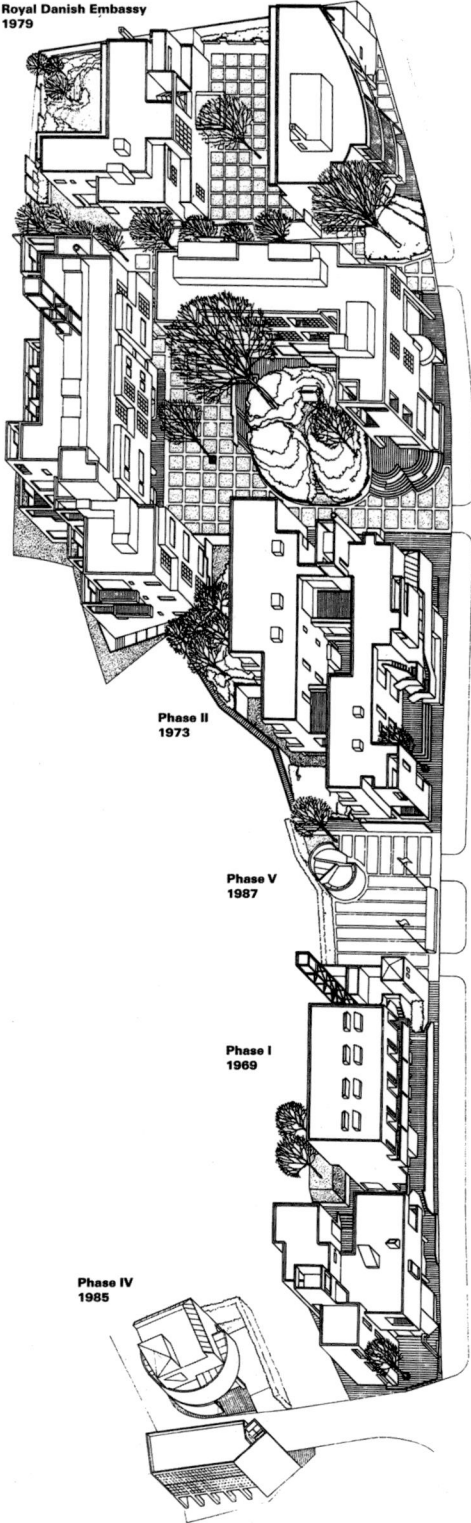

Royal Danish Embassy
1979

Phase III
1977

Phase II
1973

Phase V
1987

Phase I
1969

Phase IV
1985

Maki created his own version of collective or group form in a complex named Hillside Terrace. Located on a single site in Shibuya, one of Tokyo's wards, Hillside Terrace is "a medium-density mixed-use development of apartments, shops, restaurants, and cultural facilities." The complex is the result of a twenty-five-year multi-phased construction process.[121] Hillside Terrace has some qualities of plural urbanism: the ensemble was constructed and evolved over time, a quality that Maki noted in his *Investigations*, but in all other ways it was a unitary project, albeit an unusually long-lived and consistent one. Group form was not widely appreciated at the time; Reyner Banham dismissed it as "the unavoidable image of Italian hill-towns cited by Maki and practically everybody else at that period,"[122] implying that group form was little more than historic revivalism. Nostalgic as it might have seemed, Maki's group form idea did have some substantial content beyond historic imagery: the second half of the pamphlet was a careful study of compositional patterns or "operational categories" for future group forms. Maki showed these operational categories both in traditional settlements and in megastructures, a somewhat idiosyncratic and inaccurate comparison given that vernacular settlements are essentially pluralist spaces while megastructures are unitary.

A second understanding of urban design beyond the bounds of unitary projects and megastructure came from a well-known episode in urbanist thought in the mid to late 1970s.[123] The young Rem Koolhaas collaborated with architect Oswald Mathias Ungers on a project called *The City in the City: Berlin, a Green Archipelago*. The archipelago was motivated by the peculiar state of Berlin in the postwar period. Divided in two, the western part of the city was a political enclave with a badly damaged, incomplete urban fabric and a shrinking population. Koolhaas had visited the city in 1971 and found the Berlin Wall, only ten years old, "heartbreakingly beautiful."[124] In 1972 he contacted Ungers in the United States and in 1977 the two met in Berlin for a summer workshop,[125] one product of which was a (mostly) jointly composed manuscript that Ungers would publish in its final pamphlet form later that year.

The "archipelago" proposed a Berlin composed of a "federation of urban entities with different structures, developed in a deliberately antithetic manner." These entities or "islands" were chunks of cityscape, some surviving from before the war, others newly created, to which the architects would give a "true configuration" or "identity of [their] own." While the urban design approach of the archipelago was consistent, the

◀ **2.33** Fumihiko Maki realized his concept of "group form" in his Hillside Terrace complex in Tokyo over a period of twenty-five years. The complex resembles a hybrid between a vernacular village and a modernist megastructure.

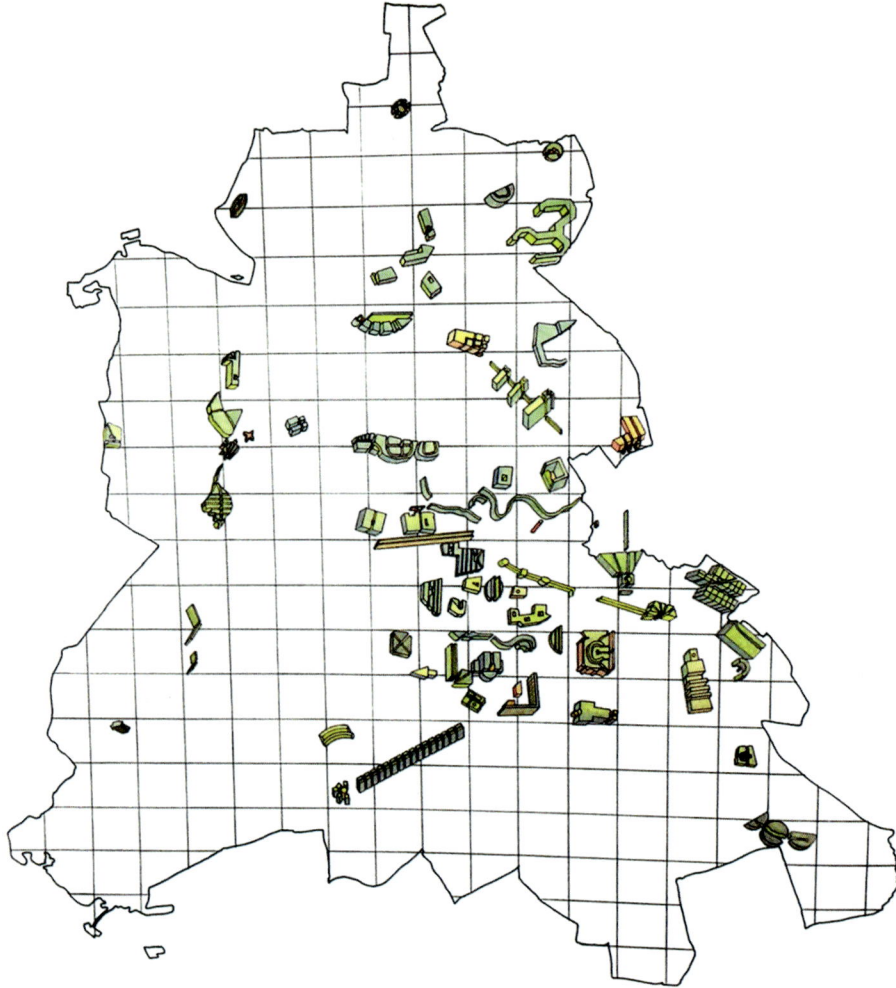

2.34 In 1977, Rem Koolhaas and Oswald Mathias Ungers envisioned the shrinking city of West Berlin as an archipelago of iconic architectural projects and Platonic forms surrounded by green space. Yet the pieces of the archipelago never cohered into an overall composition.

architectural design of its "islands" was diverse, reflecting the aesthetic proclivities of its two authors. Koolhaas preferred that the archipelago's entities be versions of polemical urban projects from early modernism like works of Ivan Leonidov and Mies.[126] Ungers, on the other hand, saw the archipelago's "islands" as being typologically based, derived from different iterations of past settlement patterns from Berlin's history.[127]

The innovative qualities of the archipelago are clear. First, the archipelago is less a particular formal scheme than it is a conceptual framework for urban and architectural design, where the particular content of the islands does not really matter, whether they are polemical projects, typologies of settlement, or something else. Both Koolhaas and Ungers saw the archipelago reflecting theoretical interests, but each would move forward in a different way: Koolhaas toward bigness, Ungers toward what he called the "dialectical city," which allowed architects to identify existing qualities of the cityscape and "evaluate the reciprocal effect of superimposed systems," including elements of historic fabric.[128] This was a kind of contextualism in which the architect accentuates elements of the historic city, making design a process where, as Ungers said, "rational decision-making replaces subjective feeling."[129]

The fact that the archipelago's architectural content does not really matter is part of the power and flexibility of this concept, and Koolhaas, at least, took this flexibility as license for architectural exploration. The same quality, however, that gave the archipelago its architectural power, namely isolating discrete chunks of city fabric and placing them into building-like entities subject to architectural control, turns out to be a weakness at the urban scale. A city composed of discrete chunks of monumental or otherwise distinctive architecture is certainly a showpiece for architects, as Koolhaas's *S,M,L,XL* essays argue consistently, but the archipelago does not necessarily constitute a beautiful, ordered, or comprehensible urban fabric. In fact, the *Archipelago* pamphlet took little position on urban fabrics per se, recommending only that the interstices between the chunks of architecture be filled with "natural zones and pastures" containing everything from suburban housing to "shooting preserves" and "Disneyland type"[130] amusement parks—a sort of throwaway landscape not so different from that of *Learning from Las Vegas*. It is far from clear that this green archipelago would have been an enjoyable or beautiful place, and also far from clear that its authors wished or cared if it was.

Both group form and archipelago concepts reached beyond the traditional conception of urban design as a "compositional approach" of buildings organized on a unitary site. But neither could fully escape the architectural origins of their authors. On the one hand, Maki recognized in vernacular settlements a dialogue between the different pluralities of the city—multiple time periods, multiple authors, multiple properties and structures—but could not project such a relationship into contemporary terms except in the form of a relatively traditional campus with multiple properties designed by a single architect, himself. Ungers and Koolhaas, on the other hand, conceived of a city where the ordinary dichotomy of building and street no longer applied, and where designers were freed to convert elements of the cityscape into diverse and contrasting chunks of fabric. Neither of the two seemed interested in making their architectural assemblages cohere into something more than a collection of parts. Ultimately, the Archipelago failed to recognize that pluralism in urban design could transcend an assemblage of monuments.

Toward Plural Urbanism

The plural form of Hillside Terrace and the Archipelago offer important lessons for the plural urbanist. But cities are more than a large-scale analogy to an architectural site plan and more than an assemblage of monuments or megastructures. Cities are not limited to unitary design at the intermediate scale; they are more than a frustrating set of fixed forms that can only be altered in fragments. And cities are certainly not an object to be designed as a work of architecture, nor a collection of obsolete structures to be cleared for tabula rasa design.

Instead, cities are living entities, forever growing and changing. They can be designed, but only by a designer who acknowledges their numerous plural dimensions and who designs within them rather than against them. Without acknowledging pluralism, urban design will forever be limited to the "intermediate scale" of Solà-Morales. Many urban designers would happily confine themselves to this scale, but such a limitation would prevent the design of larger-scaled areas as well as design in those places where plural dimensions dominate—most of the city, far away from large unitary sites.

Plural urbanism is the key to an urban design that exists within pluralism rather than against it. Only plural urbanism views the city as a collective of many different structures, some vernacular, others more purposeful. Some of these structures are buildings or parks, and some are elements like streets or infrastructure. Each of these is complete in itself, yet each may also be engaged in a larger-scale relationship with another element, making each of them constituents of a larger work of urban design. Shaping such a larger work from amidst the city's many elements is the task of the plural urbanist.

Such plural urbanism shares many attributes with architectural or landscape design, but it also differs in fundamental ways from these unitary building arts. Plural urbanism might possess each of the dimensions explored in this chapter. Like the archipelago, plural urbanism would possess a *plural form* comprised of different formal elements, but, unlike the archipelago, with each element of plural form contributing to the larger whole. Such a project would also possess *plural scale*, perhaps consisting of an individual component (a building or open space), a pair or group of components, or perhaps the entire composition. Such plural form would also be multitemporal, in the same manner as Maki's group form. Elements of the urban design composition might change, adapt, and grow as a result of new elements being added over time. Similarly, elements of plural form might fail to be constructed or might be added later without having been part of the initial composition. Plural form might be located on plural properties: components might be located on different city blocks or even several blocks apart, with many parcels and structures in between. And while architectural assemblages are the work of a single designer, plural form could be unified by many factors other than a single designer: common design strategies, programs, clients, purposes, and materials could all define its sense of commonality. In other words, *plural agents* could create plural form.

Plural urbanism would have many more potential sites than conventional forms of urban design occupying unitary sites. Most urban sites that exist in the world today are in fact pluralist, whether they are low-density urban peripheries like the American suburb, densely developed grids like that of Manhattan, or informal settlements in a developing-world city. Plural urbanism is possible on all sites, while unitary urban design is not.

Plural urbanism is also distinct from architecture and landscape in additional ways that differ from unitary urban design. Plural urban designers need not design individual buildings or the open spaces that lie between them. They need no longer concern themselves with the detailed resolution of form and compositional strategies that characterize architecture. Yet the plural urbanist is a designer of the same order as all of the other building arts: the plural urbanist retains the same aesthetic concerns as architecture and landscape. Plural urbanists need be committed to compositional innovation, to spatial exploration, to the meshing of form and function, and to creativity broadly considered.

The following three chapters explore plural urbanism in greater detail through the lens of exemplary built projects, urban design practitioners and theorists, and design scenarios for three imagined sites. The five dimensions of plural urbanism discussed above will be examined further in the cases and stories that constitute the rest of this book. We will see that many different designers have realized plural urbanism in many places, and will see how differently they have approached their mandates. In chapter 3, we will encounter plural urbanism first as a sculptural ensemble constructed in a small industrial town; then as social housing built to replace demolished slum dwellings in an impoverished neighborhood; and finally, in a regional capital proudly shaping its own destiny after centuries of subjection. The settings and forms of these pluralist projects are varied, but they share a commitment to exemplary design as well as to shaping a new understanding and aesthetic of the cityscape surrounding them.

Three Pluralist Projects

Urban design should be grounded in ideals, but like all building arts, it should also be made real through the construction of projects. Our understanding of plural urbanism grows in this chapter as we explore three urban design projects built at different times, in different places, for different purposes, each of which embodies many of the dimensions of plural urbanism that we addressed in chapter 2. In Romania during the 1930s, sculptor Constantin Brancusi constructed a sculptural ensemble that reshaped his hometown. In the troubled Bronx of 1970s New York City, a team of urban designers created a revolutionary social housing project to revitalize a neighborhood. And in the capital of Slovenia between 1928 and 1943, architect Jože Plečnik remade the city of Ljubljana with a series of works whose collective impact remains unequaled. Each of these designers, whether sculptor, architect, or urban planner, was acting as a plural urbanist. Learning about their respective works helps us see what plural urbanism looks like.

Constantin Brancusi and Târgu Jiu: Sculpture as Urbanism

Târgu Jiu, a city of approximately 78,000 people located in the Carpathian foothills of western Romania, is an undistinctive place. The 1933 *Guide Bleu* called it "a small city that has little of interest in and of itself, though it is a popular center for excursions."[1] At the time, Târgu Jiu was a city on the edge of a dramatic transformation resulting from the collaboration of an activist citizens group, the National League of Gorj

Women (Gorj being Târgu Jiu's province), and an individual, Constantin Brancusi, viewed by some as "the greatest sculptor of modern times," who was born near Târgu Jiu in 1876.[2] Brancusi's commission was simple: to construct a memorial to the defenders of Târgu Jiu during the First World War.[3] Together, the National League, acting as client, and Brancusi would shape a sculptural ensemble that scholar Radu Varia saw as "legendary, a pilgrimage destination for lovers of modern art."[4] The ensemble was to be located in the center of the city, forever transforming it and setting the stage for a new perception of Târgu Jiu and of sculpture's potential to act as a formative element in urban design.

Brancusi's acclaim is longstanding and continues. As early as 1910 American collectors began to purchase his sculptures, and his work remained in the limelight up to and after his death in 1957. His work remains relevant: several recent studies have recast his work in light of contemporary understandings of art and society.[5] One of the reasons that Brancusi's work has retained broad interest is because it addresses diverse audiences—critics, patrons, and the overall public—at once. His sculpture, which is simultaneously abstract, representational, and ancient in its references, also invokes contemporary technologies and aesthetics. The design of the sculptures is abstract, yet the sculptures themselves have a visceral materiality that is grounded in their source materials of metal, stone, and wood.

Like much modern art referencing so-called primitive traditions, Brancusi's art is also global in multiple senses, at home in the wealthiest collector's home, yet visibly conscious of "'ancient' cultures such as Egypt and Classical Greece, even of 'Negro Art.'"[6] His art is also understandable as local, sourced in Romanian folk traditions and continuing those traditions in a new way. Without pain, Brancusi's work embodies the paradox of societies wrenched into the twentieth century, incorporating ancient traditions while existing easily in the modern world. More simply, Brancusi's sculpture also appeals on an aesthetic level, even to a child. Whether it is made of metal or stone, his art is gentle in appearance, soft to the touch; works such as *The Kiss* offer a sense of "innocence … frankness … [they are] sweet and stately … undisguised and so discreet."[7] *The Kiss*, in one of its many versions, brings tears to the eyes; it is ample evidence of Brancusi's genius.

The Târgu Jiu commission, offered in 1935, was swiftly completed by 1938. It gave Brancusi the opportunity not only to express his genius at a larger scale, but also the privilege, rare for a sculptor, of shifting beyond the "studio and the private homes of the … collectors of [his or her] work,"[8] into the public space of Târgu Jiu. There, sited in

3.1 Constantin Brancusi in his studio in 1946. Brancusi's sculpture is simultaneously abstract and referential, dematerialized and tactile, local and global, accessible and remote. His Târgu Jiu sculptural ensemble possesses all of these ambiguous qualities.

3.2 Brancusi realized many versions of the *Kiss* during his lifetime, including one in Târgu Jiu.
The sculpture of intertwined male and female figures grew steadily more abstract over time.
This version from the early 1940s was clearly influenced by his Târgu Jiu work.

a "conspicuous location," his work could "survive and acquire a sense of permanence,"[9] and it would attain a public visibility and renown so great that in 1996 the World Monuments Fund placed it on its watch list of threatened monuments in need of restoration. Eleven years and over $5 million later, Brancusi's Târgu Jiu works were restored, and a globally significant ensemble returned to the world's notice right as its host nation of Romania prepared to enter the European Union one year later in 2008.

Brancusi's ensemble in Târgu Jiu consists of three sculptures: the *Table of Silence*, the *Gate of the Kiss*, and the *Endless Column*. They span the width of the small city in a roughly east-to-west direction, from the Jiu River, once an important crossing point for the Roman army, to a former hayfield on a small rise on the former edge of town. The *Table* and *Gate* sit in a public park, Parcul Municipal, located near the city center and which today "bustles with activity throughout the year."[10] Today the *Column* too sits in a park, adjoining a factory, wide roads, and a low-density, almost village-like residential area near the city's edge.

From the *Gate*, which sits about 15 meters inside the edge of Parcul Municipal, an almost straight street named Calea Eroilor (Avenue of the Heroes) leads to the *Endless Column*. Created in tandem with the construction of Brancusi's sculptures and understandable as a processional axis between them, this street was little more than a village road in 1938;[11] a photograph from that time shows a family of geese in the dirt roadbed.[12] Today the Calea holds a diverse range of architecture including grim, idiosyncratic housing blocks from the country's Communist era (1949–1989) as well as quasi-Oriental houses and urban blocks typical of fin de siècle Romanian revivalist architecture. Part of the street, near the Parcul, has been closed off as a pedestrian mall, signifying Calea Eroilor as a Main or High Street for Târgu Jiu.

The iconographic interpretations of Brancusi's work at Târgu Jiu are as wide ranging as is his larger oeuvre. Brancusi himself "rejected any attempts to interpret" his work, arguing that visitors should simply "look at them [the sculptures] until you see them."[13] The *Endless Column* is, of course, a memorial column according to its original commission, but it can also be seen as a more abstract marker, referring less to traditional forms than to "a sensibility that seeks to escape earthly confines and longs to be united with the infinity of space ... a sensibility that Brancusi encountered in ... mystic philosophies and Buddhism."[14] Critic Radu Varia took this line of interpretation further, seeing in the *Column* a "cosmogonic [i.e., relating to cosmic origins] architecture ... producing its own field of gravitation, and a consequent modification of time and space."[15] Such grand interpretations aside, the column also recalls the primordial

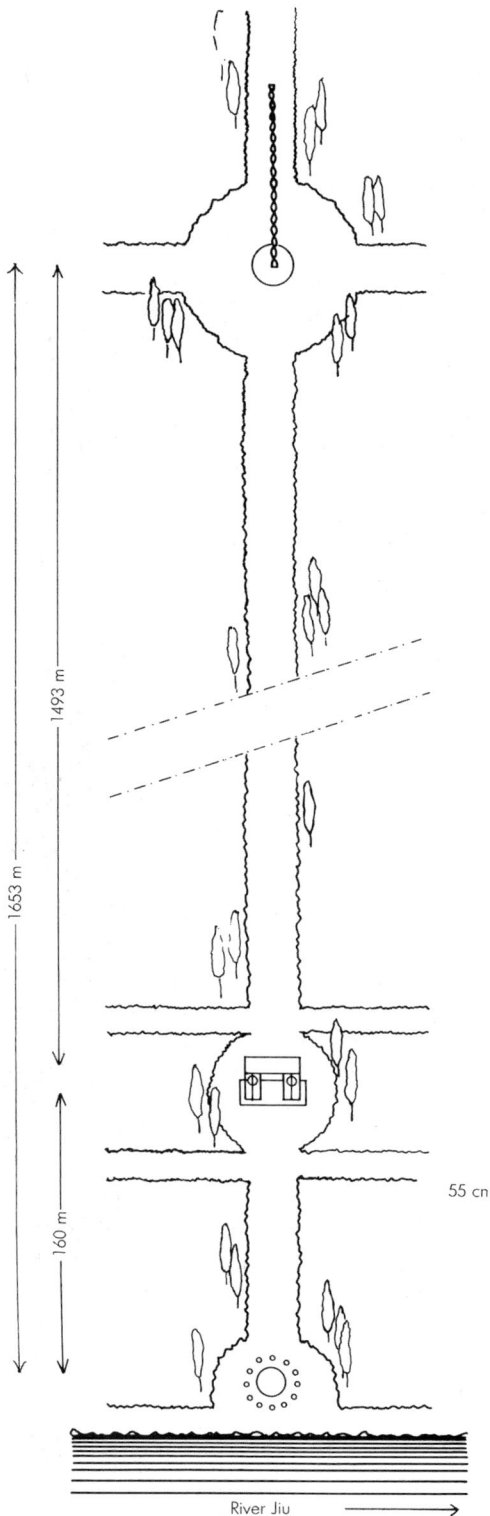

1493 m

1653 m

160 m

55 cn

River Jiu →

◄ **3.3** Abstract plan of Brancusi's Târgu Jiu ensemble, by scholar Radu Varia. Three sculptures are located on a single axis that extends from the Jiu River, through a city park, along a city street (Calea Eroilor) to end in a park atop a hill. Other structures also contribute to this axis of space.

▲ **3.4** The *Table of Silence*, with twelve circular stools arrayed symmetrically around a circular table. There are many interpretations of the *Table*'s potential symbolism, but it also provides a simple place to sit and rest.

▲ **3.5**   Located near the edge of the park, the *Gate of the Kiss* spans a busy pedestrian path. A version of the kiss repeats on both columns, and the abstract ornamentation above has been linked to cultures as diverse as Egypt, Rome, and rural Romania.

▶ **3.6**   *The Endless Column* is sheathed in a medium-yellow bronze finish and stands alone atop a hill, providing a clear conclusion to Brancusi's axis, but also implying a repetition of form and space that continues forever.

Romanian forest with its tall trees, and perhaps the pagan symbol of a "garlanded young fir pole"[16] once used by the region's Celtic inhabitants and still seen today. Critic Sandra Miller rejected all such interpretations, arguing instead that the *Column* is simply a "triumph of modern engineering."[17]

The *Gate of the Kiss* garners a similarly rich range of interpretations. Apart from continuing motifs from Brancusi's earlier sculptural work, it bears a resemblance to the triumphal arches that once adorned every Roman city, typically found at the edge of the city much as the *Gate of the Kiss* is found near the city's edge today. At the same time, the abstract art around the frieze of the gate recalls Romanian folk architecture (the barns and farmhouses of west Romania) and the ancient Egyptian funerary monuments at Dendera, Deir el-Bahri, and Philae.[18]

The *Table of Silence*, in contrast, seems to have been explicitly intended by Brancusi as just that, symbolizing nothing but a table itself. Alexandra Parigoris saw a "representation of [an] object and not [an] actual object or representation of furniture,"[19] while Sandra Miller, a skeptic of overinterpretation, claimed that "as for [the table's] symbolism, [Brancusi] intended none."[20] Yet Varia saw in the table and its twelve stools "the experience of communion [i.e., recalling the twelve apostles of Christ] … [or] the central radiant sun around which the twelve signs of the Zodiac revolve … [or] the Celtic mystery of the twelve Knights of the Round Table [i.e., of Arthurian legend]."[21]

As with most of Brancusi's art, the richness, complexity, and dimorphic quality of the Târgu Jiu ensemble rewards a diverse range of iconographic interpretations. Yet the public nature of Târgu Jiu's sculpture also leaves it first and foremost open to everyday use, where it needs little interpretation at all. The monumental column commands its amorphous park space irrespective of its meaning; the table permits one to simply sit without further ado. And the gate invites passage; according to artist and writer William Tucker, many of the couples who pass under it pause to kiss.[22] Such public quality and popular appeal, according to Tucker, helped the sculptures survive the very difficult sixty years that followed their construction; they were subject to another war, then to one of the grimmest and most oppressive Communist dictatorships of the Eastern bloc. Isolated from the West, Brancusi's Târgu Jiu ensemble nevertheless survived by becoming a recognizable and meaningful part of this small city's life.

Brancusi's work, though marking the beginning and end of an important urban axis in Târgu Jiu, does not occupy that space alone. East along Calea Eroilor, up the slight rise that will culminate at the *Endless Column* stands the Church of the Apostles Saints Peter and Paul, a medieval edifice whose reconstruction occurred at the same

3.7 The *Endless Column* seen in relation to Târgu Jiu. The reconstructed Church of the Apostles Saints Peter and Paul is visible at far left on Brancusi's axis, and a railroad, difficult to see in this image, also crosses this path. The heterogeneous, vernacular nature of Târgu Jiu is clearly visible.

time that Brancusi's works were erected.[23] The church is not architecturally significant, but in the context of Brancusi's urban ensemble it plays a noteworthy role, diversifying the sculptural axis and adding a referential, religious dimension to Brancusi's abstract, monumental art. But the church also occupies the axis of the street, preventing any visual connection between the *Gate of the Kiss* and the *Endless Column*. This connection would have been difficult even had the church not existed; the *Gate of the Kiss* is difficult to see even from Calea Eroilor because of its low topographical position and the screening trees. Likewise the narrowness of the *Endless Column*, though visible from the church, gives it only a relatively modest presence; in photographs it marks the avenue's end with much less force than does the reconstructed church. The procession toward the column is also weakened by a wide bed of railroad tracks running across the avenue, crossed only by a pedestrian path.

Brancusi's ensemble, in other words, while visible as such on a map and perceptible once one has moved from one sculptural group (the *Table* and *Gate*) to the other (the *Column*), is hardly a conventional architectural axis. This must have frustrated Varia: clearly wishing the sculptures to be within sight of each other, he produced a doctored photograph showing all three sculptures in what he called an "ideal view."[24] Nor does the Calea Eroilor have an appealing aesthetic quality—the street is small-scale, architecturally inconsistent, and interrupted by utility poles and infrastructure. Adding insult to injury, the sculptures' settings, a well-used but somewhat pedestrian downtown public park, on the one hand, and a workaday, open space on the other that adjoins a factory, do not seem to provide suitably respectful or monumental surroundings for the ensemble. In fact, the entire Târgu Jiu setting is underscaled, seemingly undeserving of the quality of the art bestowed upon it by Brancusi, and unrelated to its globally important monuments. Miller, viewing the sculptures before their recent renovation, saw them as "almost like objects from outer space, refusing to integrate with the life and atmosphere of the town."[25]

The recent (1996–2007) World Monuments Fund renovation of Brancusi's ensemble responded to Târgu Jiu's perceived shortcomings by appointing both architecture and landscape architecture firms to "restore the dignity and serenity"[26] of the sculptures' surrounds, an effort undertaken in tandem with the cleaning, restoration, and stabilization of the sculptures themselves. The landscape architecture team—headed by Laurie Olin—responded by treating landscape as a supporting element of the sculpture, using plantings as a mediating device between the sculptures and their surroundings. The workaday park of the *Endless Column* was redesigned with trees intended to "form

► **3.8** Renovations to Brancusi's Târgu Jiu ensemble between 1996 and 2007 undertook a laudable restoration and stabilization of the sculptures, but treated Târgu Jiu's cityscape as something to suppress, ignore, or domesticate.

Phase A

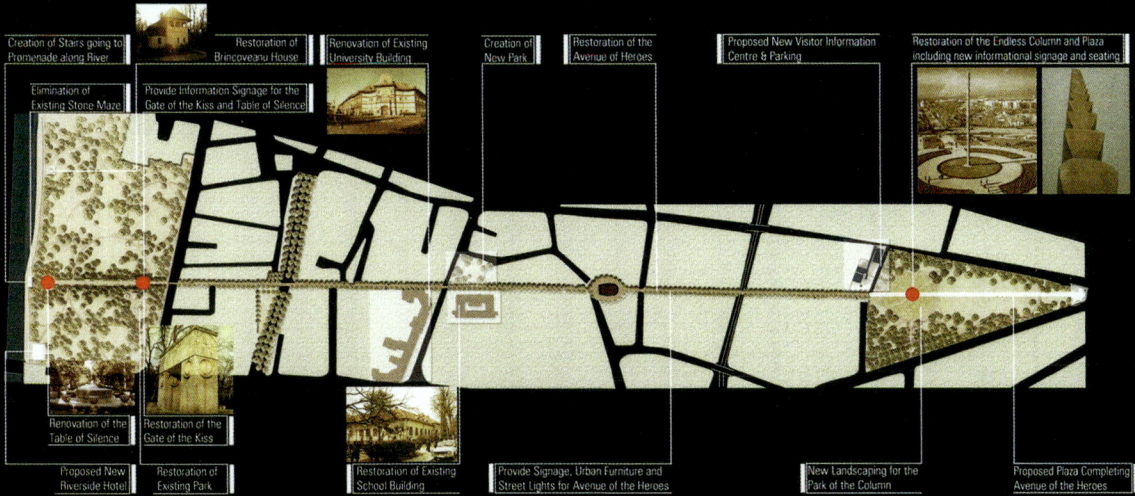

Creation of Stairs going to Promenade along River

Restoration of Brâncoveanu House

Renovation of Existing University Building

Creation of New Park

Restoration of the Avenue of Heroes

Proposed New Visitor Information Centre & Parking

Restoration of the Endless Column and Plaza including new informational signage and seating

Elimination of Existing Stone Maze

Provide Information Signage for the Gate of the Kiss and Table of Silence

Renovation of the Table of Silence

Restoration of the Gate of the Kiss

Proposed New Riverside Hotel

Restoration of Existing Park

Restoration of Existing School Building

Provide Signage, Urban Furniture and Street Lights for Avenue of the Heroes

New Landscaping for the Park of the Column

Proposed Plaza Completing Avenue of the Heroes

Phase B

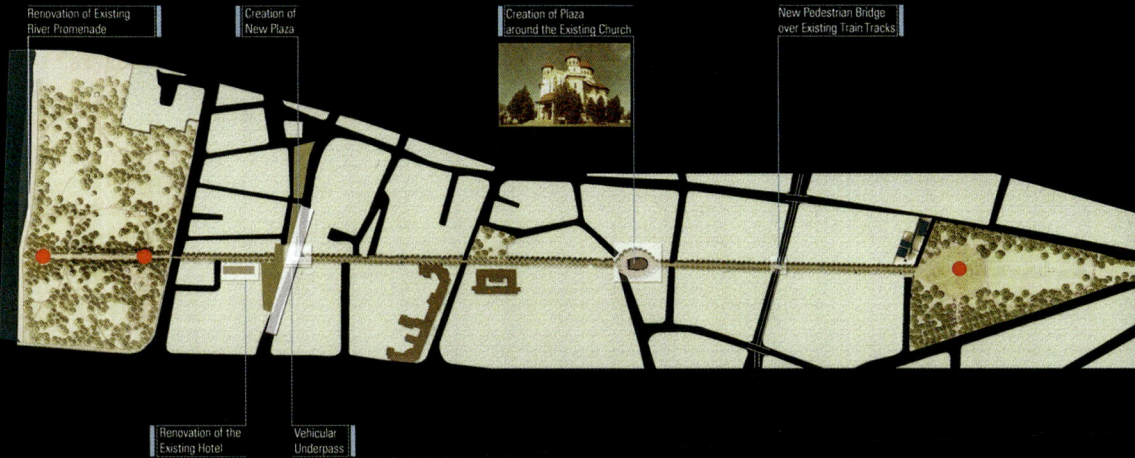

Renovation of Existing River Promenade

Creation of New Plaza

Creation of Plaza around the Existing Church

New Pedestrian Bridge over Existing Train Tracks

Renovation of the Existing Hotel

Vehicular Underpass

Phase C

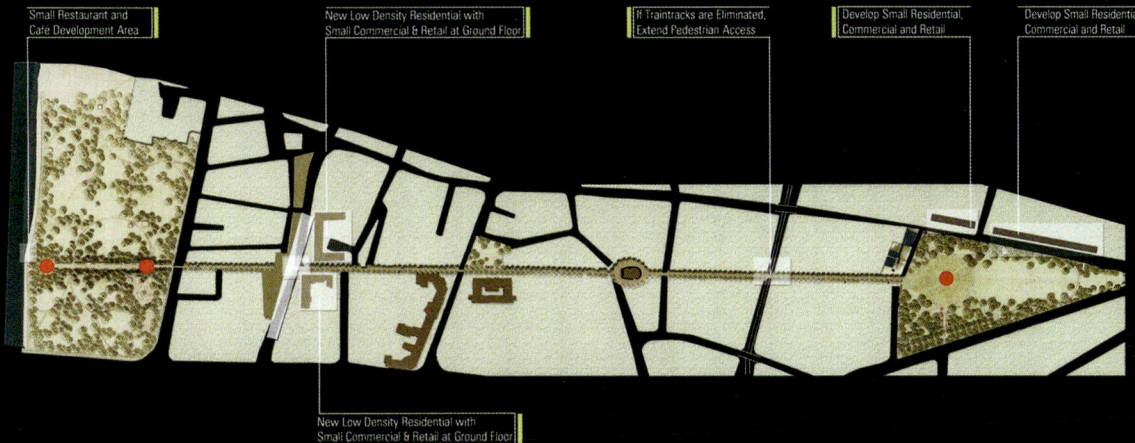

Small Restaurant and Cafe Development Area

New Low Density Residential with Small Commercial & Retail at Ground Floor

If Traintracks are Eliminated, Extend Pedestrian Access

Develop Small Residential, Commercial and Retail

Develop Small Residential, Commercial and Retail

New Low Density Residential with Small Commercial & Retail at Ground Floor a seasonally changing backdrop and to screen out the surrounding buildings. ... [The plantings] will grow together to form a woodland around the *Column*. ... [I]t will once again be seen against the vast horizon, distant mountains and sky."[27] This work was completed in 2007. The same team proposed that the equally unprepossessing Calea Eroilor have "vehicular access be managed ... [with] trees on either side of the avenue to give it a more sympathetic and humane character."[28] Ultimately, Olin sought to "provide a 'green' link between the two parks ... [once again allowing] visitors to view them quietly and without the intrusion of the modern context ... editing this context and clarifying the situation in order to allow Brancusi's work to dominate."[29]

Mihai Radu, a New York-based Romanian architect charged with generating a supporting urban plan for the Calea Eroilor, felt similarly about the urban context of the Brancusi ensemble. Downtown, reconstructed during the Communist era, was for Radu little more than "a mix of poorly maintained paving, disheveled mass housing, jumbled signage and buildings of every size and description."[30] His urban plan proposed several changes to this setting, including renovation of existing significant civic buildings, new "signage, urban furniture, and street lights" for the Calea, contextual buildings in the city center and around the borders of the *Endless Column* park, and a bridge over the existing train tracks: in short, in Radu's words, a "reconfiguration of the town centre that is more respectful of the original urban fabric."[31] Most significantly, Radu proposed a visitor's center for the ensemble on a vacant lot bordering the *Column* park. But none of Radu's improvements appeared to have been implemented by 2012.[32]

The designers' suppressions of the contemporary townscape are unsurprising. Târgu Jiu is not conventionally beautiful, and it holds nothing else aesthetically comparable to Brancusi's ensemble. It seems only natural that Olin would wish to protect the *Endless Column* from its "disheveled"[33] surroundings while at the same time exposing the *Table of Silence* by clearing out the plantings that seem to occlude its beauty. Nor should one be surprised at Mihai Radu's desire to introduce some order into the clearly fragmented surrounds of the Calea. Parks are conventionally understood to be more attractive if clearly bounded by buildings, just as streets are understood to be more attractive when lined with a consistent, clear building wall and appropriately scaled plantings.

These urban desires can also be placed in a national historical perspective. Since its independence in the nineteenth century, Romania has always looked to France. Their shared Latin heritage and language notwithstanding, France's high state of development provided a clear path of improvement for a Romania seeking to recover a European heritage in the face of the nation's more than three-hundred-year domination by the Ottoman

Turks. Bucharest, in its late nineteenth-century renaissance, had already modeled itself as a miniature Paris, complete with boulevards, palaces, and a monumental riverfront. Brancusi, long-time resident of Paris by the time of his commission, may have envisioned the Calea Eroilor as bringing a bit of Parisian grandeur to his hometown. At a modest scale quite appropriate to their setting, his sculptures do define the town's civic spaces in the same manner that the Arc de Triomphe and Place de la Concorde define the much larger Grande Axe, or Great Axis, of Paris. In this sense, the designers' early twenty-first-century moves to tame, correct, or at least disguise the seemingly provincial setting of the town could be seen as a natural and appropriate way of respecting Brancusi's masterwork.

More critically, one can also view the World Monuments Fund's restorative measures, however well-intentioned, as failing to grasp the true urban design relationships between Tárgu Jiu and Brancusi's sculptures. Radu certainly realized that these works represented a unique approach to urban design. He said:

> Brancusi's ideas about the urban fabric of a city involved making small-scale interventions connected by an overall idea about the structure and life of a contemporary city. His position was a radical one relative to urban design dogma of the twentieth century, which seemed to assume that only large-scale interventions were consequential. A key example of such unfortunate large-scale intervention is the destruction of a substantial portion of Bucharest's centre during the Ceaucescu [sic] period...Brancusi was ahead of his time when he conceived the notion of transforming the urban landscape through the introduction of significant art elements....this concept of modern monumental public art as urban catalyst is still a valid urban theory today and has guided our work in planning for urban redevelopment.[34]

Radu's words are well taken. Brancusi's work in Tárgu Jiu is absolutely revolutionary: the sculptures simultaneously exist in public space as conventional public art, providing multiple, ambiguous meanings to multiple audiences, while also serving prosaic functions (seats, gateway, monumental marker) and, most importantly for the town's urban design, shaping a larger urban structure. The sculptures' relationship, conducted through the "interior space of the ensemble"[35] defined by the Calea Eroilor, spatially integrates them with Tárgu Jiu's urbanism, such as it is, in a dramatic and fundamental way. Simple in form as Brancusi's axis is, and uninspiring a street as the Calea Eroilor is, one's progression through the lower group of sculptures, through the city's downtown, along the Calea, to the *Endless Column* is a spatial experience rare in any contemporary city.

Yet suppressing and disowning the setting of Tárgu Jiu does Brancusi's work a disservice. Disheveled as the landscape and townscape of Tárgu Jiu may be, it is this very townscape that lived with Brancusi's work, and very likely supported its survival, for over sixty years until the time of the sculptures' restoration. The proposed landscape and urban design ideas that followed the very worthy restoration of Brancusi's work seek not to bring the reality of Târgu Jiu further into the world of the ensemble, but to push it away. Vegetation is meant to screen the offending factory surroundings of the *Endless Column*; the construction of a revivalist visitor center—a conventional touristic trope if ever there was one—is meant to restore another boundary. The Calea, unacceptably vernacular, is to be prettified and thereby made more acceptable for the tourist groups that would walk from one end of the axis to the other. And within the municipal park, long a center of Târgu Jiu civic activity, the sculptures are to be isolated from surrounding uses, placed on a pedestal as it were, though they are not actually fenced off. The existing Târgu Jiu, in other words, offers the World Monuments Fund designers little or nothing of note; the town is to be negated, aestheticized, gentrified. Perhaps unconsciously, the Parisian-revivalist spirit of old Romania infected the designers' intentions. Certainly one can see a negative attitude toward Communist-era construction, which is unsurprising but still somewhat insensitive in light of the increasing appreciation of this era's admittedly bombastic design.[36]

One can appreciate the designers' and the World Monuments Fund's desire to convert Târgu Jiu into something resembling a more conventional tourist attraction, a location deserving of the sculpture it boasts, and also to rationalize the Fund's decision to spend several million dollars restoring Brancusi's work. On the other hand, the urban proposals accompanying the restoration fail to comprehend the most important urban content of Brancusi's work: the sculptures' peaceful coexistence with, and transcendence of, their mundane context. Târgu Jiu can only be itself; the city will never be a beautiful place, not even a miniature Bucharest. At the same time, the contrast between this mundane, but vibrant and no doubt livable cityscape and the "alien," but at the same time appropriately scaled work of Brancusi is what lends his sculptures their attraction. Were the *Endless Column* or *Table of Silence* sited in just another expensive corporate plaza in an American city, they would resemble a legion of other modernist sculptures in similar straits, a destination for harried office workers at lunchtime. In the admittedly provincial, even bizarre setting of Târgu Jiu, they assume a whole new meaning: a link to Brancusi's personal history (why else would they be there?), a dialogue with the Romanian countryside and its architectural vernacular, and even a comment upon Romania's somewhat poignant history as a would-be outpost of the West. Through Brancusi's work, East and West meet in Târgu Jiu in a unique and never-to-be-repeated way. Târgu Jiu's seeming imperfections reinforce, rather than reduce, his ensemble's place in this messy history and cityscape. Might not the workers in the still-functioning factory enjoy seeing the *Endless Column* from the factory yard, rather than a screen of trees, just as couples downtown enjoy a kiss under the *Gate*? Does not the Calea's double status as a prosaic neighborhood street and *grande axe* make this axis a part of residential Târgu Jiu's very heart? And are not the overscaled, hulking Communist buildings of downtown not as legitimate a piece of Romanian architectural and urban history as the smaller-scale, more sympathetic, revival buildings of the earlier decades?

Brancusi's ensemble—intact, well-used, and juxtaposed against the messy urbanism of its city—is pluralist urbanism in its finest form. The work has a plural scale, existing either as stand-alone monuments, as a duo (the *Table* and *Gate*), or as a triad. Brancusi's ensemble is civic in every way, and closely enmeshed with Târgu Jiu's everyday life. In blending into Târgu Jiu's often dissonant street pattern and urban fabric, the ensemble also reduces the difference between what constitutes Brancusi's sculptural urbanism and what does not. The clarity of the axis, and the presence of the three elements of Brancusi's ensemble at the ends of this axis, necessarily oblige subsequent elements of this plural urbanism to participate in the scheme. Are not the looming Communist buildings and the reconstructed church too, part of this plural urbanism? And does their presence, together with the *Table*, *Gate*, and *Column* not provide the entire axis of the Calea an aspect of *kairos*, a multitemporal quality?

The World Monuments Fund designers' attempts to rationalize, subdue, and homogenize the Târgu Jiu axis are appropriate in light of contemporary ideals, yet they also unconsciously attempt to apply a unitary urban design aspect to what is a clearly pluralist setting. But all is not lost: Târgu Jiu will not be tamed so easily. Its imperfect urbanism may yet prove resistant to further rectification, and international sponsors like the World Monuments Fund will likely be disappointed at this vernacular place's seeming resistance to improvement. Târgu Jiu's plural urbanism, a small-town Romanian fabric meshed with a globally significant sculptural ensemble, will continue to astonish for some time to come.

Learning from Brancusi

Târgu Jiu's meaning in the larger world of urban design may not be apparent at first. Brancusi's sculptural ensemble was in every way atypical, both in the life of the sculptor and in the life of cities. He never built another comparably scaled ensemble, and the circumstances under which he was able to build at Târgu Jiu were accordingly highly unusual. And few other sculptors have had the same opportunity either: it is certainly rare to come across such a sculptural ensemble by a single artist in a city, never mind one where the sculpture has shaped the urban fabric to such a degree. One might argue with some justification that Brancusi's ensemble is a strange exception rather than a useful lesson. What could such a grouping of special sculptures possibly offer the urban designer?

Yet if we look again, Brancusi's work does offer valuable lessons. His work in Târgu Jiu was subject to the limitations that affect urban designers everywhere. The urban setting was undistinguished and undesigned. The local populace was unfamiliar with the artist's aesthetic, and not necessarily inclined to be sympathetic to it. The available sites for his work were scattered and not immediately monumental or significant. And, of course, his budget was limited and the country was relatively poor. None of these conditions necessarily provided the most fertile setting for urban design.

How did Brancusi overcome these obstacles? First, the sculptor was fortunate to have powerful sponsorship with local legitimacy—the high social status and credibility of Mmes Tătărescu and Petrașcu (heads of the National League of Gorj Women, the sponsors of his work) were no doubt key in overcoming any local opposition and ensuring that there was a constituency to support the work.[37] Brancusi thus succeeded in his appeal to an important aspect of plural urbanism—a plural populace, albeit powerful elements within that plural populace. Second, the sculptor was able to intervene in the urban setting with design elements that were relatively small—not buildings, but sculptures. At the same time, these sculptures were absolutely unprecedented compared to the scale at which Brancusi was used to working. Brancusi of course did not consider himself an urbanist, although he became one in constructing his ensemble. An advantage of Brancusi operating as a sculptor-urbanist was that the relatively small scale of the sculptures made it easier to insert them into existing settings without much disruption, while retaining and even accentuating their visual power through their location in important civic settings (or in the case of the less centrally located *Endless Column*, through their dramatic form). And Brancusi's siting of his *Column* on a somewhat remote eminence clearly accentuated its vertical nature.

Brancusi's small-scale intervention—again, in conventional urban design terms—provided the additional advantage of allowing the sculptures to be constructed quickly. Like Manuel de Solà-Morales's work referred to earlier, this scalar limitation defied the risk of incompletion and the lack of aesthetic continuity and meaning that would have ensued. At the same time, the clear spatial organization of the ensemble, aligned along the kilometer-and-a-half "memorial axis" of the Calea Eroilor, by necessity brought other elements of the cityscape into the ensemble, such as the Church of the Apostles Saints Peter and Paul. The street itself is also part of the ensemble, and given the inherent instability of the cityscape along the street (for example, the replacement of older structures by the large-scale, Communist-era architecture downtown), the entire ensemble assumed an aspect of formal, temporal, and scalar pluralism while also retaining the entirety of Brancusi's aesthetic intentions.

Brancusi's sculpture, distinct and unique as it is, offers several simple lessons for the aspiring pluralist urban designer. First, with a relatively high degree of design control, shape small-scale elements that are meaningful and, ideally beautiful and functional. These elements provide the recognizable nuclei of the scheme that allow it to be recognized as a single design concept (rather than as a series of designed, but unrelated elements). Second, integrate these small-scale elements into a larger-scale spatial construct (in this case, the memorial axis) that embraces other elements of the cityscape. Third, construct the small-scale urban design elements on multiple properties within the larger-scale spatial construct. These lessons seem relatively straightforward, but as architect Mihai Radu noted, urban design constructed according to these ideas is relatively rare.[38] At the same time, the straightforward lessons above offer an almost infinite variety of design opportunities to urban designers. These principles will animate the work of the two projects that follow, as well as that of the designers whose work we will examine in the subsequent chapter. Simple principles, simple form, but abundant meaning, interpretation, and intersection with setting. Such is the richness of Brancusi's work at Târgu Jiu.

Twin Parks: Reformed Modernism in the Bronx

Twin Parks, another significant project embodying many principles of plural urbanism, is located in the Bronx, the northernmost borough of New York City. In the 1960s and 1970s the Bronx's physical, social, and economic troubles made it a notorious example of urban decline. The dramatic demographic changes that the Bronx experienced between 1970 and 1980, losing a fifth of its population within the space of ten years, provide some clue to the trauma that the borough experienced during that time. Public policy and urban design played a substantial role in attempts to address the Bronx's problems. Throughout the 1950s, '60s, and '70s, in addition to being the victim of widespread highway construction famously demonized by Robert Caro in *The Power Broker*,[39] the Bronx was the site of numerous urban design efforts to redevelop areas in the borough's southern and western areas. One of those projects is a "scattered site" housing development known as Twin Parks whose history and architecture have been the subject of recent study.[40]

The fourteen buildings of Twin Parks, containing 2000 housing units,[41] were constructed between 1970 and 1973 in an area between Bronx Park and Crotona Park in the borough's south-central area. Master-planned by a team of urban designers headed by Jonathan Barnett, the complex ultimately enrolled a number of architects and architecture firms, including Giovanni Pasanella, Richard Meier, James Stewart Polshek, and Prentice & Chan, Olhausen. Richard Meier in particular was to become very well known as one of the leading architects of the 1980s and 1990s, and his Twin Parks work stands as an early and important landmark in his oeuvre. It is this combination of larger-scale urban design with individual buildings by several notable architecture firms, all in the service of neighborhood social improvement, that lends Twin Parks its substantial interest.

Twin Parks' origins lay in several convergent aspects of New York City's redevelopment planning of the mid-1960s and have been well summarized both by participants in the development's planning and design process[42] and others.[43] The ultimate motive for the project lay in urban renewal policy, for which planners conducted studies determining levels of neighborhood blight, a designation that made neighborhoods eligible for federal funding for site acquisition, clearance, and construction.[44] Mixed-use neighborhoods like Twin Parks were inconsistent with modernist planning ideologies that advocated single-use communities with substantially more open space and housing quality than Twin Parks provided. As a typical aging, lower-middle area of the Bronx containing heterogeneous housing mixed with small-scale neighborhood retail, auto repair facilities, and small-scale manufacturing (these activities may all still be found in the area today), Twin Parks, or Bronx Park West as it was initially called, attracted the interest of urban renewal officials. The Bronx Park West area was consequently singled out for urban renewal designation in 1963, with additional areas designated in 1966.[45]

A few years earlier, conventional modernist ideology would have recommended total site clearance of the blighted area of Twin Parks and its replacement with large-scale building complexes with structures arrayed to provide maximum amounts of light, air, and open space. Such clearance and construction efforts had been under

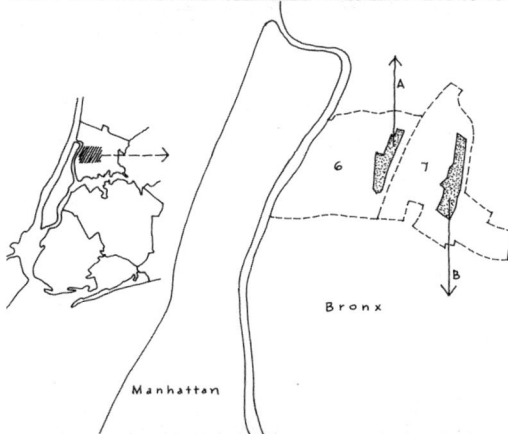

The two major areas for "vest pocket" housing in East Tremont are Twin Parks West (A, above), and Twin Parks East (B, below). The aerial photos show both areas before new housing was constructed, revealing the many places where land was vacant or under-utilized, and thus a potential vest-pocket housing site.

3.9 New York City's Urban Design Group selected the Twin Parks area of the Bronx for a novel experiment in social housing that formally engaged with its neighborhood both through architectural design and through the siting of different project elements.

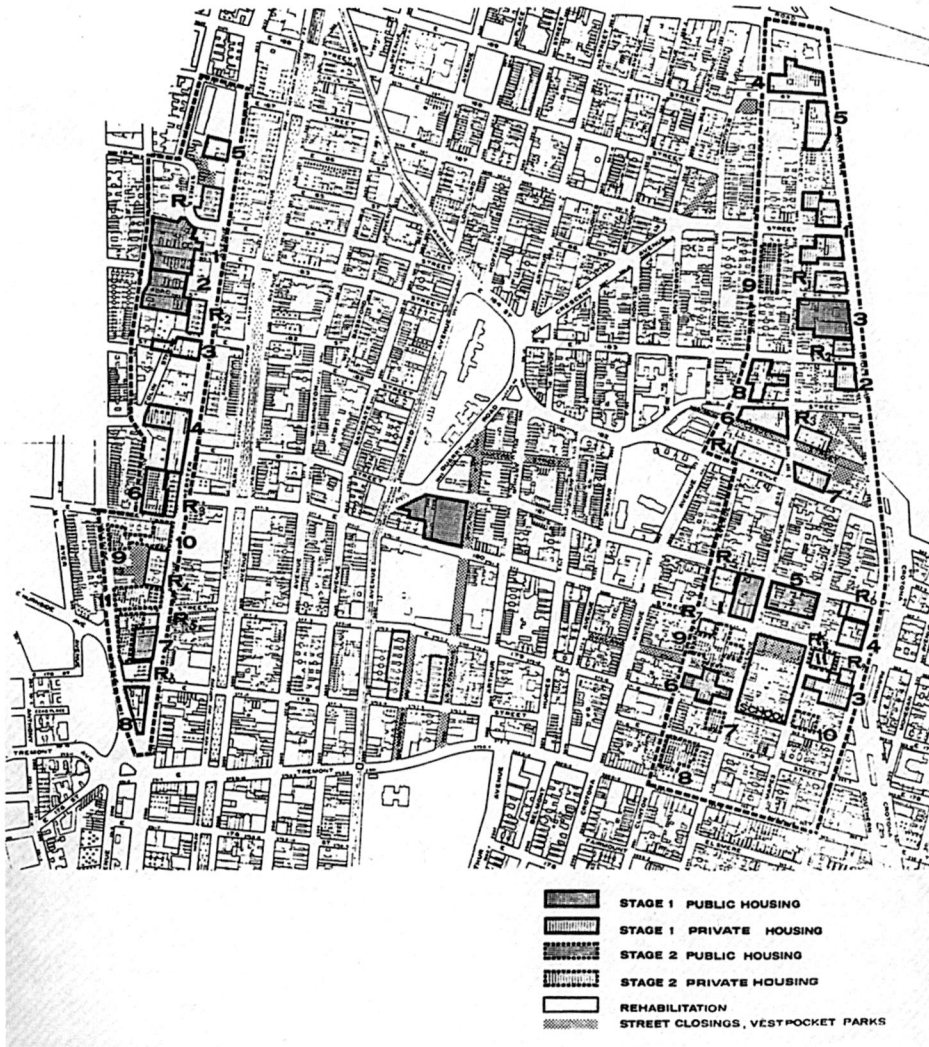

	STAGE 1 PUBLIC HOUSING
	STAGE 1 PRIVATE HOUSING
	STAGE 2 PUBLIC HOUSING
	STAGE 2 PRIVATE HOUSING
	REHABILITATION
	STREET CLOSINGS, VESTPOCKET PARKS

3.10 By the late 1960s, wholesale clearance of distressed neighborhoods was no longer socially or politically acceptable. In Twin Parks, housing planners selected two strips of neighborhood, each with several available sites, for rehabilitation.

way in New York for over twenty-five years by 1966, perhaps most spectacularly so at Stuyvesant Town in Lower Manhattan, where in the midst of World War II eighteen blocks totaling 600 "outmoded" buildings, 500 "stores and small factories," and 3,100 families[46] were displaced for a development that ultimately provided 8,755 apartments for 24,000 people, with many fewer stores and no small factories at all. Such projects were widespread in the Bronx as well. Not far from the Twin Parks site sits the cheerless Concourse Village, a complex of over 5,000 apartments in six gargantuan, monotonous, gray slabs constructed over railroad tracks to the southwest of Crotona Park. High modernism's coda in the South Bronx was the even bleaker Morrisania Air Rights housing near Concourse Village, a row of three towers containing 843 units. Morrisania Air Rights—completed in 1980 after years of delays[47]—provided strong arguments against the further imposition of Corbusian urban design on the varied, human-scaled Bronx cityscape.

Stuyvesant Town and Concourse Village's spectacular Radiant City iconography was decreasingly practicable in the mid-1960s. Resident perceptions of acceptable levels of neighborhood change and social perceptions of acceptable standards of justice for lower-income populations had both changed.[48] Nor was it at all clear that Bronx Park West was as blighted as had been the Gas Works district in Manhattan (the area eliminated to construct Stuyvesant Town). In fact, much of Twin Parks was a decidedly stable and politically empowered neighborhood of Italian Americans. As Jonathan Barnett—the municipal urban designer who eventually shaped the urban renewal plan for Twin Parks—noted wryly, "there was a lot more to the Italian neighborhood than met the eye, some of which I won't repeat here."[49] Barnett also drew telling analogies between this part of Twin Parks and Boston's North End, another concentrated area of Italian Americans that had avoided urban renewal clearance in the 1950s. Ultimately the Italian part of Twin Parks, called Belmont, was not designated for urban renewal, but the less politically empowered blocks to its east and west were.

The greatest influence on the design of Twin Parks was the ongoing shift in architectural ideology taking place during the 1960s away from doctrinaire high modernism toward what has been called "reformed"[50] or "responsive and reflective" modernism.[51] The first generation of architectural modernists was dying off,[52] and the stage was set for a new generation of architects, coming of age as designers in the 1960s, to take stock of America's troubled urban landscape and to address it, the best they could, through architectural means. The somewhat troubled Twin Parks area of the Bronx became a laboratory for what its framers saw, and what remains today, as a

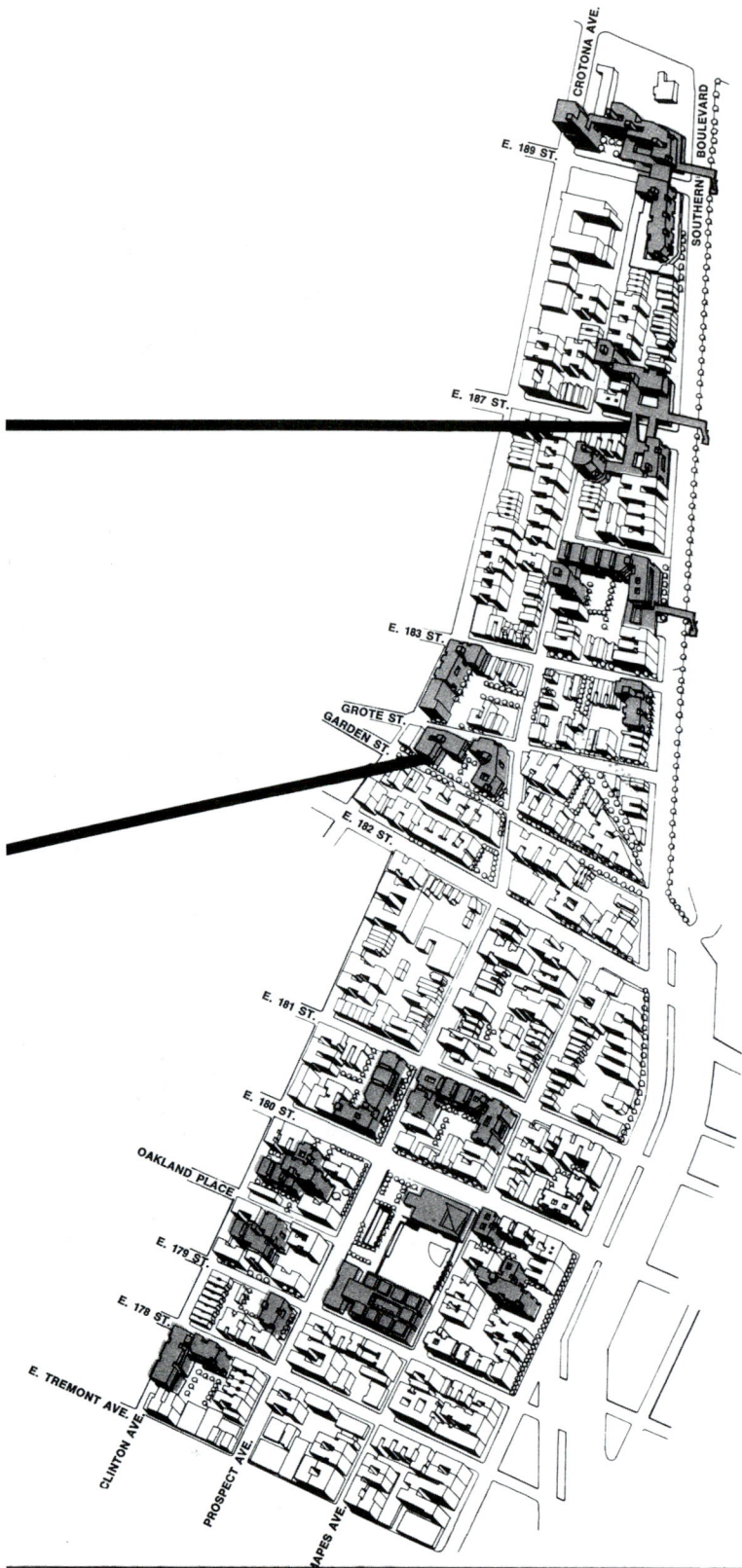

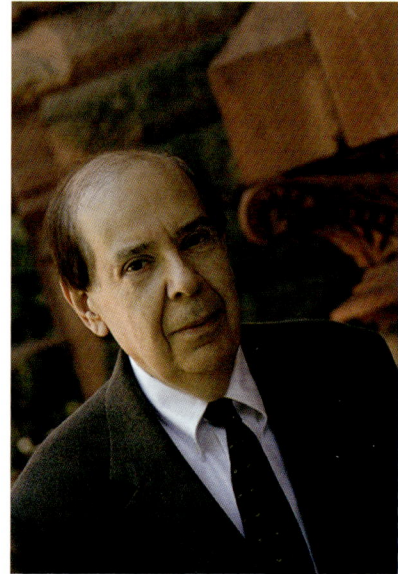

◄ **3.11** Twin Parks was shaped by a variety of policy and design actors. Funding was provided by the federal government; redevelopment areas and sites by housing planners; overall massing by the Urban Design Group; and project designs by individual architects.

▲ **3.12** Jonathan Barnett was the principal urban designer in charge of Twin Parks. Until the early 1970s, New York's urban design had the fiscal backing of the federal government. This would collapse after 1974, and urban designers would shift to regulating private-sector building.

new kind of urban design and architectural approach to the problem of urban redevelopment. Twin Parks' planners, many of whom were also architects, and the designers who eventually worked on the project were united in their sense that Twin Parks was important. Barnett, the most visible and eloquent of these planners, was a staff member of the City's newly formed Urban Design Group and a strong advocate of a new approach to urban renewal. "In terms of its stated purpose ... the East Tremont [i.e., Twin Parks] experience has been successful," he stated guardedly in 1974, while admitting that "in terms of its implied purpose, the conservation of a whole neighborhood, success is far from certain."[53]

Leaving aside for now Barnett's "implied purpose," the architects involved also saw much of merit in their work in Twin Parks. Richard Meier, for example, was still a young architect in his mid-thirties in the late 1960s.[54] In his first monograph and again in later reflections on his career, he seems to view his commission for Twin Parks—a slab and tower combination of 523 units occupying most of three city blocks—as a significant but unfortunately isolated episode in his career, both in terms of his project's relationship to the urban fabric and in its social function as low-income housing. "Twin Parks Northeast," he wrote, is "a place of urban continuity. In both its form and organization, it expresses the attitude that ... a building in an urban milieu is ... a generator of social and communal values."[55] Meier regretted the later demise of the urban policy structure that permitted Twin Parks to be constructed: "Looking back, I now realize that the public housing experiment of this period—using respected architects and providing adequate funds—was unique. In those days, we naively took it for granted and it is nothing short of disastrous that housing of this order is no longer being provided."[56] Architect Giovanni Pasanella, who designed several buildings in the complex, must have agreed: Twin Parks buildings comprise the majority of structures in his 1983 monograph *Pasanella + Klein*, and Vincent Scully's essay in the book makes it clear that the Bronx housing was the centerpiece of Pasanella's work up to that time.

Critical views of Twin Parks agreed wholeheartedly that the project was exemplary, both at the time[57] and more recently.[58] Certainly Twin Parks was in some ways very easy to like, particularly when contrasted with recent and still contemporary models of large-lot, Radiant City-type development. Critics particularly admired the plan's principal design concept: the removal of only small-scale buildings in underbuilt areas. This was a departure from the previous model of wholesale removal of an existing urban fabric. And where previous projects had simply repeated one or two tower models seemingly ad infinitum, the architecture of Twin Parks housing was far more sensitive, differentiated,

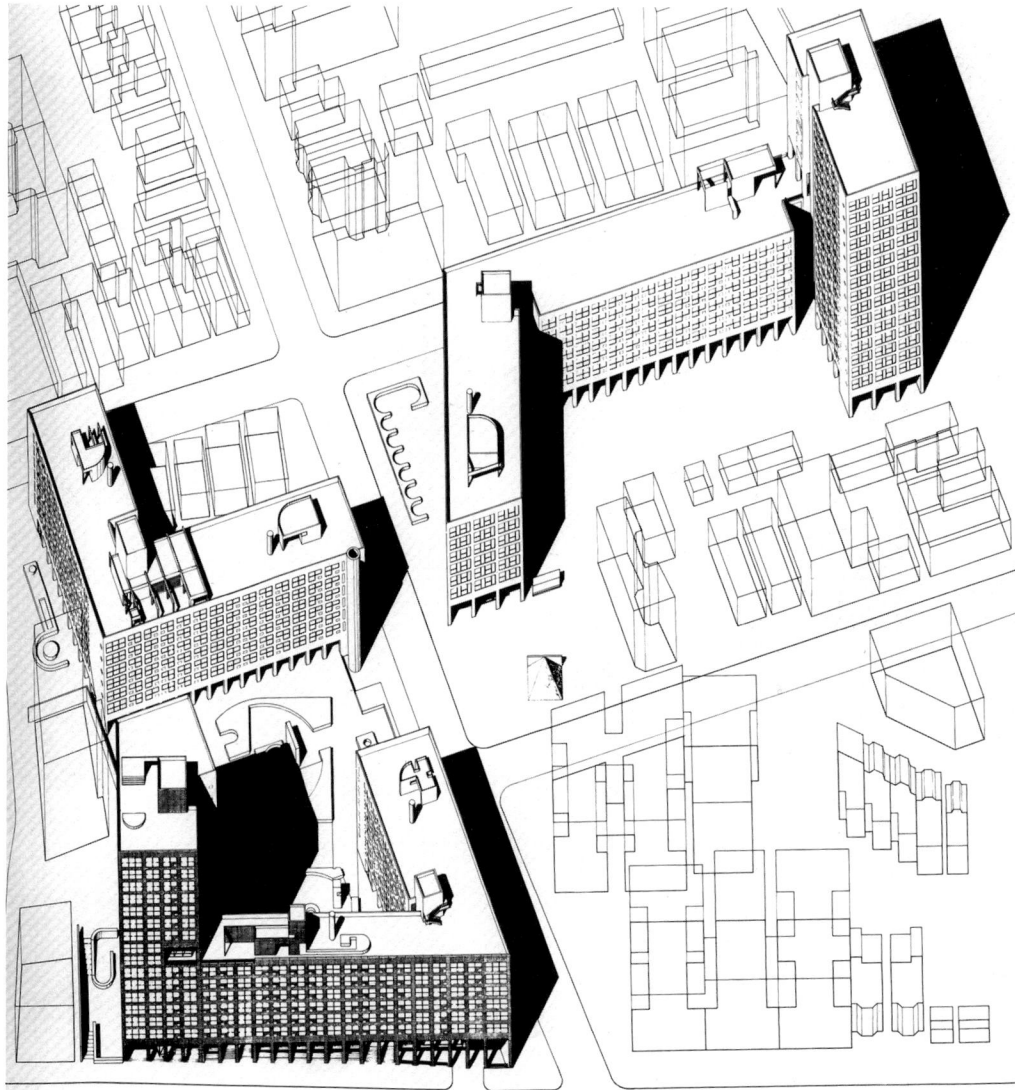

▲ **3.13** Some of the architects working at Twin Parks would go on to achieve substantial fame, including Richard Meier, whose housing complex is shown here. Meier would never again design social housing of this quality.

▼ **3.14** James Stewart Polshek's housing at Twin Parks reflected both a Radiant City tower design approach and an emerging contextual model, where buildings mirrored the scale, material, and spatial relationships of their surroundings.

▶ **3.15** Most dramatic of all Twin Parks housing was Giovanni Pasanella's work. Several of his buildings formed gateways to the Twin Parks area. Even so, Pasanella attempted to relate the scale of his work to nearby older buildings, as can be seen here.

and interesting than contemporary high-density housing. Each complex of buildings reacted to its context in individual ways, whether this context was existing structures or the Bronx's dramatic topography and rock outcroppings. The result was a series of apartment buildings that differed not only between the various sites, but also within individual complexes. In fact, no building at Twin Parks was exactly like any other, though some, like Pasanella's gateway buildings on E. 187th Street and Southern Boulevard, effectively mirrored each other's massing and materials. The differences among the clusters of housing were as notable as the differences within them. Like Meier and Pasanella's work, Polshek's complex was formally diverse, and comprised a tall tower and a slab fractured into a rough courtyard shape. But, while his complex was far from being the most formally successful of the different Twin Parks ensembles, its buildings' tan- and brown-striped brick facades did distinguish them from the others. New York State redevelopment head Edward Logue disliked the complex,[59] but one could argue that Polshek's brick patterning at least tepidly explored the potential for greater visual variability than other mass housing of the era.

Assessing Twin Parks

Twin Parks is certainly important as an episode in subsidized housing construction,[60] changing notions of public space,[61] and a step in the break away from high modernism.[62] But it is of greatest interest to us as an essay, partly conscious and partly not, in plural urbanism. The project's success lies in realizing many of the same spatial principles as Brancusi's sculptural ensemble, but at a much greater scale and with a much greater complexity of components. Perhaps the fact that Twin Parks was constructed at all despite its complexity is its greatest achievement, yet at the same time, we will see that this complexity also makes the project harder to replicate.

Twin Parks is understandable first and foremost as an urban design project with plural scale, though the project does not succeed entirely in realizing this dimension of plural urbanism. Where Twin Parks does succeed is that no single building within the project represents either the core or the entirety of the project's meaning: the project has multiple centers and is understandable in at least two scales. Twin Parks is a cluster of clusters, made up of related groups of structures that are themselves related. In the clarity of this relationship of cluster to larger cluster, Twin Parks attains a quality of plural scale akin to that realized at Târgu Jiu. Given that each parcel at Twin Parks was allotted to a distinct architect (though Pasanella designed several parcels), it is not surprising

3.16 In the socially troubled Bronx of the 1970s, the Twin Parks housing was a landmark social housing effort with diverse and sensitive urban design. Each part of the project demonstrates a present-future duality that scholar Peter Rowe called "being and becoming."

ranged from Pasanella's experimental, controversial (for the era) skip-stop[70] slabs to Prentice & Chan, Olhausen's rather conservative low-rise courtyard housing, a precursor of the architectural postmodernism that was soon to come. Such experimental housing developments, where multiple architects tried their hand on a similar problem on a single site, had a long legacy in Europe going at least as far back as the Weissenhof-siedlung in Stuttgart (1927), but analogous demonstrations of aggregated, experimental architectural solutions to social issues were almost unknown in the United States. It is this aspect of Twin Parks that architects such as Meier and Barnett found so satisfactory at the time and what critics today similarly appreciate.[71]

Twin Parks itself was constructed quickly, in only six years, from the 1967 planning study that identified sites for the clusters to the opening of the clusters themselves. As a single project constructed rapidly, Twin Parks does not reflect the dimension of plural time that is so critical to plural urbanism, instead acting as a single work of architecture in which the project as constructed represents the entirety of the designed concept. This endows Twin Parks with the air of a valuable history lesson, but this same historic quality also makes the project seem less contemporary, less of a changing, evolving lesson in urbanism for the city today.

Twin Parks' insertion into the vernacular fabric of the Bronx does mean, however, that the site as a whole will continue to evolve as individual structures around the Twin Parks clusters are replaced or removed. Abandonment in the area was never as widespread as it was in the South Bronx, either at the time of Twin Parks' construction or since, perhaps because Belmont's Italian Americans remained in their neighborhood and stabilized the social mixture of the area. As a result, many of the early twentieth-century tenement and row house blocks in the Twin Parks area are intact, though real estate prices remain low enough so that extensive market-rate developments have not yet been built since Twin Parks. In time, however, Twin Parks' early 1970s towers may sit in the midst of a changing cityscape not unlike the change that Brancusi's sculptures have witnessed in Târgu Jiu during their eighty years of existence. Whether Twin Parks will be more distinctive or less when that additional development occurs remains to be seen. In the meantime, the neighborhood is still an architectural time capsule, an intermingling of two eras of construction: the tenements and row houses of the early twentieth century and Twin Parks.

Whatever changes do occur in the surrounding cityscape, Twin Parks' formal character as an architectural assemblage means that these possible future changes are not likely to be perceived as having any relationship to the Twin Parks houses themselves. This is very different from Târgu Jiu, where the sculptures' orientation to an axis through the city also provides that axis with meaning. The diffuse site planning of Twin Parks does not make any surrounding area of Bronx Park more or less meaningful: there is no contextual consideration to apply to the project. One might decry Târgu Jiu's unruly growth for its deleterious impact on Brancusi's sculptures and on their relationship to their original setting, but one could hardly criticize future development in Twin Parks for the same, since neither the development's relationship to its context, nor the context itself, seems so significant. Twin Parks was intended to save or at least stabilize its surroundings—the "existing neighborhood conservation" that Barnett mentioned—but its buildings did not necessarily provide a formal precedent for further development. In fact, the few developments constructed subsequently along Southern Boulevard have matched the scale of the original tenements, not Twin Parks. Perhaps the original context was too uniform for Twin Parks' new scale to set a new precedent, or perhaps the Twin Parks housing had too much plurality of form (buildings ranged in height from low-rise courtyards to tall towers) for a new formal scale to be perceptible.

Twin Parks did not set a citywide precedent either. Its high-rise, scattered-site, diverse-designer experiment was never repeated for a number of reasons, including the collapse of its institutional sponsor, the New York State Urban Development Corporation, less than two years after Twin Parks opened.[72] As financing for social housing disappeared in the late 1970s and planning and development bureaucracies shifted into defensive or maintenance modes, the architect-planners like Jonathan Barnett who had curated the Twin Parks process moved toward regulation, shaping urban design through zoning where the private market was willing and able to provide it. In the 1980s and afterward, this market dependence meant mostly that "urban design as public policy," as Barnett titled his 1974 book,[73] would be restricted to Manhattan until the real estate boom of the twenty-first century returned high-rise development to the outer boroughs.

What might Twin Parks' planners and architects have done better? As we already noted, the project must first be lauded for its very existence. Had any of the actors involved come along even a couple of years earlier or later, the project would very likely not have been constructed. Earlier in the 1960s, neither scattered-site ideology nor neighborhood participation had advanced enough for Twin Parks' novel site selection to have been a reality. Nor would the architects involved have been likely even a few years earlier to have considered the kind of architectural differentiation that made the project so unique—early 1960s urban renewal projects such as Concourse Village were more or less doctrinaire Corbusian or Miesian in form. And had Twin Parks been delayed by only a few years, it might have been left incomplete or unconstructed due to the Urban Development Corporation's financial collapse in the early 1970s, part of the nationwide oil crisis that led to grim fiscal times for New York City in the late 1970s.

Ultimately, Twin Parks is valuable as a subsidized housing development that achieves notable architectural distinction, and as a collection of architectural works that achieves a commitment to social benefits. But Twin Parks is arguably most important as an example of plural urban design. The construction of Twin Parks demonstrated what was at the time a new ability of urban design to set new scalar and aesthetic standards, as well as to demonstrate how a neighborhood could be redesigned and improved without being demolished. Our assessments of Twin Parks' design shortcomings should be tempered by its pioneering accomplishments; the shortcomings ought to challenge urban designers to attempt other such essays. Twin Parks is a notable step in demonstrating how urban design can achieve multiple aspects of plural urbanism at a large scale, in a heterogeneous setting, and in a difficult socioeconomic context.

Our next and final example of built work shows how these shortcomings can be overcome. In the work of Jože Plečnik in the Eastern European setting of Ljubljana, Slovenia, we will see how plural urbanism can be realized through the construction of a full range of those typological elements comprising the city fabric.

Jože Plečnik and Ljubljana: Plural Urbanism as National Project

Ljubljana, Slovenia, is one of those small European cities that seem to have been tailor-made for the three-day visit. Both its name and location are pleasingly exotic to the typical European or American tourist. The city is just across the former Iron Curtain, in a Slavic country with a language unfamiliar to speakers of English; even its country's name, Slovenia, is sufficiently unfamiliar and so similar to Slovakia that former US President George W. Bush confused the two.[74] In the twenty-first century Ljubljana's cityscape, location, culture, and low prices have made it a tourist destination of choice and an easy place for low-budget travelers to reach.

Ljubljana's urban fabric does not disappoint tourists upon arrival. The writer Colm Tóibín, heading to Ljubljana in the early 1990s, described Slovenia as "a country made up by Borges … or a playful Central European novelist and miniaturist." Tóibín liked Ljubljana even more: "The view … was more like a scene out of Hans Christian

Andersen than anything out of Borges … the atmosphere was of civility and comfort, a world untouched by any of the wars … the lights of the castle above the city … made the bridge[s] and the willows [on the river] seem part of an illustration or a dream."[75] Twenty years after Tóibín, the *New York Times* praised the city for "its fair share of charming Old World plazas, baroque churches and dramatic castles," together with "remnants of a Roman wall … boxy Communist office buildings and Art Nouveau mansions," finding that "such juxtapositions contribute to the city's distinctive character."[76]

Ljubljana's "juxtaposed" urbanism seems to represent a happy mixture of historical events, but in reality the city's twentieth-century history was painful indeed. Ljubljana's destiny has long been tied to the East, not the West; the city's river, Ljubljanica, flows not toward Venice but to the Sava, a river that flows through Slovenia, past Zagreb in Croatia, before entering the Danube at Belgrade. A boat cast adrift on the Ljubljanica would end up in the Black Sea, and Slovenia's twentieth-century history was a tug-of-war between East and West, a pawn first in Germanic schemes of a greater Austria, then of Serbo-Croatian schemes for a greater Slavic nation, the former Yugoslavia. World War II interrupted this struggle, when Fascist Germany and Italy partitioned Slovenia between them. Only after 1991 was Slovenia permitted to pursue its own destiny.

Given this trauma, even a cynic could forgive the city for its apparent overdose of easily digestible tranquility and charm. Slovenia is part of the European Union, and uses the euro. It is seemingly ensconced in Europe's embrace, with a parliamentary democracy, a liberal and well-educated populace, and tolerance of diversity. Slovenia even ranks twenty-first, or "very high," on the United Nations Human Development Index, above Spain, Italy, the United Kingdom,[77] and every other former Communist country. Like Brancusi, Ljubljana and Slovenia mesh old and new, embracing an obligatory modernity without abandoning the past.

Ljubljana displays splendid urbanism. A regular and picturesque urban fabric, studded with markers of its people's struggle for what Lawrence Vale called "national identity" and Peter Rowe called "civic realism" dramatically accents its hills, valley, and water.[78] Like Barcelona, also studied by Rowe, Ljubljana is the historical, cultural, and psychological capital of small peoples who have been subject to larger states. Both Slovenia and Catalonia have had intermittent and only occasional independence, and both have employed urban design and architecture to define their central city and their nation's place in the world.

Ljubljana, like Barcelona with Gaudí, had the good fortune to possess a talented architect, Jože Plečnik, who spent a good portion of his life improving his national

3.17 Slovenia's capital of Ljubljana was described by writer Colm Tóibín as "a scene out of Hans Christian Andersen...an illustration or a dream." Architect Jože Plečnik's diverse works throughout the city make Ljubljana an exemplar of plural urbanism.

capital even as he constructed much notable work elsewhere in Yugoslavia and Eastern Europe. Today the work of Jože Plečnik is recognized as representative of the "spatial meaning," as Rowe put it, of its locale.[79] Plečnik benefited from fortunate timing and an abundance of talent, both enabling him to act as architect and urban designer. His work in the city, spanning a wide range of civic structures, monuments, landscapes, and infrastructure, all constructed almost entirely in a brief span of fifteen years between 1928 and 1943, is an appropriate culmination to our triad of built projects embodying plural urbanism. Plečnik's Ljubljana work represents as complete a realization as one could expect of plural urbanism in a single place by the hand of a single individual.

As with Brancusi in Târgu Jiu, much of the literature on Plečnik's work in Ljubljana concentrates on the aesthetic qualities of his individual works, not on their collective quality.[80] Yet there is as much to understand about Plečnik's urbanism as there is about his architecture: in scale, ambition, complexity, and sheer quantity his Ljubljana work is a tremendous achievement. As plural urbanism, Plečnik's work displays a profound relationship with the existing older city, manifesting dimensions of plural scale, time, form, and property. Yet Plečnik's position as effective state architect of Slovenia and therefore as the principal designer of Ljubljana's urban design ensemble makes his work somewhat remote from the dimension of plural agency that characterized Twin Parks.

Born into the aesthetic ferment of the Viennese Secession and into the political ferment of early twentieth-century Slavic nationalism, Plečnik's work achieved great renown in its day. Today we can perceive him as a mediator between the romanticism of the Secession and the functionalism of modernism, a living remnant of a grander age.[81] Plečnik survived both World Wars I and II, saw his work flourish in the newly independent nations of Czechoslovakia and Yugoslavia, and saw it decline under the cloistered Communism of Josip Broz Tito after World War II.[82] During this time, first in Prague, then in Ljubljana, Plečnik realized an architectural oeuvre of broad scalar range, high programmatic variety, and immensely rich tectonic and material expression. This work reflected both an intensely personal aesthetic vision and a deep attunement to the sites, often profoundly historic, within which he operated. Plečnik practiced less in the mode of contemporary global professionals, flying to and fro wherever their commissions took them, than in the more grounded mode of a local architect, one who dedicated more than a decade to an accumulated architectural oeuvre within a constricted location. The result of Plečnik's approach in Ljubljana shows urban design's extraordinary potential to shape a city in unforeseen and unanticipated ways through individual, highly diverse acts of construction.

3.19 This pyramid designed by Plečnik (1934–1937) sits atop Ljubljana's restored Roman wall and has obvious classical antecedents, but it is also a timeless Platonic form whose location and design also makes it a popular civic space in a well-used park.

While Plečnik's work was the inspiration of a single individual, its relationship to time, to scale, and to the city's many neighborhoods was manifestly plural.

Plečnik's position as effective city architect[90] was unusual, but he was far from omnipotent. While his role as premier designer of his small region's capital is not one that most architects or city designers might reasonably hope to possess today, he operated under notable constraints, including funding limitations, occasional public opposition, changing municipal priorities, and eventually competition from fellow architects, many of whom were former students, who felt that Plečnik was providing too much competition and was taking advantage of his position.[91] These resentments likely inhibited Plečnik's larger-scale city plans from being further implemented.

Of the three designers or sets of designers whose work we have examined in this chapter, Plečnik is unique. Both architect and city planner, he was able to design individual works of sculpture or architecture in exquisite detail, like Brancusi or the individual designers of Twin Parks, but also to envision those individual works within complex urban design concepts at multiple larger scales, somewhat in the manner of the Twin Parks planners. But at the architectural and urban scale, Plečnik's Ljubljana improvements are far more complex than either of the two preceding projects, and it stands today as not only a historical monument, but as a laudable goal for future plural urbanists.

The heart of Plečnik's work in Ljubljana is a series of axes composed of different elements—architecture, sculpture, and infrastructure—that emerge as one strolls along the Ljubljanica river in the heart of the city.[92] Walking into downtown from south of the city, along the river one encounters in sequence a sculpted curvilinear riverbank (1930);[93] the channelized, regimented riverbed and mouth of the tributary Gradaščica (1929–1931)[94] with an ornamental bridge upstream; the end of a redesigned Zoisova Cesta, featuring an abstract pyramid, street widening, and tree plantings; the dramatic Cobbler's bridge over the Ljubljanica; then an extraordinary combination of elements: the unique Triple Bridge[95] directly adjoining the city market, all built into a designed river embankment together with the landing for another bridge projected by Plečnik but only recently constructed. Further downstream, the water axis ends at Plečnik's Greco-Egyptian sluice gates, constructed in the depths of World War II and slowing the river's flow. This is an extraordinary sequence and its juxtaposition with the picturesque heart of the city and the delicately scaled Ljubljanica, makes this work by Plečnik a pleasure to experience.

The sequence of works along the river was not the only one that Plečnik created through the city fabric. Perhaps the best defined of these is a sequence that extends from his own house, south of the Gradaščica at the edge of the 1930 city, over that stream on a bridge of his own design that also marks the culmination of one branch of the river sequence. Continuing north, one crosses Zoisova Cesta, another branch of the water axis or itself a partially realized axis, into French Revolution Square. This place, widened and landscaped by Plečnik, contains a number of his works: a monument to Slovenia's brief period of independence under Napoleonic France, a memorial to Slovenian poet Simon Gregorčič, a monastery whose renovation in the 1950s was one of Plečnik's last works, and a fragment of the city's Renaissance wall converted into a small park and boulevard.[96] Most visible of all in French Revolution Square is the city's National and University Library, a monumental Renaissance-type urban block, whose interior is filled with exquisitely realized spaces and rich details. Continuing on from this rich cluster, the axis passes along the widened Vegova Street, with busts of Slovenian musicians and scholars, to Ljubljana's most beautiful public space, the paved Congress Square adjoining the planted Star Park. Plečnik paved Congress Square with a black-and-white grid like that used in Prague Castle's Third Courtyard. Here the land axis ends, but only a short block away to the east lies the halfway point of the water axis between Plečnik's two river bridges.

Understanding these axes, or "promenades" as sociologist Lucius Burckhardt called them, may seem difficult.[97] The diversity, number, and location of Plečnik's interventions are astonishing for so small an area and within a period of some fifteen years. The axes do not read as traditional urban design axes, with their characteristic regularity and predictability. But Plečnik's work need not be understood through the axis idea alone in order to arrive at an appreciation of its individual and collective effect in the city. One might also understand Plečnik's work as a series of clusters of designed elements, often organized around city spaces and contributing to, if not wholly creating, those spaces through their design.

The real pleasure of Plečnik's work in Ljubljana is not necessarily found by walking from the end of one axis to the other—this is no Parisian Grande Axe, nor even Târgu Jiu's modest Calea Eroilor, and Plečnik's axes do not always begin or end at any significant point; neither the visitor nor the resident is likely to experience them in this way. The real experience of Plečnik's plural urbanism in Ljubljana comes from wandering through the city, finding again and again a Plečnik-designed civic feature, building, space, or monument, at times where one least expects it. The collective effect of such a ramble, as I myself have experienced, is the feeling that Plečnik is present everywhere in the city—one comes upon his work so unpredictably that one fairly expects to come upon it almost anywhere. It is rare to sense such a strong role of a designer's hand in a place: a sense that a designer took a city in its totality, correcting in small ways here

3.20 Plečnik's Ljubljana architecture was often contentious; structures such as his National and University Library (1936–1940) were disparaged by functionalists. As urbanism, however, works like the Library are merely one part of a larger sequence of exemplary projects organized within the city.

and there, changing things significantly at important points and introducing totally new elements and understandings as well. Ljubljana provides the sense of Plečnik's total command over the capital, even as his hand and touch were also very light, leaving the city's basic appearance and function unchanged. For an urban designer, this total inter-relationship of Plečnik and Ljubljana is the city's most magical aspect.

The city's plural urbanism takes many forms. Its pluralism of scale is wide; whether one understands Plečnik's work as a series of axes or not, his work ranges from the relatively small (paving, lampposts, stonework) to the quite large (street segments, park allée, river improvements, public spaces). His work similarly incorporates plural instantiations of time, from the entirely new (National and University Library, city market) to the rebuilt (Triple Bridge, Congress Square) to the reshaped (Tivoli Park, Zoisova Cesta, Ljubljanica riverbank), to the reinterpreted (Roman Wall, Gradaščica). Working in urban environments that have existed since at least Roman times, Plečnik's work consciously embraced a range of histories and time periods, itself entering the stream of time in a multiplicity of ways. The fact that subsequent urban design has directly stemmed from Plečnik's work (e.g., the 2002 Butcher's Bridge in the market, and extensions of the Ljubljanica riverbank) is an additional sign of Plečnik's work's engagement with the plural time of Ljubljana. Plečnik's work also possesses a rich range of forms through its typological breadth and wide distribution.

Despite the success of Plečnik's oeuvre in Ljubljana, he experienced much frus-tration as a designer. His city plans of 1928–1929 and 1943–1944 show a great deal of unrealized projects. Plečnik proposed park improvements, a new university campus, suburban subdivisions, and a new Parliament Building for Slovenia. None were ever constructed.[98] He was also frustrated by Ljubljana's plural actors; scattered property owners frustrated his subdivision plans, and the public sometimes resisted his more grandiose ideas. Although Plečnik was never provided the master planner powers that he was permitted as an architect, this failure to achieve widespread spatial planning powers was actually Plečnik's greatest success. By failing as a unitary urban designer, he was able to concentrate on siting smaller-scale interventions at strategic points in the city, and on linking these interventions together via a series of larger-scale spatial concepts (e.g., the river sequences). The limitations imposed on Plečnik resulted in an urban center whose designed elements provide ever greater pleasure with time's passage.

Brancusi, Twin Parks, and Ljubljana are only three episodes in a much wider world of urban design. Hardly typical projects, they have always existed at or beyond the

▶ **3.21** Sociologist Lucius Burckhardt perceived Plečnik's work in Ljubljana as a series of "axes." The one along the river Ljubljanica includes the city market (top), Cobbler's Bridge (middle), and Embankment (bottom), among many others.

▲ **3.22**   Plečnik's Triple Bridge (1930–1932) provides a functionally important and visually ceremonial connection between the Ljubljanica's east and west banks. Today limited to pedestrian traffic, the bridge also serves as a lively public square and marketplace.

▼ **3.23**   Many of Plečnik's more ambitious design visions for Ljubljana, such as the Parliament Building for the Republic of Slovenia, never came to pass. World War II and the onset of Communism frustrated and then marginalized him.

▶ **3.24**   Plečnik never managed to become a conventional master planner, but the finely scaled and closely coordinated urban projects that he did realize constitute one of the most highly significant works of plural urbanism.

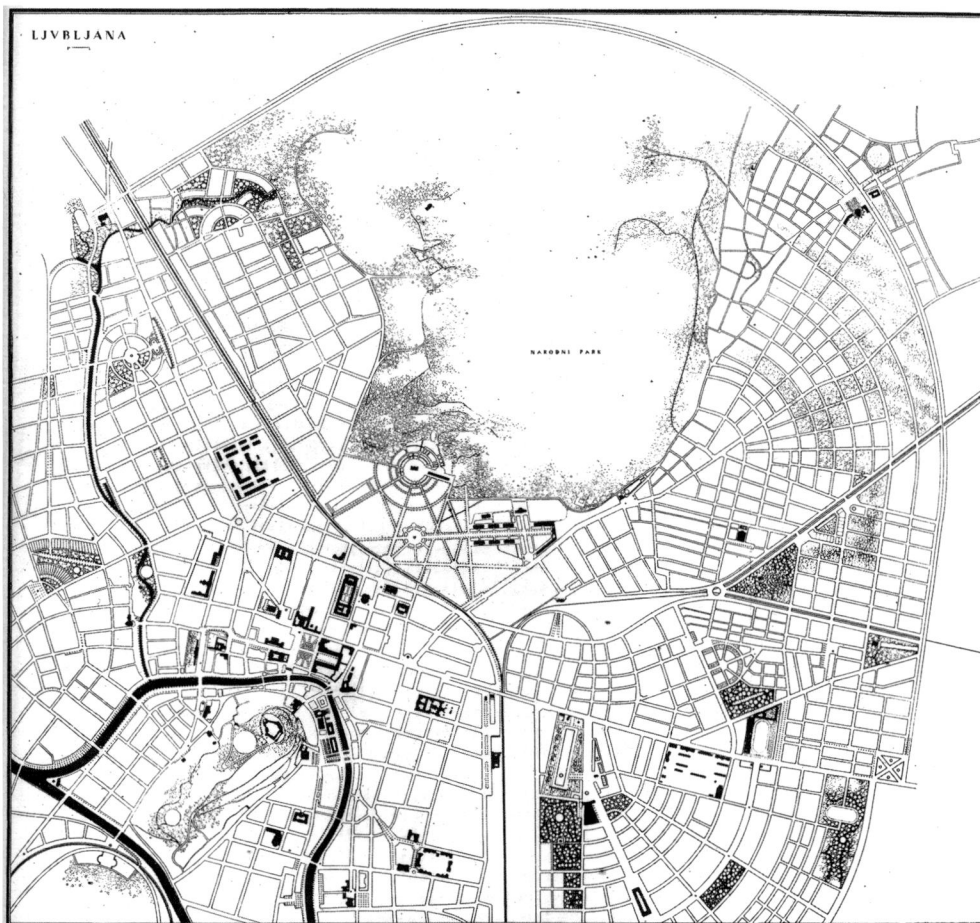

LJVBLJANA

NARODNI PARK

margins of surveys of the field. But viewed through the lens of the urban design principles explored in chapter 2, these three projects are valuable and instructive exemplars of plural urbanism. Ranging from the small-scale to the ambitious, each of them possesses a rigorous attention to design detail as well as a sophisticated understanding of the relationship between individual elements and the larger city in which they are located. Each project is also transformative at multiple scales; as an individual work of art, as a definer of public space or natural features, as a provider of valuable social or economic goods, and as an element of a larger-scale approach to urban design that embraces the city's multiple spaces, actors, or properties rather than ignoring or attempting to suppress them. This chapter has explored only these three works, but there are many more such pluralist projects to uncover, and even more projects to create.

Plural urbanism is not a new concept. Although the dominant thread of urban design thought during the twentieth century favored unitary urbanism, whether modernist or neotraditionalist, some designers have thought and acted otherwise. The era of late modernism, from about 1960 onward, was a particularly fertile time for such thought, as orthodox principles of design diversified and expanded in many different directions before dissolving in the 1970s, in concert with modernism itself. The next chapter explores the work, writings, and principles of three nascent, though undeclared plural urbanists—David Crane, Edmund Bacon, and Kevin Lynch—whose ideas and work were well known in their time and still partly known today. We will reinterpret and reexamine them within the context of the plural urbanists qualities and projects explored thus far. Each of these designers offers valuable lessons for the application of plural urban design principles in the contemporary city.

Three Plural Urbanists

David Crane: The City of a Thousand Designers

In 2006 the Graduate School of Design at Harvard University commemorated the fiftieth anniversary of the school's first urban design conference.[1] The commemoration engaged several eminent practitioners of urban design, some of whom had decades of experience in the field, including Denise Scott Brown, whose work *Learning from Las Vegas* we discussed in chapter 2. Looking back, she reflected upon her own fifty years in urban design, drawing both conclusions and directions forward. Her essay, "Urban Design at Fifty," could easily be read as nostalgic, an elegy for what Scott Brown perceived as a lost art and, to some extent, her lost career as an urban designer. But her essay was also quietly provocative, for it highlighted the work of an urbanist, David A. Crane, whom Scott Brown called "among the foremost thinkers and philosophers on urban design of the twentieth century."[2]

David Crane wrote no books on urban design, and he does not appear to have ever built much of lasting importance at the urban scale. His firm's archives at the University of Pennsylvania contain many ambitious but unbuilt urban projects, and at first glance the work appears mostly conventional. Much of it reflects American architecture and planning practice of the 1970s and 1980s, shifting from publicly financed projects to campus planning, office and retail development. Crane's career path was similar to that of Scott Brown, and she doubtless sympathized with Crane's need to take on institutional work as public funding dried up in the 1970s. While Crane remained closer to

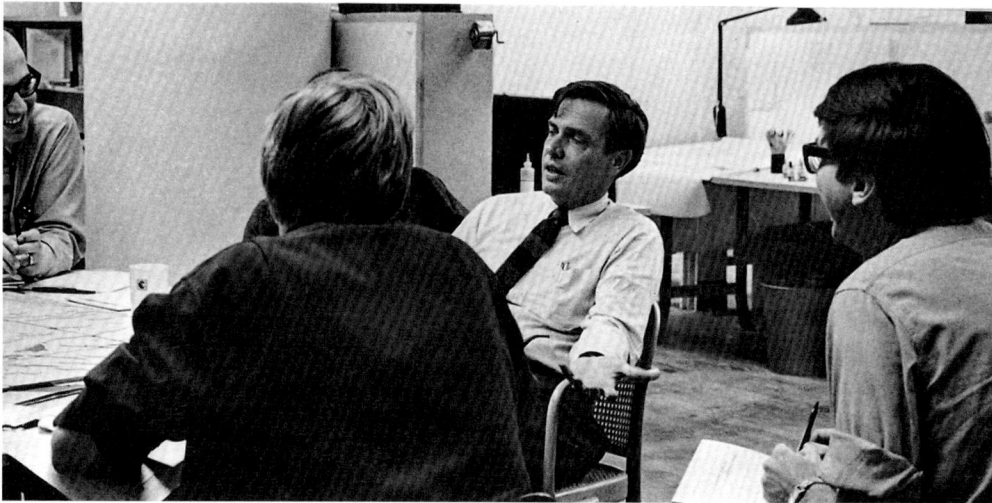

4.1 David Crane and office staff around 1970. After a brief period as a full-time academic, Crane balanced teaching, academic administration, and practice for the remainder of his career. Crane died in 2005.

academia than Scott Brown, he appears to have always centered himself in practice, an easier balance perhaps in an era when academic positions could be had by simply "asking if I could teach," as Scott Brown said.[3] Crane remained linked to both academia and practice throughout his life, with posts at the University of Pennsylvania in the 1960s, Rice University in the 1970s, and the University of Tampa in the 1980s, while his firm continued during the same period.[4] But unlike Scott Brown, Crane never published much. For a "foremost thinker on urban design," he is strangely invisible as an intellectual. He wrote four articles in all, between 1960 and 1964 when he was on the University of Pennsylvania faculty, a position he held on and off until the late 1960s. This assortment of articles and the mostly unbuilt urban design projects he carried out in the years after constitute most of Crane's intellectual urban design corpus: a seemingly weak legacy. But the content of these articles rewards further investigation, and what they tell us places Scott Brown's high praise on firmer ground. Crane's modest articles comprise an abbreviated and unfinished manifesto for plural urbanism, and one can only regret that Crane never developed his ideas further, a regret that Scott Brown seems to share.

One would hardly expect David Crane's mere four essays, however well-conceived, to define a wholly new understanding of urbanism. But Crane's sparse written record is packed with revelatory understandings of both the city as a physical entity and of the act of urban design as a physical art. In his essays, Crane uses three terms—the *city of a thousand designers*, the *dynamic city*, and the *capital web*—to refer to his particular conceptions of urbanism. The first two terms are analytical descriptors of the city as it is, and therefore an acknowledgment of forces that urban design must harness and incorporate to succeed, while the third is a neologism that provides Crane's best guess as to how his new approach to urbanism might be accomplished—an approach that Crane himself would attempt to practice in his city-building efforts.

While Crane's terms are not entirely novel, nor his ideas fully new—we will see that Kevin Lynch was developing similar notions nearly in parallel—Crane's conceptions signal powerful differences between his understanding of urban design and those of Josep Lluís Sert (whose near-contemporary formulation became a formal academic program at Harvard). And while Crane's terms do not fully encapsulate plural urbanism as we will come to understand it, it is clear that Crane grasped many, if not most, of the essentials that differentiated the act of designing a *city* from that of designing a *site*, however large that site. We can thus see Crane as a nascent theorist of plural urbanism, a practitioner whose theories were never fully placed into practice, in part for reasons that were little fault of Crane's own.

In chapter 2, we developed an understanding of the city as a single space filled with a multiplicity of actors, each beholden to his or her own particular, personal needs and answering to those needs or to those to whom he or she is responsible. This is one concept of a plural society, and Crane recognized the design of cities as being subject to the whims and wills of this diverse polity. What he called "the city of a thousand designers" was a place in which pluralism represented—just as it does in the political sense of democracy—a "complexity, multiplicity, and power."[5] One of the urban designer's principal tasks, according to Crane, was to harness this fractious energy to the task of generating an aesthetic whole, a "structure of esthetic and utilitarian continuity," to improve upon the "uncoordinated cacophony"[6] that currently comprised the modern metropolis, and that seemed to make the very act of urban design a quixotic, unsatisfying exercise.

Crane was well aware of the emerging appreciation of the vernacular among modernist architects, including Peter and Alison Smithson. Scott Brown would later found her Las Vegas studio at Yale on a similar appreciation. But there is no indication that Crane was enamored of the vernacular: he rather pejoratively refers to Indian cities, for example, as "mud and dung hovels,"[7] though of course he sought to improve such conditions. And unlike architect Christopher Alexander, who would in

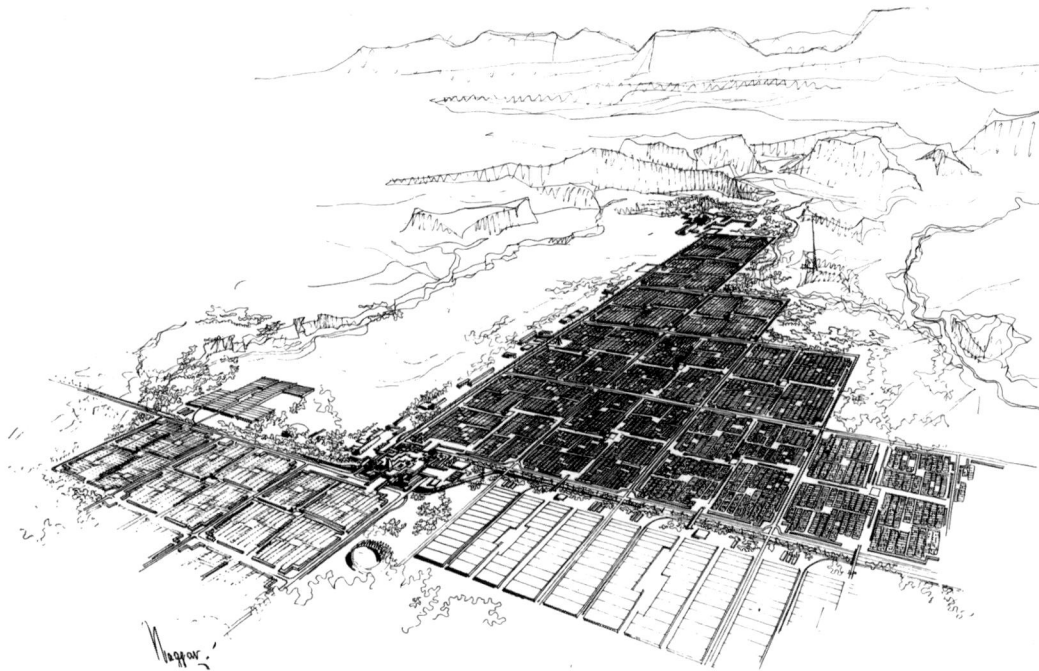

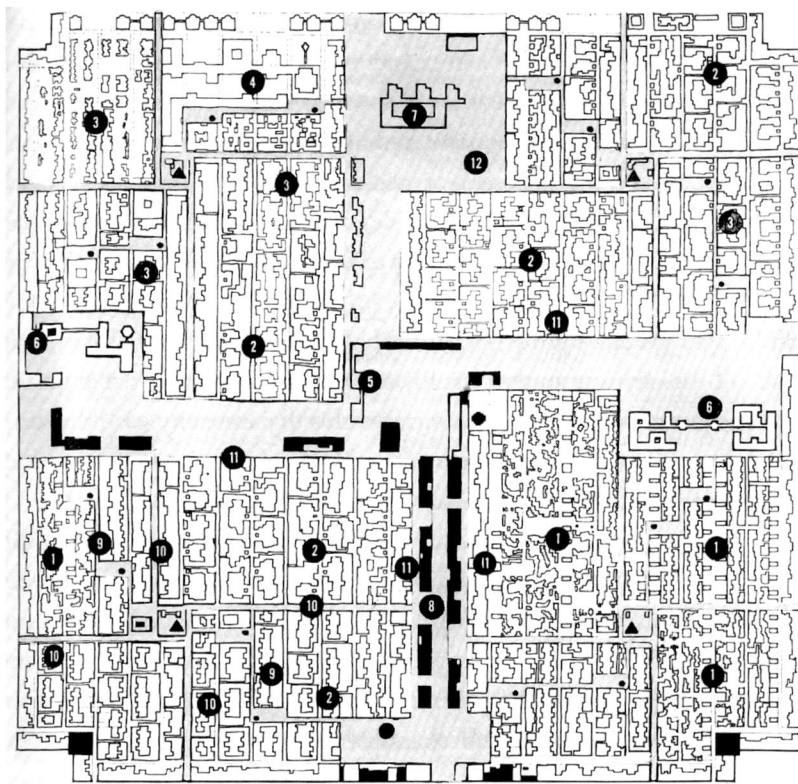

A typical residential sector showing control through "capital design"—Circa. 1970. **1** *planned squatter area* **2** *aided self-help housing* **3** *private housing* **4** *public and experimental housing* **5** *health center-library* **6** *elementary school* **7** *middle school* **8** *shops and small industries* **9** *pedestrian-cycle distributor* **10** *vehicular distributor (sub-sector)* **11** *vehicular distributor (sector)* **12** *floating land reserve (varies different sector locations)*

land uses or an architect's organization of monumental structures in appropriately monumental locations—though those considerations, too, were part of New City's design, since its program dictated that it was to be both an industrial center and a government capital. Instead it was even more important to accommodate "time as a fourth dimension of design," to permit whatever types of future change might occur, including "replacement," "entirely new purposes," "the unknown," and the choosing of alternatives.[18] Thus New City provided space for everything from (potentially) equally monumental structures as Le Corbusier's capitol complex, all the way to land planned, but otherwise left open and available, for squatters. Rather than projecting a purely monumental city that would inevitably be polluted by reality, Crane argued that the designer's eyes should be open throughout the design process to social realities like India's endemic poverty and to the physical consequences of those realities.

Social contact between income groups and gradual improvement of social conditions, Crane believed, could be accomplished by the urban designer organizing the city as a series of "successive layers and scales of parts where change and stability seduce and sweeten each other."[19] Thus New City's planned squatter areas were adjacent to major roads and employment centers, in order to make squatting there more desirable and logical than in the city's major public parks.[20] Adjacent to these districts were those of "more fortunate people," presumably the middle or lower middle class, whom the squatters could aspire to be. This vision was a tad patronizing, dictating that the poor look up to and learn from their economic betters. But Crane's design for what we would today call mixed-income districts, as well as his hope that the poor could incrementally improve their dwellings over time, mirrors contemporary best practice and accurately reflects what has actually happened over time in most squatter settlements.[21]

Crane required comparatively radical formal measures to permit the dynamism and unpredictability that he saw as a formative element of urban design. New City thus featured a "special physical commitment" of "*free edge*[s]" adjacent to significant elements of the city plan—for instance the city's two industrial belts, and New City's public belt of institutions.[22] This openness was intended to permit inevitable expansion, but also unforeseen shifts, for example, if the city's industrial sector were to expand and its institutional sector decline. Even New City's civic spaces, unlike the frozen monumentality of Chandigarh's actual capitol, left "room for the city fathers to embellish [them] as time went along."[23]

◄ **4.2 and 4.3** New City Chandigarh, a Crane studio conducted at the University of Pennsylvania in the spring of 1959, applied Crane's ideas about infrastructure and public buildings providing an armature around which the rest of the city's plural actors could build both formally and informally.

Like any urban design scheme, Crane's scheme for New City can be critiqued in hindsight. Certainly Crane accorded far too much capacity to the institutional structures that he felt would shape the city's development over time. "Time-space scheduling of land units to be developed" and "floating land reserves" that provided additional space were processes unlikely to be adopted, never mind implemented, by the dysfunctional Indian bureaucracy of midcentury. Even New City's "free edges" were in reality just as likely to be encroached upon by squatters as they were to provide expansion space for industry thirty years down the line. Crane's New City plan paradoxically assumed the uncontrolled rural-urban migration that was and remains typical of India as well as a governance structure able to implement and administer an urban design framework over a series of decades. Postindependence India saw the migration, but for the most part it lacked effective governance of settlement.

Today Crane's New City scheme, apart from its representational qualities and somewhat dated economic assumptions, merits interest both for its declared interest in incorporating the constructions of the city's plural actors, particularly its underprivileged population, and for its acknowledgment of urban design's inability to completely predict the built results of those actors. Crane admitted that drawings depicting the "tropical tree" of the city would be insufficient to represent its perpetual growth, because such "drawing fails to express the fourth dimension of time, like all other design communications to date." And in its description of time Crane's language conveyed a sense of city-building quite different from static, conventional urban plans. His city possessed instead a "generality and flexibility of parts, strong and permanent locational rhythms, less permanent superimpositions, and a dynamic balance of mass."[24] Here Crane might be describing a symphony, not a city—and perhaps the core elements of both are in a sense the same: a long-term process in which time's passage and the existence of sound or mass are the only constant, with a changing cast of participants and an evolving, path-dependent progression toward a later event. Or perhaps New City is less a symphony than a musical improvisation, where the future leads somewhere, but nowhere for certain. Whatever the outcome, Crane's idea was certainly no static architectural portrait. His thousand designers' dynamic city was an exciting, though thinly developed, exploration of pluralist urbanism.

Chandigarh was an appropriate urban symbol of an era in which governments—particularly those of the European welfare state and the Communist bloc—were the initiators and funders of much urbanism. Especially in the postwar era, the rise of expanded governmental power, rapid population growth, technological shifts, and aggressive ideologies all placed the state in a position of substantial power to shape cities. Crane's writings occurred within this penumbra of state-financed urbanism and much of his early practice would as well. It is of little surprise that Crane's theory of urban design implementation, which he termed the "capital web," would rely heavily on the state as that principal actor. He explored the potential of this web in two post–New City essays that he completed in 1960 and 1964.

Crane understood the city as pluralist and dynamic, and accordingly the act of urban design would never be a simple one: "composing a painting on a flowing river" was his summary of the urban designer's task.[25] How then was the city to be shaped, particularly if its many actors were resistant or immune to coercion, if zoning was overly restrictive, and if time's passage was sure to erode any singular design vision? Crane felt that the answer lay in the city's visible infrastructure, in those "streets, public buildings, and open spaces"[26] where the state was responsible for both maintenance and improvement. This was a logical step to take, for American urban design had long been dependent on infrastructure construction.[27]

What then was new about Crane's idea of a capital web of roads, open spaces, and public buildings shaping new or remade city areas? His was not a painterly depiction of an entire area unified under a single aesthetic banner like Jules Guerin's images of Chicago or Le Corbusier's City for Three Million. The capital web was as noteworthy for what it did *not* depict as for what it did. Crane's images of a second New City studio project, for the Four Corners area in the southwest United States, feature a near-total absence of buildings in favor of a detailed skeletal roadway and transit structure. Crane's dynamic city principle stated that the city's private fabric would shift and change, and that closely designing this fabric was therefore not particularly feasible or particularly important. Instead, the private structure of the city would develop and evolve according to large-scale infrastructure generated by the state for state purposes on state land. This infrastructural idea is pragmatic, for even the most conservative American politician would agree today that government intervention in infrastructure is legitimate, and that this intervention can and should stimulate privately financed development.

Le Corbusier's urban vision derived from an architectural understanding that spiraled outward in scale to encompass urbanism with the same degree of attention as that accorded to the individual building. His design for urban projects such as Chandigarh, Saint-Dié, and Algiers incorporated urban-scale elements, but always through architecture's lens. For him, architectural projects were essential to establishing larger design moves at an urban scale: Le Corbusier's buildings at the center of Saint-Dié

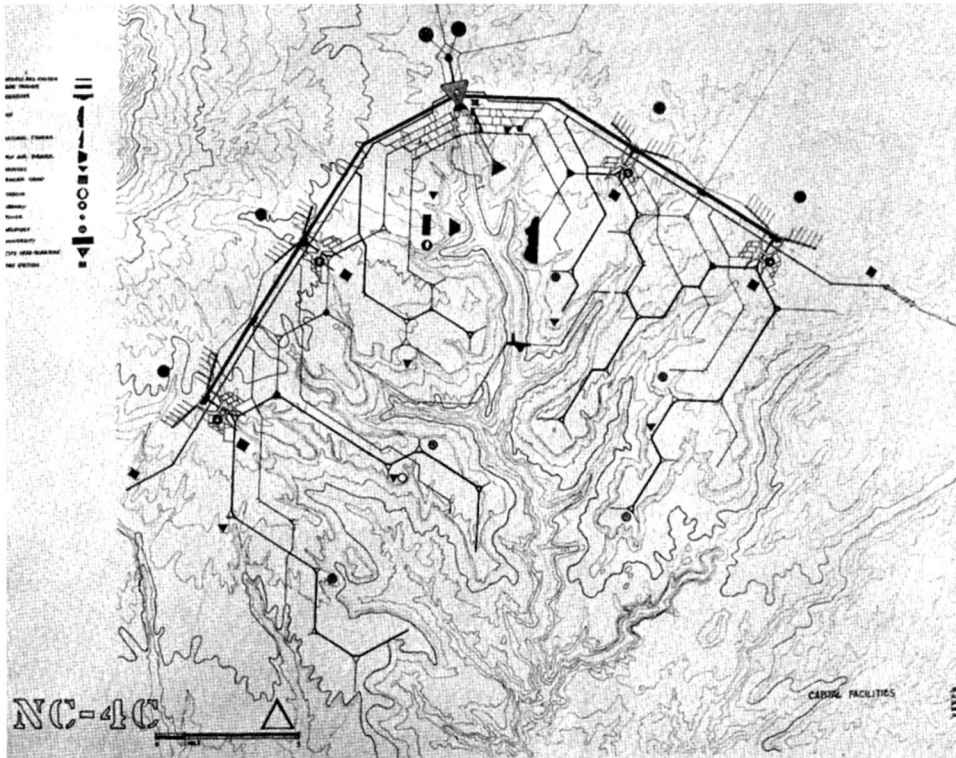

4.4 In another Crane studio at the University of Pennsylvania, sited in the Four Corners area in the American Southwest, one student detailed a hexagonal formal structure with gateway buildings or complexes at multiple scales. At least three or four scales can be seen in this drawing. Additional construction was left unspecified.

were not stand-ins for works to be built by another but Le Corbusier-designed building proposals; and the city itself was an extension, a scaling-up, of those projects. Sert may also have slightly shifted the language and scalar concern of his urbanism, but he did not shift its architecturally centered origin. In contrast, Crane's urban design work showed no such concern. Buildings might be designed in detail or not; the city's design did not depend on the architectural design of individual major buildings. Public projects in New City Four Corners were mere glyphs signifying location, program, and prominence. Anchored to the roadway system, they provided an impetus for architectural resolutions to an infrastructure scheme, but Crane's urban design was primarily a designed framework, a capital web, that would in turn eventually shape both architectural monuments and the city of the thousand designers.

Conventional land use maps and zoning, never mind the "thousand obscure" provisions of detailed design regulations, are also notably absent from Crane's 1960 depictions of the capital web. Only capital projects, Crane thought, could provide sufficient "context for private creativity":[28] a strategic location for a capital element was far more meaningful than a zoning provision that might ultimately be only occasionally and episodically enforced, particularly in a developing country. Crane called his spatial allocation of capital projects a "symbolic order,"[29] generating a clear rhythm and thereby understanding of city form in the city-dwellers' mind. As an example, Crane noted that in New City Four Corners a "strong symbolic order in the location of parking garages" would permit the city-user to easily find them, "even though their designers give them the shapes of neoclassic temples."[30] This concept of symbolic order was likely influenced by Kevin Lynch's 1960 published work on city image, which proposed that precisely such symbolic order already existed in the mind of city-dwellers.

Crane's capital web concept is idiosyncratic and demanding. Idiosyncratically, it denies the conventional tools of the architect-urbanist, particularly monumental buildings, as well as those of the planner, particularly zoning. Yet the capital web also paradoxically requires an architect's spatial and compositional expertise together with a planner's tolerance for uncertainty and public input. Additionally, Crane's concept not only requires substantial knowledge of a city's engineering components, but demands that these elements be treated aesthetically, not just technically. In short, the capital web requires the determination of a master builder to build, but with enough modesty to know that the future is not totally knowable. The capital web is design at the urban scale, but it is not an architectural design, nor is it a planner's rationally determined balance of land uses derived according to a formula. The capital web is not a large-scale architectural diagram; nor is it a drab, technical projection of infrastructure. It is a unique work of art that is both eternal and incomplete, a novel conception and lesson for urban design that we will explore further in this book's final chapter.

Demanding yet inspiring, denying yet encouraging, Crane's concept of urban design seems intended for a professional who did not yet fully exist, an architect perhaps who had surrendered hope of designing buildings, who had maintained the breadth of vision and commitment to innovation of modernism, and yet who was prepared to engage enthusiastically with the clamor of the thousand designers. This ideal of the urban designer was conceptually leagues ahead of Sert's rather simplistic notion of the urban designer as an ambitious, highly powerful architect. And it is small wonder that nascent urbanists such as Denise Scott Brown or Tunney Lee (later head of planning at MIT)—both committed to creative design *and* democratic participation—found Crane's vision so exciting.[31]

A capital web, defining an ideal spatial disposition and sequence of public facilities within an infrastructural system, is more appropriate for new settlements than for existing ones. Existing cities such as Plečnik's Ljubljana are so constrained by previous settlement and construction decisions to make imposition of abstract design ideals difficult or impossible. Even Plečnik, with his great power as effective city architect, had little success with conventional master plans. Like an actual new settlement, Crane's capital web is a unitary concept that evolves over time, but one that does not dictate architectural details, and that is not dependent on a final form to reach completion.

How was Crane to put his ideas into practice? America's federal government was not (yet) building all-new cities in the early 1960s—it was rebuilding existing ones, particularly older, built-up northeastern cities such as New York and New Haven, Connecticut. These and other similar cities would not appear to be particularly promising settings for a capital web. In 1961, however, Crane was offered the opportunity to put his ideas into action on just such a city. It was in that year that he became the Planning Administrator for the Boston Redevelopment Authority (BRA).[32]

As Kevin Lynch had already shown,[33] Boston was a paradigmatically confusing city, constructed on a series of drumlins and mudflats, which were gradually and opportunistically filled by industry and railroads. With few connecting roads, navigation between these islands of settlement is a challenge, and residents of one neighborhood may often not visit another for years simply because existing street systems make such travel inconvenient. To make matters worse for the urban designer, the region's feisty heritage of independent towns has left central Boston riddled with independent municipalities uninterested in being annexed (e.g., Cambridge and Brookline). Boston's isolated neighborhoods and village-scaled neighbors create warm senses of community, but the city as a whole is less accommodating to large-scale design than even the average American settlement. Crane did his best in this comparatively unfavorable setting, directing neighborhood plans for blighted areas with requisite new facilities such as schools, reconstructed housing, wider roadways, and highways.

One neighborhood in particular, Washington Park in the Roxbury area of Boston, served as a test bed for Crane's ideas, receiving a swath of new public facilities along a new boulevard, now named after Martin Luther King, Jr. Like many such urban renewal areas across the United States, the BRA's intention was generous, the dollar

4.5   In Boston's early 1960s master plan, Crane was able to site his "capital web" concepts within the framework of an existing city that was actively reconstructing itself. But Boston's confusing development pattern presented difficulties to the clear implementation of Crane's ideas.

4.6 One of Crane's most completely constructed neighborhoods was in the Washington Park area of Boston's Roxbury neighborhood. Unfortunately, the disparate structures do not cohere either spatially or architecturally, and the resulting ensemble is only weakly recognizable as urban design.

amounts expended substantial, and the construction extensive. But the urban design impacts were at best mediocre and at worst disastrous. With little room to maneuver for new building, Washington Park was less a capital web than it was a piecemeal replacement of a typical Bostonian urban fabric with modernist facilities of varying architectural quality and little aesthetic unity. The Washington Park capital web subtracted from rather than added to its historic neighborhood, and in a depressed area of the city it spurred little subsequent development activity. One might blame bureaucratic interference, but little of Crane's genius and none of his concept is visible today; the urban design elements are mediocre, strongly antiurban in quality, and the whole is a poor neighborhood center for Washington Park's mostly low-income inhabitants. The project does Crane little credit, and it is little surprise that analogous efforts elsewhere in Boston led to widespread rejection of urban renewal in the city soon after Crane left the BRA in 1965.

The comparative failure of Crane's attempt to implement a version of his capital web ideas in Boston could easily be chalked off to recalcitrant bureaucracy, but this would be unfair. Twin Parks, conceived and implemented just a few years later in the at least equally complex setting of New York City, was a notable success, and it offered some lessons for Crane. Twin Parks achieved two aims that eluded Crane at Washington Park: it was programmatically homogeneous, comprised of moderate- and low-income housing, and Twin Parks was also formally consistent, with generally mid- to high-rise buildings built primarily of brown brick. Twin Parks also displays notably more architectural quality than any of the Washington Park projects. This latter aspect of quality would be particularly successful in the work of Edmund Bacon, the plural urbanist that we will examine next.

Crane would test his capital web approach again in the early 1970s in his firm's schematic design for the proposed new town of Lysander, New York, not far from Syracuse. Headed by Ed Logue (Crane's former superior at the BRA), the New York State Urban Development Corporation (UDC) commissioned the project. The UDC formulated its new-town plans under a federal program that promised to subsidize much of the costs of the enterprise.[34] Today one would not imagine Syracuse to be in much need of expansion; the city is losing population, and upstate New York as a whole is economically unhealthy. But in the 1960s the region's industrial infrastructure was robust, and a garden city adjacent to the newly constructed New York State Thruway must have seemed consistent with a vision of a growing constellation of prosperous manufacturing hubs.

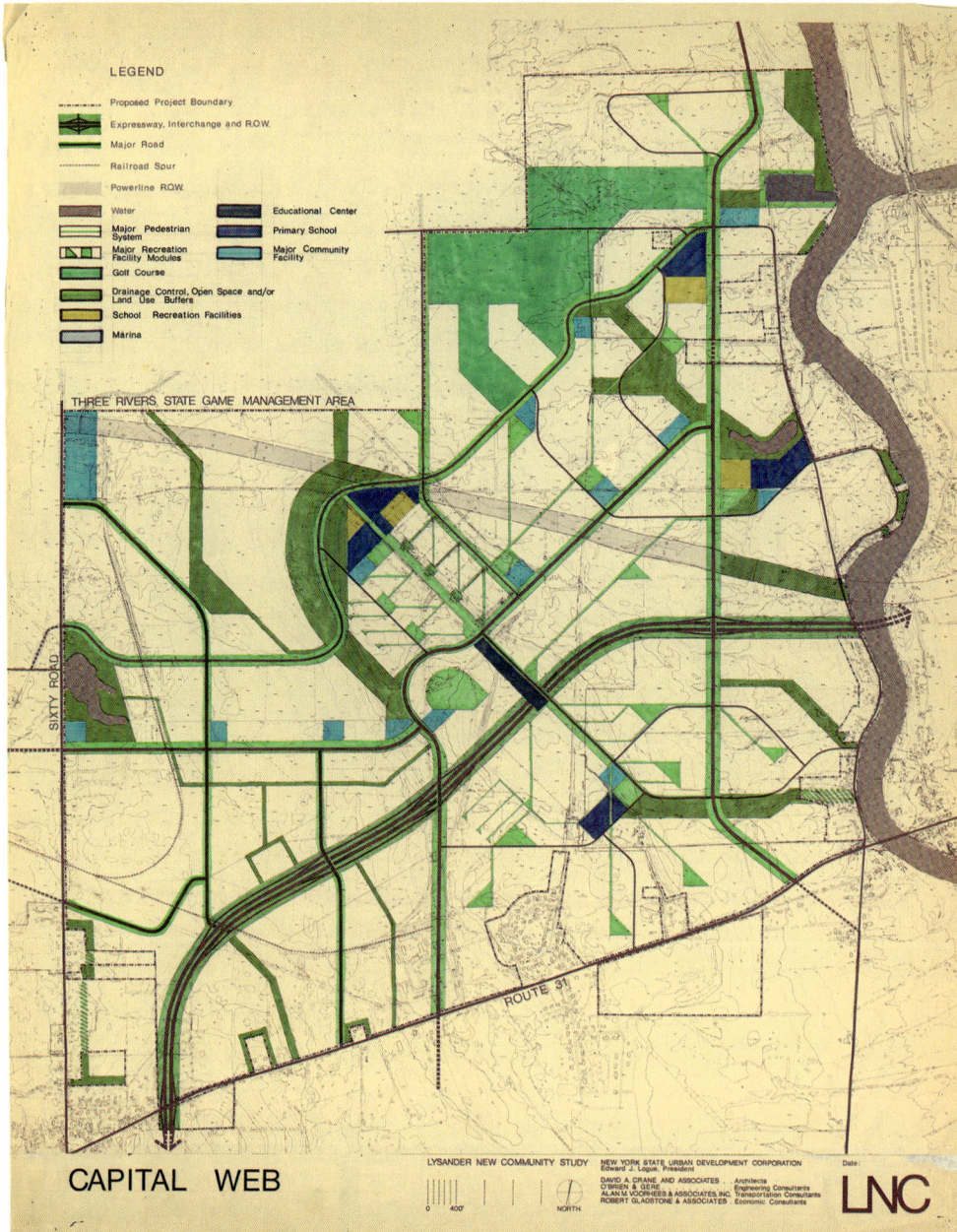

LEGEND

Proposed Project Boundary

Expressway, Interchange and R.O.W.

Major Road

Railroad Spur

Powerline R.O.W.

Water

Major Pedestrian System

Major Recreation Facility Modules

Golf Course

Drainage Control, Open Space and/or Land Use Buffers

School Recreation Facilities

Marina

Educational Center

Primary School

Major Community Facility

THREE RIVERS STATE GAME MANAGEMENT AREA

SIXTY ROAD

ROUTE 31

CAPITAL WEB

LYSANDER NEW COMMUNITY STUDY

NEW YORK STATE URBAN DEVELOPMENT CORPORATION
Edward J. Logue, President

DAVID A. CRANE AND ASSOCIATES . . . Architects
O'BRIEN & GERE . . . . Engineering Consultants
ALAN M. VOORHEES & ASSOCIATES, INC. . Transportation Consultants
ROBERT GLADSTONE & ASSOCIATES . Economic Consultants

Date:

0   400'

NORTH

LNC

4.7 The capital web was a stronger idea when applied to new settlements. Crane's new town
of Lysander in upstate New York would have been a striking project had it been constructed.
Unfortunately, the fiscal slowdown of the early 1970s cancelled Lysander.

Crane poured his heart into the "Lysander New Community"; the firm's archived drawings of street, path, and open space networks are exquisite, particularly those diagramming what he labeled the new town's "capital web."[35] Had it been built, Crane's new town would have been a worthy parallel to those being constructed in the United Kingdom at that time. Lysander's road, path, and open space networks were woven into clusters of housing, retail, and manufacturing, all built at relatively low densities. The formal vision is not particularly novel; other new towns such as Columbia, Maryland, and The Woodlands, Texas, were designed along similar lines. But the capital web concept makes sense at Lysander. One can easily imagine the city's capital web growing outward and evolving over time, as its new roads and path networks extended into the agricultural landscape and as its civic facilities expanded to accommodate growing residential populations. One can see Crane's excitement as he applied his New City concepts from his time at Penn to a greenfield site poised to make the capital web real.

Unfortunately, it was not to be. As I have detailed elsewhere,[36] the mid-1970s were not propitious ones for American urbanism. Both economics and ideology conspired against realizing Lysander: the oil crisis of 1973 precipitated a real estate crash, dampening demand for development in new towns, and the parallel divestment of the federal government from urban renewal left developers of places such as Lysander without markets and without financial backers. Few of Crane's ideas were implemented; the new town today is a collection of ordinary subdivisions adjacent to an industrial park, and only a strangely wide, straight roadway ("Willet Parkway") cutting through the subdivisions hints at the vanished new-town intentions for the place.

The capital web is not universally applicable to the contemporary city. Built-up areas will resist imposition of a clearly perceptible infrastructural framework in the same way that Twin Parks' "gateways" and "axes" are only partially perceptible. As the failed Washington Park project shows, a capital web in an existing network may not be perceptible at all, nor will the capital web always spur additional development in disinvested, depressed areas of the city. But the capital web is a very sound concept for shaping the form of unfinished large-scale areas in a way that accommodates architectural diversity, permits diverse patterns of private development, and evades any pretense or assumption of finality. Appropriate settings for the capital web are widespread, particularly in the developing world where additional settlement, whether formal or informal, is often inevitable and where simply leaving settlement to its own devices results in visual and functional disorder, as in typical informal settlements. The capital web establishes order, but also provides for an almost infinite variety of aesthetic visions

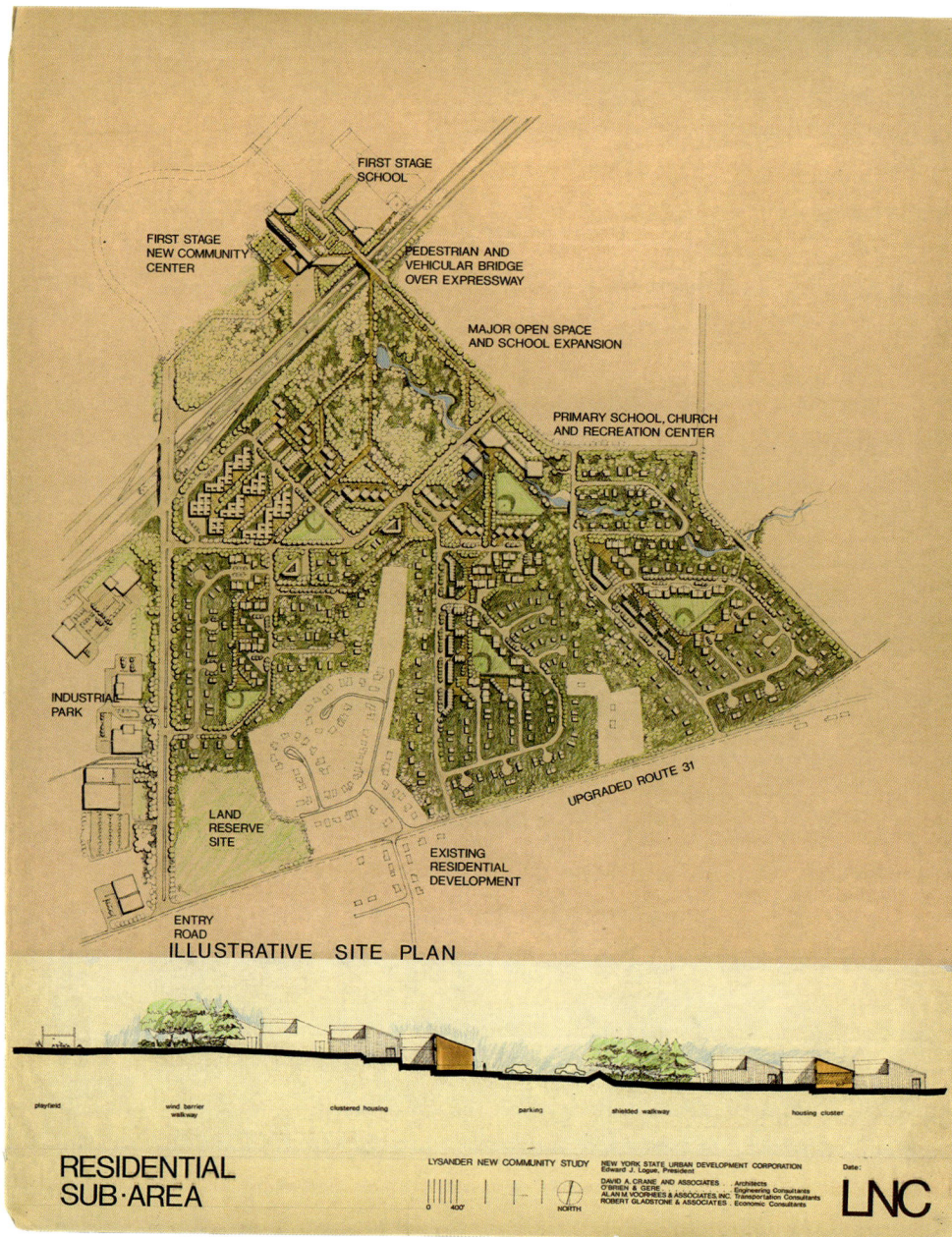

FIRST STAGE
SCHOOL

FIRST STAGE
NEW COMMUNITY
CENTER

PEDESTRIAN AND
VEHICULAR BRIDGE
OVER EXPRESSWAY

MAJOR OPEN SPACE
AND SCHOOL EXPANSION

PRIMARY SCHOOL, CHURCH
AND RECREATION CENTER

INDUSTRIAL
PARK

LAND
RESERVE
SITE

UPGRADED ROUTE 31

EXISTING
RESIDENTIAL
DEVELOPMENT

ENTRY
ROAD

ILLUSTRATIVE SITE PLAN

playfield   wind barrier   clustered housing   parking   shielded walkway   housing cluster
                   walkway

RESIDENTIAL
SUB·AREA

LYSANDER NEW COMMUNITY STUDY

NEW YORK STATE URBAN DEVELOPMENT CORPORATION
Edward J. Logue, President

DAVID A. CRANE AND ASSOCIATES . Architects
O'BRIEN & GERE . Engineering Consultants
ALAN M. VOORHEES & ASSOCIATES, INC. Transportation Consultants
ROBERT GLADSTONE & ASSOCIATES . Economic Consultants

Date:

0   400'   NORTH

LNC

▲ **4.8** In this site plan of Lysander, Crane demonstrated one potential set of architectural outcomes that could stem from the construction of the capital web shown in figure 4.6. Lysander is a convincing demonstration of Crane's urban design concepts.

▶ **4.9 and 4.10** Another compelling Crane project was Washington, DC's Fort Lincoln new town. Fort Lincoln and Lysander demonstrate that the capital web idea could generate a range of formal concepts. Neither project was constructed.

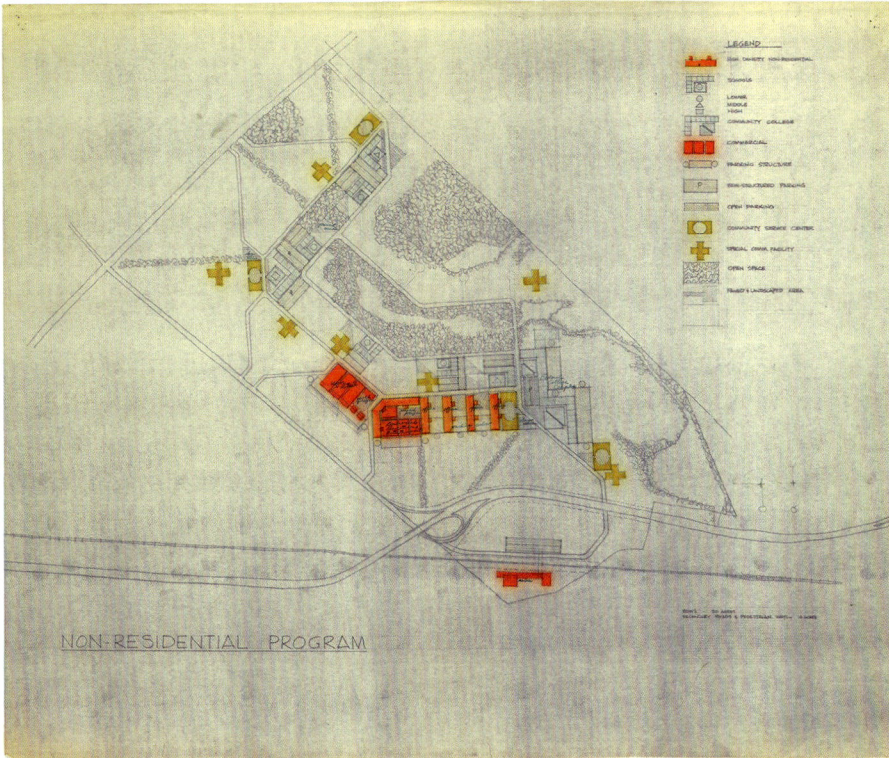

NON-RESIDENTIAL PROGRAM

LEGEND

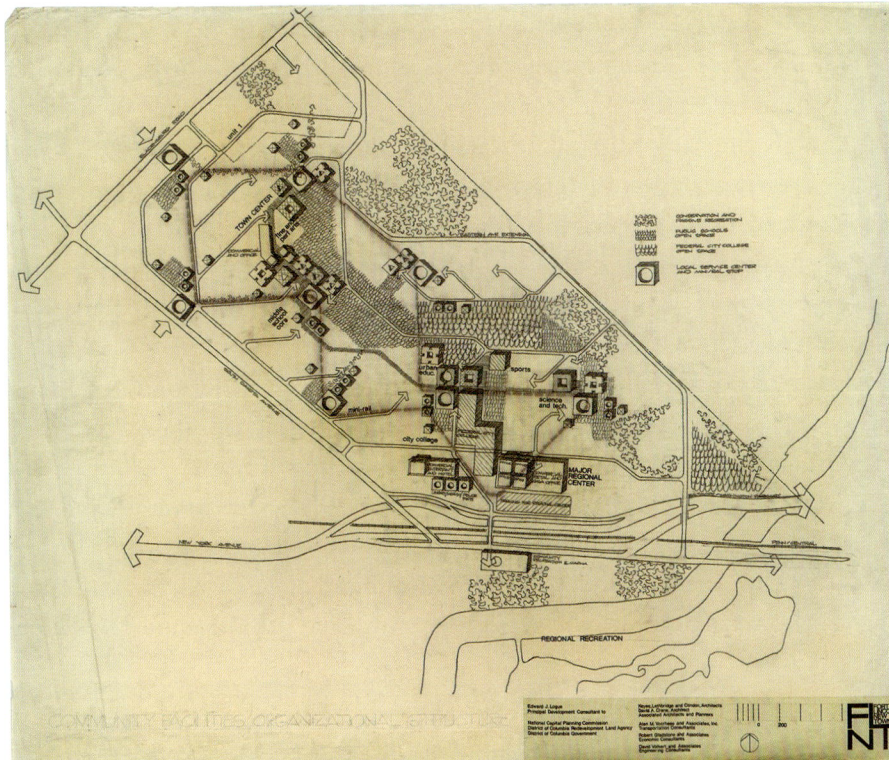

COMMUNITY FACILITIES / ORGANIZATIONAL STRUCTURE

to be imposed at scales larger than that of the individual project site. By shaping what is admittedly a unitary concept—an infrastructural system—the capital web allows for all five of plural urbanism's dimensions—scale, time, property, agency, and form—to flourish amid its branches.

Though his ideas have not gone unrecognized,[37] David Crane is an underestimated figure in urban design thought. Divided, like most urban designers of the time, between education and practice, he ultimately had only a momentary impact on teaching, a parsimonious published record as a researcher, and a legacy of constructed projects that reflect the vicissitudes of their time more than they do Crane's creativity. But his unfulfilled legacy in no way diminishes the promise of the capital web as a direction for realizing plural urbanism in today's world. Crane firmly grasped the city's essential pluralist character in its "thousand designers," and in the time span required for meaningful change. Integrating these realities into an urban design philosophy was no small accomplishment, particularly at the height of influence of modernism's unitary approach to urban design. Our understanding of Crane's relationship to plural urbanism allows us to reassess his intellectual legacy, one that is well worth exploring and expanding in tandem with the expanding cities in which he took such interest.

Edmund Bacon: The Movement System

In 2003 Philadelphia's retired master planner, Edmund Bacon, provided a cameo appearance in the documentary film *My Architect*. Nathaniel Kahn, third child of long-deceased architect Louis Kahn, had embarked on a poignant quest to recapture his father's memory, and the documentary featured many of Kahn's past associates' laudatory recollections of their past friend and colleague. The architect's personal life, as depicted in the film, was certainly flawed, but memories of the master's commitment to architecture and the poetry of his built work spurred more than one interviewee to tears.

Bacon reacted somewhat differently. Nathaniel Kahn interviewed Bacon in downtown Philadelphia's City Hall Plaza to reflect on his father's contributions to urbanism. Kahn had been a consultant to the Philadelphia City Planning Commission in the 1950s, and his drawings of traffic flows and sketches for monumental parking garages set like city gates against the new city walls of interstate highways are powerful and canonical visions. In Brownlee and DeLong's 1991 exhibition and catalog of Kahn's work,[38] his traffic studies are the *only* work shown prior to the architect's well-known late-1950s buildings, such as the Richards Lab and the Yale Art Gallery. But Kahn's Philadelphia garage towers were never built, and Bacon made that perfectly clear to Nathaniel Kahn. "By the way," he said, "there's not a single shred of any way in which Lou influenced downtown Philadelphia." Urged on by Kahn, Bacon added, "It would have been an incredible tragedy if they had built one single thing that Lou had proposed … [his ideas] were all brutal, totally impractical, totally insensitive … [the ideas showed] absolutely pure ignorance on Lou's part."[39]

Bacon's unfair and somewhat irrational denigration of Louis Kahn accurately reflects the former's hierarchical approach: urban designers, particularly Bacon himself, were clients, and architects merely customers. Bacon was also an architect, but he was one who was above others, a bureaucrat who could make an architect's career by appointing him to design in Center City (downtown Philadelphia). And appoint them Bacon did. In his twenty-plus years as Philadelphia's chief planner, he pursued an approach to urban design that combined aspects of Jonathan Barnett's work at Twin Parks and Jože Plečnik's in Ljubljana, using the machinery of American urban renewal politics to rebuild different areas of Center City with programmatically diverse ensembles of urban design created by talented architects, ensembles that embody all five of plural urbanism's dimensions.

This legacy of built work, combined with Bacon's own theoretical principles of urban design that we will examine here, make him a plural urbanist par excellence. Like David Crane, Bacon was able to define a third way between the large-scale architectural projects of the Josep Lluís Sert school and the regulatory tedium of the typical master plan. And like Crane, Bacon understood the city as an entity that existed in both space and time, an entity that could never be designed by a single individual or assume a single form for eternity. In order to accommodate these urban realities, Bacon developed a design concept that he called a *movement system*. But Bacon also transcended Crane, who was never able to make his permanent mark on any of the cities in which he worked.

Bacon's career has come to be seen—not inaccurately—from two perspectives. As executive director of Philadelphia's City Planning Commission from 1949 to 1970 Bacon carefully nurtured an image of a powerful bureaucrat, which accorded him the power of public opinion in addition to his somewhat limited statutory power. Public visibility even landed Bacon on the cover of *Time* in 1964 as the chief architect of downtown Philadelphia's rebirth. But the nationwide public image of the master planner soured in the late 1960s. Social discontent with strongman city rebuilding made highly visible planning directors soft targets for vulnerable mayors and changing electorates, and so Bacon stepped down in 1970 at age sixty, never to regain his professional footing. For the next thirty years he was a marginal figure in the city to which he had dedicated the best years of his professional life, a symbol of a discredited era of master planning living out a very long retirement.

Still, almost every reputation is redeemed in time. Philadelphia's post-1970 history was difficult, as political turmoil and economic decline gave the city a reputation as an urban embarrassment.[40] But in the late 1990s the city's economic climate improved in tandem with historiographical reassessments of modern master planners such as Robert Moses.[41] As a safely obsolete public figure who was amazingly still around and more opinionated than ever, Bacon's 2002 protest of a skateboarding ban in Center City's Love Park provided him with national attention. Nathaniel Kahn's film, while not painting Bacon particularly positively, put the master planner on the same plane as Philip Johnson, I. M. Pei, and other titans of midcentury architecture and urbanism.

With resurgent Philadelphia in a mood to reassess its recent past,[42] the time was ripe for Bacon's reputation to be redeemed. Following Bacon's 2005 death, two books (an edited volume, and a biography that started as a collaboration with Bacon himself) presented the master planner in more favorable terms. According to these books Bacon may have been "iconoclastic," but he did have a "remarkable vision" for Philadelphia, a poignant image of what "might have been, and what could yet be in the city's future."[43] In a new era of Philadelphia optimism, Bacon no longer seemed so problematic: he did after all create some of the city's more significant downtown spaces, and he created a public voice for city betterment that has never been replaced. In his home city's reconstituted historical narrative, Bacon is now a quixotic Philadelphia visionary, a cranky but city-loving booster, who can be safely praised for his optimism and energy by contemporary politicians, just as Robert Moses was by New York's post-2001 Bloomberg administration.[44]

Bacon's work in Philadelphia did have enormous local impact, and his local importance is deserved. But to portray Bacon as merely a local actor is akin to depicting Kevin Lynch, the subject of this chapter's next and final section, as little more than a Boston-area academic. Philadelphia was Bacon's canvas, but the ideas with which he painted derived from a much greater scope of thought, drawn from Bacon's experiences in Europe and from other cities around the globe, particularly in Asia and South America, and they deserve greater appreciation. These ideas, formulated early in his career, shaped much of the work in Philadelphia that we shall explore.

One can read Bacon's ideas most easily in his 1967 classic *Design of Cities*, particularly in that book's loving interpretation of Rome, explained further in a later film *Rome: Impact of an Idea*. Bacon was a true student of Rome; what he found there, and how he transformed those findings into a larger theory of urbanism that he put into practice, mark him as a central figure in plural urbanism. Bacon's long-term dedication to somewhat provincial but still large-scale Philadelphia yielded a substantial body of built work that derives directly from his thought, and that bears his direct imprint. In the democratic and rapidly changing politics of American cities, this achievement is no small feat, and it places Bacon alone among the three plural urbanists of this chapter.

Design of Cities is on first glance a misleading book. Its title, as well as its cover copy, alleges that it is a sort of compendium of urban design history, a textbook of ideas offering contemporary urban designers a pattern book of paragons drawn from every era. Were this to actually be the case, Bacon's book would have been little different from already existing compendia of the time, such as Paul Spreiregen's *Urban Design* (1965) or Frederick Gibberd's *Town Design* (1953). In fact, Bacon's book is quite distinct from its peers. A cursory read finds the book organized around a seemingly idiosyncratic selection of designed cities, albeit in roughly chronological order. But Bacon's progression through time is peculiar and disconnected. He includes several cities of classical Greece, while classical Rome is almost entirely absent. The European fifteenth through eighteenth centuries, Renaissance and baroque, are present in splendid detail, but the nineteenth and first half of the twentieth centuries, eras that typically occupy a great deal of space in urban design histories, are nearly entirely overlooked. Le Corbusier is mentioned but then summarily dismissed within the space of a few pages, while other paragons of modernism (e.g., Mies and Sert) or modernist urbanism (e.g., British new towns) do not appear at all. The book's interrupted chronology resumes with the late 1950s and moves up to the then-present time of 1967.

Interspersed in Bacon's selective chronology are a series of other themes that do not at first accord with the book's allegedly historical progression. The work of German-Swiss artist Paul Klee features heavily, with a few stand-alone pages and many other diagrams matched with those of cities or city areas. Much of the beginning of the book discusses "involvement," "ways of perceiving one's self," or "psychology of space."[45] First readings of *Design of Cities* may leave readers puzzled by these apparently unrelated discussions and eager to get to the more comprehensible history of urban form at the book's core.

With its seemingly idiosyncratic selections, staccato history, and disparate discussions, *Design of Cities* is unlikely to be the result of accident or ignorance. Bacon was doubtless appraised of the same urban history and contemporary projects that occupied his contemporaries' books; after all he was a practiced urban designer who had traveled much of Europe and Asia and whose career had commenced almost thirty years before

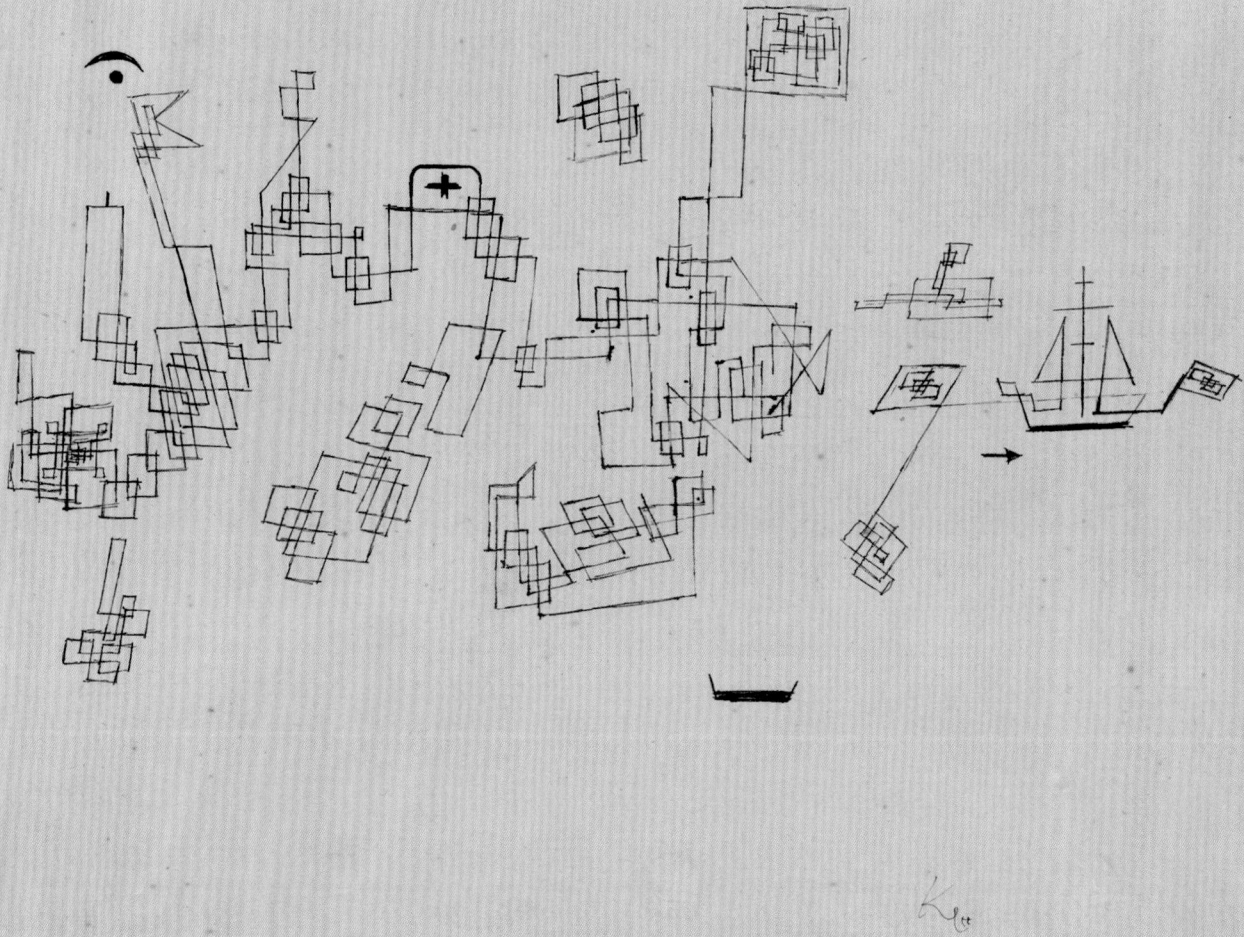

4.11 The drawings of German-Swiss artist Paul Klee play an important role in Bacon's book *Design of Cities*. Much of Klee's work, as in this drawing, is concerned with the way in which space is contained and directed by relatively simple formal gestures — a lesson that Bacon applied in his work.

Design of Cities was published. Nor was Bacon's selective discussion likely to be the result of ideological bias steering the reader toward a preferred settlement pattern. Bacon was no Lewis Mumford, attempting to posit a single settlement pattern such as the garden city as the apotheosis of urban development. Bacon was more all-embracing and more complex than that. He was certainly a modernist, but he also respected historic fabrics, and while he may have been cranky and imperious, he was hardly doctrinaire.

Design of Cities is nevertheless at least partially readable as a history of urban form. Bacon's publisher likely preferred such a depiction, since history is a traditional and comprehensible means of explaining the substantial body of information required for understanding urban form. And Bacon does much more in his carefully designed, carefully structured, carefully selected book. *Design of Cities* contains historical information, but it does so as a gentle manifesto describing a single and singular theory of urban design that goes very much against the grain of contemporary urbanism in the mid-1960s, of which Bacon clearly saw Le Corbusier's work as representative. And like Crane, Bacon does not favor particular contemporary constructed projects, except for those deriving from his own ideas. In the end Bacon is less a historian than a designer who sees past cities offering lessons for his own design approach—in development since the late 1940s. Ultimately *Design of Cities* is a peculiar but landmark book on urban design, simultaneously history, manifesto, and monograph, and reinforcing Bacon's unique position as a hybrid of bureaucrat, designer, and theorist.

This alternative reading of *Design of Cities* paints a clearer picture of Bacon's understanding of urban design and its engagement with the built structure of the city. He wished to communicate that human understandings of space had changed over time from static to dynamic, and that this dynamic concept of three-dimensional space constituted the conceptual frame around which urban design must be constructed. This progression is explained in brief from pages 15 to 20, and again in greater detail in the core of the book, beginning at page 66 with classical Athens and ending around page 215 with post-eighteenth-century Paris and London. Here one can see the difference between a conventional urban form history and Bacon's manifesto: where a typical history would simply describe a temporal progression of buildings or urban spaces, Bacon shows a teleological progression toward an apotheosis of urban design. Tucked away on pages 82 and 83 is an explanation of this progression, which Bacon shows as six "concepts" or "basic themes," the last of which was first realized in eighteenth-century Paris.

Bacon's teleology is an extension of the thinking typical of conventional histories of architecture. The Renaissance has long been understood as the era in which spatial perspective was discovered and made manifest in the form of both drawings and constructed works. Similarly, the baroque has conventionally been taken to be an era of space unleashed into infinity from its Renaissance boundedness. In this sense Bacon's understanding of spatial evolution is conventional, even conservative. But while Bacon particularly admires the baroque, his concept of urban design evolution differs from that of architectural history, since he emphasizes that the city's form is not the result of a single actor but of many, and that the experience of the public in space is therefore crucial.

Bacon expands his definition of urban design in the book's next section, "Involvement."[46] Here he emphasizes the social force of public opinion. As he explains, "the city is a people's art, a shared experience, the place where the artist meets the greatest number of appreciators … it is the function of the designer to conceive an idea, implant it, and nurture its growth in the collective minds of the community so that the final product has a reasonable chance of coming close to his original concept." This is a dramatically different understanding of urban design than in unitary thinking, one that emphasizes, even advocates, the actions of plural agents in realizing urban design. Bacon said as much when he described the city not only as a "shared experience" but one with a "number of appreciators," those who might also become actors in the enterprise of the city's plural urban design. Bacon maintains a careful balance, retaining the designer's concern for formal control, but acknowledging some release of this control by necessity. On the one hand, Bacon believes that no design concept can exist without a formative thought and an active agent (the designer) promoting that thought. On the other hand, the designer alone cannot realize this design idea, because urbanism is a "people's art," and urban design's plural actors and scales inevitably result in imprecision of design resolution. No design idea, says Bacon, is likely to be realized in complete or detailed form: "coming close" is likely the best that the urban designer can expect. This lack of resolution, Bacon adds, spurs the urban designer; it is a "severe discipline" that obliges creation of "coherent vision of a finer, healthier, more inspiring city." In other words, urbanism's complexities do not relieve the designer of providing a powerful formal concept and may even emphasize its importance.

In "Involvement" Bacon also emphasizes time's particular influence on urban design. "The designer," he notes, "functions in time and space … [he or she] brings into full focus the physical realization of an idea which had been implanted long before and establishes a glimmer of the vision of the development to come." City-building, Bacon notes, is similar to music, since both occur over time and are irreversible; the city is thus a cumulative composition made up of thousands of elements, "a vast number of separate acts of city-building brought into relationship with each other over a considerable span of time."

"Involvement" is a critical and underappreciated passage in *Design of Cities*. In this brief section Bacon demonstrates his clear grasp of the same truths of urbanism that Crane had noted in his four essays: the multiple actors participating in the city's construction, the necessary imprecision brought about by these plural actors, the long span of time required for realizing urban design, and the relatively limited ability of an individual design to effect large-scale change, thus necessitating a certain economy. These truths are combined in Bacon's book with an astute understanding of spatial principles for cities derived from architecture and grounded in architectural history. Bacon did not see the different qualities of urbanism as constituting a rejection of the formal principles that shaped urban architecture, but as elements that established urban design as a clearly autonomous, yet related spatial art.

Bacon believed in the importance of a designer's will, but by 1967 he had also operated for almost thirty years within the rough-and-tumble world of municipal politics and, at a larger scale, within the democratic setting of American society. Bacon was no dreamer wishing for the power of Louis XIV, though we will see that he was not averse to the urbanism that could be created under such autocratic circumstances. Thus Bacon did not merely acknowledge the necessity of involving a democratic public, he personally advocated it. As he notes, the "safeguards and processes of rejection" of contemporary politics makes any "forc[ing of a designer's] ideas on a community [and] overriding the sentiment of the community extremely unlikely."[47] With the lessons of Philadelphia in mind, Bacon emphasized that only the designer operating within and with a plural public could achieve success.

With involvement firmly established as a baseline condition under which urban design need occur, Bacon proceeds to develop his "movement system" as a guiding concept. Bacon disowned cities designed by the static method of the plan view, arguing instead that movement through space alone permitted pedestrians (and other types of urban travelers) to perceive the larger design within which they exist.[48] Bacon explicitly criticized plan-centric designs such as Vällingby (Sweden), Chandigarh, and Brasília, though Brasília's all-uniting sky did, Bacon believed, excuse it to some extent. Movement systems were necessary in contemporary urban design because the scale of modernist development had broken the traditional tie between a plan view and human experience. Whereas Renaissance urban spaces such as Italy's Pienza or the Campidoglio in Rome were small enough to be entirely perceptible from a static viewpoint, such understanding was impossible within the vast scale of the contemporary city. At the same time, Bacon noted, extending design ideas over a larger geographical space than in the Renaissance necessitated a certain economy: movement systems marked by individual elements at intervals "enabl[ed] the designer to establish a central design structure without attempting to cover the entire area." Thus movement systems, in Bacon's eyes, answered urban designers' needs to shape contemporary cities in a manner that was visually and experientially perceptible, as well as realizable, economical, durable, and democratically acceptable.

The historical survey of urban design contained within *Design of Cities* provides (in the words of Koolhaas) a "retroactive manifesto" for Bacon's explanation of movement systems. The book is beautifully illustrated and designed, and Bacon's exploration of Rome through the obelisks of Pope Sixtus V is particularly detailed, occupying over thirty pages (Paris and London together, by contrast, occupy only twenty-six). Bacon's book demonstrates a love of Rome and deep knowledge of the city's "design structure,"[49] and his 1983 film *Rome: Impact of an Idea*, part of a five-part series, is by far the most inspired episode.[50] Bacon was particularly enamored of the sculptural and architectural elements added to the city by Pope Sixtus V during his five-year reign from 1585 to 1590.[51]

Sixtus V's design ideas are explained at length by Bacon,[52] but it is not necessary to detail them here. The economy of Sixtus's methods is of substantial interest because this economy relates so closely to Bacon's perception of the position of the contemporary urban designer, drawn no doubt from his own experience. Sixtus V reigned for only five years: he was sixty-four when he became Pope, and he was elected in part because he was not expected to live long.[53] Yet he had had much time to consider his ideas, and he acted swiftly. Sixteenth-century Rome was a much-reduced city from classical times, and its frontiers were weedy wildernesses in between high-ranking churches (San Giovanni in Laterano, Santa Maria Maggiore, and others) marking significant Christian sites or relics. Pilgrims would walk the paths between these sites in medieval fashion, much as they did to the tomb of St. James along Spain's Camino de Santiago, or to the tomb of St. Thomas Becket in Canterbury, England. Sixtus V marked four of these sites (including St. Peter's Basilica) with obelisks that had lain in Rome since classical times, reerecting them to serve as vertical markers of a single urban spatial structure.

▼ **4.12** Paris contains a number of interlinked axes and spaces organized by monumental structures. Bacon found this type of "design structure" to be spectacular, but also too costly and time-consuming to be applied in the more economical context of American cities.

▶ **4.13** Bacon took inspiration from five ancient obelisks reerected by Pope Sixtus V in late sixteenth-century Rome. These small-scale design moves organized city spaces and provided a series of axes around which later growth could coalesce—what Bacon called a "movement system."

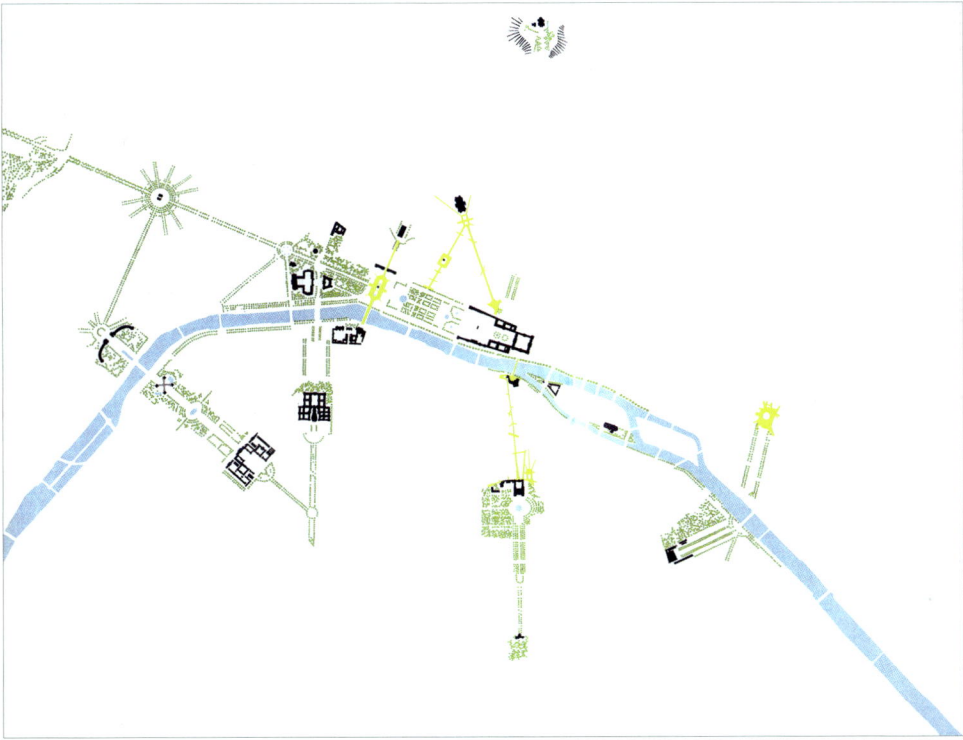
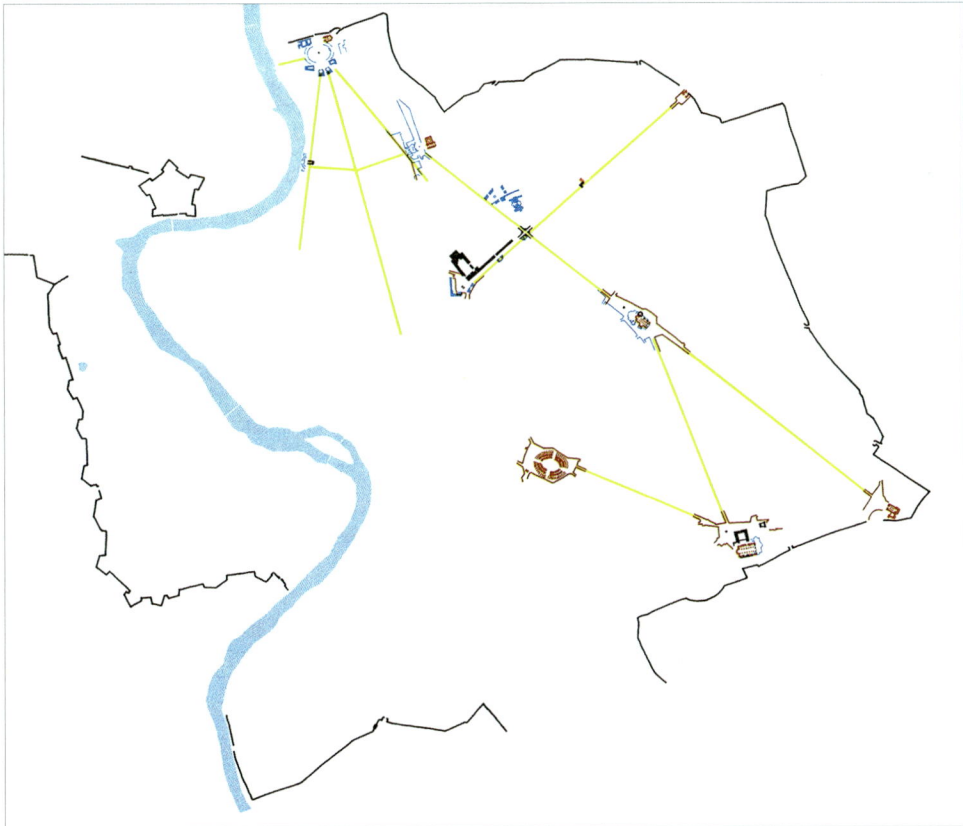

4.14 Bacon's 1983 film *Rome: Impact of an Idea*, a still of which is shown here, succinctly states his ideal of the urban designer: a visionary who could shape space with limited means, and around whose interventions even monumental architecture, such as St. Peter's Basilica, would fall into place.

It was in this "connection of nodal points," with the "obelisks as points in movement systems" that Bacon saw the establishment of Rome's urban design order. And indeed, the establishment of all urban design order, for he noted in *Design of Cities* that the "essential nature" of connected "points in space" was easily transferable to the contemporary city, with "points of production in regional economy," or "centers of regeneration in blighted areas" substituting for pilgrimage monuments. Achieving this connection provided multiple benefits to the urban citizen, giving them not only an "aesthetic physical design entity," in other words the built entities themselves, but also "an awareness of the structural relationship of functions" emerging from "a chaotic distribution of independent functions."[54] Order from chaos: this primal urge was also Bacon's as he sought to make sense of the jumble of urban functions that comprised twentieth-century Philadelphia.

Today, either in an automobile or via online street view images, we can travel among Sixtus V's nodal points much more swiftly than could the sixteenth-century traveler. And from this perspective, as well as in the book's wonderful diagrams (e.g., pp. 128–129; see figure 4.13), Rome's urban order is quite clear. Doubtless sixteenth-century pilgrims, with their next destinations and their spiritual significance well in mind, also anticipated and appreciated this consistent marking of sacred sites. These sites have less meaning today, and the obelisks themselves are diminished in importance because of the clamorous city that has grown up around them, but Bacon would argue that this diminution does not matter because this clamor was itself organized by the now shrunken nodal points, which nevertheless remain visible. In similar fashion, we saw that Târgu Jiu's Calea Eroilor has grown up in part around the nodal points established by Brancusi, though Brancusi's sculptures are smaller than and lack the sacred significance and literal utility of Sixtus V's pilgrimage churches. These nodal points comprise very little of the building mass of the cities in which they are located, but their intersection with sites of great importance (votive churches in Rome, a city park and hilltop in Târgu Jiu) provides them with greater visibility and significance, and encourages responsive additional development.

In the United States, electoral cycles often place planning directors or high-ranking municipal staff in office for only a short number of years: sometimes as few as four or five. Bacon, in office through parts of four different mayoral administrations from 1949 to 1970, was a skilled survivor of political change. But he also recognized that an urban designer's time in office might be short, and the economy and an inspired design strategy could work together in powerful combination to establish an urban order that might long outlast the political administration and even the life span of an urban designer. This, Bacon believed, was what Sixtus V had achieved so successfully during his short reign, and what others could achieve in their turn as well. Center City Philadelphia was Bacon's own exercise in movement systems, and the outcome of his efforts there provides a useful illustration of the movement system's promoting of the different dimensions of plural urbanism in Center City.

Bacon's 1949 appointment as executive director was extremely well timed, though he could not have known it then. The federal government had just passed the first of several laws that would steer hundreds of millions of dollars to older cities, and the ascendance of modernist ideology provided a convenient and convincing formal rationale for urban rebuilding. Like planning directors elsewhere, Bacon almost immediately had a significant role in determining how federal money would be spent to rebuild

Philadelphia. Over the next twenty years, he would make his mark in many areas of Center City as well as large areas of North Philadelphia and outlying areas of the city. Like most cities in the American northeast, Philadelphia was mostly a nineteenth-century city, and it was hobbled both by obsolete infrastructure—in particular a plethora of rail lines leading into and around downtown—and by a lack of limited-access highways. Bacon attacked this infrastructure problem with vigor, and Philadelphia spent the 1950s and 1960s in a frenzy of rebuilding and modernization, much of it intelligently directed by Bacon and encouraged by the publication of two master plans for the city in 1960 and 1963.

But in more ways than one, Philadelphia was not Sixtus V's Rome. The city was at its population peak under Bacon, not its low point, and it was heavily and densely developed with row houses and industry. Nor was Philadelphia's urban development chaotic: it was one of the few British colonial cities in North America to be shaped by an initial street plan, and most of the city followed a consistent grid of square blocks derived from the street plan of Center City. Thus where Sixtus V's urban design was in essence additive, Bacon was required to be subtractive. Whether Bacon recognized this foundational difference between his efforts and those of his papal model is unclear; perhaps he was too enmeshed in the realities of modernist master planning to see the distinction. Almost all of Bacon-era urban design in Philadelphia involved much destruction of the existing building stock, including the city's principal nineteenth-century railroad station and much of its historic banking district. The removal of these architecturally significant buildings is to be much regretted; it almost certainly would not be permitted today. So Bacon's Philadelphia urbanism can be evaluated as much for what it removed as for what it added.

But the executive director's work was not all destruction, nor is it all to be regretted. Though Philadelphia was densely built and spatially quite organized, Bacon's city did in a sense resemble Rome in that its historic center was studded with a variety of colonial-era (eighteenth-century) monuments that had played important roles in the American Revolution, but that were mostly lost in its twentieth-century fabric. Rehabilitating and exposing these monuments was a federal priority in the 1950s, and the juxtaposition of colonial landmarks with a then-deteriorated waterfront neighborhood provided Bacon with a unique opportunity to link his own city's pilgrimage points, such as Independence Hall, Christ Church, and the First and Second Banks of the United States, via a new movement system of pedestrian paths. Even better, the deterioration of the surrounding neighborhood, known as Society Hill, allowed Bacon to replace

4.15 and 4.16 As effective chief urban designer of Philadelphia, Bacon played a substantial role in shaping major infrastructure and redevelopment efforts of the 1960s, such as the construction of the Penn Center office district adjacent to City Hall.

many of these older buildings with new, higher buildings, thus providing contemporary monuments of a different scale. But again, Philadelphia was no Rome, and the American city's monuments did not have boulevards linking them, unlike the votive churches of Sixtus V. Instead, the city's selective removal of intervening buildings in the 1950s and 1960s, combined with the wholesale clearance of blocks with high densities of preserved monuments, created a patchwork of pedestrian paths and parklike grounds that provided pastoral settings for restored colonial landmarks.

Much of the new construction envisioned by Bacon in the city's 1963 *Center City Philadelphia* plan and in *Design of Cities* did not occur, but that which did is significant, and additional construction since Bacon stepped down in 1970 has continued to, albeit weakly, respond to the design moves that he established in Society Hill. By far the finest ensemble in terms of individual architecture and the larger urban condition are the Society Hill Towers and surrounding townhouses designed by I. M. Pei & Associates and Louis Sauer & Associates, respectively. While the scalar and material clash between the thirty-two-story towers and the minute brick row houses seems somewhat abrupt today, the design quality of both, together with the drama of their juxtaposition, location amid the urban grid, and generosity of open spaces is notable. Society Hill's quality is certainly much higher than similar work achieved elsewhere in Philadelphia, or indeed almost anywhere in the United States outside of a few developments in New York City and Chicago. Bacon provided this work with pride of place among his Philadelphia accomplishments in *Design of Cities*, and rightfully so.

Yet the limitations of Bacon's approach in Society Hill are also painfully apparent, quite apart from the destruction of historic structures mentioned earlier. Whereas Sixtus V's movement system consisted of straight streets with immediate utility as well as visual connectivity, the pedestrian paths of Society Hill are difficult to perceive as a network, and their comprehensibility pales in comparison with that of the seventeenth-century street grid. Admittedly the paths and parks are pleasant landscape elements, and they provide patches of green that are rare elsewhere in Center City, but they are not used much as a circulation system, and they certainly do not structure movement in Society Hill. The towers are stronger as a reference point; visible from afar, they provide orientation and also an indication of activity, for at their feet is a commercial center. Unfortunately, Bacon could not provide further clusters of towers of equivalent quality and meaning; another cluster around Washington Square is low-quality and relates poorly to the existing street and open space system. New open spaces, such as Independence Mall (itself far too large), do not relate well to older spaces, for example the directly adjacent

4.17 The reconstruction of Society Hill, a deteriorated eighteenth-century neighborhood, provided Bacon the opportunity to place his movement system ideas into practice with some success through a combination of new towers, row houses, and pedestrian paths.

Franklin Square. And the overall district has a distinct sterility in contrast to the bustling commercial streets of Old City, an adjacent district that was spared colonialist restoration. Perhaps the Philadelphia grid was just too dominant; the city's blocks are very small, and the city did not really need a new movement system in addition to its dense networks of streets and alleys. But this was the canvas that Bacon had during his twenty-one-year term in office, and he deserves significant praise for shaping rebuilding efforts that were both more sensitive and sophisticated than those of his peers in other cities.

Bacon's design vision for Philadelphia extended far beyond Society Hill. There is a fascinating diagram in *Design of Cities* showing a range of rectangles of different colors, overlaid across Center City Philadelphia and extending from the Delaware River on the east all the way across the Schuylkill River on the west, encompassing nearly the entirety of downtown. Bacon labels these areas "architects' hegemonies," where "one or another designer is dominant."[55] Here, beyond the scale of any single movement system, Bacon depicts an urbanism of multiple design concepts: they are organized by a hierarchy of design thought, overlapping and intersecting in what is ultimately a comprehensive and ideally consistent formal vision for a significant scale of space, effectively the entire downtown of a major American city. This is no totalitarian fantasy for the wholesale replacement of a downtown; in fact, the architects' hegemonies are surprisingly modest. Here, the urban designer's touch is light, but it is spatially and conceptually wide-ranging. Rather than heavy-handedly replacing a pluralist fabric with a massive unitary architectural project, Bacon deftly reinterprets the city's form, structure, and function using architectural and landscape means that are extremely economical compared to the mass of the city's construction.

Bacon's diagram reflects significant achievement, but it is also incomplete. As Bacon said, his urban design "is not a final form ... it makes no claim to finality." Not all of Bacon's Center City architects succeeded; Louis Kahn in particular was frustrated, and Philadelphia is the worse for it. Nor are the "architects' hegemonies" always visible to the same degree as Plečnik's wonderful work in Prague and Ljubljana. But Bacon's diagram is both surprising and beautiful, particularly in a gritty, industrial city with only an intermittently positive self-image. Bacon concludes: "on the highest level, the design of this kind of activity is, of itself, a work of art," and this is also a fitting conclusion for our understanding of Bacon's work. In the difficult setting of a single American city, no urban designer ever achieved so much, nor achieved it so well. Though he was long slandered as an arrogant master planner, both the language of *Design of Cities* and Bacon's built work reflect not arrogance but the measured, mostly implemented vision of an experienced, ambitious, dedicated architect who devoted his career to public service, and whose work made downtown Philadelphia a promising example of plural urbanism.

Kevin Lynch: City Design and Place Utopias

The day before Kevin Lynch died at age sixty-six, he tended to his garden.[56] Like many such gardens, Lynch's was neat, ordered, and predictable; its vegetables were planted in straight rows, and each row was cleanly segregated by type of vegetable. These clean rows possessed a rigor and an order that had little in common with the scrubby island forest of their surrounds on Martha's Vineyard. Nor did Lynch's garden bear a likeness to the form of his ideal city, which was everything that his garden was not: disordered, shapeless, forever in flux, unpredictable, even messy. Lynch's ideal city was atypical; it resembled neither the modernist urban visions that were predominant during his early career, nor the postmodern reaction of his later years.

Like his ideal cities, as an urban designer Lynch too was atypical: primarily an educator, he spent comparatively little time in practice, and he taught within a planning, not an architecture, department, beginning his career a decade before the establishment of Harvard's urban design degree. Lynch seems to have always been a leader: he attained early recognition for his bachelor's thesis, and in his early forties he became internationally known with his canonical book, *The Image of the City* (1960).[57] Over the remaining two decades of his career at MIT, Lynch secured his status with an active publication record and involvement in a variety of professional projects.

Every urban designer knows Kevin Lynch through his first book. Concise and compulsively readable, *The Image of the City* is nearly required reading for students and practitioners interested in city-shaping. Lynch's readers quickly grasp his argument that city residents hold a physical image of the city in their minds, and that urban designers should understand this image to incorporate the citizen's view of the city into their schemes. The book's perspective dovetails neatly with planner-advocates working to represent the poor, and it also meshes well with architect-urbanists who appreciate that citizens, too, have a sense of the city's design. Whatever the normative truth of Lynch's "city image" concept, its simplicity and utility make it an obligatory touchstone for analyses of city form.

But success, as is often said, is a double-edged sword, and so it proves with Kevin Lynch and his ideas. The limelight shone on *The Image of the City* leaves his other ideas

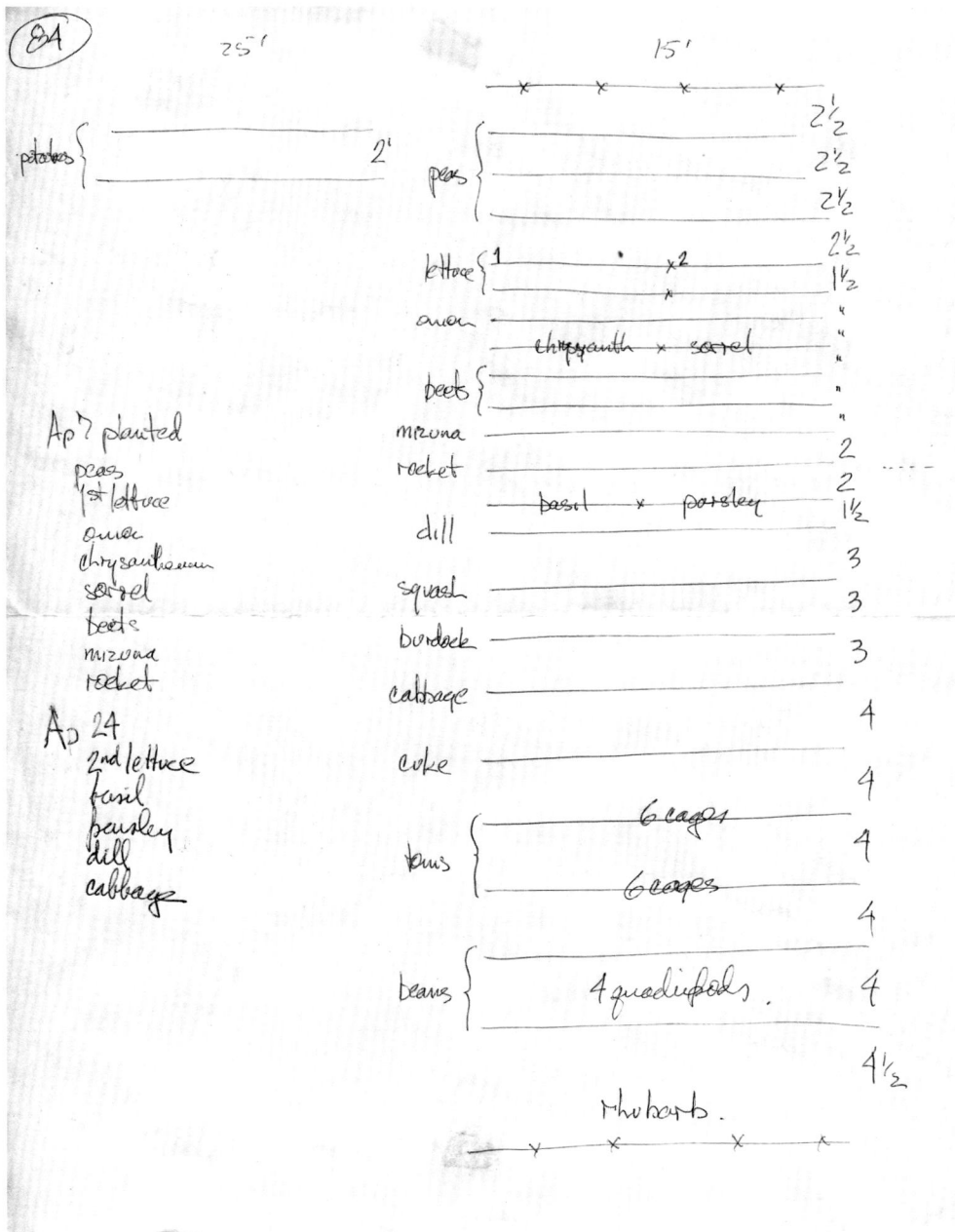

8A

25'   15'

potatoes {   2'   peas {   2½
                                                                          2½
                                                                          2½

                                                lettuce { 1   x2   2½
                                                                          1½
                                                onion   "
                                                chrysanth x sorrel   "
                                                beets {   "
                                                mizuna   "
Ap 7 planted   rocket   2
  peas   dill   basil x parsley 2
  1st lettuce   1½
  onion   squash   3
  chrysanthemum   burdock   3
  sorrel   cabbage   3
  beets   coke   4
  mizuna   4
  rocket   6 cages   4
                                                toms {
Ap 24   6 cages   4
  2nd lettuce   4
  basil   beans {   4 quadrupeds   4
  parsley
  dill   4½
  cabbage
                                                     rhubarb.

4.19 Urbanist Kevin Lynch lived a comparatively tranquil life as an academic at MIT, retiring on weekends to a rustic house on Martha's Vineyard. His garden there, sketched by Lynch just before his 1984 death, was a neatly organized ensemble of different vegetables.

4.20 Lynch's calm personal demeanor was mirrored by his approach to urban design, which advocated an openness to participation by many different actors and an absence of strong doctrine regarding conventional urbanist concerns such as density, monumentality, and building form.

on urban design in the dark, as with Jane Jacobs's lesser-known sequels to her famous work.[58] This occlusion of Lynch's other books is all the more regrettable because, whereas David Crane's and Edmund Bacon's intellectual productivity was limited by the demands of professional practice, Lynch had few such limitations. His corpus of published work is rich and voluminous, ranging from studies of time and cities[59] to thoughts on the ideal city.[60] Even his numerous articles and unfinished works were gathered up and published by former students after his untimely death in 1984.[61] Those who wish to read Kevin Lynch find that there is much to read indeed.

Yet Lynch's writing is also peculiar, as much for what it does *not* contain as for what it does. A reader familiar with urban history and theory will be surprised at

Lynch's silence on urban renewal, political struggle, and neoliberal capitalism, even though these topics dominated the planning field in the 1970s and 1980s.[62] Such serenity distances Lynch's writing from that of his contemporaries, giving his work a distinctiveness, but it also gives it a sense of remoteness from concerns of the time. This is not to say that either Lynch or his ideas are abstract or uncaring; Lynch's writing is plainspoken and sensitive, much like, to all accounts, the man himself. But for whatever reason Lynch distanced himself from the turmoil and excitement of late modernism.

Those interested in Lynch face another challenge: unlike Crane and Bacon, Lynch left little recognizable built work to his name. Some of the professional studies authored principally by Lynch are noteworthy, in particular those for Brookline, Martha's Vineyard, and San Diego.[63] But none of these studies was implemented, and much of the other work of Lynch's consulting firm is conventional in content, indistinguishable from other work of its day, and seemingly unrepresentative of Lynch's thought.[64] Lynch's urban design ideas seem to have been difficult to translate into reality; we will see that even his most noteworthy studies contain only limited implementable ideas.

For a voluminous writer with a strong concern for the practice of urbanism, it is surprising how often Lynch's significance is reduced to five concepts, all drawn from *Image of the City*: path, node, landmark, edge, and district. Yet beyond this book, there is much, much more to Kevin Lynch's thought, as Michael Sorkin recognized in 2006, when he called Lynch's work "critical" and "fundamental."[65] Lynch's independence from the mainstream of urban design thought and practice, together with his own keen intellect, gave him the space to formulate an alternative to the unitary urban design practices that composed late modernism. Lynch called his alternative "city design," and we can recognize in this concept many of the foundations of plural urbanism that this book explores. Lynch himself never fully explored or explained his city design concept, though he remained interested in it to the end of his life and published several articles on the topic, gathered together in the posthumous *City Sense and City Design*.[66]

Two of Lynch's concepts of urbanism are particularly relevant to us here. The first is his understanding of metropolitan form, explored in some early work and again in his final book *Good City Form* (1981). Nearly alone among his colleagues, Lynch grasped that static models of the city, such as that of Le Corbusier, were inaccurate, for the simple reason that cities are always changing. Lynch was the first to postulate that urban designers must intervene in this living fabric rather than try to wrest the city into the shape of a static form, as at Brasília. At the end of his career Lynch revisited this notion when he posited a city model that incorporated all of the "good city form" values of his

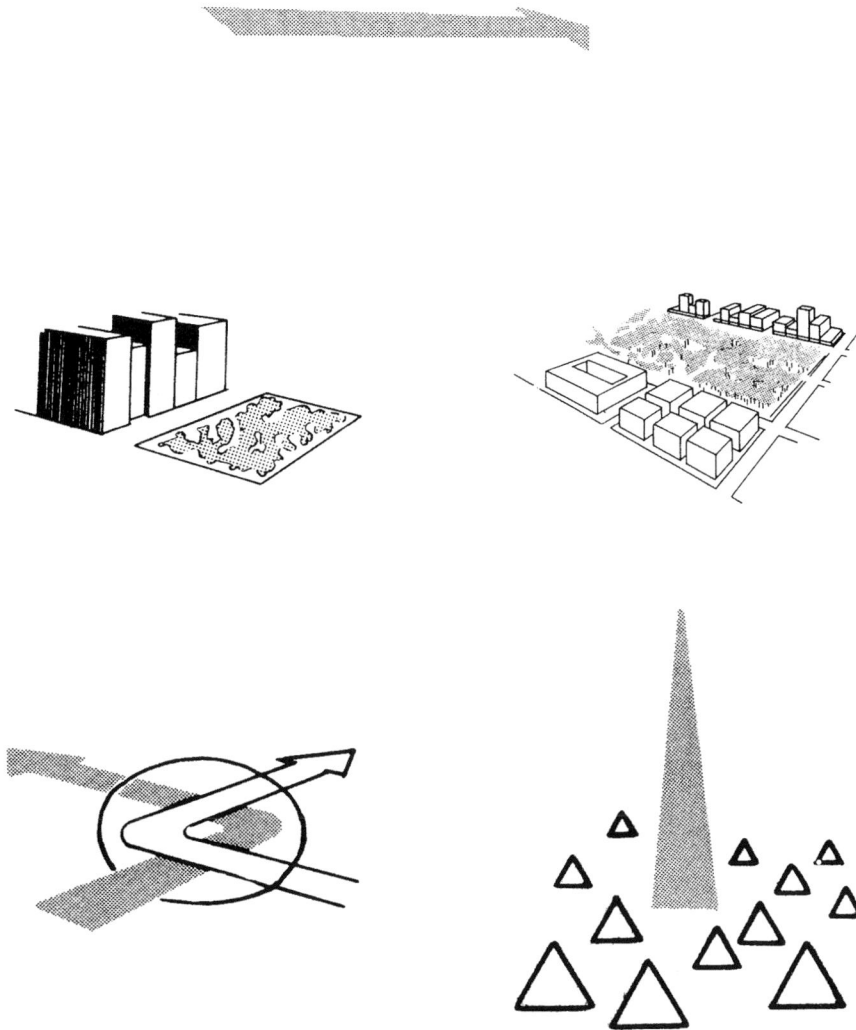

4.21 The canonical dimensions of path, landmarks, and so forth developed by Lynch in *The Image of the City* provided a firm basis for analysis of urban space, but Lynch later admitted that they could provide little guidance in actually shaping cities.

final work. Second is the notion of "city design" itself, which Lynch saw as that version of urban design that would attempt to shape the living fabric of the city. In a series of essays beginning in the mid-1960s and extending for twenty years until his death, Lynch spelled out the qualities and skills that a city designer would need, though he remained stymied by precisely what formal concepts a city designer might use in shaping urban space.[67] In *Good City Form*, Lynch called for additional "models and theoretical constructs" for the "scarcely developed art" of city design.[68] He was unable to develop such models himself; his professional studies were frustrating, only lightly developed efforts to apply ideas like city image to actual places, and in his later works Lynch was increasingly influenced by ecological thinking that was not his own.

Lynch's concept of city design has had little influence since his death. It is both open-ended and inclusive; Lynch included nearly any physical improvement to the city as part of the idea. While perhaps effective as a means of widening participation in urban design, the breadth and generosity of the idea also dilutes its effectiveness as a model for shaping the city. But Lynch himself recognized that his definition of city design was not final; it was only the beginning. His work opened a door for the further exploration of plural urbanism, a challenge and a potential that this book attempts to fulfill.

Metropolitan Form: The Unfinished City

While much of the twentieth-century debate on city form witnessed a back-and-forth between modernist and traditional views of urban design, Lynch transcended this struggle early in his career by generating formal models of the city with little relationship to either modernism or traditionalism. His first concepts for "The Pattern of the Metropolis" were published shortly after *The Image of the City*, and Lynch reprised and expanded these ideas twenty years later in *Good City Form*. While the formal content of Lynch's metropolitan pattern is interesting, the concept is significant principally for its incorporation of the city's perpetually changing fabric as an element of urban design, and the ensuing redesignation of urban design itself as an art that must not only shape formal patterns, but accommodate change as a fundamental aspect of that art.

The 1950s were an era of rapidly expanding cities in the United States, and of expanding confidence among urban planners that city complexity could be understood and commanded.[69] In 1961, with city rebuilding on the national agenda, the American Academy of Arts and Sciences published a special issue of *Dædalus* on "the future metropolis" with Lynch as a guest editor.[70] His contribution, an article titled "The

Pattern of the Metropolis," stands out among the generally clinical speculations of the rest of the issue, portraying a novel approach to urban form that is little known even today. Lynch's question in "Pattern" is quite simple: If one is to shape metropolitan or city form, then how should we do so, and what ideal forms might the metropolis take? The timing for Lynch's investigation was excellent: the 1950s had seen several experiments in shaping metropolitan form, particularly in the United Kingdom, where the construction of new towns and the imposition of the London Green Belt imposed a spatial structure on much of the nation; and in the Soviet Union, where Khrushchev's prefabricated housing program exploded the empire's scale of urbanization.

Lynch posited several relatively simple shapes as potential formal options: the ring, core, star, dispersed sheet, and galaxy. Each was an abstraction of existing approaches to metropolitan form—Lynch noted the analogies of his concepts of the *ring* in the Dutch Randstad, the *core* in many a highly centralized city, the *star* in Copenhagen and Amsterdam, the *dispersed sheet* all over America, and the *galaxy* emerging in the United Kingdom through its new towns. Lynch noted the potentials of each before proposing that a sixth form called the "polycentered net" would "better satisfy our aspirations," at the top of which were the qualities of "choice" and "interaction."[71]

The polycentered net contained formal elements of many of Lynch's other, simpler metropolitan forms, but it differed in having no ultimate spatial configuration. The net was instead in a perpetual process of "growth and decay … undergo[ing] periodic renewal" where it "would continue to specialize and grow"; it was unbounded, characterized by "indeterminacy." The components of this "rhythmically pulsating" city were traditional components of the city including dense areas, open space, suburbs, and transportation arteries, but within the polycentered net these components were spatially organized in novel fashion, with contrasting areas often directly adjacent. Consistent with Lynch's qualities of choice and interaction, "many types of flow [traffic, people, water, etc.] would be provided for. Densities would have a wide range and a fine grain, with intensive peaks … but with extensive regions of low density." The communication arteries of the polycentered net facilitated both flow and contrast: organized as a triangular grid, roadway infrastructure meshed with "another type of grid" composed of "belts and tongues of open land." In Lynch's city "the general pattern would resemble a fisherman's net, with a system of dispersed centers and intervening spaces."[72]

The polycentered net is a fascinating concept for many reasons. First and foremost, it frees urban design from the static inheritance of architectural diagrams; the city is ever changing. Buildings must remain stable, but the city, as Lynch perceived,

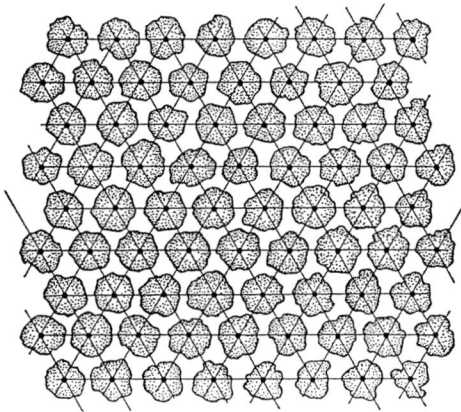

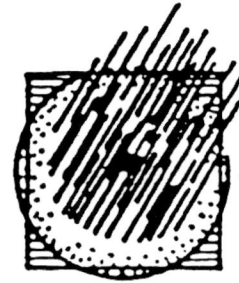

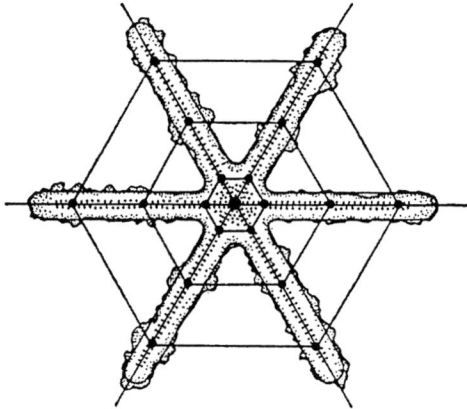

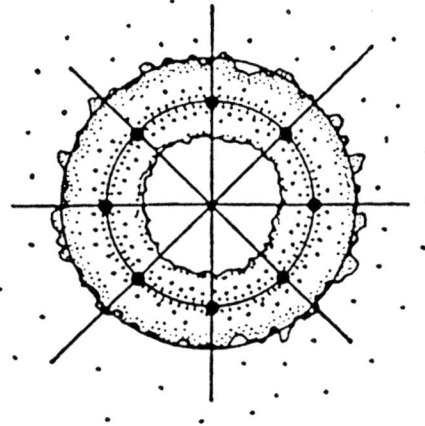

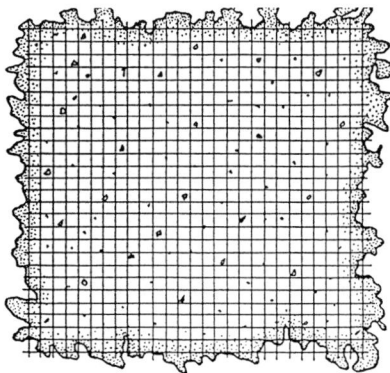

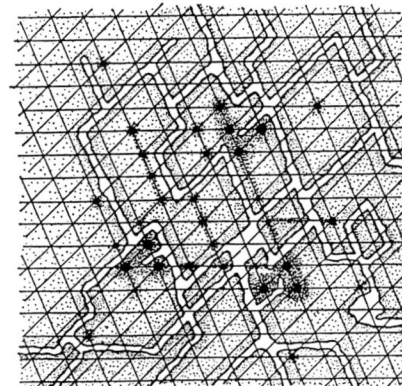

4.22 Early on, Lynch spelled out a compelling and radical concept of metropolitan form that he called the "polycentered" or "alternating" net (at lower right in this figure), permitting formal variation across both space and time. Lynch believed that the ideal city would permit maximum flexibility and choice for all its inhabitants.

was entirely different. Static formal arrangements such as rings and stars were, Lynch believed, both difficult and costly to establish and even more costly to maintain as city-regions grew. The polycentered net dissolves the city's relationship to static form. In doing so, the net also necessarily dissolves the city's formal relationship to the traditional bounded, pedestrian city of history, since contemporary development patterns no longer generated such urban form. Lynch's city did not abandon the traditional city—pieces of which might continue to exist as elements of the net—but it did not resist the inevitable growth of such contemporary urban elements as office districts, industrial areas, or whatever else might arise in the future. The net does not claim preeminence for any time of movement, whether pedestrian or automobile or other, nor for any type of living environment, whether high- or low-density. Lynch's polycentered net destroys many of the distinctions that bedeviled urban designers and urban planners both before and since; should the city be modern or traditional? High- or low-density? Natural or artificial? Beautiful or ugly? The polycentered net tells us that the city can be all of these, and that providing for this plurality does not mean the end of urban design, but instead releases design to confront an entire range of new concerns. Little recognized, the polycentered net deserves a place among the greatest and most radical formal visions of the twentieth-century city.

The perpetual change of the polycentered net would place substantial demands on its inhabitants. Dwellers within such a city-region would have to be comfortable with change, since all areas are constantly in flux, and the fixed form of any neighborhood is never guaranteed. Such a city would be inconsistent with zoning, unless that zoning permitted any and all development to occur. The net would also offer many advantages to its citizens, those of the senses above all. A resident of the net could shift from urban excitement to quiet countryside and back again, maximizing both choice and interaction. Such experiences are all too rare in the cities we possess, but one can get a sense of Lynch's desired contrasts if one emerges from the wilds of Central Park into the tumult of Manhattan; or takes the ferry from packed Lower Manhattan to the relative quiet of Staten Island. Lynch himself enjoyed such experiences as he traveled from Boston to Martha's Vineyard and back, and his polycentered net reflects a generous desire to afford all city-dwellers such experiences.

Of course, a polycentered net would face many barriers to realization. Change is uncomfortable to many citizens; it destabilizes real estate values, and wealthy areas especially wish to preserve their status and appearance, as Lynch ruefully observed in a later book *Managing the Sense of a Region* (1976).[73] In Manhattan, zoning was created to resist just such destabilizing change. And yet cities do grow and decay in ways Lynch's vision seems to acknowledge. Change happens despite the best efforts of those who wish to halt it, and the polycentered net thus represents a characteristic possessed by all cities. The polycentered net would also present a barrier to conventional urban design, whether modernist or traditional, that depended on a static model of city form to sustain its formal quality.

Lynch did not explicitly revisit the polycentered net during the next twenty years, though his 1976 book did examine cities' nascent attempts to shape regional form. When in 1981 he did revisit the now "alternating net" in the form of what he called a "place utopia,"[74] his metropolitan formal ideal had expanded to incorporate an equally ideal vision of society. This double vision addressed what Lynch saw as one of conventional utopias' principal shortcomings: either a radical society in an ordinary city, or a radically changed city that left society unaltered. But the twenty years between 1961 and 1981 sent a clear message that society and space were tightly interwoven; changing urban fabrics changed society, and changed societies could have an impact on the urban fabric as well. Lynch's place utopia thus obliquely reflected the tumultuous changes in urbanism that by 1981 had ended planning's rational dreams together with those of high modernist urban designers.

Lynch's dreamlike portrait of the place utopia's "alternating net" occupies the final chapter of *Good City Form* in the form of a "personal statement" liberated from any burden of proof or empirically demonstrated findings. In his place utopia Lynch describes a society where the conventional boundaries, associations, and divisions between groups have broken down, much like their physical analogues are dissolved within the polycentered net. In this utopia, property is voluntary; children have substantial liberties; people shape their own environments or live in tall towers; animals coexist with people, and habitat for both is abundant. Nations are dissolved, as are factions; poverty is gone, and people disown great wealth. Technology, or the abandonment of it, is omnipresent; transportation ranges from bicycle to lightning-fast trains. One may enjoy excitement twenty-four hours per day or wander in wildernesses that might be filled with the ruins of now-abandoned cities or suburbs, for no environment is ever what it once was, and all places are always becoming something else. People find meaning everywhere in this landscape; everyone has a place that speaks to one's innermost being, in sacred places of one kind or another.[75]

All of this sounds impossible, yet Lynch makes clear that the place utopia is merely a concatenation of things that already exist, if only at intervals, in scattered places around the world. Many such place utopias, Lynch emphasizes, are commonplace: "the farm, the garden, the 'urban village,' the tribal territory, the summer house, the wilderness camp, the weedy vacant lot and the remembered landscapes of childhood, the sacred precinct, the historic city, … even the despised North American suburb" are among the environments contributing elements to this utopia.[76] According to this formulation, Lynch's place utopia does not require images because pieces of it are all around us, whether in our hometown, or across the world in radical environments such as the former Soviet Union or Cuba. Lynch, an astute observer, had seen much during his career, and he carefully selected elements from his journeys and experiences that contributed to his ideal. And while no single environment on earth closely resembles Lynch's vision, its closest analogues may perhaps be communalist settlements such as the Israeli kibbutzim that flourished for a few postwar decades before falling before political and economic pressures.

The social imaginings of Lynch's place utopia step far beyond his own polycentered net. His utopia is a physical one, grounded in the dynamic qualities of city space that Lynch defined in "The Pattern of the Metropolis." But the utopia is even more remote from conventional urban design; it occupies the realm of futurism or philosophy as much as it sits within the space of conventional urbanism. The place utopia confirms Lynch as a broad and unusual thinker, and it remains today one of the more compelling images of a built environment that meshes closely with a still-desirable vision of society. The chapter is deep, well thought, and merits repeated reading. But like the polycentered net, it remains abstract; it lacks physical specificity, and as a physical model it is too remote from the reality of contemporary places to provide guidance to urban designers. Lynch acknowledged as much; this conclusion to his thinking on urban design was an assemblage of best practices as much as it was a utopia, and he never intended for it to provide instructions for professional action; such was to be left to others. But beyond the place utopia, Lynch did articulate a vision of what he thought the profession of urban design should be, and he spelled this out in his writings explaining the "art of city design."

City Design: An Unfinished Profession

Lynch's dynamic city would require a special kind of art to shape it. What was this art to be, and what kind of professional would carry it out? Lynch's vision for what he ultimately called "city design" cohered over the course of his professional career, taking initial shape as early as a 1968 essay "City Design and City Appearance," and made into a comprehensive vision in the later "City Design: What It Is and How It Might Be Taught" (1980). Yet he continued to express continued uncertainty in the validity and extensibility of his own concept: his final essay on city design labeled it an "Immature Art," providing a clear sense of issues yet to resolve and questions yet to answer.

Lynch's thoughts on city design centered around three issues: subject, action, and training. Subject treated the *object* of city design: what part of the city, what kind of experience, and what aspect of city form should city design seek to affect? Lynch especially sought to distinguish city design from what he called "project design," or the act of generating static, three-dimensional arrangements for "defined geographic areas."[77] Project design was effectively the subject of conventional urban design, which Lynch saw as being closely related to architecture. Action, on the other hand, treated the *way* in which a city designer carried out an act of city design. Here again he moved beyond the typically architectural modes of enacting project design such as schematic designs, renderings, and ultimately construction drawings. City design's actions were instead much broader, ranging from detailed building controls to less direct means such as design review and public participation. And the environmental and infrastructural content of city design allied Lynch's art with environmental science and engineering as well. Given city design's aesthetic focus but broad subjects and actions, Lynch also pondered how existing training for architects, planners, and urban designers was appropriate, or not, for generating professionals with the skill set, interest, and ability to enact the kinds of wide-ranging aesthetic goals of city design. A city designer should not simply be an architect interested in the city, as Sert's urban design program proposed; yet planning education was not closely linked to the built environment either. Spanning this divide presented a dilemma for Lynch.

Lynch was cautious about limiting city design's subject to those elements of the cityscape (i.e., "boulevards, parks, civic centers, cultural institutions, waterfronts, and garden cities")[78] that had traditionally been the province of the architect-as-urban-designer. No doubt he was leery of having city design merely replicate or replace the City Beautiful or modernist plans that often included elements such as boulevards and parks within their unitary schemes. Lynch thought that the design of these facilities was the province of "project design," and that attention to project design alone neglected other areas of the city, particularly bland or low-income areas. *The Image of the City* had identified the lack of design in such areas as contributing to a sense of confusion or indistinctiveness, as in Jersey City.[79] Yet excising project design elements from city design would also mean excising many of the buildings or city spaces where city governments traditionally sought to apply design attention, and Lynch himself acknowledged that the "direct design" of these kinds of city elements was the most productive way for designers to strongly and clearly shape city form.[80] And city design concerning itself with enhancing the "legibility" and "meaning" of less visible city areas would by necessity weaken the focus and intensity of design efforts, a paradox that Lynch addressed only lightly in his 1968 essay.

By 1980, influenced by the bureaucratic adoption of city image studies by planning departments across the United States,[81] Lynch saw city design as taking the form of a benevolent management of the built environment, with the abiding goal of enhancing that environment in a manner that meshed with the principles (of access, fit, vitality, etc.) found in his 1981 book *Good City Form*. In his 1980 essay "City Design," he described the city designer as a "manager, user, or developer"—distinctly not the architect that he saw as the subject of most urban design programs. The entire essay is suffused with a sense of benevolence, generosity, and public-spiritedness that conveys many of the values of urban planning, and urban planners. But the "City Design" essay is also replete with an ambiguity, even confusion, about the importance of design and by extension creativity. One keeps getting the feeling that Lynch wished to have his cake and eat it too; to generate a profession that would never offend and never violate the public trust in the manner of the now-departed modernists, but that would also remain inspired by the spirit of visual thinking and creative intervention in the built environment. This was not an impossible vision; in fact Lynch's thinking was quite consistent with the restorationist view of urbanism that took firm hold in the 1970s and 1980s. Doubtless many architecture graduates sympathetic with these ideas filled Lynch's courses throughout this time.

But this emphasis on values and modes of action said little about the kinds of ideas or formal direction that city designers should actually take. An attractive sidewalk or contextual zoning ordinance may be appropriate in certain circumstances, but such small-scale and restoration-based actions cannot shape new cities or direct the growth of existing ones. To the end of his life, Lynch remained befuddled regarding the formal directions that such city designers should take. In his final city design essay,[82] he presented six "possibilities" that might animate city designers. The first two, "perceived structure" and "journeys," reiterated findings from Lynch's first two books, *The Image of the City* and *The View from the Road*.[83] These were both valuable works, but both had limitations for shaping new areas, since city image essentially described problems in

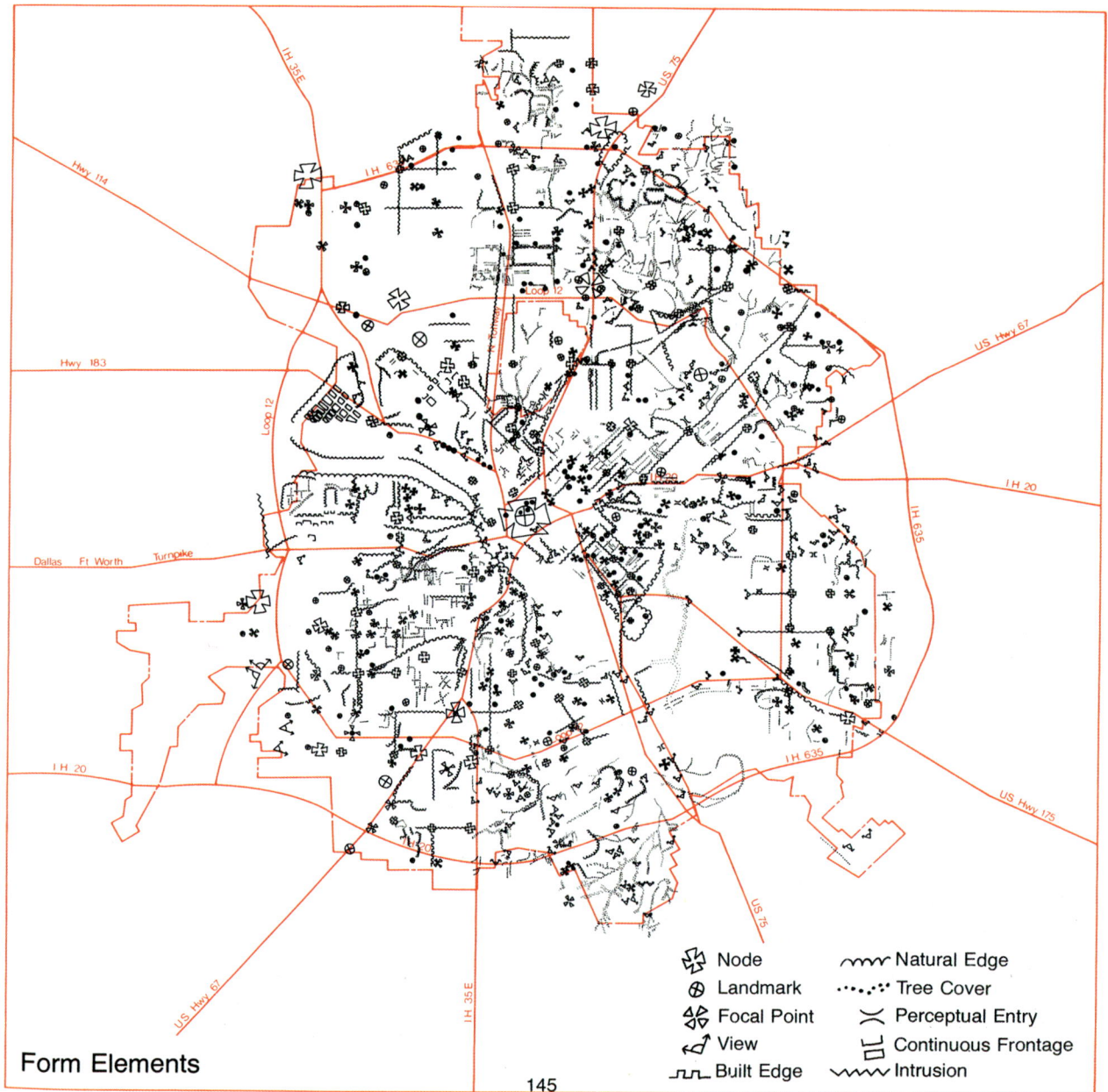

Form Elements

Legend:

- ⊛ Node
- ⊕ Landmark
- ⊛ Focal Point
- ↙ View
- ᴧᴧ Built Edge
- ∿ Natural Edge
- ⋯∴ Tree Cover
- ⋊ Perceptual Entry
- ▭ Continuous Frontage
- ∿∿ Intrusion

145

4.23 Application of Lynch's city image concepts, as here in a study ca. 1973 of Dallas, reveal the complexity and confusion that results from applications of city image at large scale. The use of Lynch's ideas by public agencies waned after the early 1980s.

existing structure, not the direction of new ones, while journeys were far too single-variable a mode of shaping urban space.

Lynch repeatedly attempted to utilize his city image ideas in his professional work, but with only limited success. City-image-based urban design, sampling citizen perceptions of the quality and success of existing environments, could clearly identify underperforming areas of the city, such as a roadway connection that seemed like it should exist but did not. An urban designer following city image findings could therefore be corrective, a direction that Lynch pursued in his 1965 study for the town of Brookline.[84] This town was an essentially complete environment in need of some patching and fixing, and Lynch's methodology was ideal for noting the fuzzy areas of the built environment. But the city image method, as Lynch himself noted in another late essay, seemed only "to have some characteristic that adapt[ed] it for research, not for policy."[85] At the end of his career in 1984, it was apparent to Lynch that identifying city image problems could not provide a clear direction for urban designers to project modes of city growth, never mind shape new settlements. Could a city image study direct an urban designer, for example, to permit a new hundred-story residential building, or to envision the transformation of a derelict railway into a linear park?

The limitations of city image as a method for shaping growth were made clear by a 1973 study of Lynch's examining Martha's Vineyard.[86] The island was facing extreme growth pressures, and badly needed a design vision that could accommodate this pressure while retaining the qualities that new island homebuyers were seeking. Lynch's study shows a variety of research findings based on city image as well as journeys, but his ultimate scheme for the island had little to do with either. It was an ecologically based concept that keyed development form to the existing biotopes of moors and pine forests, and it seems to have been based on the ecologically deterministic design ideas of landscape architect Ian McHarg.[87] Whatever the merits of McHarg's ideas, the Vineyard study illustrated the limitations of Lynch's city image and journey methods. Ultimately both were research methods for the built environment more than they were models for projecting new places.

Lynch presented four other possibilities that might shape formal directions for city designers: renewal (restoration), events (festivals, spectacle), systems (details such as bus shelters), and prototypes (generic models).[88] Each of these modes of city design has value, and each comprises a sector of professional work: historic preservation and urban revitalization are both examples of renewal, and one can see nearly any planned activity in an urban space as an example of an event. Systems too are common; Lynch

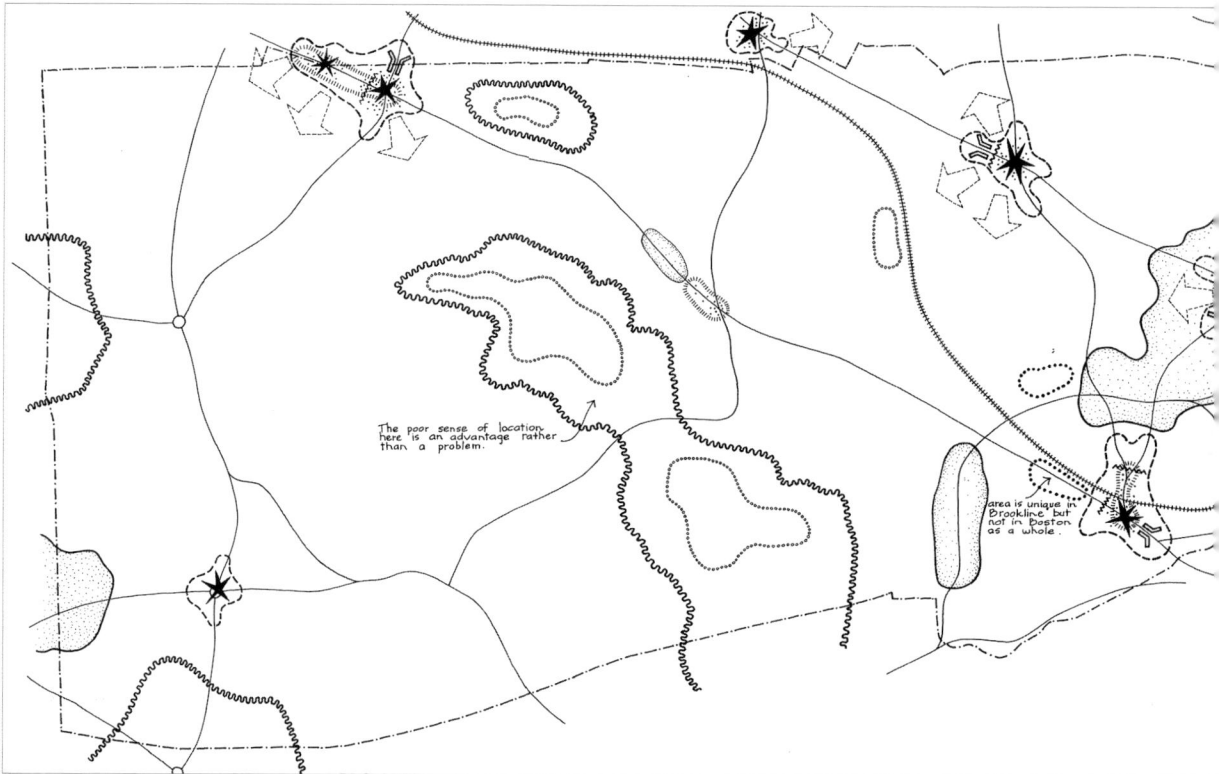

The poor sense of location here is an advantage rather than a problem.

area is unique in Brookline but not in Boston as a whole.

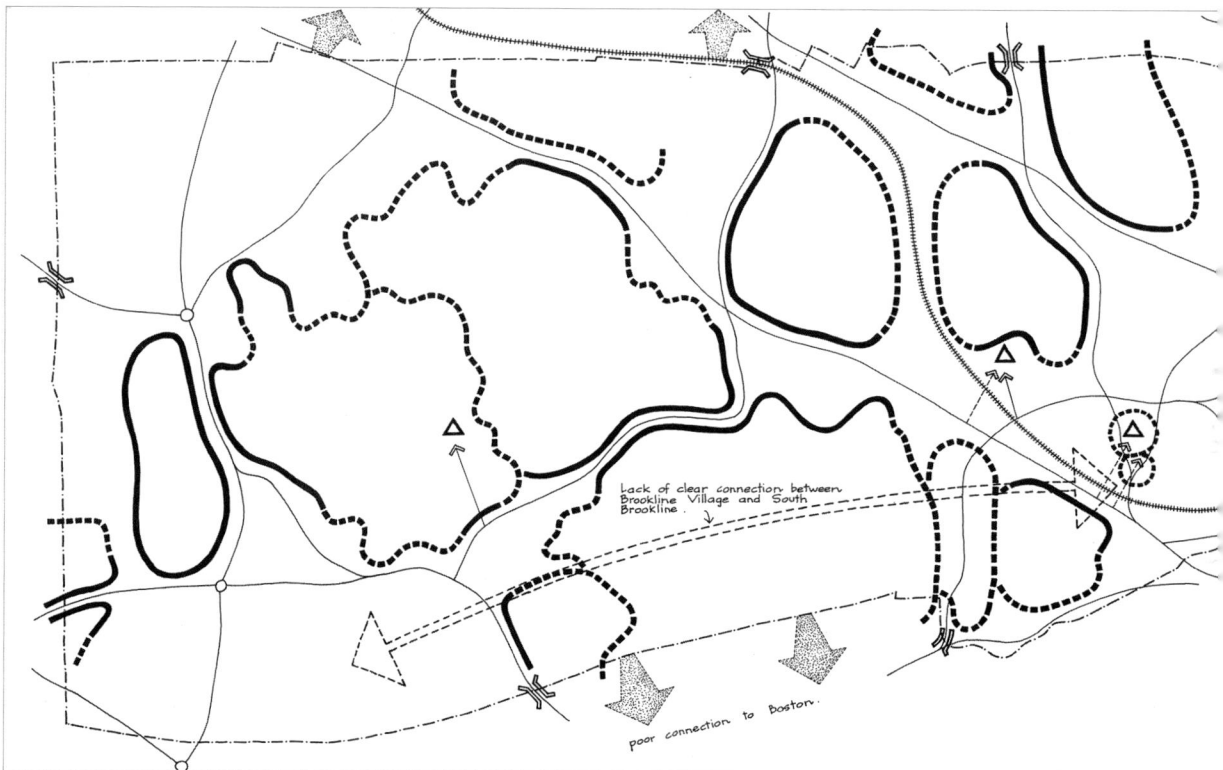

Lack of clear connection between Brookline Village and South Brookline.

poor connection to Boston.

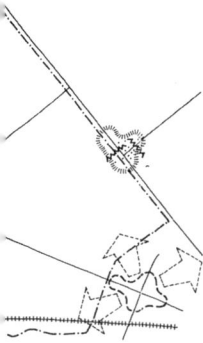

COMMUNITY RENEWAL PROGRAM

Town of Brookline , Massachusetts

CRP | THE PROBLEMS OF EXISTING CENTERS AND DISTRICTS | FIG 6

PERCEPTUAL OVERLOAD

NOISE AND FUMES

AREA LACKS SENSE OF CALM OR HAS MICRO-CLIMATE PROBLEMS

LITTLE CHOICE IN ENVIRONMENT

AREA OR CENTER LACKS IDENTITY

NO SENSE OF LOCATION

INADEQUATE REST AND SHELTER

LACKS WELL FORMED PUBLIC OPEN SPACE

POOR CONNECTION TO SURROUNDINGS

NO CLEAR ENTRY

DIFFICULT PEDESTRIAN MOVEMENT

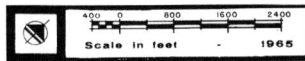

400 0 800 1600 2400

Scale in feet - 1965

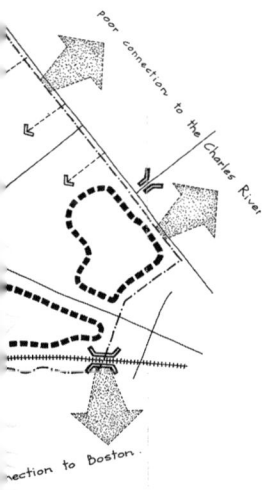

Poor connection to the Charles River

nection to Boston

COMMUNITY RENEWAL PROGRAM

Town of Brookline , Massachusetts

CRP | THE PROBLEMS OF VISUAL CONNECTION | FIG 8

AREA OR CENTER NOT VISIBLE FROM THE MAJOR PATH SYSTEM

AREA PARTLY VISIBLE FROM THE MAJOR PATH SYSTEM

INSTITUTION OR LANDMARK NOT VISIBLE FROM THE MAJOR PATH SYSTEM

EXCEPTIONAL VIEW OF AN OTHERWISE INVISIBLE LANDMARK

LACK OF DIRECT VIEW OR VISUAL EXPOSURE

POOR CONNECTION TO SURROUNDINGS

LACK OF SENSE OF ENTRY OR EXIT

LACK OF CLEAR ENTRY

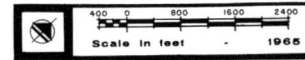

400 0 800 1600 2400

Scale in feet - 1965

4.24 Lynch's own professional work, such as this 1965 analysis of Brookline, Massachusetts, showed both the potential and the limitations of his ideas in professional practice. Lynch's most compelling ideas regarding city form were abstract and open-ended, making them difficult to enact.

	DEVELOPMENT DENSITY, TYPE OF CONTROL	SITING AND FORM OF BUILDINGS	ROAD AND PATH CHARACTER, PARKING	CLEARING AND PLANTING	MATERIALS AND DETAILS	ACTIVITIES
THE SALT LANDS	LOW DENSITY, NO DEVELOPMENT OR VERY LITTLE. RIGID CONTROL.	NONE ON BEACH, DUNE, MARSH, POND, GRASS. ONLY VERY SMALL, LOW CLUSTERS BACK IN THICKETS.	ROADS VERY LIGHT, MOSTLY IN THICKET. FOOT PATHS TO POND AND BEACH. NO PARKING.	LEAVE ALONE. NO EXOTICS.	EARTH, GRASS, WOOD. EARTH COLORS.	MEN ONLY TEMPORARILY PRESENT. NO CARS, ENGINES. ENCOURAGE BIRDS, DOMESTIC ANIMALS, SMALL BOATS. QUIET ACTION, SWIMMING AND OTHER WATER-ORIENTED ACTIVITIES.
THE BLUFFS	POSSIBLY SOME CLUSTERS OF MODERATE DENSITY, LITTLE OR NO DEVELOPMENT ELSEWHERE. RIGID CONTROL.	GROUPS OF HOUSES RELATED TO GROVES OF TREES OR LAND FORMS. LOW OR STEPPED UP SLOPES. NEVER ON CRESTS.	PARKING AND ROADS NOT VISIBLE FROM SHORE. NO ROADS RUNNING UP THE SLOPE.	NO TALL VEGETATION ON CRESTS. MAKE MORE OPEN.	NO PAINT OR METAL. MATERIALS WHICH BLEND OR WEATHER. NO LARGE, LIGHT SURFACES.	BOATS, FISHING. NO CARS. SOME RESIDENCE.
THE MOORS	LOW-MODERATE DENSITY, SOME DEVELOPMENT. CAREFULLY MANAGED.	LOW IN VALLEYS. NONE ON HILLS. CLUSTERED. ROOTED.	TRACKS IN GRASS, NARROW, LOW WITH LAND. HIDDEN PARKING, NEVER ON TOPS.	KEEP OPEN. NO EXOTICS OR TREES. MOW OR GRAZE.	WEATHERED WOOD, STONE. STONE, EARTH FENCES.	RECREATION. GARDENS, PASTURE. DOMESTIC ANIMALS. RESIDENCE.
THE HILLY THICKETS	CLEAR TO MOOR OR: MODERATE DENSITY IN DISTRIBUTED OPENINGS. INVENTIVE CONTROLS.	EDGES OF PRIVATE CLEARINGS. LOW, TALLER IN VALLEYS.	NARROW OR TUNNELS, WINDING. OPPORTUNITY FOR CARVING SEQUENTIAL OPENINGS. DEVELOPMENT SCREENED.	CLEAR ALL OR ONLY VALLEYS. NATURAL PATCHES. "DWARF" LANDSCAPES.	WOOD SHINGLE ROOFS.	PRIMARILY HOUSING. PRIVATE, SCATTERED.

4.25 Influenced by 1970s-era ecological thinking, Lynch used landscape and natural systems as a guide for shaping human settlement, as in this strategy for Martha's Vineyard. While appropriate for low-density areas, this approach also reduced designers' agency in shaping urban form.

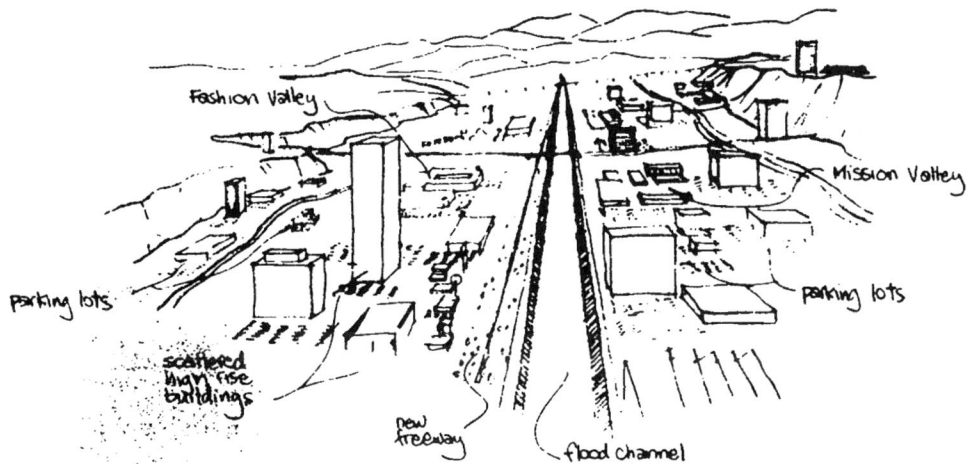

Fashion Valley

Mission Valley

parking lots

parking lots

scattered high rise buildings

new freeway

flood channel

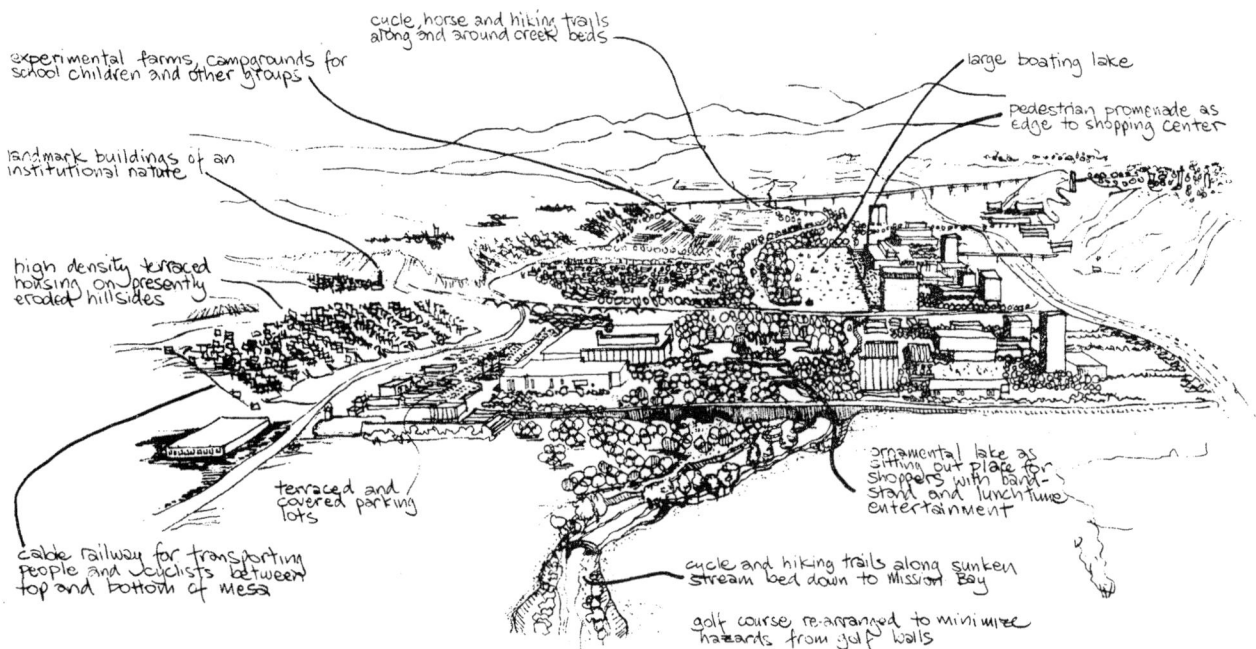

cycle, horse and hiking trails along and around creek beds

large boating lake

experimental farms, campgrounds for school children and other groups

pedestrian promenade as edge to shopping center

landmark buildings of an institutional nature

high density terraced housing on presently eroded hillsides

ornamental lake as sitting out place for shoppers with band-stand and lunchtime entertainment

terraced and covered parking lots

cable railway for transporting people and cyclists between top and bottom of mesa

cycle and hiking trails along sunken stream bed down to Mission Bay

golf course re-arranged to minimize hazards from golf balls

4.26 While Lynch's proposals were often difficult to realize, his writings and theories show that he grasped many of plural urbanism's essential qualities. These images from his 1974 proposal for rapidly growing San Diego show one possible negative future for Mission Valley north of the city (top) and the valley's positive potential (bottom).

noted that these elements require near-constant replacement, and that they might be visually or functionally coordinated to great effect. Prototypes might also prove valuable if widely taken up by different actors; Lynch was clearly thinking of the same engaged homeowners or citizen-activists for whom Christopher Alexander intended his *Pattern Language*, and perhaps he was thinking of the Pattern Language itself.[89]

But at the conclusion of Lynch's essay, one senses that city design is a more "uncertain art" than ever. The six possibilities are highly different in nature, and one has difficulty imagining how two models (for instance city image and systems) might be coordinated, much less three or more. Some of the possibilities are abstract or indirect, while others are restorationist or simply small-scale. The whole seems a collection of only loosely related approaches to improving city spaces rather than a comprehensive ideology. The whole approach, in fact, seems characterized by modesty and indirectness, even a reluctance to take bold steps or to shape great things; an ideology so diffuse and discerning, in other words, that in the end it does not comprise an ideology at all.

And that is the paradox of Kevin Lynch, an astute thinker who grasped the plural nature of the city, and who clearly saw the potential for urban design to interact with that plural city, but who was ultimately unable to formulate an ideology to supplant or replace the project design paradigm of which he was so skeptical. In many respects, Lynch was correct; the city was a physical space quite different from that of the unitary site or "project," and to shape this space aesthetically would require an art very different in both degree and kind than the urban design that had guided urban renewal. But something held Lynch back. Perhaps it was a reluctance to propose substantial change when the social skepticism of change had grown so great. Or perhaps it was the development of robust, revolutionary research methods, such as city image and journeys, that generated impressive tools for the analysis of city space but provided little guidance for transforming it. Or perhaps it was his own instinct, a temperamental reluctance to generate a grand pronouncement or manifesto that might be mistaken for yet another modernist diatribe. But the city design substitute that Lynch devised suffered from the very breadth of scope that Lynch found so essential. Ultimately, nearly any physical improvement to the city qualifies as city design, whether it is a responsible real estate development, a contextual rezoning, or a guerrilla garden created under the cloak of night. But an assemblage of benevolent urban actions does not an urban design make. Just as Frank Lloyd Wright's architectural assemblage in Oak Park fails to cohere into more than the sum of its parts, so too does Lynch's city design.

Lynch occupies the culminating section of this chapter because of the depth and profundity of his thinking on urbanism. Crane and Bacon both recognized that urban design must transcend the unitary site, and both sought to design cities in a way that recognized their plural nature. But their thinking was necessarily constrained by their focus on practice. Lynch had greater freedom to think and write, and he took full advantage of this privilege. Lynch was generous and open-minded. From his perspective within an academic planning department, he was appropriately cautious of the mistakes that he saw occurring through overambitious urban projects. His ideal city was the antithesis of brutal urban renewal; Lynch's imagined citizens, whatever their views and preferences, possessed a physical and social consensus that permitted an ever-flexible, ever-evolving city shaped by a single aesthetic purpose.

But the real world was and remains far messier than Lynch's place utopia, and the decades since Lynch's death have shown that his concept of city design is too diffuse to resist or direct forces such as the conservative market instincts driving neotraditional design, or the ever larger and more complex cities of the world outside the Anglo-American sphere. The gentle environmental management that Lynch advocated, and as he himself observed, has operated in favor of wealthy areas with abundant political and social capital,[90] while disempowered, undesigned areas remain as undesigned as ever. Lynch is not to blame for the continuance of trends that were well under way when he was alive, yet we cannot look to his work to find an easy solution to the design of plural space. Ultimately, Lynch's thought and work provide support, sympathy, and information to plural urbanists, but the completing creative spark must come from designers themselves, as we will see in the next chapter.

Designing Pluralist Urbanism

Kevin Lynch's place utopia was an imaginary arena that embodied the ideals, consequences, and variables of his *Good City Form*. While his place utopia could never fully exist, Lynch recognized that articulating its dimensions through extensive description of that place was important to "further illustrate the theory" and "performance dimensions" of *Good City Form* by illustrating "how concrete proposals may arise from very general statements."[1] Lynch, in other words, felt the need to make his abstract, performance-dimension ideals real through describing a scenario for a built environment, however imaginary that place might be.

Resolving general statements or conceptual ideas into concrete, defined proposals is the task of every designer. In that spirit this chapter absorbs and expands the dimensions, projects, and designers of the previous three chapters by describing the design of three imaginary places, each embodying different qualities of pluralist urbanism. While this chapter's three pluralist places are not real, one may identify elements of real cities within each, just as Lynch's place utopia reflected aspects of many places. Here, each pluralist place embodies an urban condition typical of many cities and regions around the world: the first, a low-density, decentralized suburbia; the second, an urban grid in a post-Socialist state; and third, a rapidly growing city in an equally rapidly developing nation.

These three design stories illustrate how plural urbanism might radically improve the aesthetic appearance of different urban conditions. Each of these plural places is imperfect, and like most places, each is in need of urban design; they certainly could never be labeled utopian. Plural urbanism cannot promise to perfect these places; in each place the intervention of design is gradual, even piecemeal. The urban design of these places is incomplete and imperfect at the beginning of each story, and it remains incomplete and imperfect, though improved, at the end of each. This imperfection and incompleteness, which might frustrate an urban designer seeking to impose a unitary scheme, is part and parcel of plural urbanism.

The illustrations of this chapter communicate in graphic form the qualities of plural urbanism explained in the text. These drawings were conceived but not executed by the author, just as actors other than the individual or individuals who originally conceived of those ideas realize many urban design ideas. The drawings have a particular graphic quality; they are meant to convey the sense of each of the three plural design strategies, not a final outcome. They communicate plural urbanism's particular quality of imprecision by depicting formal concepts that might shift in scale or number of elements without losing their integrity. Like this chapter's stories of three plural places, the drawings are defined yet open-ended, conveying plural urbanism's infinite potential for design creativity. In short, this chapter's stories are meant to communicate plural urbanism's potential to reshape a better design for any space inhabited and constructed by human beings. From these three stories could come many more; this chapter's pluralist places are just a beginning.

Island: Green Avenues to the Sea

This place is shaped by nature, not by man, or only secondarily so. Eons ago the area was volcanic: the resulting stone was soft and glaciers carved it away, leaving the land on either side and fragments of surviving rock, islands in the stream of ice. As the ice melted, the sea returned; what were islands in ice became islands in the sea, teardrops of land within a deep-set waterway cutting into the continent. The resulting archipelago was favored by the land's original inhabitants and then by its European colonizers; here was the natives' last redoubt and here, too, one of the first colonies, today a seemingly ancient city in a still-young nation. The islands were convenient by ship, but inconvenient by every other means; settled early, they flourished in the era of steam, becoming a tourist mecca for the great cities north and south along the coast. But the islands' geography was hostile to rail and to automobile. Only one railroad arrived: little used, it was abandoned early. Not until midcentury was the great bridge constructed that finally allowed mainland traffic to flow onto the largest island. The floods of day-trippers found a place that, if not preserved in time, was certainly different from the rapidly suburbanizing cities whence they came.

The largest island in the bay is a high place, shaped almost like a whale breaching the sea; when it was mostly farmland, the long roads that traversed the landscape provided vistas down the slopes to the ocean, occasionally giving views to both sides. Despite the island's size, the presence of the sea is strong; fishing and boat building were long the mainstay of its economy, and tourists today come for the beaches, to see old houses, or simply to feel like they are in a different place where nature and humans have a more intimate relationship than they do elsewhere. But this mostly rural place was ill prepared to confront the rush of cars that came with the great bridge. For fifty years suburbs have been appearing in its landscape; traffic on its roads has grown heavier and heavier, houses have appeared on former farmland, and commercial sprawl has slowly spread. As in many places, the tourists and residents who have come to enjoy this unique landscape have also spurred the development that is slowly degrading it. At the same time, residents and tourists perceive the island's different character. For the most part they share the perception that the place is special and should stay that way. They are also cognizant that modern development trends, necessary as they are, are reducing this character and have little to do with what they feel the island really is.

The island is beautiful by nature, but its human institutions are ill equipped to confront its contemporary problems. The place certainly is geographically cohesive, and the boundary for any potential regional design is equally strong: the limits of concern are the island, all of it, and nowhere else. But the island is politically divided into three municipalities, each firmly grounded in history but with very different environmental and political characters. The early colony, now a small city, is the locus of tourist traffic and settlement; every officially sanctioned historic district and nearly every historic building may be found there, as well as almost all commerce. At the other end of the island, another municipality was almost entirely rural until very recently; even today, it houses only a few stores, and farming is still strong there. The middle town has the best and worst of it; stunning views and beaches, but much traffic and much sprawl. These three municipalities, so different from each other, share a geographical space and also the need for their home, this island, to be shaped in common. Following an especially active cycle in the real estate market and new cries of overdevelopment, the three municipalities—spurred by a nonprofit, open space preservation organization—decide to appoint an islandwide regional design committee to shape a strategy for the island's future.

The committee's membership spans the range of constituencies concerned with the island's future. Each municipality is represented, together with representatives of the state's environmental, housing, and transportation departments, the island's open space and heritage nonprofits, a few concerned citizens, and an urban design firm hired from outside the state. The risk of design by committee is avoided from the outset: the committee's recommendations will be strictly advisory, and final recommendations will come from the design firm. Even in this democratic, actively participatory context, the committee recognizes that action is more important than discussion.

The committee has some cause for concern. Precedents from other coastal areas that have attempted to control development and better shape the form of their future are rare. In many places the most politically palatable option has been to slow down or stop all development: to declare urban areas historic districts, to rezone open spaces for very low-density residential use, and to require that developers set aside open space, in the hope of diffusing suburban sprawl and preserving vistas of agricultural land. But these strategies have not worked out as planned; the low-density houses quickly consume developable land, leading to rapid escalations in land prices and even more development than before. Economic diversity has declined and intense gentrification has resulted, making the areas too expensive to live in for most citizens. Real estate prices in some of these coastal areas are now the highest in their respective states. And much of the land preserved by developers has been relatively low in quality, far from scenic areas, and fragmented. The public's use of this land preserved by developers is limited, and its visual quality is often poor. Overall, development pressures have overwhelmed unprepared coastal areas and short-circuited or overridden strategies to alleviate growth pressure. Yet the alternative strategy, to simply purchase all remaining land for open space to be preserved at public expense, is not an option: only the national government could achieve that, and both political will and local acceptance for such heavy-handed strategies are absent. But the price of inaction is high: most agree that this island becomes both less interesting and more crowded with each passing year. An alternative future must be possible.

The island's first problem is political. How are three different municipalities to agree on a collectively built future for the island when the tradition of individualism is so strong in this place? This may not be impossible: there is already an islandwide open space nonprofit, as well as a heritage organization. The open space organization has a partial trail network in place and conservation easements on a few properties, while the heritage organization owns many of the designated historic homes in the city, including

5.1 The island today. Undesigned growth erodes views of the sea and conceals the landscape behind settlement.

5.2 Absent designer intervention, the island's unique views, terrain, and settlement will be drowned in a generic sea of shops and houses.

some on spectacular coastal sites. The state also governs the provision of some collective goods, including requirements for construction of social housing. And islanders already seem agreed on the qualities of the place that they like the most: quiet places, trails for walking and hiking, ocean access, broad beaches, a sense of a place distinct from both the city and the suburb. These are islandwide qualities.

But residents are not the only constituency here: the island's summer population is much larger than its year-round one. On busy summer days tourists outnumber permanent residents three to one. It is harder to get a sense of what these more diffuse constituencies want, and year-round islanders are disinclined to consider the opinions of these other so-called communities. The committee decides early on that political realities cannot be ignored; any islandwide design or development concept will have to be ratified and enacted at the individual municipal level. All recognize that this pragmatic reality clashes with the poetic reality of the island as a unified historic, geographical, and cultural space; the collective conclusion is that all are islanders, but that they are islanders separately. This seems paradoxical, but committee members are also confident that this bicameral structure, where a unified spatial vision is applied at intervals, represents any islandwide design concept's best chance at actually being enacted.

The designers conduct an initial survey of the public—residents, tourists, workers—about their feelings for the place. They are careful to sample different publics in different places, and they find that many tourists and workers never visit the island's more rural areas; indeed they often do not know that these places exist, nor do the activities and scenery there hold interest for them. Those most knowledgeable about these hidden spaces tend to be longer-term residents, but these residents have their own myopias, for they often neglect to visit the city, and these residents have comparatively little knowledge or appreciation of those parts of the island that are, paradoxically, most well-known. The result of this divided public is a divided sense of the place: visitors love the city, and residents love the quiet, hidden areas of the place. But there are also areas of the island that both of these publics appreciate. Everyone is eager to glimpse the sea, and everyone appreciates opportunities to access the water, whether to simply see it from afar, walk along its shores, or actually touch and swim in the water along the island's abundant public beaches. The urban designers realize the paradox of this place: land, the space actually shared by the public, is perceived as divided, but water is something that the public all sees themselves as sharing.

The island's relationship to water is multifaceted, complex, and problematic. On the one hand, water is omnipresent; one confronts it on a daily basis either to enter or leave the island, and most of the island's built environment, with the exception of some suburban sprawl, has been shaped by water. The designers estimate that roughly 90 percent of the island's residential population sees the ocean on a daily basis. Yet this experience is episodic. One may only see the water at high speed from a bridge or as a brief vista from a major island road. Within the city, development crowds out much of the water views that one might expect. Paths and public beaches along the water are confined mostly to the island's south end, while access to water on the island's northern two-thirds is often secretive or difficult. All of the residents know a beach where they can go and find almost no one else, but these beaches are often far from their houses and, conversely, most residents are unable to access the water nearest to their house even when it is close by. The designers also observe that the island's agricultural space and its water are closely related, at least visually. Where there is agriculture, there is often water in some form; the largest farms have open lands that permit the water vistas that islanders find so satisfying. In some areas, roads through farm fields lead down to the waterside; vistas of water are complemented by access to it. Yet this water access is vanishing as open space disappears, and the public perception of its existence fades. Tourists traveling at the island's northern end are often unaware that there is any access to the sea there at all.

In the formulation of their design strategy for the island, the designers are inspired by the work of Kevin Lynch, particularly his concept of city image and his lesser-known ideals of city form. Understanding the image of such a relatively large and fractured place is important; this is also an important means of assessing public opinions about their perception of the built environment. The designers carry out an image study with members of a willing public drawn from a sample of the island's multiple constituencies: open space advocates, downtown tourists, members of a private library, and shopping mall employees. The findings are interesting; some are exactly what one might expect, such as the city being the best-known place, and the positive perceptions of the island's large public beaches and grand mansions. The image study also confirms the designers' suspicions regarding the water: it is less visible, accessible, and present than islanders might wish.

The designers also look to Lynch's "polycentered net,"[2] an ideal built environment concept that found its way into his final work on good city form. Lynch depicted a landscape composed of both city and countryside, where dense city land was interspersed with open space, where nature was accessible to the city and vice versa. Lynch's polycentered net was in a perpetual state of growth and change. The polycentered net was not a final built environment; growth and change were ongoing, and areas might decline and be abandoned, or areas that were empty might be later developed. Lynch made no recommendations about how the polycentered net might be achieved, but he clearly felt that such an urban structure meshed the best features of urbanization with the best aspects of wild lands, and that such an urban pattern would satisfy a wide range of constituencies. The net was an ideal pattern for a highly plural place, with a plural population.

The designers are provided additional inspiration by the concepts of both David Crane and Edmund Bacon. The island has a strong infrastructure composed not of town centers but of roads. The roadway experience is a principal means of both accessing and experiencing the island, especially its northern end. Crane's "capital web,"[3] where infrastructure is an armature for a dependent, loosely shaped settlement pattern, has many analogies to the relationship between the island's road structure and its subdivisions. What the island lacks is a hierarchy of settlement: current development is almost all low-density, and the experience of this roadway infrastructure is uninteresting, unpredictable, and increasingly homogeneous. The designers also note Bacon's concept of the "movement system," where urban design operates at intervals via carefully designed, relatively small-scale projects, and where axes of open space link these designed areas almost in the manner of beads on a string.[4] The designers would like to introduce axes of space into the island, particularly those that might connect busy places with open water or open land. But to do this, some agent or agency will need tight control, perhaps ownership, over certain parcels of land, just as Bacon had in urban-renewal-era Philadelphia. Yet property condemnation is neither a fiscal nor political reality on this island; land will have to be acquired via other means.

The designers also look at another, widely promoted means of guiding development decisions in relatively natural landscapes. This method depends on cumulative mapping of natural features to determine those areas that are least ecologically sensitive or valuable. The intention is to center settlement according to nature, to preserve sensitive areas such as wetlands and wildlife habitats. The method is not oriented toward human use of the land; commonly shared pleasures of vistas, scenery, or the simple experience of open space play little role and are not incorporated in this method. Nor does the method treat areas that are already developed; these are off limits, already subtracted from the equation, so to speak. Although this ecological method is held up as a means of living sensitively, even sustainably, within a natural landscape, the urban designers find it has little utility on this island. The island has very little ecologically sensitive land per se; the most sensitive places, such as wetlands and shorelines, are already protected by state environmental laws. Nor is the island a particularly unique place ecologically; there are no endangered species here, at least none that are any more endangered than on the mainland, half a mile away. But the island is visually and scenically unique, and the designers resolve that their design strategy will incorporate the visual aspect of nature even if their design does not pretend to be dependent on nature's ecological qualities.

Before forming a detailed strategy for the island, the designers first propose three framing parameters for design to the larger committee. First, they propose that the islandwide design process must be more than just an agreement to meet again, or to let things remain the way they are. The committee must agree that the design generate a particular and unique form for development on the island that both reflects its special qualities and is different from what was there before. The island's design, in other words, must shape something recognizably new. The designers also propose that any islandwide design cannot concern itself with architectural particulars: there will be no design review committee arguing over paint colors or square footage, nor can the architecture of individual buildings be part of an islandwide spatial design. Lastly, the designers propose to the committee that their islandwide design strategy should shape both open space and developed space. This spatial design will not be a conventional conservation plan protecting land from development while ignoring the form of creeping subdivisions, nor will it be a conventional urban design plan overly concerning itself with the form of buildings while ignoring the larger spatial organization of the island. On this island, the designers declare, both built space and open space matter: How could it be any other way, when both residents and tourists agree that the historic city and the wild views of the ocean are equally valuable?

Reflection takes time, but ultimately the designers propose a single, overarching spatial concept for the island that they call "green avenues to the sea." The idea of green avenues to the sea captures several existing positive qualities of the island and also sets a strong agenda for future development. Avenues or roads are already a strong feature of the island; one of the city's principal streets leads past the island's largest houses to end at the sea. This avenue is an attractive place that is also the best-known street on the island. The island also possesses many roads leading to and then over the sea on one or another of the island's bridges. The term "green avenues" suggests a second infrastructure, a doubling of road with field or path, and thus a mesh of passages of east-west natural space with north-south roads throughout the island. This mesh of green avenues and automobile roads will possess a clear relationship to the water, giving both a perceptual and physical link to the island's most widespread but underutilized asset. The presence of multiple green avenues also implies a rhythm of green avenue and settled area, perhaps even a large-scale grid, generating predictability to the island's form that is currently absent. The green avenues imply that the remainder of space on the island will be occupied by development, and that this development might consciously face the green avenues in the manner that city buildings front streets. Where the island's open space is currently ignored by development, perhaps because it is never certain when such space will or will not be preserved, the green avenue concept promises that openness can become a permanent feature of the island, creating a rhythm of settlement and space, with intervals of housing or shops interrupted by bands of green and vistas to the sea.

The green avenue concept contains elements of concepts from plural urbanists Crane, Bacon, and Lynch. Crane proposed infrastructural systems that shape a place at large scale and that determine the location of subsequent development. The island's green avenues will be this new islandwide infrastructure, forming a loose grid or branching structure of open land, with development eventually bordering this space. In Philadelphia, Bacon proposed and constructed a network of spatial axes that linked closely designed areas of cityscape, both architectural and landscape.[5] The island already possesses such designed areas in the form of preserved open spaces managed by the land conservancy; these can act as reservoirs from which avenues of open space may lead to the sea or connect to other such reservoirs. From Lynch's polycentered net, the designers derive the idea of polycentricity, of the island as a place with green and built space, where development and fields interlock or overlap. The island that the designers seek to create is one much like Lynch's place utopia: not a very dense place overall, but a place where people can find the kind of environment that they are looking for.

To realize the green avenues to the sea, the land that will comprise the avenues must be designated and acquired. But neither the number nor the location of the green avenues is specified; the islandwide design does not require a master plan whereby a single, highly detailed static future is projected. Instead the designers argue that the island should have up to ten green avenues, but that only three to five need exist in order for the design concept to be readable on the ground. This lack of specificity is not intended to reduce the three towns' responsibility for realizing the design, but to provide flexibility and imply that there is no right or wrong number of green avenues needed for the concept to be effective. There are many places on the island where a green avenue might exist, but not all of these locations need be acquired. Some future green avenues are located where land is already held by the open space organization; others may be active farms, or patches of woods that

5.3 The first green avenues to the sea will ensure visual and physical access to water and enhance amenities of development along their edges.

5.4 In the future, additional green avenues will provide a rhythm of views and paths to the sea along principal roads.

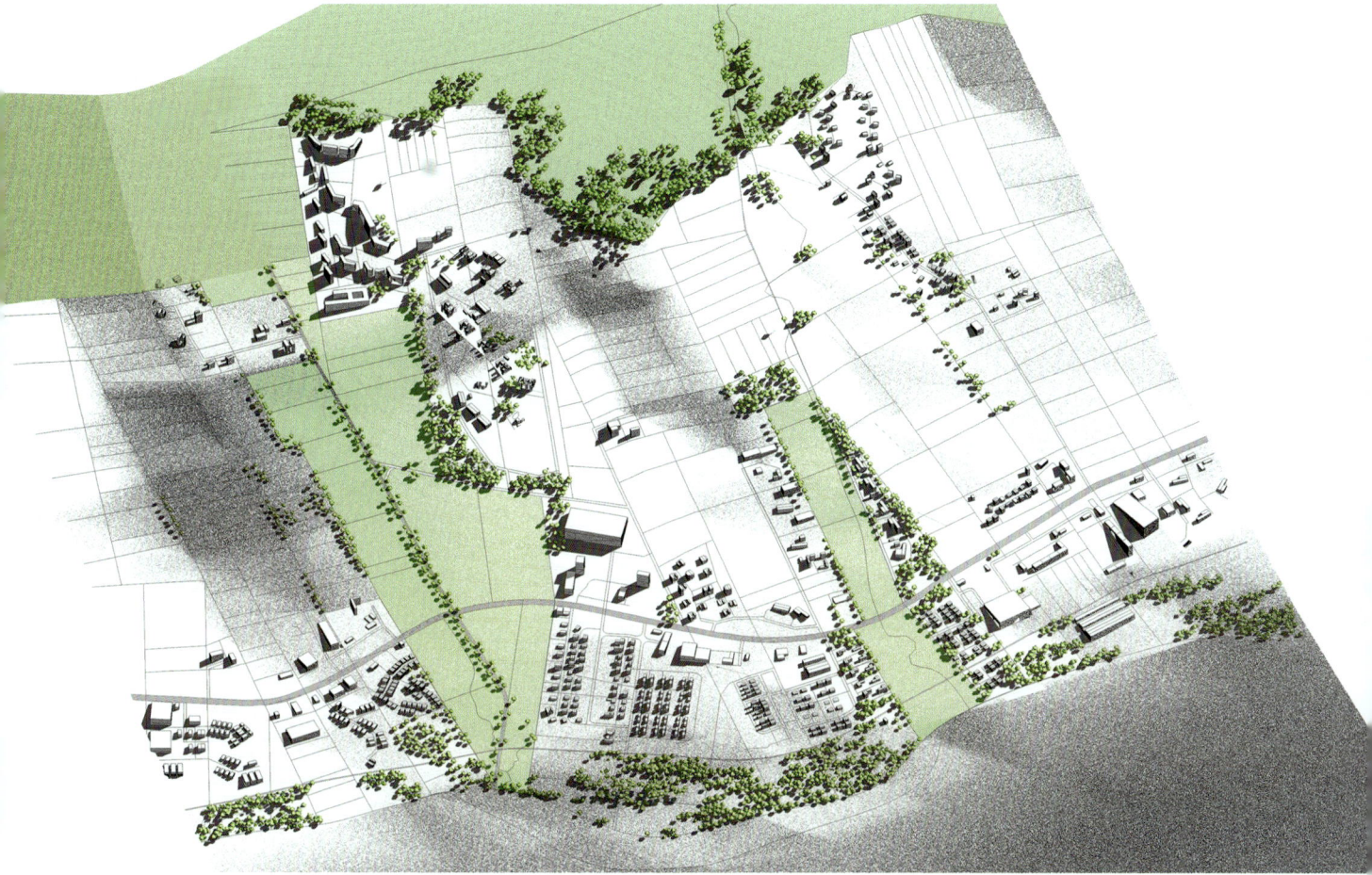

◄ **5.5**   The island's plural urbanism will frame intermittent-quality development with vistas, paths, and promenades linked to water.

▲ **5.6**   Inland reservoirs of open space, preserved farms, and forests organized as green avenues flow down to the sea, shaping islanders' senses of their home's unique geography.

are currently for sale and available for development. So long as green avenues are distributed north-south along the island, a driver will regularly experience them, and they will be reasonably accessible to all island residents. The avenues may be visual instead of experiential; in parts of the island where the sea is visible from a hilltop, an avenue need not extend fully to the sea. In other, flatter areas, a continuous band of green will provide water access. In many places, existing roads will adjoin open areas; in others, pedestrian paths might be constructed to allow water access from a green avenue.

Constructing this plural urbanism will not be simple. Land must be acquired or marked for conservation by either town government or the islandwide open space organization; to enhance vistas, vegetation in some cases must be cut back, removing trees from the road and providing visual access to fields and the sea. Areas where development can occur may be reregulated to permit greater densities or changed site designs, in the hope that developers will respond by constructing housing or commerce that faces open space rather than turning away from it. Islanders must also confront the reality that the green avenue concept will be constructed at intervals; it will never be completed, and some parts may never be realized.

But even if only pieces of the design are built, the designers' intentions will start to become clear: this island is different from the mainland. It is a place where not every road is for commerce and not every field is destined to become a subdivision. Nor is the entire island a nature preserve where only the wealthy may choose to live. On this island, views and access to the water will define the character of the place: if one can see the water, then one can be sure of access to it. The future built environment of the island may not be distinctive; developers are conservative after all, and there is little chance that automobile dependence will wane in future decades. Ultimately the designers, and the committee that ratifies their strategy as a path to the island's future, hope that this place can be at least partially reimagined and physically restructured, even if incompletely; that the island will be filled with active and quiet areas, a place where both residents and tourists can enjoy both settled and open places, and where enveloping ocean vistas, wind, and waves are open to all, for all time.

Grid: Adding Multiscalar Islands

Speculators shaped this place in the long-ago past, pioneers who ventured into an unsettled landscape and hacked a city out of hostile forest and plains. Their work was successful; today the city is the center of its region. Much has transpired since the city's founding; political regimes have come and gone, the country and city have been both rich and poor, but the city has always grown and for much of this time it retained its grid, a relatively simple plan of slightly rectangular blocks, as the framework for its growth. Ultimately the grid was abandoned, at least as a model for the future; the city's periphery is a mix of small-scale housing and larger-scale apartment blocks structured around superblocks, the result of stronger state intervention during the twentieth century. Still the grid comprises several square kilometers of the city, including the city's entire center, almost all of its public waterfront, and the entirety of its small office district and tourist area. This is also the most distinctive area of the city, whereas the periphery of small-scale housing and large-scale apartments are generic environments found across the country.

While the grid is extremely regular, its built fabric is extremely heterogeneous. Most of what tourists would regard as beautiful are surviving older buildings built in the nineteenth and early twentieth centuries before a period of national economic and social turmoil. These are often smaller-scale, heavily ornamented structures painted in lovely colors. Even if they are not open to the public, and most are not, these buildings are cheerful reminders of an idealized period in the country's history. Unfortunately, many are dilapidated; the twentieth century was not kind to them, and they are often near collapse. Much of the rest of the grid's fabric is less attractive. There are many mid-twentieth-century housing structures constructed according to minimum standards; these grew more elaborate over time, but they all seem dated today, a reminder of a time when just getting by was the best that most citizens could hope for. And there is an abundance of more recent construction, the result of the building boom of the past decade and a half. The architecture of each of these buildings is only as good as the developer who constructed them, so aesthetic standards are mostly low. The city's economy is not growing rapidly; an energy boom in the region has mostly passed the city by, and the large industries that thrived in the twentieth century are declining due to global competition. As a result the urban fabric of the grid is filled with vacant lots and the remains of old buildings that have simply collapsed in the harsh climate or have been demolished for development schemes that did not come to pass.

Democracy has never had much of a foothold in this place, and the current government, while professing participation and free speech, in reality promotes little of either. At the same time the city has many wealthy private landowners; some, profiting from economic turmoil, have purchased many properties at low prices. Other, mostly residential properties have been partially or wholly privatized; and still others are owned by various branches of government ministries, who are often eager to shed ownership of what are perceived as liabilities. The government is not in an acquisitive mode; it does not intend to purchase more properties but rather to sell more, in the hope of balancing its books from many poor real estate decisions in the past. At the same time, the government is extremely powerful when it wants to be, both at the national and local level; the city is geographically distant from the country's economic center, but it has good transport links, and the city government wishes to increase its own national visibility for political purposes. An urban design strategy for the city center seems the perfect device to solve all problems: to increase the city's reputation, attract additional visitors (domestic tourism is growing by leaps and bounds), rein in out-of-control developers, and assure the population—most of which is moderate-income and unsure about its future—that the city is headed in a positive direction.

Commissioning an urban design strategy for the grid is not a problem. The government has substantial leverage over large landowners; it can make things very difficult for them if it wishes simply by changing permitting procedures or by exerting other political pressures. A committee of large landowners quickly agrees to finance an urban design strategy and another committee is formed, in which government ministries form the majority and large landowners the minority. Civic and resident groups have but a single representative on this committee. A prestigious urban design firm from another country is hired to carry out the plan, and the urban designers are provided with an abundant budget.

A greater problem than the strategy's financing is the urban fabric itself. Apart from the regularity of the grid, there is little aesthetic consistency to the urban fabric; the city's heritage of turmoil and its changing approaches to construction have left it a very heterogeneous place. And there are plenty of problems: the general condition of buildings is poor, and the public realm is even worse, with fragmented sidewalks and wide streets that are difficult to cross. There are signs that development is spiraling out of control; a couple of well-placed developers have built extremely tall, characterless structures at important intersections, angering other landowners who were not permitted these liberties. And, in contrast to past eras, the government is not interested in assuming control of additional properties.

The challenge to any coherent urban design approach would seem substantial, but the urban designers see several positive aspects to the city's grid, all of which aid in the formulation of a formal strategy for this pluralist space. First, landownership is less fractured than one might think. In addition to the large private landowners, municipal

5.7 The grid today. Developers are constructing tall buildings in seemingly random locations amid older, low-rise buildings, while open space is sparse and wide roads speed traffic.

housing companies often manage a cluster of buildings collectively. The country has never had a tradition of decentralized private ownership except at the periphery, so parcels are often large as well. Decisions that impact a single landowner can often have a large effect. Second, the country has a tradition of centralized decision making. The government has not always made correct decisions, but there is broad social support for the government to make them, even among powerful private developers. Lastly, the building fabric, though heterogeneous in its details, has mostly conformed to the street line, and it is mostly below eight stories in height simply because there has been little economic demand for taller buildings until quite recently. Much of this fabric, built in the mid-twentieth century or later, is unworthy of preservation; it could be easily replaced for newer, higher quality buildings without much loss of local character.

The designers, afforded substantial liberty in their decision making by the government-dominated committee, frame their design strategy around three premises. First, the regularity of the grid must serve as the springboard for additional regularity in the future urban design of the city. This will not become a Manhattan-like place, where development of whatever stripe and height appears wherever landowners demand it. State control is stronger here, the city more regular, and a clearer design strategy more attainable. The nation's tradition of large-scale decision making can and should be registered in the future form of the city. Second, individual sites within this grid may be very important, but not all of them will be under the control of the government, nor will most of these sites be redeveloped by the public sector. Private developers will construct most future buildings. Third, the designers see that much of the fabric will simply remain the way it is; this is a slow-growth place, and some lots contain old buildings that should be retained, although it is far from clear that there are means to ensure their preservation. Other lots contain tired old buildings that may hold hundreds of moderate-income housing units, even if they are architecturally unworthy. Housing structures cannot be demolished at will, and the designers vow that they should not be demolished at all unless there are very good reasons for doing so.

The urban designers center their strategy around a concept of a multiscalar grid. The street grid provides the principal generative scale, since it already exists, and growth is structured around it. The grid divides the city into blocks, and the urban designers elect to promote the creation, or at least the perception, of additional grids at additional scales both above and below block scale, while operating within the constraints of the existing plural fabric with its various owners and buildings. Within the block, the designers insert new elements into the public realm that they call "islands." These islands occupy public land that is currently divided between streets and sidewalks, both problematic elements in the existing city. The city's streets are wide, and road margins and sidewalks are often wastelands of parked cars, broken pavement, and fragmented plantings. At the same time traffic often speeds down the wide streets. The resulting public realm is an unattractive and little-used place. Badly needed in this impoverished streetscape are places where public amenities can be concentrated: plantings, seating, orderly parking spaces, small playgrounds, and space for the tiny kiosks that have sprung up in the past twenty years.

The designers are particularly inspired by urban design precedents that are small-scale, yet that have provided broad public benefits and are widespread within a city fabric. They find the precedent of Savannah, Georgia, particularly attractive.[6] This city has a unique urban design possessing regular blocks and planted squares that provide a sense of respite within an episodic urban fabric. These squares act as islands of green amid the pluralist fabric of Savannah. Yet these islands also have their disadvantages; they require enough otherwise developable land that later developers stopped constructing them. They also provide substantial obstruction to traffic, and several were removed to permit easier traffic flow. At the same time, Savannah's squares are mostly ornamental; they provide shade, but little other practical amenity besides some seating. Perhaps, the designers think, smaller islands in this larger city's more regular grid can provide many of the same advantages with fewer of the disadvantages. The designers are also inspired by the New York City playground strategy of Robert Moses.[7] Though possessed of great power, Moses was delicate and pragmatic in his construction of playgrounds; he constructed them in marginal spaces around the city, often where there were existing parks or land left over by overly wide roads. Yet Moses was also socially insensitive and constructed his playgrounds to placate wealthy New Yorkers rather than constructing them where they were needed most. Can this city's islands meet the needs of both the powerful and the needy? The designers resolve to try.

The designers recognize that they cannot place one of these islands on every block, nor can they ultimately hope to improve more than a small part of this disparate, dilapidated public realm. In a sense they are renovating the urban fabric by adding to the space outside of it, rather than replacing its constituent buildings or reshaping large areas of public space. By influencing the urban public realm at intervals with the construction of islands, the designers hope to achieve several aims at once. First, they hope to increase the level of amenity for inhabitants of buildings on the blocks, who are more often than not moderate-income and long-term inhabitants.

Second, the designers aim to provide a relatively concentrated area of public amenities that may be easily maintained and secured, in strong contrast to the fractured, poorly maintained, and often absent existing public realm. Who might maintain these islands, and how, are issues that need to be resolved as well. Lastly, the urban designers wish to convey the sense to passers-through that the city's blocks are places for rest and inhabitation as well as for passage. The city suffers from wide roads and aggressive traffic; many places in the city are beyond reclaiming for pedestrian use. But within the grid, the islands will restrict traffic speed to the scale and pace of the block itself.

Through the island concept, the designers wish to emphasize the advantages of a grid system: predictability, orientation, and redundancy, by adding elements that will regularly enhance residents' and passersby's level of amenities. At the same time, the islands, with their different features and distinctive design, will reduce some of the disadvantage of grids: their monotony, overexposure to traffic, and confusing similarity to each other. Islands can be as diverse as the urban fabric within which they exist, with larger playgrounds on residential streets, or more kiosks in commercial areas. The islands effectively break down the city grid into smaller segments, each of which becomes more useful and comfortable. The islands provide a means for different blocks to identify themselves and a common meeting ground for residents of a block, who are too often confined to their own housing complexes. The islands have an additional advantage: the construction of even one provides a level of amenity at the local scale. Islands do not need to be constructed all at once, nor can the island concept ever be conveniently finished; there could be no final number of islands until every single block had one, which is neither possible nor desirable. There is an additional advantage to the islands; they are relatively inexpensive to construct, and they are a readily identifiable improvement. Each island can potentially have a sponsor: a public agency, a large private landowner, or perhaps a prosperous housing association. An archipelago of different islands dotting the city grid will reflect the city's archipelago of large property owners.

How to site islands within the grid? The designers have two goals in mind: first, to place islands where they are most needed, but also to place them where they will be most highly visible. This will demonstrate the success of the strategy and encourage the construction of additional islands. They therefore decide to encourage a limited number of initial islands, around ten, each one sponsored by a large landowner so that once the urban design scheme is published, construction can begin immediately. These islands are sited according to simple rules: each must be either near a large concentration of multifamily dwellings or on a busy street with commercial activity. No islands

5.8 Additional tall buildings located on wide roads mark important corners, while nearby green islands slow or stop traffic and provide needed neighborhood amenities such as playgrounds.

are placed in forgotten or low-activity areas. Each island must additionally be within a block or two of a property owned by its sponsor, so that the benefits of the island can impact the landowner's property as well. This strategy may seem overly pragmatic, but the designers hope that the public relations accruing from the construction of the first islands will make the construction of subsequent ones—perhaps financed by the city government—easier. Ultimately the designers project that the city grid will accommodate up to forty islands.

While the island strategy generates a smaller-scale grid within the city's street network, the designers also hope to generate a larger-scale grid as well. The city's urban fabric is so regular that important streets are relatively imperceptible; they are often lined with buildings of the same height and architectural quality as buildings on smaller streets. Looking at the city's skyline, one cannot discern where important streets are, nor does the homogeneous fabric aid drivers in their navigation of the city. The street grid is heterogeneous at a small scale, with buildings of different types and eras scattered throughout, but also homogeneous at a larger scale. Because a building of a certain type might be located anywhere in the grid, all of it has a monotony that is only exacerbated by its regular street pattern.

At the same time, the more or less random construction of high-rises by developers with political influence is introducing additional confusion into the urban pattern. Already the city has four or five new towers of mediocre design, containing mostly offices, since people with money live not in the city center but at its periphery. The city administration is concerned about the proliferation of high-rises downtown; construction of such buildings was historically the privilege of public agencies, linked to the provision of space for prestigious bureaus or apartments for well-connected people. This regime is gone, and public agencies no longer have the will, the funds, or the need to construct such buildings. In an era when high-rises can be easily built, what rules will shape their construction in a city fabric that is still mostly low-rise and where the visible impact of high-rises matters greatly? Could such rules make the city fabric more comprehensible and easier to navigate?

The designers are inspired by city grids that provide as much clarity of orientation as they do regularity of pattern. They especially note New York City's grid, where rectangular street blocks and streets with differing widths shape an urban pattern of very tall buildings along wide streets, and much lower buildings along narrow streets. This hierarchy is one that the designers hope to generate in their own city, despite its more homogeneous fabric. The designers also find similarities between the placement

5.9 As development continues, additional towers mark additional corners, creating a rhythm of tall buildings along the avenues, while a network of islands connects parks and enhances tranquility.

of ancient obelisks by Pope Sixtus V and their modern parallel in Edmund Bacon's work in Philadelphia, with the "city image" concept suggested by urban design theorist Kevin Lynch.[8] Sixtus V's pattern of obelisks placed around Rome for the orientation of pilgrims attracts the designers for its economical system of wayfinding through iconographic clarity.[9] The religious purposes of this iconography are of course obsolete and inapplicable in a contemporary city, but the idea that similar elements placed in different locations around a city might serve as a marker and guide seems wonderfully relevant to the designers. Lynch of course recognized the importance of such markers where they already existed, labeling them nodes or landmarks, but he never formulated strategies for the placement of additional such elements. But the designers recognize in Lynch's analytical system a means by which additional tall buildings, if strategically placed, might serve as orienting elements in the otherwise homogeneous grid, particularly for automobile drivers whose field of vision and need for orientation is greater.

The designers' strategy for this larger-scale grid is relatively simple. By permitting taller buildings to be constructed on important streets and in enough locations within the grid, the chance is high both that important streets will quickly gain one or more taller buildings, and also that the several large-scale landowners who control much of the city center's commercial frontage will each benefit by constructing a taller building. At the same time, by allowing tall buildings if they are in an appropriate location, the designers remove the current incentive for undue political influence that has led both to power for some landowners and to resentment by others. The logic for tall buildings on important streets is clear; they serve as a visual marker of the importance of those streets, and they generate less shade on neighboring buildings, an important consideration in a cold climate. There are several streets within the grid where such buildings are appropriate; many of these streets are also the location of important public buildings from the previous era of greater government power. The designers are not particular about the height of these tall buildings; as long as they are greater than ten stories and less than twenty they will achieve their purposes of orientation and hierarchy. Nor do the towers need to be constructed all at once. All that is needed is that the government permit towers in certain areas and forbid them in others. The relatively low economic demand for such towers also means that their construction will be limited, unless the economy of the city and region should shift dramatically.

The urban design strategy that is ultimately published is extremely pragmatic. The designers recognize that they have an imperfect city, the result of many past decisions

▶ **5.10** The grid's plural urbanism provides vistas of towers along streets punctuated by islands of open space, giving a formerly homogeneous place a memorable and humane character.

5.11 The grid's character is not rigid or chaotic; it is an ever-evolving archipelago of towers speaking to each other across neighborhoods punctuated by green.

that cannot be undone and whose logic was sometimes flawed. At the same time the new design strategy recognizes the city's grid as a special area; not only is it the home of most of the city's significant architecture, but it is also the center of public attention and certainly the center of the city's public image. As such, this area of the city is worth treating with special care even if the means for changing its design are limited. The designers are confident that their multiscalar grid strategy speaks to as many constituents of the city center as possible. It speaks to uncertain residents, most of whom are unlikely ever to leave; to the oligarchy of wealthy landowners, each insecure of the power of others and each eager to gain power and influence; and to the city government itself, a political regime whose democratic legitimacy may be limited but whose decision-making power is still strong. These government officials' interest in making the city more attractive, if only for venal political purposes, is the strongest motive for urban design and the likeliest guarantee that this pragmatic urban design strategy, intended to please both citizens and developers, will come to pass.

The designers' strategy also acknowledges several qualities of plural urbanism. The grid, as we observed earlier, is a plural site with thousands of individual properties and residents in addition to the greater public that travels, works, and shops there every day. The multiscalar grid strategy introduces plural scales into this plural site by breaking the grid down into smaller components through islands and by reinforcing one's understanding of the grid with the towers at major intersections that create a larger-scale grid on top of the existing grid. Plural time is also registered in this strategy, given its retention of structures dating from as long ago as the nineteenth century all the way up to the present decade. The new strategy also enriches the plural time of the site by adding additional built elements to those from older eras. The multiscalar grid incorporates multiple properties, ranging from the public property of the street and sidewalks to the numerous private properties that will be redeveloped for towers. And the strategy engages the city's plural actors and methods of construction: city government will construct islands, perhaps with private or institutional actors; private owners that are regulated by the public sector will construct towers. Lastly, the new multiscalar grid will be plural in form, constituting an archipelago of scattered interventions, indeterminate in form, number, length of time of construction, and located in an ever-changing pattern around the city grid. In a nation and in a city that once viewed all power and decisions as stemming from a single source, this new urban design strategy registers the city's equally new recognition of its plural nature.

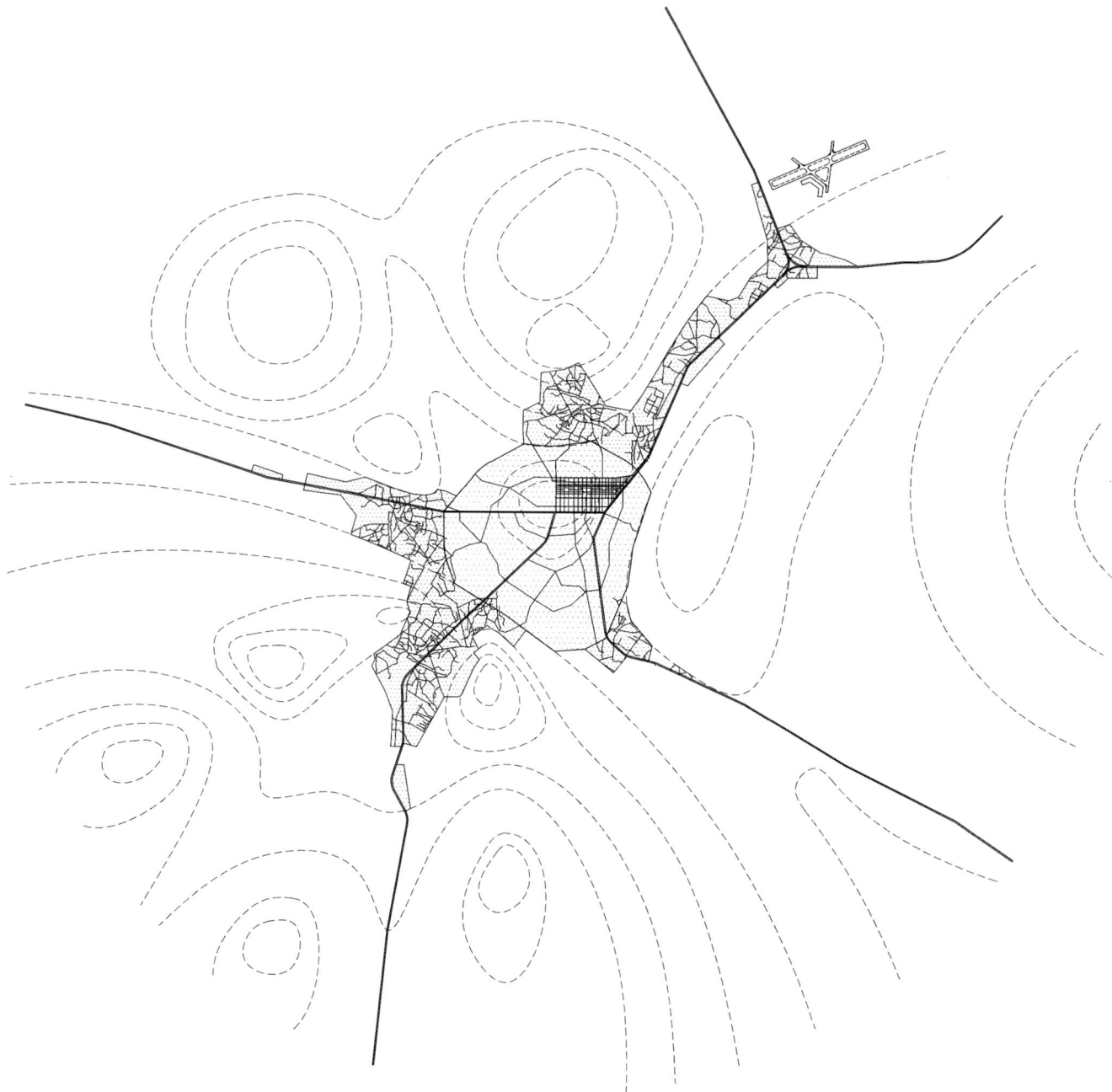

5.12 The growing city expands along arterial roads and up hillsides. With a rapidly growing population, the periphery of the city is in constant flux.

they are in rural areas. True, these settlements are slowly upgraded by their inhabitants, but more often than not their inhabitants never attain full ownership of their property, and they are always at risk of displacement by a more powerful actor.

The government, imperfect as it is, is inspired by the experiences of nations on other continents, also emerging from poverty and colonialism, that addressed their housing problem through the construction of large-scale settlements or "new towns" inspired by European examples. These new towns were not elaborate by the standards of wealthy nations, but they overcame several disadvantages of existing urban patterns of the time. First, the housing was constructed on land owned by the government, with secure land tenure and no risk of resident displacement in the future. Second, the housing was built of durable material, almost always concrete, with built-in electricity and running water; a much higher standard of living than was typical in the settlements. Third, the housing was constructed at large scale and in large numbers, with supportive activities (commerce, recreation, etc.) included within the development. The new towns were constructed in convenient areas, where transport to the city center was relatively easy, thereby reducing commuting times and improving the lives of residents. Eventually these nations were able to construct mass transportation networks to the new towns, increasing their desirability even more. To government officials, a new-town program seems like the perfect solution to the problems of this rapidly growing city, and a group of urban design consultants are engaged from a technical institute overseas with expertise in this area.

The consultants are not initially inspired by the prospect. The country's record of achievement in housing construction is poor; a few developments were constructed in the 1970s but little formal housing for the poor has been built since then. And the city administration is not able to provide clear information on land tenure in the areas that they are suggesting for new-town construction; it is not clear that land records exist, nor is it clear that the administration is inclined to respect property rights. Lastly, the country's overall human rights record is poor, and the government is not elected democratically. How can it be ethical, the consultants wonder, to participate in an urban design process where great power imbalances exist between government and citizens, and where it is uncertain that constructed housing will benefit the neediest citizens?

The consultants have other, more practical problems as well. The government has never successfully constructed an urban design project of this scale, and it is unclear that it has the capacity to do so. It promises a private partner in construction, an international infrastructure company with experience constructing dams and roads in

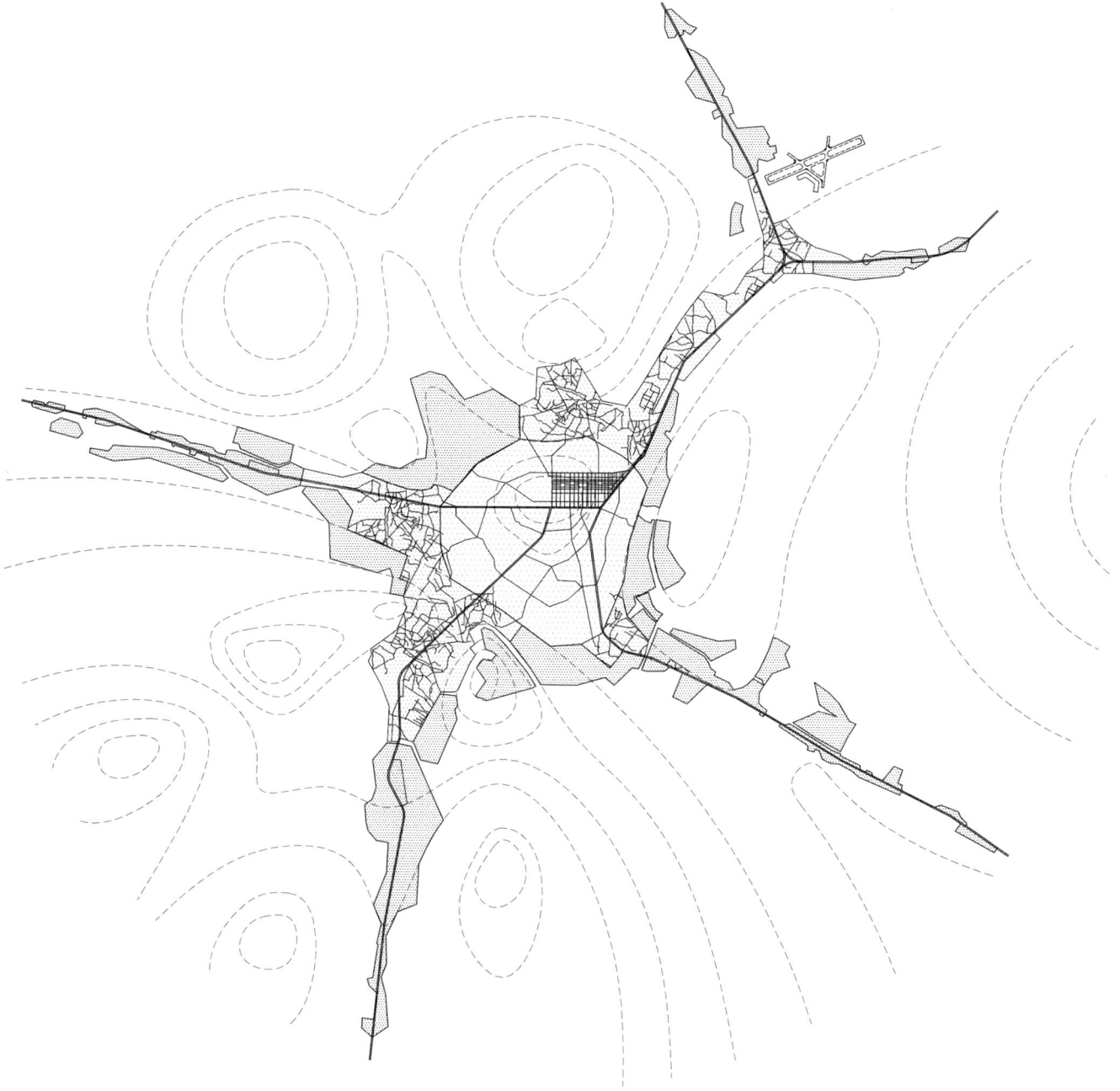

5.13 Like many such cities, this place could continue to grow outward and upward, with ever-increasing traffic and expanding undesigned settlements.

the region. But there appears to be little profit potential for this company in the construction of a new town for low-income residents of the urban periphery. The project is paradoxical: from a social and political perspective it makes sense, particularly if the government is interested in gaining additional legitimacy with its citizens, but from an economic perspective it does not appear to make any sense at all. The designers wonder whether an urban design strategy can address these structural problems. What if the project is constructed partway, then abandoned? What if a design is published, but the project is not constructed? The continent is littered with the remnants of grand ideas only half constructed and with projects that are very different than they were intended to be. How will the designers overcome these obstacles? Is overcoming them even possible in this less-than-ideal situation? The inspiring projects on other continents were different; where there was a tradition of governmental stability and responsibility, strong bureaucracies remained from the colonial era, and there were important reasons to demonstrate these other new nations' legitimacy in the international arena. These advantages do not exist in the current situation.

Despite the unpromising circumstances for the new-town program, the consultants are particularly inspired by the urban design concepts of plural urbanist David Crane. In his concepts for extension of the new city of Chandigarh, Crane defined a theory of what he called the "Dynamic City ... of a Thousand Designers."[10] The dynamic city emphasized two aspects of plural urbanism: plural actors and their methods, and plural time. Crane believed that cities could not be constructed principally by governments or private companies, but only by what he called "sub-manufacturers," or myriad small-scale builders, designers, and residents who made up the city. He suggested that the largest-scale elements of the city (the "capital web") be constructed first, as a "basic control" on the plural designers who would subsequently fill in the web with individual structures.[11] His greatest concern was for urban design to establish a logical "philosophy of hierarchical change" in which "successive layers and scales"[12] of city growth generated additional specialization at smaller scales. Crane was referring here to urban design's plural scales as a formative concern in the art.

As we saw in chapter 4, Crane placed his dynamic city ideas into practice in his New City proposal for Chandigarh published in 1960, where a capital web for a new sector of the city was constructed with the following hierarchy of urban design elements: a major vehicular intersection, linking the new sector to other elements of the city; "inter-sector trunk ways" lined with community facilities such as health centers, schools, shops, and small industries; and a range of housing, including "public and experimental housing," "aided self-help housing," and "planned squatter areas."[13] The form of the new sector was in reality indeterminate; a full build-out was provided for illustration, but this build-out was not necessarily the sector's final or optimal form. Other drawings indicated full sector build-outs with alternative structures, or partial sector build-out scenarios. The remainder of the scheme would be more or less informal, though necessarily guided by the form of preexisting infrastructure. Crane's scheme did not pretend to be a unitary, large-scale architecture project along the lines of Manuel de Solà-Morales's intermediate-scale work, nor did it pretend that the city could be shaped all at once by a single designer. Instead, Crane's proposal incorporated the realities of plural scale, plural time, and plural actors and their methods, while also shaping a strong, distinct formal direction for the new sector.

The design consultants also note the clear relationship of Crane's thoughts to the contemporary thoughts of John Habraken, published in his 1961 book *Supports*.[14] As we saw in chapter 2, Habraken conceived of design as a ladder of decisions ranging from the smallest scale—the arrangement of furniture in a room—to the largest scale of a city region. Habraken was most interested in providing users of mass housing with the autonomy to avoid the aesthetic monotony and social repression that he saw in mass housing in developed countries such as Holland and the United States. Like Crane, Habraken was interested in design as a process involving a hierarchy of decisions of both user and architect, not in a particular design aesthetic. Of course, aesthetic outcomes were encoded into Habraken's work, particularly in cases where users were afforded a high degree of autonomy in determining the design of exterior spaces outside the dwelling itself. Habraken's mass housing was constructed from the inside (structure) out in the same manner as all buildings: users of a building inhabit not the positive spaces of the building—its structure or other solid elements—but its negative spaces (its rooms, stairs, and other interior spaces).

Cities, however, are constructed from the outside in. Because they are larger in scale than buildings, both their negative spaces (streets, squares, parks, open spaces, etc.) and positive spaces (buildings) may be inhabited. A building's structure is positive space, but a city's so-called structure is negative space. A city's positive spaces (buildings) cannot be shaped by a single designer, since this positive space is more often than not, as we have already seen, determined by the thousand designers. But a city's negative space *can* be shaped by a single designer. When viewed from the perspective of unitary design, the city's duality leads to obvious difficulties for the urban designer, since unitary urbanism charges the designer with shaping both negative and positive space. Indeed, at the intermediate scale, urban designers acting as architects constructing at large scale may succeed in designing both positive and negative space. But Crane recognized that urban designers would customarily be fortunate just to design even the negative space—the capital web—of the city, leaving the thousand designers to build the rest. Crane accorded the same autonomy to the submanufacturers of city space that Habraken accorded to the housing inhabitant in his supports conception of architectural space.

Crane's capital web concept has a third difference from Habraken's, apart from that of scale and the distinction between positive and negative space. This is an aesthetic difference founded on the fact that the designed negative space of the city is its most public area, whereas the negative space of a house—its structure—is inaccessible to the user. In other words, if the urban designer begins by shaping the largest-scale elements of the city—its main vehicular intersections and its district-scale commercial streets, for example—then the designer's work will be the most visible part of the city rather than its least visible. This accords Crane's urban-scaled strategy a signal aesthetic advantage over Habraken's architecturally scaled one. Whereas Habraken's designer-first, user-second strategy runs the risk of occluding the designer's ideas behind a mass of user accretions, Crane's parallel strategy, operating at larger scale, means that users of city space experience the city's designed elements before they experience informal or less designed aspects. A user who never leaves a city's principal streets might not experience its less designed areas at all.

Crane's strategy might be criticized by comparing it to a monumental building whose sides or back are undesigned, or even to a Potemkin village (a seemingly ordered, prosperous environment masking poverty and squalor). But, whereas a building with a designed facade and undesigned rear implies superficiality and a lack of attention to the deeper qualities of a structure, the city again performs in the opposite fashion, because its facade—its public streets, infrastructure, and major buildings—is also its structure. The city, in other words, is a structural inversion of a building. The city is not a larger-scale replica or parallel of architecture, allowing us to see that Crane's capital web strategy is not a superficial masking of true urban conditions that ignores the deeper functioning of the city, but its opposite. In Crane's city the urban designer shapes the most important structural *and* visual elements of the city first, leaving its dependent elements (housing, smaller-scale commerce, etc.) to subcontractors, the city's plural actors.

One might criticize Crane's strategy for shortchanging the smaller-scale fabric of the city—housing and commerce—in favor of infrastructure. In this sense Crane's concept of the capital web bears similarity to earlier modes of urban design that shaped

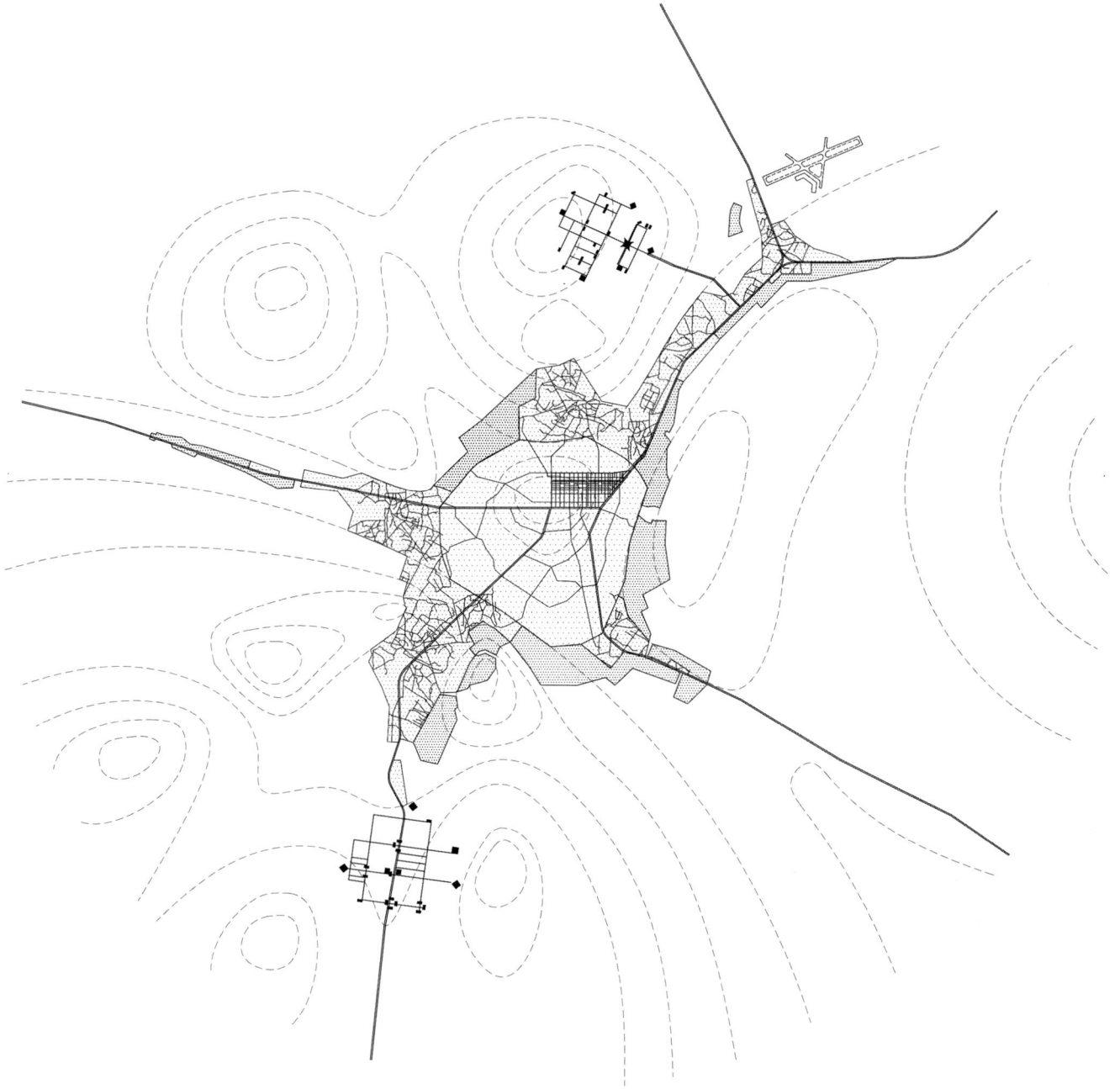

5.14 One urban design strategy might shape and direct growth with infrastructure and public facilities constructed on hilltops or in valleys.

only large-scale streets and facing buildings while neglecting smaller-scale elements. Haussmann's Paris boulevards and the Burnham and Bennett *Plan of Chicago* come to mind.[15] But these older capital webs have an important difference from Crane's idea: both were urban reconstruction projects that reshaped existing cities instead of generating new areas of the city. In other words poor quality housing came first in both of these earlier urban design schemes. The capital web of grand boulevards and buildings came afterward, either destroying or neglecting this first, poorer phase of urban development. Crane's scheme does the opposite, using the capital web to shape later, less formal developments. This has two advantages over these earlier schemes. First, of course, in the capital web the subsequent housing fills in between the larger scale elements rather than being destroyed by it. Second, the capital web can benefit smaller-scale development, whereas the earlier Haussmannian projects were a form of gentrification, often bringing in higher-income development to supplant poorer-quality housing. Crane's scheme thus possesses a quality of social justice that these earlier schemes lacked.

The capital web provides the urban design team with a clear framework for constructing new towns at the periphery of this rapidly growing city. But Crane's theory of plural urbanism is a theory of design action, not a set of instructions. It does not provide guidance for additional decisions such as where new towns might be located, what particular combination of elements might be provided in each new town, how the new towns might relate to each other or to the central city, or even how many new towns there might be. The urban designers are reminded that design can never be simply the rational outcome of a process: no equation can provide the perfect solution to a design problem. Determining the location, content, relationship, and quantity of new towns around this city will require additional design thinking. The designers might apply Crane's thinking further, guiding their placement of new towns by thinking of the entire city as an even larger capital web where constructing a new town is an act of subcontracting analogous to the smaller subcontracting decisions that occur as individual builders construct buildings within the new town's capital web. Perhaps the designers decide to site new towns at the junctions of major roadways leaving the city in order to maximize transportation connectivity. Or perhaps they decide to site the new towns where land is emptiest in order to minimize land acquisition costs and to provide the most space for construction. The designers might even decide to construct new towns in relationship to the city-region's topography, perhaps at the tops of hills so that visibility from the civic center at the center of each new town will be highest. Or, perhaps, they might locate the new towns in the lowest, flattest places, to minimize

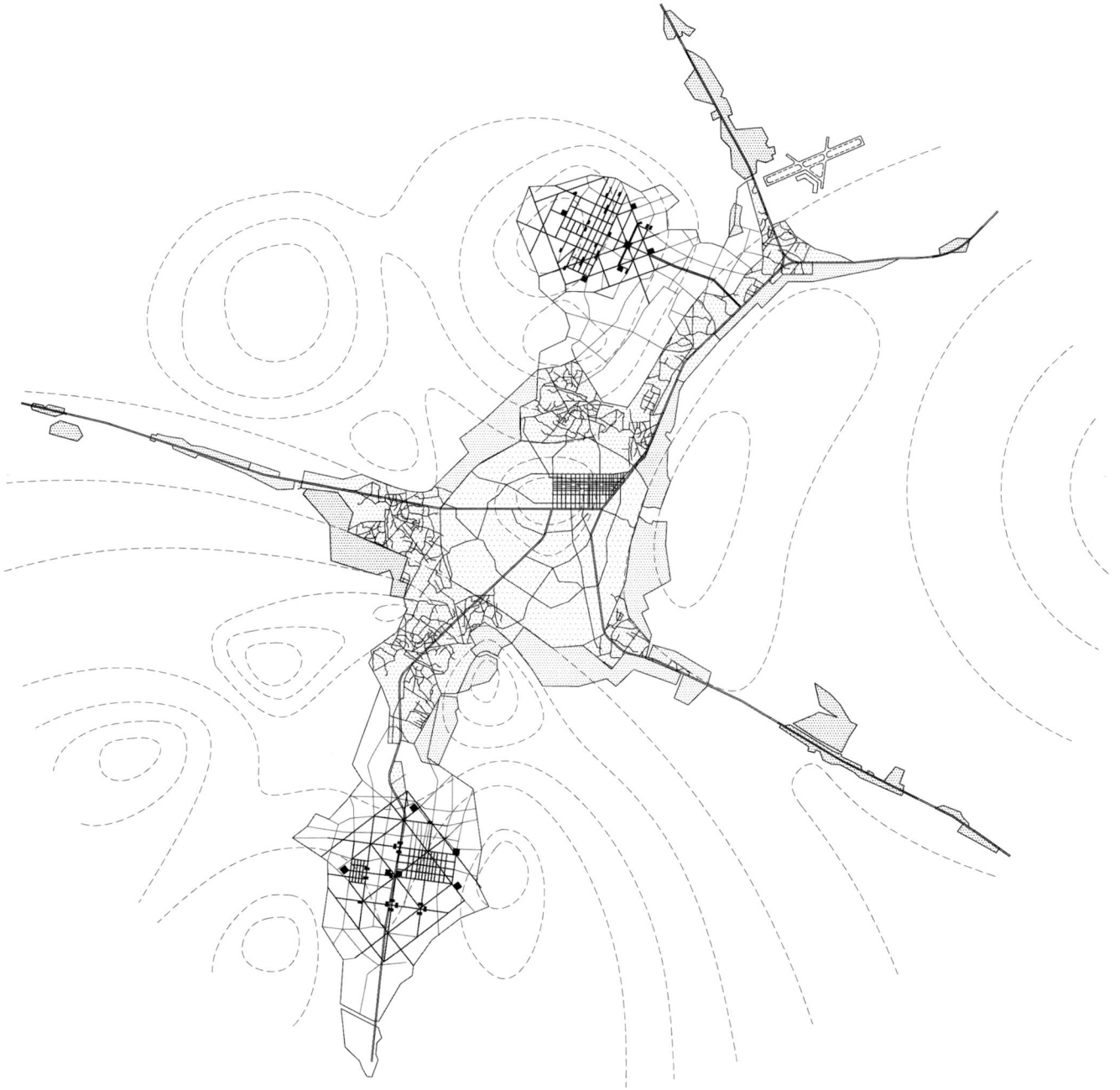

5.15 The city will grow in all directions, but purposeful plural urbanism can distinguish the city with new peripheral centers that emphasize nature and organize building.

undevelopable parcels and to ease the traffic that doubtless will soon be flowing in and out of each new town.

Why do we not here define the decisions of the designers more closely? Do these decisions not matter? Of course they do, but in addressing the question of design at the periphery of a growing city the designers decide to first understand their particular design problem through the lens of plural urbanism, discovering that the particular prescriptions of David Crane might give conceptual guidance in shaping their strategy. Plural urbanism acknowledges indeterminacy as a reality of urban design, but this does not mean that plural urbanism is itself indeterminate, or that design can conversely be resolved simply as a series of empirically derived decisions with rationally determined outcomes. And understanding a new town as a design problem that differs not in degree but in kind from an architectural, unitary design problem does not absolve these urban designers from the responsibility—and the privilege—of making creative decisions.

We might project many design paths for our new town at the periphery of a developed, undemocratic nation. Perhaps the urban designers decide to integrate additional plural urbanist strategies, introducing the theories of Bacon and Lynch with those of Crane. The city might be designed as a series of settlements occupying different hills, with major transportation arteries in between and with settlement on the slopes. Such a strategy might designate the city's hilltops as parks or recreation spaces, a retreat from urbanity rather than a concentration of construction as at New York's Central Park. Civic spaces would then be located in the lowlands, adjacent to the transportation arteries, in an inversion of Le Corbusier's acropolis concept at Chandigarh. Or the new towns might be designed as settlements that communicate to each other, visually and functionally, from different hilltops. One could even understand this rapidly growing city's new towns as a larger-scaled version of Sixtus V's obelisks, with roadways connecting the two in both cases at different scales. At the periphery of this growing city, as in any other example of plural urban design, are many possibilities and opportunities for creativity.

Just as the number of cities in the world is nearly infinite, so are the potential scenarios for plural urbanism to improve the design of those cities. In the final chapter of this book, we will consider three principles—change, incompleteness, and fidelity—that can further guide the urban design of pluralist places.

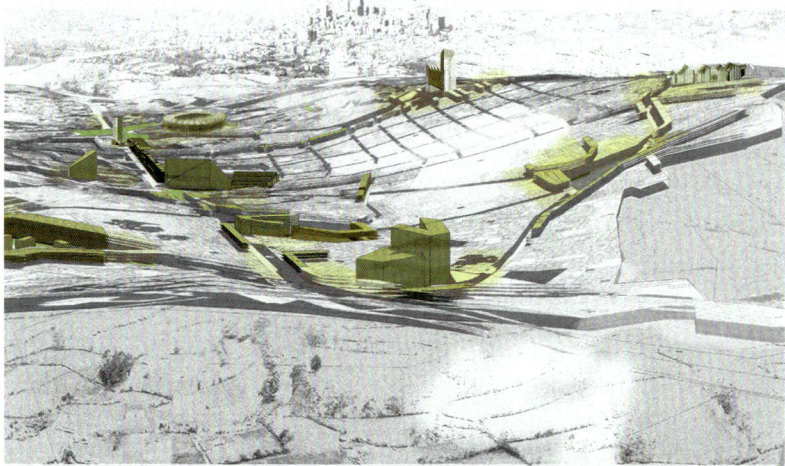

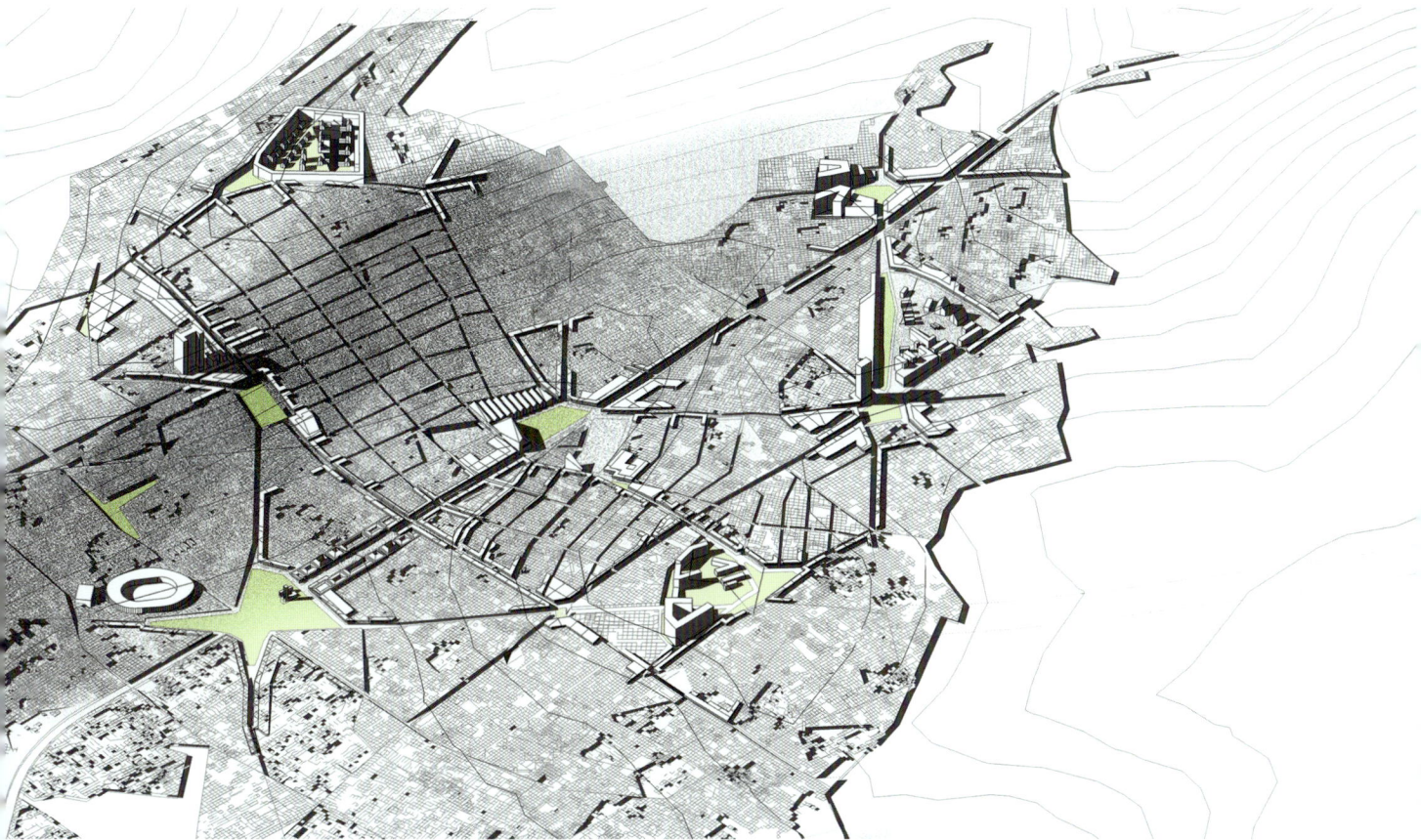

◄ **5.16** The generally undistinguished visual character of the cityscape will be clarified and visually organized by larger-scale civic complexes constructed on hilltops or at major intersections.

▲ **5.17** New centers organized as a web within an otherwise lightly designed city reinforce topography and strengthen the city's relationship to its site.

Principles and Potentials of Plural Urbanism

The previous three chapters have shown that imagining a world of cities shaped by plural urban design is less difficult than it may seem. Chapter 3 showed examples of plural urbanism already existing in many places, even if those examples have not been previously understood explicitly as such. In chapter 4 we saw how previous urban design thinkers have understood many of its dimensions. And with its three semi-imaginary scenarios, chapter 5 showed how rich is today's potential for plural urbanism in a range of diverse places. Now we will explore three principles that characterize all urban design and especially plural urbanism: the principles of eternal change, inevitable incompleteness, and flexible fidelity. In explaining these three principles, this book's definition of urban design as a distinct, different, independent building art will be complete.

Change Is Eternal: Reforming Representation

David Crane's term "painting on a river" indicates a peculiar tension between the representation of urban design and the reality of the city. Such representations as one sees in renderings or plans are by nature static, usually depicting a vision of the city in an ideal state following the realization of the urban design. Jules Guerin's images from Burnham and Bennett's *Plan of Chicago* are iconic and typical, showing a splendidly remade Chicago ranging from the scale of individual buildings up to the scale of the entire region. Burnham's plan was intended for implementation, but whether or not an urban design vision is intended to be realizable does not change the nature of representation: Antonio Sant'Elia's imagined Città Nuova represents the city in as static a manner as Burnham and Bennett's *Plan*. But urban design, as we have already seen, is far from static, because cities are dynamic and ever-changing. In fact, the discipline's historic dependence on static representational methods is artificial and problematic, and urban designers might do much more to incorporate the reality of eternal change into representation.

Artists have long struggled to represent a dynamic subject matter through a static medium. Painters such as Frederic Church and Winslow Homer depicted dynamic natural entities—waterfalls, raging seas—with just the right balance of monumentality and vivacity. Looking at a painting of ocean whitecaps could not bring Victorian viewers into the world of a storm, but perhaps it could evoke just enough of that storm's impression to capture their emotions. With the advent of the moving image, painters' struggles to capture the multifaceted nature of an active subject drove their art in more and more abstract directions, first toward cubism, in which multiple aspects of a subject were represented simultaneously, and ultimately toward abstraction, in which the painter no longer attempted to represent reality at all, placing the burden of imagination upon the viewer.

Painting's tradition of representing dynamic events through a static medium would shape the way in which architecture, and then urban design, would be represented in the late nineteenth century. First architecture and then much larger-scale designs for cities came to be visualized in static, painterly fashion. In this manner a static representational medium (the painting or drawing) became firmly encoded as the means of representing the dynamic subject of the city. Yet architects had an aim, and a responsibility, that painters did not: their drawings represented a vision of the future instead of an interpretation of the present. The challenge of representing a raging sea or stormy sky is representational, but it is not conceptual: painters are not projecting an ideal future condition at the same time as they represent it. Thus Winslow Homer's paintings were not design intentions for the sea in the same manner as Jules Guerin's paintings were for the *Plan of Chicago*, nor did Homer's paintings bear the same burden of "conformance with reality" that is borne by representations of a city's ideal future.

Architecture and urban design's inheritance of painterly traditions of static representation can be seen in the *Plan of Chicago* of 1909. The plan's drawings of Chicago

6.1 Frederic Church's 1867 painting *Niagara Falls, from the American Side* captures an active subject—the falls' thundering rush of water and swirling mist—through the static medium of painting.

6.2 An imagined aerial perspective of the Chicago region in the 1909 *Plan* conveyed humanity's growing ability to intentionally shape cities and landscapes.

emerged directly from a tradition of architectural representation, that of the Beaux-Arts of nineteenth-century Paris, which refined and perfected the representational traditions of plan, elevation, section, and perspective. All of these modes were abstractions, of course; real buildings are always seen in three dimensions, with three or more vanishing points, and it is impossible to cut through walls in the manner of a plan or a section. These representational abstractions are among the first rules of visualization learned by architecture students, and they are also among the most difficult for laypeople to understand. This is because plans and sections do not show reality except in one important sense: they show a building in static pose, much the way it actually is when constructed. The monumental solidity of Chicago's proposed Beaux-Arts edifices was mirrored by the monumental, static representations of those structures in plan, section, and elevation.

It was natural for Burnham, an architect of monumental Beaux-Arts structures like the grandiose 1893 World's Columbian Exposition, to represent his plan for Chicago in a manner similar to how he would have represented a building. The *Plan*'s representational devices are different in scale from those used for architectural drawings, but they are not fundamentally different in kind. In fact, Burnham's plans for "the Heart of Chicago" are literal Beaux-Arts drawings: figures CXXIX ("Business Center plan"), CXXI ("Civic Center elevation") and CXXX ("Civic Center Plan") would not have looked out of place in the annual competitions for the Prix de Rome, whose increasingly grandiose building designs mirrored the *Plan*'s own elephantine scope.[1]

Architects have never seriously questioned the validity of the representational conventions of plan, section, elevation, and perspective, even as perspectival techniques have grown so photorealistic that it can now be difficult to discern a rendering from the built reality. Representational conventions remain intact primarily because they work well: a building's fundamental nature as a three-dimensional, static object has not changed. Though the 1960s Archigram group and many since have projected buildings that were inflatable, mobile, or otherwise active, as of 2017 most buildings remain more or less stable and immovable, though they do of course change slowly over time.[2]

Nor have urban designers ever seriously questioned the static representation of the dynamic city through the discipline's representational conventions of plan and perspective. And while buildings may evolve somewhat over time, cities change constantly, in ways that cannot always be foreseen by urban designers. The static quality of city plans has thus proven perpetually problematic to urban designers and urban

6.3 Daniel Burnham's civic center plan uses representational conventions directly derived from nineteenth-century Beaux-Arts architectural drawing. Burnham's 1909 *Plan* began the conflation of static representations—the plan drawing in particular—with the dynamic entity of the city.

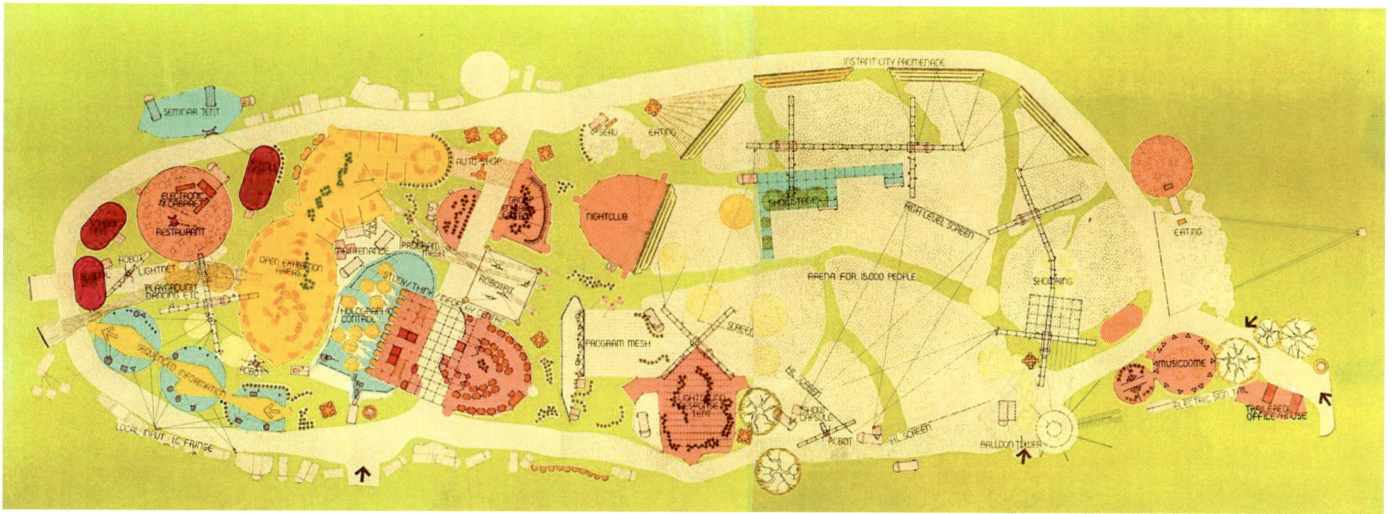

6.4 Though avant-garde modernist architects such as the 1960s Archigram group dreamed of buildings that could grow, shrink, assemble, and disassemble with the ease of a carnival or fairground, architecture has remained primarily a static art.

planners. City plans are "too quickly outdated," "obsolete before they are printed," or "unable to keep up with the times"—never mind that such plans too often "sit on the shelf," as planners say, or remain unimplemented—an issue we will confront later in this chapter. But the problem of plans' persistent lack of connection to reality is not just a problem of implementation, nor one of professional ineptitude. The real problem with the *Plan of Chicago*'s representations, and by extension with all urban design dealing with pluralist space, is that the visual conventions they use were developed to depict building designs, not city designs. This is a fundamental misfit, for any static representation will inevitably be left further and further behind by the reality of the city, in which change is eternal.

Urban designers need to acknowledge the basic contradiction between the reality of an object that is always changing (the city) and the projection of a fixed future for that object (urban design). How is this contradiction to be resolved? If the city's plural space is ever changing and ever evolving, then is the effort to shape its ideal future too quixotic to merit designers' energy? Might urban design be subject to a different kind of "end" than Michael Sorkin suggested, an end resulting not from exhausted ideology but from an impossible quest?

From a practical perspective, this end seems not to have arrived—yet. Many areas of cities require design for practical reasons, and design of these spaces cannot simply be abandoned. And the differences between static representations (urban designs) and dynamic subjects (city spaces) are not as drastic as they may seem: many city spaces are substantially stable, making static representations of their future potentially meaningful. Trafalgar Square in London is just one example of a plural space whose form is relatively fixed, even if the larger skyline of London is much more dynamic. Most open spaces and monumental plazas within cities rarely shift either their location or their form.

Urban design at the intermediate scale need not be inconvenienced by the eternal quality of change in the city. Manuel de Solà-Morales's static, architectural representations of spaces such as his railway square design for Leuven, Belgium,[3] were not made irrelevant by the fact that small-scale change would later occur there in the form of changing shop fronts, maturing plantings, and weathering of buildings. Such small-scale change occurs in every urban space and indeed every building, but this small-scale change does not fundamentally alter the configuration of these spaces. Thus, urban design's historical dependence on static, architectural conventions of representation need not change fundamentally if the space concerned is relatively small in scale and unitary in nature. Because the change experienced by these spaces is not substantially different from that experienced by a building, such change will not make a static representation of that design meaningless.

But larger scales of urban design are difficult to maintain unchanged. The difference between a static design concept and a dynamic entity (the city) becomes more consequential when urban space becomes more plural in nature, as in any of the dimensions described in chapter 2. Time's passage will replace, remove, or otherwise alter spaces, structures, and streets within such an urban design ensemble according to the demands of different property owners or changing needs, even if the overall urban design ensemble, encoded into property boundaries and existing buildings, remains more or less intact.

Change is inevitable even in urban design districts developed with great rapidity, such as the three Levittowns built postwar in the New York and Philadelphia metropolitan areas. Though Levittown was constructed with essentially identical houses, each individual house was highly plastic in form, available for alteration as owners added to or remodeled their homes. By 2007, Long Island's 17,447 Levittown houses were almost

◄ **6.5 and 6.6** Static representations of architectural and "intermediate-scale" urban design projects are accurate, since change is relatively limited. Manuel de Solà-Morales's Leuven Stationsplein in Belgium is unlikely to grow or shift dramatically, apart from routine weathering and replacements.

6.7 Large-scale works of urban design will inevitably change due to small-scale, incremental action. The 17,447 originally identical houses in Long Island's Levittown are now all different due to the addition of floors, garages, screened porches, and ornamental details.

all different, with a plethora of additional floors, garages, and screen porches added to the original modest homes.[4] Such individually motivated alterations are nearly universal in neighborhoods where buildings are relatively cheaply constructed or subject to few regulatory restrictions, or both, as in many cities in the developing world.

Manhattan too is constantly changing, with buildings going up and coming down all the time, even as the grid remains the same, as Rem Koolhaas and Zoe Zenghelis noted in their 1972 *City of the Captive Globe* project. Manhattan's grid is an urban pattern in perpetual transformation as new buildings of various heights are incrementally added to the urban fabric.[5] All designed city districts display a similar pattern of small-scale change and large-scale resilience.

Change can be painful, particularly for advocates of historic preservation. In the case of Levittown, where the aesthetic quality of the overall ensemble is not perceived to be at risk, few have bemoaned changes to individual homes. But change can ultimately

▶ **6.8** Plural urbanism, too, is vulnerable to change. The late 1960s construction of the Tour Montparnasse in central Paris violated Paris's long-established height limits. No similar towers have been permitted since.

destroy the urban design quality of a once-homogenous ensemble, particularly if older buildings are replaced by larger ones of notably different aesthetic character. Paris's carefully maintained height limit, for example, was violated in the 1960s by the construction of skyscrapers. Historic preservation attempts to arrest change at a larger scale by preventing building demolition in entire districts, but as these efforts themselves grow in scale the attempt becomes quixotic and even self-defeating.

Manhattan, as Rem Koolhaas presciently observed in 2010, is in the midst of a large-scale experiment in city district preservation; the urban fabric of much of the island is now under the effective control of fifty-four different historic districts designated by the city's Landmarks Commission.[6] Koolhaas, aware of the deleterious effects that such paralysis would have on design, proposed that preservation standards be revised to encourage destruction of "junk" instead of preserving monuments. Free-market economists, eager for an unfettered market to operate, have shared Koolhaas's concerns, noting that "no city's future should be a prisoner of its past."[7]

As we noted in chapter 2, only extreme political circumstances are able to arrest change in large-scale areas of cities. Kevin Lynch noted one such extraordinary freezing of urban form in Havana, where the Cuban Revolution of 1959 nearly halted new building construction.[8] With a resilient political regime that has lasted some six decades, the entire city of Havana is an artifact, where palimpsest- and patchwork-like change of the urban fabric have been more or less arrested. Similar artifact-like cities existed in Russia and China after Communist revolutions there (in 1918 and 1949, respectively), at least for a time, so that even the giant city of Shanghai in 1972 looked much as it had in 1949.[9]

The challenge of representing urban design is thus fundamentally greater than that of representing architecture. Such representation is obligatory: architects and urban designers may build detailed small-scale models, and they may even construct 1:1 versions of small parts of a design, but they must design first in order to construct, for design and fabrication are two different things, much more so than in painting or sculpture, for instance. And both architects and urban designers need to represent a three-dimensional entity through two-dimensional drawings, creating something through drawing that is unrealizable until constructed. But only urban design will inevitably keep changing and evolving in ways that will soon bring it beyond the realm of any static representation.

Urban design is not the only art that need represent and conceive an entity whose form will shift over time in a manner beyond the designer's control. Landscape architects shape the spatial distribution and composition of living things, but they cannot fully control the growth rate, lifecycle patterns, or demise of the living things themselves. A park design will thus change inevitably over time and it is a rare landscape can retain the formal consistency of a monumental building. Central Park, seemingly a perpetually unchanging monument, is actually far from being so; its differences from the design originally envisioned by Olmsted are substantial.[10] And most large parks have experienced far more change than Central Park, much of it deleterious.[11]

It is worth noting that urban designers face the added challenge of designing something that is very likely to change even as the design is being constructed. Cities are not literally alive, but they are the product of life, and their form is far less predictable than that of vegetation. A tree will grow over time, but it will grow at a predictable rate to a predictable size, and if the landscape around it is maintained one will be able to foresee its future form with some accuracy. Even a natural ecology may reach a climax or peak state of some stability, though the degree of stability is still debated.[12] But growth and stability cannot be forecast with any great accuracy for a city, for pluralist space changes in ways that are inherently unpredictable. Lúcio Costa designed a fixed form for Brasília, and there is no indication that he considered or even was able to conceive of future growth beyond the city districts he designed. Nor can one have much confidence that any city's future form can be predicted at all.

If plural urban design is neither a complex of buildings whose form can be designed, constructed, and consistently maintained, nor a landscape that will change in a relatively predictable way, how should design for plural space occur in a way that registers and respects change? The challenge is not as difficult as it may seem. Change is eternal and inevitable in a city, but not all parts of cities change in the same way, nor do all parts of cities change at the same speed, as Kevin Lynch observed.[13] One must remember that changeability itself is constructed, and is itself changeable. Building laws that are strictly enforced can restrict height, and therefore diminish change, for hundreds of years, as in Paris.[14] But if those laws are contravened or altered, as they were repeatedly in early twentieth-century America[15] and more recently in London,[16] the form of the city can shift dramatically and unpredictably. Cities are a surprising, complex, and dramatic mix of elements that are changeable and unchangeable; of elements that are likely to change and unlikely to change; of elements that can change in dramatic ways or only in small ones; and of places where change is a regular occurrence, or very scarce.

All three of the plural urbanists of chapter 4 understood and appreciated the changeability of cities, but the most serious student of change was Kevin Lynch: his

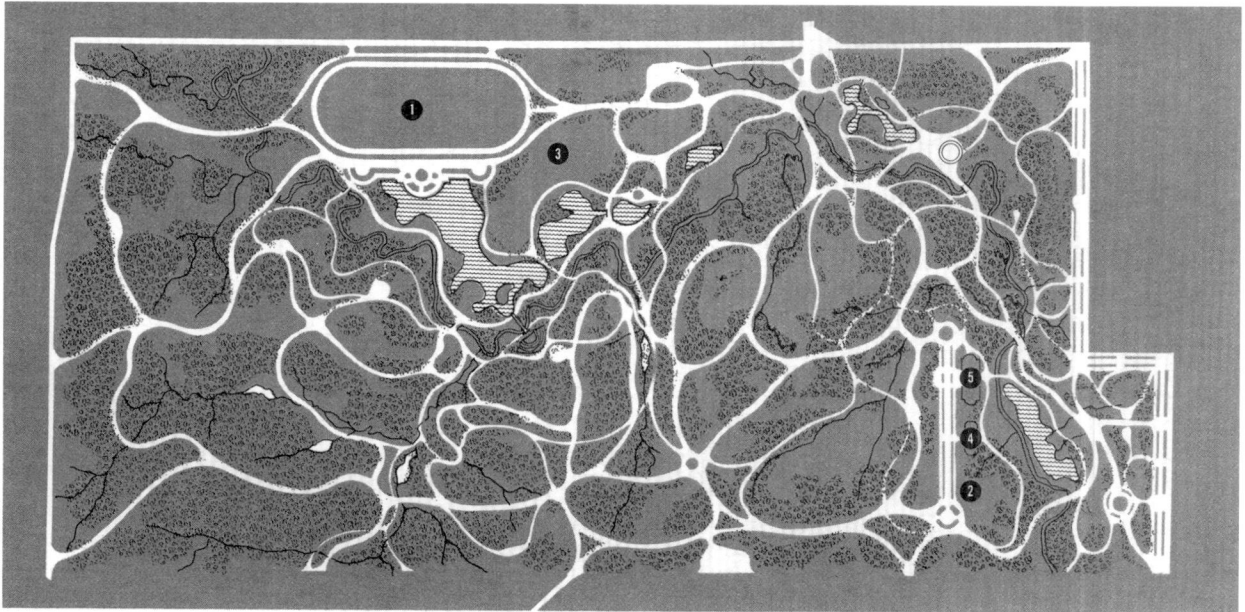

FOREST PARK - ST. LOUIS

Original design of Forest Park, greatly influenced by Olmsted, with formal elements at Hippodrome and Flower Walk.

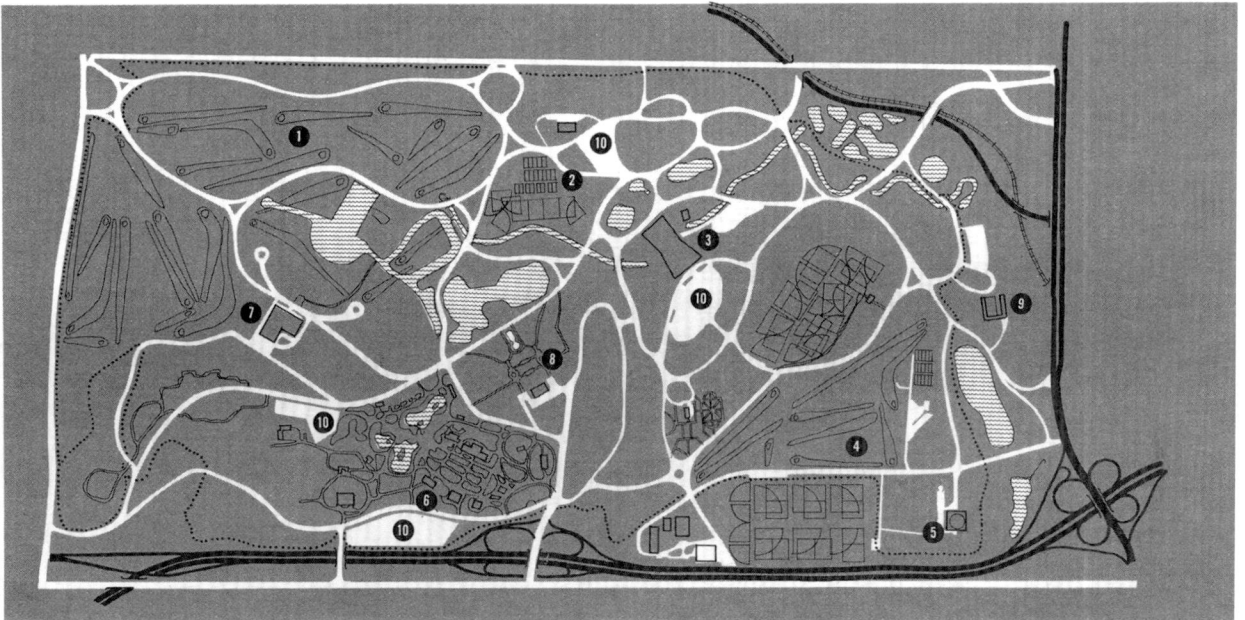

FOREST PARK - ST. LOUIS

The park today, showing multiplicity of special uses, traffic lanes, parking spaces, etc.

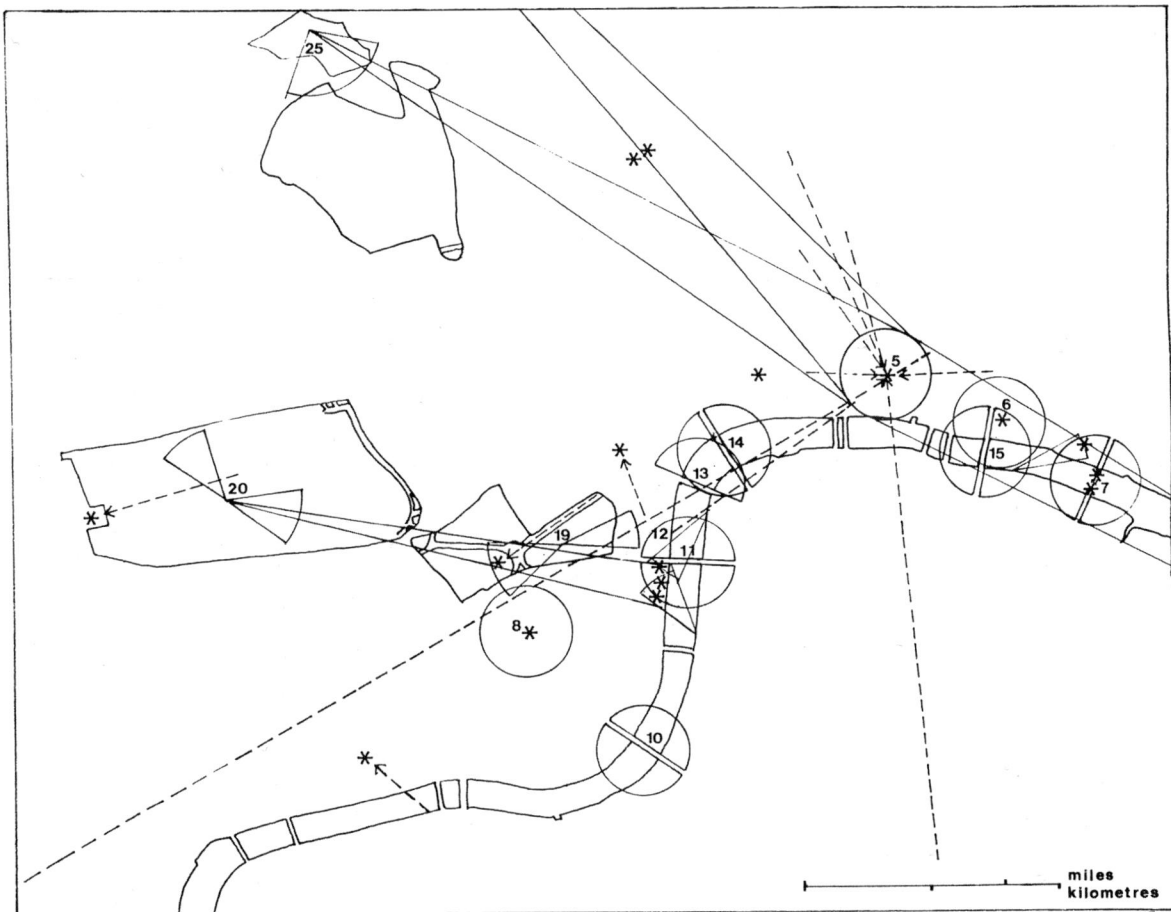

VIEWS IN CENTRAL LONDON

Strategic views (angle of view indicated)

Panoramic views from tops of buildings

Major visual cones

Major visual corridors

Major historic landmarks

Views numbered according to paragraph in text.

5   St Paul's Cathedral Gallery
6   The Monument
7   Tower Bridge Elevated Walkway
8   Westminster Cathedral
10 Vauxhall Bridge
11 Westminster Bridge
12 Westminster Pier
13 Hungerford Bridge
14 Waterloo Bridge
15 London Bridge
19 St James's Park
20 The Serpentine
25 Primrose Hill

◄ **6.9** Landscape architecture evolves according to plant maturation, but it may also be altered by human agency: Forest Park, St. Louis, has experienced substantial change, much of it deleterious, since its construction in 1876.

▲ **6.10** Economic pressures continuously drive change in city form. London's building height regulations have been revised in recent decades to permit additional towers, impacting many of the "perpetual" views outlined by urban designers in this 1987 document.

urban visions depicted cityscapes in perpetual processes of change,[17] and he dedicated much thought to understanding and diagramming time's passage in cities.[18] The plural projects explored in chapter 3 demonstrate the possibility of perpetual change that does not damage or destroy an urban design concept. But change can often damage unitary urban design, particularly if the design concept being created is Platonic and inflexible. Brasília may have been envisioned as a perfect form, but since 1960 the city has grown far beyond that original Platonic form, creating a disorganized and often unattractive place. This change marginalizes and mocks Costa's original concept.

Architects accustomed to static representations of presumably static form are likely to have a difficult time accommodating the inevitable, eternal nature of change in the city. Accordingly, plural urbanists will benefit from acknowledging that even the most well-considered and well-conceived urban design scheme is likely to change in unpredictable ways. One thing is clear: whether or not urban designers wish for plural space to become stable and changeless in the manner of an architectural monument or a simple building, the city will never become such. Our static representations and conceptions of urban space convey a wishful thinking about urban form that is not derived from the city itself, but from the architectural origins of urban design.

Urban designers shaping pluralist space might consider both formal and temporal configurations, projecting areas and dimensions for change that are not only forecasts but normative projections. For change too can be shaped, controlled, and designed for. Both Stewart Brand[19] and Anne Vernez Moudon[20] have recommended that buildings and city blocks be "built for change" by constructing relatively simple, generic, straightforward, predictable and therefore predictably alterable structures and parcel patterns; their recommendations are derived from studies of changes in nineteenth-century structures and city forms into the present day. Both have also recommended against building forms and block patterns that are too idiosyncratic or large in scale; these tend to freeze and prevent change, not promote it. But this is only one proposal for how block forms or other elements of the urban fabric might attempt to shape their future change, and there might be many others.

Figures 6.11 and 6.12, abstractions of a design for a city area, show the contrast between conventional unitary understandings of urban design and a pluralist urban fabric where change is eternal. In the first, an urban design concept is projected, then built out over time, resulting in a final form that realized in large part the ideals of the original concept. In the second diagram, we see an urban design project that has been in part realized, but that continues to change, with areas that are unfinished and others

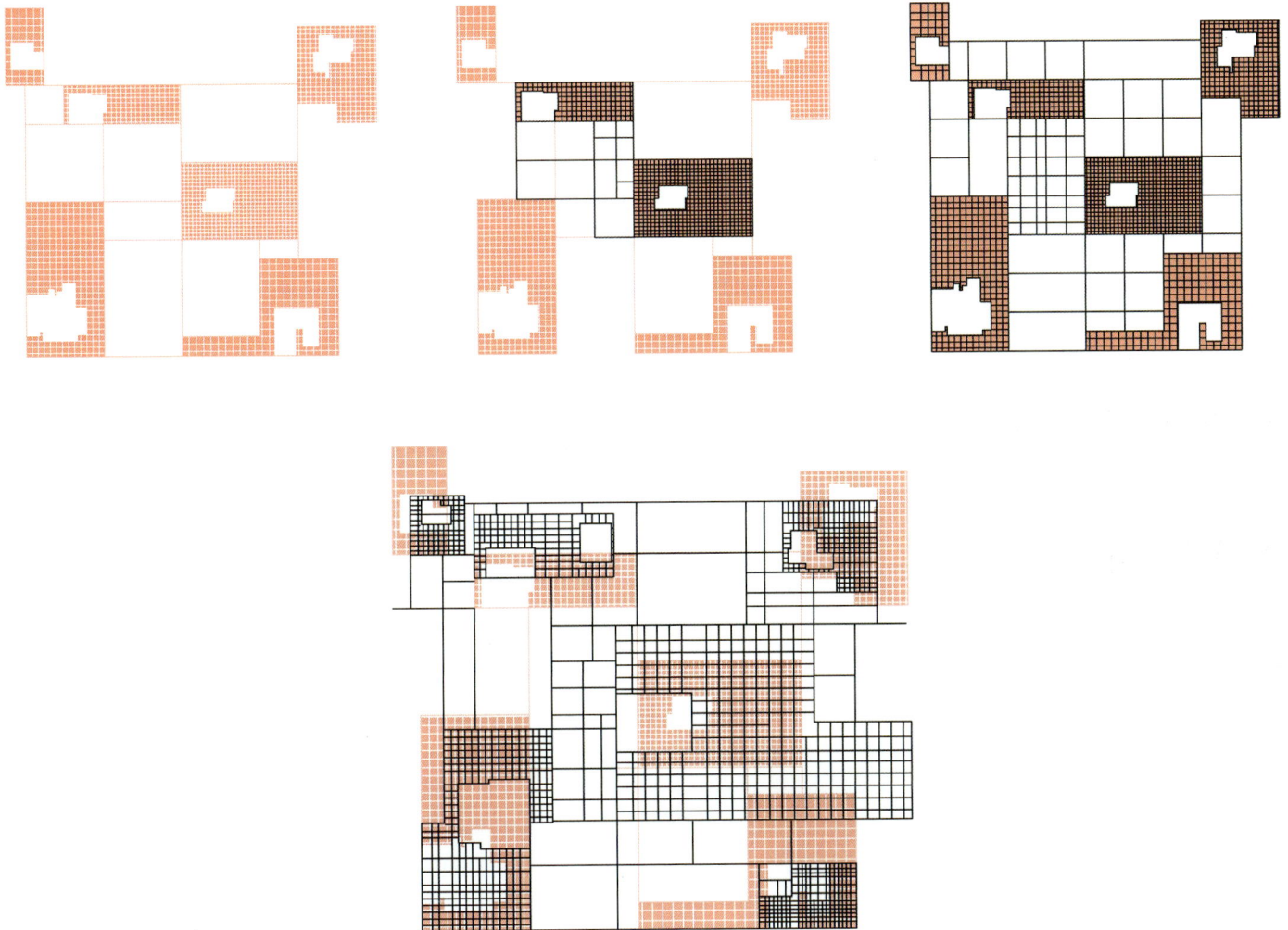

6.11 and 6.12 Change is eternal in urban design, but much current urban design thought, as shown in the first diagram, projects that urban design ideas will be built much as they are designed. Instead of resisting change or pretending that it does not exist, urban designers should conceive of new formal concepts and representational modes to reflect and accommodate change. The abstract project shown in the second diagram, though shown in static form, can be thought of as having mutated or evolved away from the original constructed concept.

that have continued to grow beyond the bounds of the original concept. The analogy to Brasília is direct, but the reality is that all pluralist city fabrics behave in this way; change will never cease.

As for representation, plural urbanists also might begin to question the well-worn conventions of static representations of city space. It is hard to imagine how one might depict urban designs in a way that acknowledges changeability, but then again nineteenth-century painters would have found the cubist concepts of the early 1900s revolutionary as well. Digital technology holds substantial promise. Perhaps new representational means might be developed to capture the city's temporal mutability and flexibility more meaningfully. Few students or practitioners thus far seem interested in computation's potential to represent and conceive plural urban design, but this may represent limitations in current design practice and education, not limitations of capacity.

Urban design's link to static concepts and projections for plural space is long-standing, but this dependence might erode and shift over time. It may seem a tall order to demand that urban designers interested in shaping pluralist space become skilled in conceiving not only formal configurations but temporal ones, but such is the reality of urban space, and therefore such is the challenge of designing it. If urban space is to be designed at all, acknowledging eternal change needs to become more than a thorn in the side of urbanists—it should become a central area of interest and one that can drive fundamental changes in conceptions and representations of urban design.

Incompletion Is Inevitable: Accepting the Unfinished

In the late 1950s the city of Providence, Rhode Island, began to issue regular urban design proposals for its downtown area. Like those of many coastal cities in New England, Providence's downtown was a combination of older housing, industrial structures, and a few high-rise office buildings intermingled with rail and port infrastructure. By the 1950s, interstate highways were being developed and abundant federal funds were available for urban redevelopment. Downtown Providence was headed for redesign. Blessed (or cursed) with political stability and a consistently engaged consortium of business and institutional leaders, Providence issued several urban design plans over the course of forty years.[21]

As we saw in chapter 1, this was a tumultuous time for design, as modernism waxed and waned and in the end gave way to postmodernism and neotraditionalism. Providence's urban design approaches to downtown accordingly shifted from large-scale

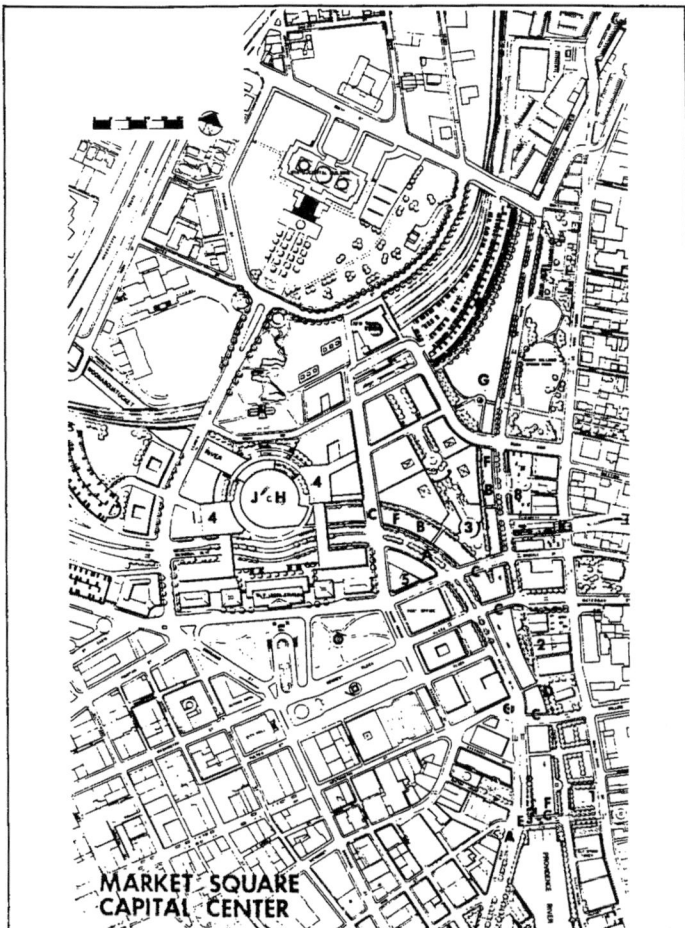

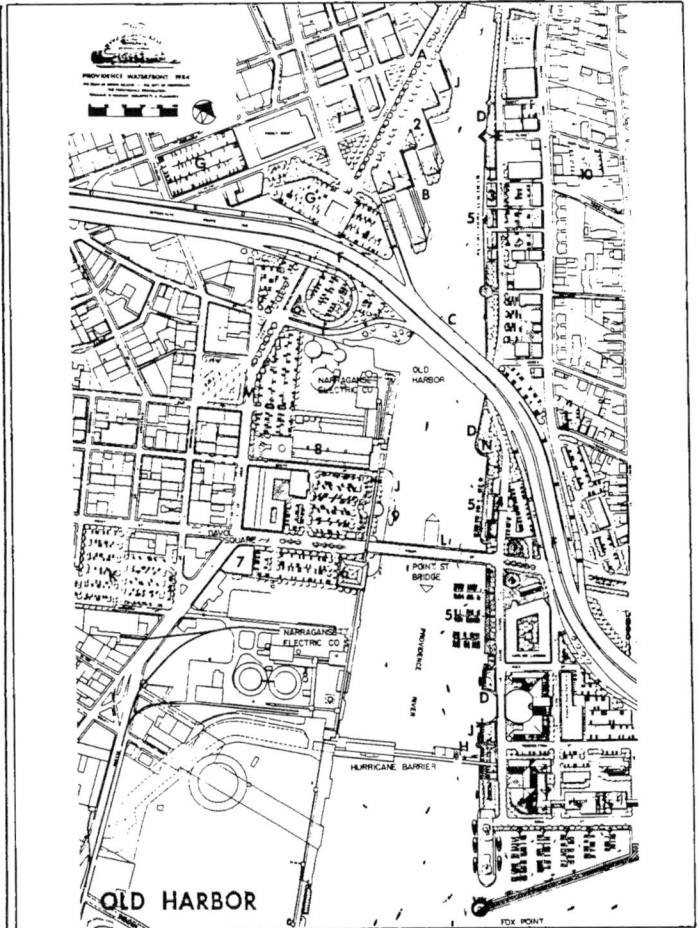

6.13 While the constructed portions of William Warner's design for downtown Providence, Rhode Island, are successful, most of Warner's scheme was never built. Providence is not alone: urban design is incomplete more often than not due to its great scale and the length of time required for construction.

clearance for tower blocks to measured preservation; then to the restoration of surviving historic areas of downtown, to the reconstruction and reopening of the city's downtown waterfront, a beginning of ecological restoration, and even to the gradual removal and reconfiguration of the belt of ugly highways that once ringed downtown.

Providence's downtown urban design plans were not particularly ambitious in scale. Its downtown is small, about one square kilometer in size, and most of the plans did not propose change over the entirety of this area. But this downtown is most certainly plural space. There are over fifty city blocks there, and most contain several parcels.[22] Every one of the urban design ideas proposed for downtown Providence involved changes to dozens or even hundreds of parcels ranging from large industrial plots to tiny plots that once held single-family houses. And transforming this aged cityscape required many to submit to alteration or even removal of their property.

The aims of Providence's urban design—beauty, order, visual unity, modernization, and creation or enhancement of public space—were similar if not identical to any number of urban design projects for similar pluralist city districts elsewhere. And Providence's urban design proposals had another commonality with these other designs: none of them was ever completed. The city's regular downtown urban design proposals over a series of decades are impressive; during the same time, no New England city of similar size was anywhere as prolific. But compared to the number of urban design ideas it created, Providence was comparatively poor at realizing them: none of its urban design plans were completely constructed, and some were not constructed at all. Even downtown's most acclaimed urban design intervention, the reconfiguration and reopening ("daylighting") of the Providence River, represented only a small part of the waterfront changes originally envisioned by architect William Warner. But incompletion did not seem to hurt Providence: its reopened, newly shaped rivers made the city famous and brought tens of thousands of spectators to its parklike riverbank for summer festivals.

Providence's urban design is not alone: incompletion is inevitable in plural urbanism. In fact, incompletion is the dirty secret of urban design, since incompletion goes against the Platonic ideal of a finished form. Yet even iconic examples of unitary urban design suffer from incompletion. Brasília may seem complete, and its *superquadra* blocks successfully reflect Lúcio Costa's neighborhood design, but many *superquadra* sites on the north side still remain vacant despite Brasília's vast growth beyond its original boundaries,[23] as do some parcels in the central business district of the *plano piloto*.[24] Most of Brasília's peer capital cities have been realized to a much lesser extent; one such,

Belmopan, is a tiny capital city in the Belizean countryside, so unfinished that it seems almost as empty as a Mayan ruin.[25]

It is hardly revolutionary to remind urban designers that incompletion is endemic to the art. Reasons for incompletion are legion: urban design takes a long time, "things change" (meaning clients, economics, design fashions, and politics), urban design is expensive, property acquisition is difficult, and so on. And incomplete urban design is still better than design not built at all: most urbanists are accustomed to the worse fate of seeing most of their ideas come to naught. Some, such as Le Corbusier's Plan Voisin or the futurist proposals of Sant'Elia, were never meant to be constructed. Yet most unbuilt urban design ideas were seemingly intended for construction but proved too difficult to build, such as the 1935 plan for Moscow or any number of more recent urban design plans like Detroit's 1969 proposal *Detroit 1990*, Kevin Lynch's 1973 *Looking at the Vineyard*, and so on.

Remaining unbuilt is a quality that urban design shares with architecture: most monographs of well-known designers, even those known for their professional success, such as Steven Holl, Rem Koolhaas, Frank Gehry, and Andrés Duany, contain unbuilt projects. Unbuilt projects are part of the reality of architectural practice, and there is little surprise in a project failing to be constructed. But among the building arts, incompletion is a problem almost unique to urban design. Buildings are rarely half completed: functional requirements, weatherproofing, and financial strictures all encourage a project's completion once it is initiated. Partially completed buildings may be tolerated in the developing world, where a building owner may wait for years before adequate funds are available to continue, as in the notorious Torre de David in Caracas. And some large buildings—a convention center or laboratory, perhaps—may have an extension temporarily or permanently suspended. But in European and American cities permanently incomplete buildings are generally embarrassing eyesores, a sign of failure, an invitation to vandalism or even demolition.

Incompletion in urban design occurs on a scale that would be surprising and likely unacceptable in architecture. My calculations showed that Warner's Providence riverfront design was left 75 percent incomplete,[26] and Burnham and Bennett's *Plan of Chicago* is equally so. The *Plan* is justly celebrated for its realized elements, including the city's parks along Lake Michigan, the double-level Wacker Drive along the river, the widened Michigan Avenue, and other arteries. But these admirable elements represent just a small fraction of the design proposals of the *Plan*.[27] Among the *Plan*'s unbuilt urban design elements are a number of axial boulevards; numerous street

6.14 Architecture is rarely left half finished: incompletion inhibits profit and invites vandalism or even informal inhabitation, as in Caracas's infamous Torre de David. Even this tower, long left open to informal settlement, has been requisitioned for eventual completion.

widenings and waterfront improvements; a unified grouping of railroad stations, and a monumental Civic Center. Today's impressive array of realized Burnham and Bennett projects is just a small fragment of what the *Plan*'s authors envisioned. This is not to mention that many realized *Plan* elements were realized in a manner different from what Burnham envisioned—an issue that will be addressed in the concluding section of this chapter.

Just as we saw that Burnham's proposal for Chicago, Le Corbusier's proposal for the City for Three Million, and for that matter most urban design images, show finished projects as static, unchanging entities, we can see that Burnham's urban design ideas, conceived as a Platonic ideal of balance, proportion and symmetry in perfect concert with Beaux-Arts philosophy, would have been incomplete even with one building left unbuilt. The conception of the *Plan of Chicago* as a unitary ideal of perfection, analogous to Versailles in form and scale, but imposed on the pluralist reality of industrial Chicago, doomed it right from the start. First, land cost and acquisition issues restricted the city from constructing more than a small portion of the plan in the twenty-year period after its 1909 publication. By the early 1930s economic conditions had shifted and construction of plan elements was abandoned. But after World War II, when Chicago might have again been able to construct more elements of the plan, priorities had changed. The automobile was more dominant, different types of roadways were needed, and the plan's overall concept of clusters of planned monumental buildings defining urban space seemed dated and irrelevant in the age of modernism.

Even the greatest political powers and funding levels in history would not have made Burnham's plan fully possible. But the *Plan of Chicago*'s incompleteness does not reduce the impact of those plan elements that were built. A citizen enjoying the city's beautiful lakefront is not likely to know or care that a monumental Civic Center capping the view inland from Grant Park was never constructed: the built elements of the plan function as intended and are very popular. In similar fashion, the crowds enjoying the "WaterFire" art events on the banks of the Providence, Woonasquatucket, and Moshassuck rivers neither know nor care that this river walk was originally projected to extend much farther north and south from where it exists today.

Urban design has been left incomplete for as long as there has been urban design; should designers, when formulating their ideas, really care if projects are likely to be left unfinished? The seemingly obvious answer to this question is no. One might argue that urban design should always be designed as a complete form, whatever the likelihood of incompleteness, simply because designs should be beautiful and because complete designs are better than incomplete ones. Just like architects, urban designers' notions of formal appeal and formal success do not include incompleteness. On a practical level, little would likely be gained from an advocacy standpoint by showing a rendering of an unfinished project: the likelihood of incompletion would hardly enthuse a client being asked to support a major design effort. From this perspective, incompletion is an uncomfortable reality of urban design. Though it is not ideal, there is not much one can do about it, so the less said about this messy reality, the better.

It does seem a curious thing, however, that urban designers would not consider accommodating the reality of incompleteness more, even if that reality were undesirable. Manuel de Solà-Morales, for one, was aware of this danger; we recall that he favored projects "small enough to get achieved in a foreseeable time period" precisely because he feared "exceeding the client's capacity for implementation."[28] Like any good architect, Solà-Morales wished for his urban design to be completed, permanent (i.e., unchangeable), and finely realized; scalar limitation was his method of ensuring that this could happen.

But other architects building at large scale do not always seem to have learned this lesson. Perhaps the lure of gigantic projects is so tempting that even the risk of incompletion does not dissuade. Richard Meier was fortunate to have the vast resources of the Getty Foundation supporting his 110-acre museum complex overlooking Los Angeles,[29] but his colleague Peter Eisenman was not so lucky. His City of Culture of Galicia, an equally massive museum and civic center atop a hillside near Santiago de Compostela in Spain,[30] was derailed by funding problems and is not likely to see completion soon, if ever. Half of the project remains unbuilt. One might indict the scale and ambition of such gigantic building programs, but such scalar gigantism is a reality of contemporary times, as Koolhaas noted in "Bigness,"[31] and incompletion therefore seems likely to continue.

Accustomed as we are to images of Platonically complete urban design, the idea of a purposefully incomplete urban design concept may seem ludicrous. But let us reconsider. Wouldn't Burnham's projects have succeeded even if they had been proposed on an individual basis, just as Providence's waterfront succeeds in its mostly incomplete state? In similar fashion, Emperor Napoleon III's Paris boulevards succeed whether or not any larger design concept, if it even existed, was completed or not. And Paris's boulevards are definitely incomplete; one 1863 map shows dozens of projected roads, only some of which were ever built.[32] Napoleon III reputedly drew a schematic plan for the city's future roadways in different colors according to their

6.15   Santiago de Compostela's City of Culture of Galicia was to be the crowning achievement of Peter Eisenman's body of work, but Spain's 2008 fiscal crisis left the project incomplete, perhaps forever.

twenty buildings instead of the thirty or so that were constructed. And Plečnik's work, as we have seen, is itself the result of incompleteness. His constructions in Ljubljana are treasured and beneficial nonetheless.

Similarly, the concepts of chapter 5 accept and welcome incompleteness. The green avenues to the sea and the multiscalar grid concepts succeed even if only one or two are constructed. Likewise Savannah's aforementioned squares succeed with no definitive or final number; squares may be subtracted or added without detracting from the integrity and interest of the design concept. The design scenarios in chapter 5 provide just a few examples of how incompletion can be integrally conceived as part of a design concept rather than apart from it. Thus does plural urbanism open new doors to accepting and welcoming, rather than resisting, this most fundamental feature of urban design.

The diagram in figure 6.17 contrasts the gradual completion of a design idea associated with conventional urban design thinking with the inevitable incompletion associated with plural urbanism. In this image, only four of the six projected urban design elements have been constructed to any degree, and only one of those has been completed as projected, while two elements are left completely unbuilt.

Incompleteness is not consistent with the idea of successful urban design, and yet incompleteness is a hallmark of almost every urban design project at a scale larger than Solà-Morales's "urban fragments." Inevitable incompleteness is a fundamental quality of pluralist urbanism and an aspect of design that urbanists should not only accept but welcome. Embracing the incompleteness of urban design ideas—and built projects—is tantamount to embracing the incompleteness of the city, and of human enterprise itself. We may one day see incompleteness—and thereby the ability to extend urban design ideas infinitely—as one of urban design's most valuable qualities. One day urban designers will routinely design projects whose incompleteness is embedded within the design.

Fidelity Is Flexible: Framing the Future

In his essay "The End(s) of Urban Design," Michael Sorkin provocatively posed urban design as trapped in a Scylla-and-Charybdis-type situation where opposing and unattractive options represented the only choices for urbanism.[35] Sorkin's outlook is cynical but also sobering. Neotraditionalism projects close control over a city's form, but the prospect of cities completely governed by guidelines dictating building form, bulk, use, facade, material, ground-floor activity, transparency, number of parking spaces, pedestrian entrances, and so on seems depressing. Such overly controlled cities—Portland, Oregon, and San Francisco come to mind—are pleasant enough but experientially quiet places, where experimentation is only rarely seen and buildings lose much of their visual interest as a result. These high-fidelity cities seem a rather passive and soporific end to urban design.

But the prospect of cities ungoverned by any aesthetic ideals whatsoever is equally unappealing. Cities that seem to have no control over building form at all, like many cities in contemporary China or Japan, are less attractive than those that are too controlled. As such cities grow larger and larger, adding more and more skyscrapers in random places, the possibility of a coherent urban design vision for these cities seems to recede into the distance. Sorkin correctly identifies the dilemma of urban designers who have no formal alternatives available other than a high-fidelity version of urban design—where the entire city is controlled and where experimentation or new formal visions are impermissible—and the zero-fidelity alternative—where urban design seems entirely absent, and architects can do whatever they want without fear of disrupting the city.

Plural urbanism provides designers with a third alternative, that of flexible fidelity. Urban design schemes need not be perfectly realized, nor do designers need give up on fully shaping the city. The past two sections on change and incompleteness have shown us that neither alternative is possible in any event: urban design is always incomplete, and eternal change will always alter an urban design scheme over time, whatever its designers' wishes. Unlike unitary urbanism whose design schemes must be realized in detail or fail, plural urbanism—whose designs possess multiple forms, agents, and scales—is amenable to flexibility because cities are plural entities with a wide range of different conditions.

Fidelity makes urban design foundationally different than architecture. In architecture, the ability to resolve a design successfully at a high level of detail is widely held to be evidence of an equally high level of ability. Similarly, the failure of architecture to reflect its designer's intentions at the scale of materials or construction details can be seen by architects themselves as a sign of failure. Paul Rudolph, a notoriously demanding and perfectionist designer, regretted some of his later buildings in Asia because associated architects, not Rudolph himself, had resolved their details. The results, Rudolph thought, did not reflect his full design intention.[36]

The most renowned architects of the modernist era, and of today, are those who were able to resolve their designs to the finest degree of detail. Certainly little is more fulfilling than the experience of a Mies van der Rohe structure for one interested in building details. Every inch of Mies's work is finely resolved, from the careful alignment of joints in the terrazzo floors to the mirrored slabs of marble on lobby walls. Potentially extraneous elements are ordered as much as possible; light switches are shifted downward to align with doorknobs, and window frames reduced so glass may meet floor and ceiling. Mies himself famously said that he wished his architecture to become *beinahe nichts* (almost nothing). To do so, Mies and his staff resolved architecture to its finest level of detail, where everything from a curtain wall to a window latch was consistently realized through clean design and rigorous fabrication.

Mies was perhaps the most rigorous of high modernists in his application of abstraction and resolution of detail, but he was not alone. Where Mies resolved architecture to a minimalist level of perfection, Finnish architect Alvar Aalto carefully and prolifically designed at multiple scales from glassware to furniture, from ornamental woodwork and metalwork to buildings, and even to small-scale civic complexes. Like Mies, Aalto's work is delightful to behold, less because of its rigor than for the variation that Aalto introduced into seemingly every scale and element of his architecture. Unlike Mies, one may not be able to predict every detail of an Aalto building in advance, but the architect's hand is abundant throughout. An apotheosis of this approach is the Villa Mairea, an early Aalto work near Turku, Finland. A critic noted every part of the house "present[ing] a remarkable array of colors, forms, textures—abstract white planes, lime-washed brickwork, weatherboarding, teak and stone cladding, assorted poles, trellises and wooden and metal railings, blue-glazed tiles, grass roofs, a spiral staircase, fragments of structure, climbing plants."[37] Even door handles were designed in various ways in different locations within the house. Rather than Mies's rigorous minimalism, Villa Mairea manifests a finely realized efflorescence of creativity at every scale.

Because carefully designed and realized details are a hallmark of successful architecture, a high level of fidelity to a designer's intentions is necessary to achieving this success. And for those architects who view building details as significant elements of their design, faithful construction monitoring from schematic design to built form is critical to achieving this high level of resolution. Fidelity is therefore an important feature of architecture: without it, even a well-designed structure may be so poorly realized or constructed that the designer's intentions will be difficult to discern, or altered beyond recognition. Quite apart from the legal ramifications of unfaithful construction, the aesthetic desire for design fidelity makes it a rare architect who approves of substantial design changes that do not come from the architect's hand or with the architect's

► **6.18** Mies van der Rohe designed his buildings down to the smallest level of detail. In the Farnsworth House, pictured here, terrazzo joints align neatly with window mullions. Such fidelity of construction is characteristic of the finest architecture.

approval. In extreme cases, a building's lack of design fidelity to its architect's intentions can even lead to it being delisted from the designer's record.

Some urban design can achieve the high fidelity found in the finest architecture. A small urban complex—such as those Alvar Aalto designed in the centers of three Finnish cities, Seinäjoki, Rovaniemi, and Säynätsalo—may faithfully reflect the architect's intentions from the scale of public spaces all the way to building details. Aalto's complexes reflect the designer's full thought, from the relationships of buildings and the city all the way to his trademark lighting fixtures. But while Aalto's complexes are generous architectural commissions, they are at best only intermediate-scale works of urban design. Perhaps their design and construction fidelity is as much as one can hope for in a work by a single designer: even Solà-Morales achieved no more.

At larger scales, retaining fidelity of design intentions is only possible by decentralizing design responsibility to multiple designers, each of whom can administer construction of their own buildings. In Chandigarh, for example, Le Corbusier designed the schematic plan of the city, but he then confined his design efforts mainly to the capitol complex, while his cousin Pierre Jeanneret designed commercial and civic structures in the city center. Similarly, in Brasília, Lúcio Costa designed the overall form of the *plano piloto* as well as the schematic design of the city's building blocks, its residential *superquadra*, but left design of individual buildings to other architects, notably Oscar Niemeyer.

Urban design is commonly accepted as a relatively low-fidelity art. Architects design buildings, while urban designers create design guidelines that may be variously strict or permissive according to the circumstances of their creation. On the one hand, in a private development such as Seaside, Florida, design guidelines may be strict enough to essentially dictate architectural style; this was certainly Duany and Plater-Zyberk's intention. On the other hand, urban design controls may be also quite loose. Some of New York City's zoning, for example, provides so much flexibility that building designs can assume nearly any shape; witness the current explosion of hysterical architectural form surrounding the High Line, as developers and their architects compete to attract well-heeled residents to what are for all intents and purposes functionally identical buildings. Citizen reaction to such zoning permissiveness has not generally been positive: over the decades since "flexible" zoning was introduced in 1961, urban designers have gradually restricted zoning to require more predictable, finely resolved building forms that more

► **6.19** Alvar Aalto was fortunate to design a civic center in Seinäjoki, Finland, in its totality, and to see the finished complex closely reflect his original vision. Opportunities to design works of urban design at a high degree of fidelity are rare.

Situationsplan des Zentrums: links Kirche (gebaut) mit Versamm-
lungs- und Gemeindesälen, rechts oben Bibliothek und Theater,
unten das bereits gebaute Rathaus, zwischen den beiden Zentren
die ausgeweitete Verkehrsstraße

Site plan of the center; left the church, already erected, with library
and theater, below the finished town hall, between the two centers
the enlarged traffic artery

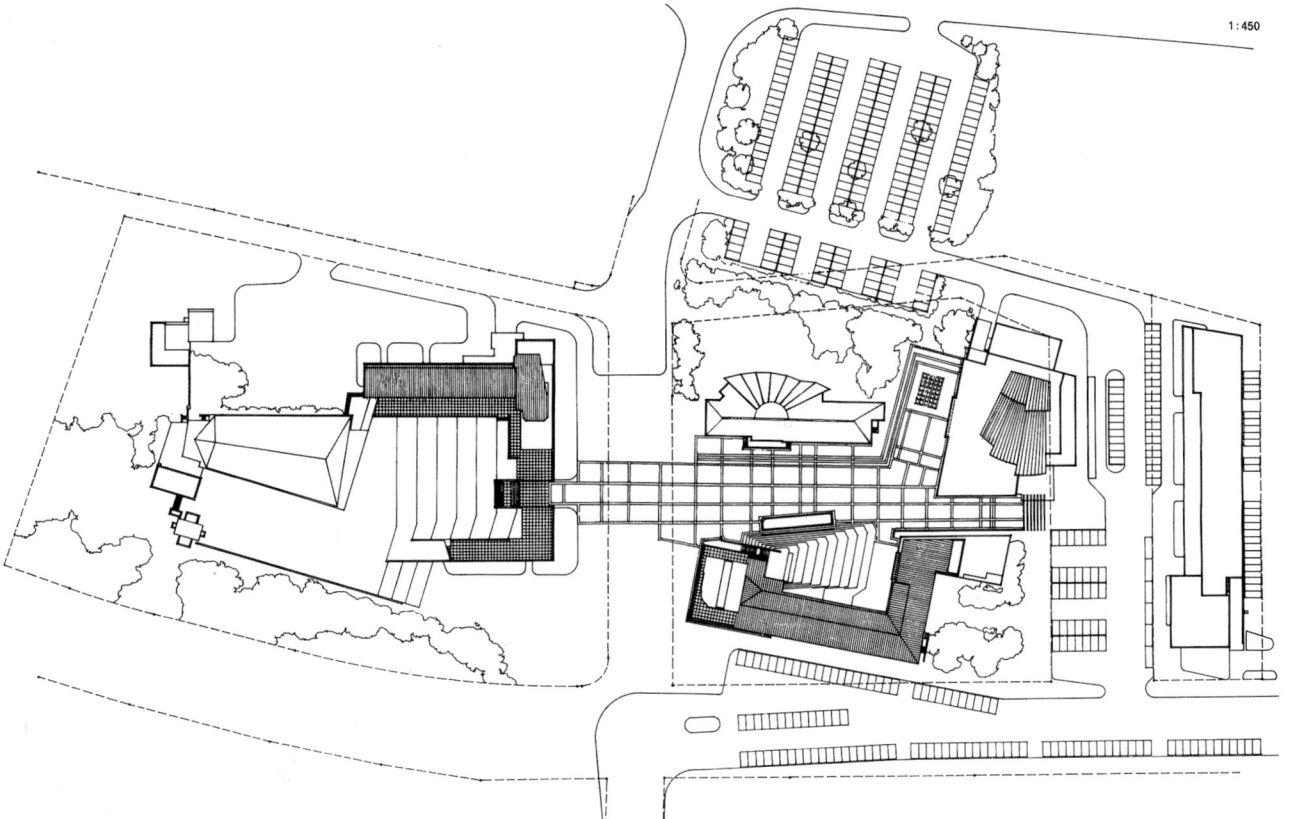

1 : 450

clearly reflect urban design intentions. Such was the aim of much of the zoning presented in Jonathan Barnett's 1974 book *Urban Design as Public Policy*.

Following on the heels of Duany and Plater-Zyberk's successfully implemented urban design controls in Seaside and subsequent new urbanist projects, the new urbanist movement has taken to the challenge of creating neotraditional, "form-based" zoning controls with great ardor. Based on the failure of typical zoning to shape predictable building form, new urbanist zoning is finding favor with Americans concerned with property values, quality of life, traffic, and other issues dear to property owners' hearts. They are joined by historic preservationists, who favor even stricter building controls in order to preserve the look and feel of landmark districts. Form-based zoning reflects a growing conformance between urban design controls and urban design conservatism, where the need for "urban design" is seen as equivalent to the need for contextualization or neohistoricism, whereas "architecture" is seen as risking variation from the historicist norm. Development in Manhattan is thus increasingly governed both by increasingly restrictive zoning and by a growing patchwork of landmark districts where all development is held to high standards of conformance with historic architecture. One can only imagine how Rem Koolhaas, who formerly saw city form as uncontrollable and now sees New York as *too* controlled, perceives the growing numbers of form-based zoning ordinances being adopted around the United States.

Current urban design approaches, based in unitary architectural concepts of order, do not lend themselves conceptually to flexibility. And even if fidelity is not critical to an urban design idea—the near-architectural fidelity of intermediate or smaller-scale urbanism is not found in all urban design proposals—its application is almost always constant. The lower-fidelity urban design resulting from zoning, for example, is almost always a field condition applicable across the entirety of a city's space. Similarly, urban design schemes intended for a particular site project a constant level of design attention across all parts of the site. Just as an architect (except, perhaps, Cedric Price or John Habraken) would never propose leaving part of a building for improvisation, urban designers rarely release design control over any part of a site, however large such a site may be.

But it turns out that fidelity is flexible in every city. Even in European cities such as Paris or Vienna, where the city centers are closely kept in more or less their historic state, many outlying districts sensibly permit a higher level of individual control over building design and an accompanying lower level of urban design fidelity. These lower-fidelity areas are hardly undesigned; the Parisian periphery, like American suburbs, remains regulated, but in a way that does not include as high a control of building form

6.20 Urban designers generally wish to achieve as much fidelity as possible. The "Starbucks urbanism" decried by critic Michael Sorkin reflects new urbanists' attempts to restrict city form to historic scales and relationships.

6.21 Ironically, while advocates of bigness like the aptly named BIG (Bjarke Ingels Group) may decry the "undesigned" cities of today, their own closely designed, massive buildings mirror new urbanists' desire to realize high-fidelity urban design.

or site planning as in the center of the city. The variability of urban design fidelity is even greater in developing nations, where state control is often quite weak and where the realization of urban design is a difficult enterprise except in the center city or in wealthy areas.

Flexible fidelity is reflected in all three plural urbanist projects in chapter 3. Brancusi's sculptures achieve a very high level of fidelity, as do the urban spaces around them since their restoration.[38] But the rest of Târgu Jiu is much less formally resolved; the buildings constructed along the axis during the 1980s are garish and ungainly, and much of the remaining urban fabric is modest, banal Romanian vernacular. But this lack of resolution and beauty in most of Târgu Jiu is not a bad thing. Were Brancusi's sculptures to be connected by a regular, monumental avenue, their power would be reduced and the viewer would likely be distracted from Brancusi's work. The sculptures' impact comes both from their individual quality and from their contrast with Târgu Jiu's typical and unassuming landscape. Amid this modesty, Brancusi's individual elements acquire more value.

Plečnik's Ljubljana is a much higher-quality environment overall than Târgu Jiu, but that city also has many districts where urban design is absent and where the cityscape is banal or even unattractive. In others, as we saw, Plečnik's work makes the surrounding city setting much more meaningful. Areas of Ljubljana where Plečnik devoted his design attention, such as the Zoisova Cesta where he placed a stone pyramid and path leading inland from the river, are much more meaningful than those where he did not. In Ljubljana one can observe three levels of urban design fidelity: a very high level, represented by Plečnik's own interventions; a moderately high level, of urban spaces influenced by or connected to Plečnik's interventions; and a low level, of urban spaces shaped by less distinctive urban design features like the street grid that are remote from Plečnik's work. Variable fidelity is exactly the sensation one experiences walking through Ljubljana's streets: there are clearly streets and spaces that Plečnik carefully considered and those that he did not.

Future urban designers could react to Ljubljana in multiple ways. In and around a Plečnik intervention one would expect some level of attention to the prior work, whether contextual in nature or not. But, in the areas of the city not influenced by Plečnik, an urban designer would be able to decide whether to attempt to impose a high level of design fidelity, perhaps in a different manner than Plečnik, or not. Except during the comparatively brief Communist era (from ca. 1950 to 1990), when large-scale urban design measures ignored Plečnik's work, it has continued to shape one's perception of Ljubljana through its careful placement and execution. Overall, Plečnik's urbanism refines and reflects Ljubljana's piecemeal, flexible fidelity of urban design, rather than resisting or reversing it.

Twin Parks also demonstrates that urban design fidelity need not be strong in order for a formal scheme to have a positive effect. We have already seen that its original plan displayed buildings quite different from those ultimately realized. As built, each individual cluster of buildings in Twin Parks reflected the design interests of its individual architect: James Stewart Polshek played with polychromy, Richard Meier explored flexible massing and different types of spatial enclosure, and Giovanni Pasanella mirrored Le Corbusier in his building's novel spatial organization. Yet collectively the projects shared much: not only their social mission to provide low-cost housing, but also their material expression of brown brick, providing a common aesthetic. Twin Parks has a comparatively low level of design fidelity. The urban designers determined the program, selected the sites, and selected the cluster architects. The architects then were permitted substantial latitude in design decisions, so much so as to sometimes displease officials in the client administration of the New York State Urban Development Corporation.[39] But Twin Parks's relatively low design fidelity does not appreciably diminish the project's impact today, particularly when compared to similar projects of the time.

The dimensions of plural urban design demonstrate that fidelity is neither absent nor omnipresent, but flexible. Many areas of the city merit a high level of urban design fidelity while other areas deserve much less. The plural dimensions of time, agents, and form permit a trajectory in which, at different times and in different spaces, design elements may be finely resolved, almost perfected, while in others the city may be left to its own devices, to be shaped as the market or as its inhabitants wish. We can begin to imagine all cities as patchworks of greater or lesser urban design fidelity. This has practical aspects, reflecting the limited ability of urban designers to exert control, and normative aspects, reflecting the desirability of urban designers to exert control in certain areas.

The diagram below represents the flexible fidelity of plural urbanism contrasted, again, with the conventional model of a fully constructed unitary urban project that is built almost exactly as designed. Plural urbanism, on the other hand, is realized at varying levels of fidelity; some areas are very close to the original design, while others vary substantially.

Variability in urban design has multiple meanings. It has conventionally been taken as more or less proportional to (even equivalent to) historic value: historic areas require very high-fidelity, restrictive controls while nonhistoric areas require much less.

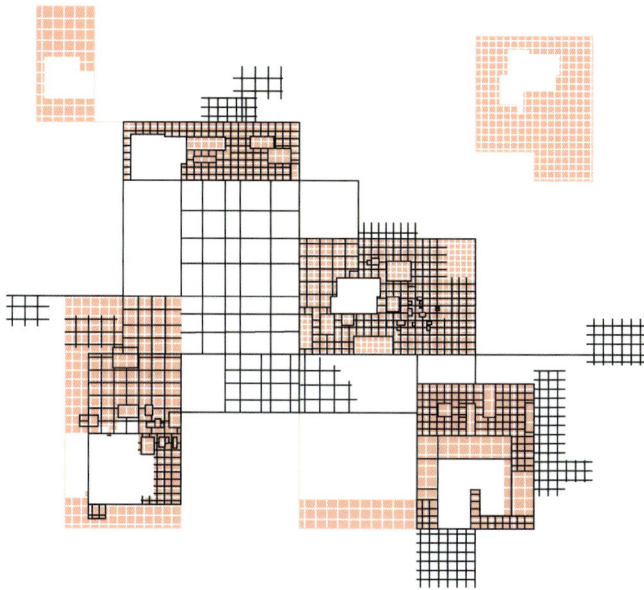

6.22 Just as cities are patchworks of greater or lesser design fidelity, so too can plural urbanism exert variable control over the form of the city. Some areas may merit close, careful design, while others may merit a relaxation or even absence of formal design control. This drawing shows an urban design scheme whose finished form varies substantially from that originally projected. Again, compare this drawing to that of the conventional urban design project shown in figure 6.11.

But this is a conservative and limited interpretation of flexible fidelity in urban design. In some settings, urban designers might decide to determine precisely the opposite, that formally irregular areas merit high degrees of urban design fidelity to permit at least a weak urban design vision to take hold, while consistent areas (say, a swath of monotonous 1960s housing) might merit relaxations of design control, to loosen up the area's appearance. While neither of the above alternatives might seem desirable to everyone, certainly the possibilities for variation and creativity in varying levels of urban design fidelity are very great, because the urban form of most cities is actually much more pluralistic than is implied by Sorkin's polemic against neotraditionalism and bigness.

All three of the plural urbanists of chapter 4 acknowledged flexible fidelity in their design schemes. David Crane was well aware of urban designers' ability to focus only on certain areas of a scheme. Crane utilized the device of the capital web in order to be sure that even the least finely resolved proposals, perhaps by builders who weren't aware of the larger urban design idea, would be consistent with that idea. The capital web acknowledged and encouraged a higher level of fidelity around infrastructure and designed community facilities, with lower levels of design fidelity around "planned squatter areas" and "aided self-help housing."[40] One can easily imagine diagrams of cities that first show where flexibility has existed historically; then a second set of diagrams that envision a projection of future desired flexibility. Kevin Lynch imagined as much in his study of postwar Cambridge.[41]

Lynch's polycentered net and place utopia also argued both for and against close levels of design, portraying the city as a patchwork of highly governed areas and low-fidelity "strips and pieces of wasteland open to spontaneous or deviant use."[42] Bacon's vision of the city as a series of movement systems between closely designed monuments clearly acknowledged a lower level of urban design fidelity in the spaces in between, which were occupied by vernacular row houses. In each case, these plural urbanists balanced high levels of design fidelity equivalent or even identical to those achieved in architecture, with very low levels allowing for city growth and development to be more or less laissez-faire.

Resisting flexible fidelity will continue to restrict urban design to scales where high fidelity can be achieved (as in Solà-Morales's urban fragments) or to field-based approaches (e.g., zoning that attempts to institute a similar, generally low, level of fidelity everywhere). Both attitudes, one favored by architects and the other favored by planners, ignore the fact that cities are composed of highly variable levels of design fidelity—areas that are themselves not fixed but variable. Ultimately, urban designers would do well to formulate new design ideals and perhaps new representational modes, which can reflect flexible fidelity as a foundational principle in urban design. Until this happens, we are likely to see continued limitations in urban design's scope and effectiveness, whether at high or low levels of fidelity. Might we not instead design cities that are both closer to reality and more ideal, as we seek to perfect pieces of the urban fabric, releasing the rest?

Conclusion: Urban Design's Plural Future

Urban design is a difficult art not only in its conception, but also in its realization. Though all the building arts (architecture, landscape, sculpture, and land art) face related challenges, urban designers face additional difficulties that make urban design, particularly unitary urban design, a scarce commodity among the world's cities. These challenges, some of which were discussed in previous sections, are endemic to urban design, but they are not insurmountable; creativity can play a role in diminishing them.

Urban design needs a special sort of creativity, a creativity that is different both in kind and degree from that needed by the other building arts. Before we discuss what kinds of creativity are needed and why, let us review some of the particular challenges faced by urban design.

Like the other building arts, urban design is costly. Large buildings are expensive, as are large parks. Urban design can be even more costly than architecture or landscape, particularly when it is constructed at large scale and all at once, as in an entire neighborhood or city. Since urban design is generally composed of several buildings, or open spaces, or sometimes both, construction of urban design usually requires much greater resources than are required for a single structure or space alone. Even if those structures or spaces are themselves city district in scale, challenges await. While unitary urban design, like a college campus, airport, or office complex such as Rockefeller Center, usually has a single owner and client for design, construction of such urban design projects within a short time frame is usually rare unless the client has very substantial means. The rapid construction of new airports in China or new capital cities and capitol complexes in developing countries are extremely expensive unitary design projects that are the exception, not the rule.

But cost is only the beginning of urban design's challenges. All of the building arts exist within economic systems, but urban design exists within social and political systems that are more demanding than they generally are of architecture and landscape. Because urban design projects can comprise the very fabric of an urban or suburban citizen's daily living space—a neighborhood center, perhaps, or a shopping district or downtown area—many citizens living near urban design projects feel that urbanism somehow has an impact on their lives, even if it is just about looking at the project every day. Urban design is thus responsible to political and social processes that may exact demands in terms of the time, scale, or nature of a design proposed for construction. This can lead to a much higher level of public questions, scrutiny, and even distrust for urban design.

Such scrutiny is particularly acute in societies whose average level of income, education, and general sense of empowerment are high, or at least increasing. Urban design, or change in the urban public environment, is particularly threatening in prosperous, democratic societies such as New York City and London. The historic districts and restrictive zoning so decried by Rem Koolhaas are a direct result of these societies' concern over change; the mismatch between growing wealth and a decreasing permission to build is becoming particularly acute, so much so that extremely wealthy Londoners are now resorting to "dig outs" or "luxury bunkers" under their mansions in areas such as Kensington Palace Gardens. The skepticism of powerful citizens generates resistant political structures that can make large-scale change to the built environment, or urban design, almost insuperably difficult: witness the decades-long struggle to add a single airport runway to London's Heathrow, a struggle that may never succeed.

To these fiscal, social, and political challenges we may add a practical challenge, one shared with the other building arts. Many clients who might commission a notable or well-designed work of urban design either do not choose or cannot afford to do so. Ironically, places where high-quality urban design might be more possible—wealthy cities like New York and London—are skittish for the reasons mentioned above. Yet, in many cities where there are large amounts of construction, there is little high-quality urban design but plenty of vernacular or undesigned development.

Under ideal conditions, all of the building arts would be well designed and well executed, well financed, and well supported by enlightened, powerful clients. Many architects have benefited from such ideal conditions when realizing their finest works, but most projects in the building arts fall short in one or more of these categories. Urban design is perhaps the most highly affected—as the largest, most complex, and expensive of the building arts, it requires particularly favorable circumstances, as well as luck, for correct execution. As a result, urban design is almost inevitably deprived in one or another of these categories—leading to the equally inevitable change, incompletion, or infidelity reviewed earlier.

With comparatively few ideal commissions available and fierce competition for them, realizing high-quality, well-executed urban design is a privilege for comparatively few designers. It is often, therefore, only achieved toward the end of a long career. While commissions may vary from country to country depending on political or economic circumstances—the 1950s, peak of the New Towns program, was an excellent time to be an urban designer in Great Britain, for example—the number of accomplished, critically acclaimed urban designers in any country at any given time is relatively small. Even in Spain, a nation with a rich design tradition and significant urban construction, Manuel de Solà-Morales had few peers.

Urban design's difficulties are perceived as structural or endemic to the field; designers accept them as part of the cost of engaging in an art that is thought by most practitioners to be a privilege. Their worthy dedication notwithstanding, it is important to ask why urban design is so difficult to carry out, and whether it must be and must stay so. It would, for sure, be foolhardy to wish that difficulties such as political pressures, economic restrictions, or resistant societies might simply evaporate. They have not, even in Stalin's Russia, and they will not so long as human society persists. But urban design's difficulties are due not only to the challenges described above but to its unitary origins, from the very conception of urban design as a large-scale or larger-scale architectural or landscape composition. It may be heretical to suggest that a substantial part of urban design's problems lie within our current conceptual framework of urban design, but I believe this to be the case.

As we have seen in chapter 1, unitary urban design is essentially an enlargement of architectural thinking. Like monumental architecture, urban design was born under conditions of great wealth and power (e.g., Louis XIV's Versailles), and it is under these conditions that it continues to achieve its greatest successes even today (e.g., China's Beijing 2008 Summer Olympics). Yet there are, and will always be, many places where the power and wealth needed to carry out conventional unitary urban design will not be available. Many societies are so poor that large-scale urban design is nearly impossible under current conditions (e.g., in Haiti). And in wealthy places, as democracy, wealth, and empowerment grow, the number of citizens willing to tolerate large-scale construction in their midst may continue to shrink. The difficult development process for new large-scale construction in wealthy cities such as London and Boston certainly seems to indicate that this is the case. Barring a flourishing of additional wealthy autocracies, in other words, conventional unitary urban design as we know it could quite possibly become an endangered species—the result of constraints in power, economics, society, patrons, and so on, but also the result of urban design's conceptual dependence on unitary models developed for a world that no longer exists, or for a world that never will.

In some ways, and in some places, unitary urban design will continue to flourish. Presumably, there will always be new suburban subdivisions, there will always be office complexes, and there will always be airports. At the same time, the world possesses a large number of comparatively undesigned or lightly designed environments, of little visual quality or interest and underperforming in terms of the aesthetic satisfaction, performative function, and efficiency that they might provide. Urban design can contribute positively to these underdesigned places. But if urban design is currently unable to contribute because these places do not possess the conditions conducive to unitary urbanism, why not reframe urban design in order to accommodate the realities of the urban conditions that need it most?

I believe that urban designers should focus on new conceptions of the art that will make it possible for this largest of the arts to thrive in a variety of other settings.

The dimensions of plural urbanism provide conceptual and practical grounds for urban design to operate in a wider variety of urban environments than are currently engaged by unitary urban design. And the principles that are inherent to urban design—incompletion, change, and lack of fidelity—provide no disadvantage to plural urbanism. Incompletion is no disadvantage because plural urbanism avoids "completion"—it is open-ended. Change is easily accommodated because cities change, grow, and shrink around plural design elements without damaging the scheme. And lack of fidelity is not necessarily damaging, because the broad aim of plural urban design concepts can be readable and meaningful nonetheless.

Plural urbanism is an art appropriate to the city *that is*, rather than one that waits for the city that may never be. Plural urbanism may be comprised of architecture and landscape, its sister building arts, but it is fundamentally different from both: this largest of the arts relates directly to the functioning and life of the city, without being an enlarged echo of its smaller peers. Plural urbanism has an aesthetic as powerful as any art, yet it is uniquely and necessarily constructed piecemeal, without demanding significant changes to the cityscape around it. Plural urbanism certainly does not demand the tabula rasa that has been an unattractive element of so much unitary urban design, yet this art can powerfully transform one's perception of the cityscape. Only a hard-hearted citizen would claim Plečnik's work in Ljubljana as meaningless or invisible.

Understanding urban design's plural qualities, and projecting urban design as a plural art, does not reduce, reconfigure, or abandon what has conventionally been considered to be urban design. Currently popular tropes of urbanism such as new urbanism or landscape urbanism—both dependent on unitary concepts and predicated on unitary sites—would not evaporate in a world further shaped by plural urbanism. Unlike the competing urban design ideologies of the past, plural urbanism is not a substitute but the opposite, an expansion of urban design thought and action that permits urban design to exist, for this art to flourish, where it never has before. Plural urbanism opens the door to new aesthetics, spatial concepts, compositional structures, and creative avenues for design to act within the world that is.

While this book is subtitled "a measured manifesto," plural urbanism is not new; urban design's plural dimensions have always existed, as have the three principles of change, incompleteness, and flexible fidelity. In time, the dominance of unitary thinking in urban design may simply come to be seen as a historical artifact, the reflection of urban design's century-plus dependence on architecture, the art from which so much urban design thinking and practice derived. Thus this book's manifesto is less a formal declaration of independence than a call for recognition of an independence that has always existed. Urban design can never be the same as architecture; this does not remove urban design from the realm of the arts, but more firmly establishes it as a different one.

Cities are wondrous creations of humankind. Quite apart from the economic and social benefits they have historically provided, they have seeded a rich ground for creativity. Humanity has long recognized that the design of the city itself can be one of these creative activities—perhaps the most demanding and certainly the largest in scale. By demanding that the largest of the arts shape cities in the manner of a large architectural composition, humanity has been asking too much. Such an act—an entire city designed in a unitary manner, such as Brasília—is so unusual that such acts cannot be the core of urban design, only an unusual branch of it. The art of urban design is much better suited as a reflection of cities than as a reflection of architecture. Cities change perpetually, and urban design itself should perpetually change. The dynamic nature of the city provides, and demands, a *dynamic* art, an art with new compositional strategies, an art with new, perpetually changing patterns and networks of aesthetic ideas that exist within the city—and improve it. This, and no less, is plural urbanism.

Plural urbanism may not be any easier to realize than unitary urbanism has been. Unitary urban design has pictorial advantages, for one—it is conceptually easy to depict through conventional means of architectural representation, an advantage for dissemination through media, particularly in the digital age. The plethora of flashy city district renderings streaming out of Asia and elsewhere is proof enough. And while it is easy to understand the changing, incomplete, flexible quality of plural urban design, it is not so easy to visually represent what such a dynamic art might look like, especially through the current convention of static architectural renderings. Plural urbanists will therefore have to be particularly creative in developing representational strategies that allow the art to be communicated and understood. This is a challenge, but not an insurmountable one. Nor are compositional challenges necessarily a barrier. The relatively few examples outlined in this book demonstrate that a variety of compositional strategies are possible in plural urban design, and that these can be easily adapted, borrowed, and further developed.

This book was in part written to dispel the current understanding that urban design is, professionally speaking, merely an architectural outgrowth. Architects (and quite possibly landscape architects as well) are very well equipped both in terms of interest and skill to become urban designers, but after reading this book it should be clear that urban design is not simply a scalar modification of either of these building arts. These words echo Kevin Lynch's over thirty years ago,[43] but they bear repeating as contemporary urban design practice mirrors many of the issues which Lynch himself observed, particularly the restricted understanding of urban design as a unitary enlargement of architecture. This unitary-only understanding of urban design is valid only in part, and it has long prevented a more diversified and sophisticated understanding of the true nature of this largest art. Fortunately, as with all professions, reality drives ideals as much as the other way around. And the reality of the city, of the comparative scarcity of urban design, and of the limitations of unitary urban design press for renewed understandings, alternative approaches, and new generations of creative ideas. These, I believe, are possible through a new understanding of urban design's plural dimensions and foundational principles.

Many professions can and should participate in the creation of plural urban design. Trained, talented designers will be central: we have seen the benefits of their involvement in previous chapters. These may be practitioners of the other building arts who relinquish the privileges of these other arts in order to embrace the privileges and responsibilities of plural urbanism—designers who can become improvisers, generating or following design decisions freely and loosely, designers who surrender the exactitude of other building arts in favor of the scalar reach of the largest art. Even artists may become plural urbanists. Brancusi already did, stepping outside of the conventional boundaries of art to see the city as a canvas for art, and art as a building block for a more beautiful city. The range of potential participants in plural urbanism is great, since plural urbanism has plural agents, and each of these agents may be a designer.

We stand here not at a conclusion, but at the beginning of a new understanding of urban design, the largest art. This book has imagined some further steps into that beginning, a potential world of plural urban design projects for multiple environments, in multiple settings, through multiple means. But it has not completed the journey. The world is not yet and will never be complete, and beyond the dimensions, projects, principles, and ideas in this book lies a world of cities awaiting plural urbanism, a world of urban design projects yet to be realized. And perhaps, in a future world where plural urbanism is widespread, everyone can live in a place that is a work of urban design, and everyone, every urban citizen, builder, or designer, can become one of those plural agents who helps design and construct their world.

Acknowledgments

Although this is my second book, it was longer in the making. Over the past twenty-five years, many individuals, institutions, and places provided insights that developed my experience and intellectual progress in urban design. First and foremost I thank my wife Lorena Bello Gomez, herself an urban designer. Over the past eight years Lorena has continually inspired me with her creativity and talent, while exposing me to Barcelona's robust urban design culture, particularly the work of Manuel de Solà-Morales and Josep Lluís Sert.

I began to think about urban design long ago. Douglas Woodward, Jeffery Sugarman, Geoff Baker, and Lauren Otis, my colleagues in New York City's Zoning and Urban Design Division, showed me how urban designers could engage with a plural public and a pluralist city. John de Monchaux and Julian Beinart were inspirational role models, architects who cared deeply about urban design and whose lectures and studios formed much of my doctoral education. In Chicago, my colleague Charles Hoch always believed I had something to say about urban design, and I will always treasure his confidence in me. The Graduate School of Design at Harvard University provided an invigorating insight into contemporary design culture; I could not have written this book without seeing the work and ideas of Alex Krieger, Jerold Kayden, Joan Busquets, Steve Cecil, and Scheri Fultineer.

At MIT, many generous and insightful colleagues, staff, and students made the writing of this book easier. My especial thanks go out to Larry Vale and Anne Spirn, both of whom read and edited substantial portions of the manuscript during busy times, and to Eran Ben-Joseph, whose confidence in my work made me more confident in turn. Allison Hu created evocative and powerful images of the book's imaginary places. Caroline Jordi's work contributed much to chapter 5's "Island." Melissa Vaughn provided valuable counsel regarding the publishing process. Talented editor Patsy Baudoin provided an almost infinite number of improvements both small and large, reshaping my manuscript into a book. Sonny Oram and Hannah Gaudet obtained almost all of the image permissions in the book, while research assistants Lilly Jacobsen, Kara Elliott-Ortega, Sara Brown, Laura Schmitz, Josselyn Ivanov, Andrea Ferreira, and Brandon Peterson contributed to the bibliography, research, and figures. Daniel Campo and Marcel Smets generously shared images.

Books require time and space for reflection and writing. An early journey to Ljubljana, Slovenia, exposed me to the wondrous work of Jože Plečnik, while a week on Prudence Island, Rhode Island, reminded me that urban design shapes more than just urban space. MIT's Department of Urban Studies and Planning provided a semester's leave for the writing of three chapters, and visits to Gdańsk, Poland, and Mount Hood, Oregon, permitted me to organize initial thoughts. I might have hoped for a more exotic locale in which to write, but my university office did provide a gateway to the world via Rotch Library and Google Maps' Street View. The latter allowed me to see almost every city in the world both from the air and from the street, and I cannot recommend it enough.

I dedicate this book to John Louis Ryan and Isidro Bello Verdeal, my inspirations in family, work, and life.

Notes

Chapter 1: Unitary Architecture, Plural Cities

1. Michael Sorkin, "The End(s) of Urban Design," in Alex Krieger, ed., *Urban Design* (Minneapolis: University of Minnesota Press, 2009), 181.

2. Both the magazine and the book were associated with Harvard University's Graduate School of Design.

3. Sorkin, "The End(s) of Urban Design," 182.

4. Alexander Cuthbert, "Whose Urban Design?," *Journal of Urban Design* 15, no. 3 (2010): 443–448.

5. Ibid., 444, 447.

6. Sorkin, "The End(s) of Urban Design," 182.

7. Ebenezer Howard, *Garden Cities of To-Morrow* (London: Faber and Faber, 1946).

8. Dora Wiebenson, *Tony Garnier: The Cité Industrielle* (New York: George Braziller, 1969).

9. R. Stephen Sennott, ed., *Encyclopedia of Twentieth Century Architecture* (New York: Taylor and Francis, 2004), 261.

10. Jean-Louis Ferrier, *Art of Our Century: The Chronicle of Western Art, 1900 to the Present* (New York: Prentice-Hall, 1988), 421.

11. Ludwig Hilberseimer, *Metropolisarchitecture and Selected Essays*, ed. and trans. Richard Anderson (New York: GSAPP Books, 2012).

12. Brian J. Bailey, *The Luddite Rebellion* (New York: New York University Press, 1999).

13. Lewis Mumford, "The Sky Line: Mother Jacobs' Home Remedies,'" *New Yorker*, December 1, 1962, 148–179.

14. Stephen A. Goldsmith and Lynne Elizabeth, eds., *What We See: Advancing the Observations of Jane Jacobs* (New York: New Village Press, 2010); Sonia Hirt and Diane Zahm, eds., *The Urban Wisdom of Jane Jacobs* (New York: Routledge, 2012).

15. Jane Jacobs, *The Death and Life of Great American Cities* (New York: Random House, 1961), 373.

16. Rem Koolhaas, *Delirious New York: A Retroactive Manifesto for Manhattan* (New York: Oxford University Press, 1978), 82–109.

17. Roy Strickland, ed., *Post Urbanism and Reurbanism: Peter Eisenman vs. Barbara Littenberg and Steven Peterson, Designs for Ground Zero*, Michigan Debates on Urbanism 3 (Ann Arbor: University of Michigan, 2006).

18. Rem Koolhaas and Bruce Mau, *S,M,L,XL*, ed. Jennifer Sigler (New York: Monacelli Press, 1995).

19. Ibid., 502.

20. Ibid., 510–511.

21. Ibid., 836.

22. Ibid., 848.

23. Ibid., 839, 841.

24. Sorkin, "The End(s) of Urban Design," 181.

25. Oddly enough, the same holds true for beautifully designed neotraditional city districts, such as the early twentieth-century Amsterdam South neighborhood designed by Hendrik Berlage. Its peaceful canals, green riverbanks, and brick housing blocks have a gorgeous harmony, but the ensemble feels artificial, too perfect, with little room for creativity or even accident. Much like Seaside, Florida, Amsterdam South feels like a stage set of urban design rather than the real thing.

26. Stella Duffy, "Celebrating Joan Littlewood: It's Time to Build Her Fun Palaces," *Guardian*, September 18, 2013.

27. Robert A. M. Stern, David Fishman, and Jacob Tilove, *Paradise Planned: The Garden Suburb and the Modern City* (New York: Monacelli Press, 2013), 950–951.

28. Andrés Duany, "The Garden City: A General Theory of Urbanism," lecture, MIT Center for Advanced Urbanism, Cambridge, MA, March 10, 2014.

29. Eugene Kinkead, *Central Park 1857–1995: The Birth, Decline, and Renewal of a National Treasure* (New York: Norton, 1990), 18.

30. Ludwig Hilberseimer, *The Nature of Cities* (Chicago: P. Theobald, 1965), 238–256.

31. David Gosling and Barry Maitland, *Concepts of Urban Design* (New York: St. Martin's Press, 1984); Paul D. Spreiregen, *Urban Design: The Architecture of Towns and Cities* (New York: McGraw-Hill, 1965); Urban Design Associates, *The Urban Design Handbook: Techniques and Working Methods*, ed. Karen Levine (New York: Norton, 2003).

32. Roy Rosenzweig and Elizabeth Blackmar, *The Park and the People: A History of Central Park* (Ithaca: Cornell University Press, 1998), 412–438.

33. Rem Koolhaas, "Bigness, or the Problem of Large," in Koolhaas and Mau, *S,M,L,XL*, 509–516.

34. Of course, despite Koolhaas's call for retreat, there has been longstanding interest in designing cities beyond the scale of unitary sites. For example, there is a long regulatory history of "coding" cities through

zoning and other regulations. (See Eran Ben-Joseph, *The Code of the City: Standards and the Hidden Language of Place Making* [Cambridge, MA: MIT Press, 2005]. Andrés Duany and new urbanists are using such coding aggressively today, as we will see in a later chapter. Urban designers have a robust tradition of using regulation to shape the same uncontrolled cityscape that Koolhaas disowned; Jonathan Barnett is perhaps the best-known of these (see Barnett, *Urban Design as Public Policy: Practical Methods for Improving Cities* [New York: Architectural Record Books, 1974]), and many European and North American cities, among them Toronto (http://www1.toronto.ca/wps/portal/contentonly?vgnextoid=3e6652cc66061410VgnVCM10000071d60f89RCRD), Vancouver (http://vancouver.ca/home-property-development/land-use-and-development-policies-and-guidelines.aspx), and Portland, Oregon (https://www.portlandoregon.gov/bps/34250), have created and enforced such urban design standards.

35. Architectural Association, "Projective Cities," Architectural Association Graduate School, 2014, http://projectivecities.aaschool.ac.uk/.

36. Pier Vittorio Aureli, *The Possibility of an Absolute Architecture* (Cambridge, MA: MIT Press, 2011).

Chapter 2: Five Dimensions of Plural Urbanism

1. Rose Etherington, "Le Corbusier's Cabanon—the Interior 1:1," *Dezeen*, March 6, 2009, https://www.dezeen.com/2009/03/06/le-corbusier%E2%80%99s-cabanon-the-interior-11/.

2. The grid of streets and parks in Savannah, Georgia, for example, was extended until the mid-nineteenth century, and later contracted as automobile needs expanded in the twentieth. See John William Reps, *The Making of Urban America: A History of City Planning in the United States* (Princeton: Princeton University Press, 1965), 199–202.

3. Bart King, *An Architectural Guide to Portland* (Layton, UT: Gibbs Smith, 2001), 275–276.

4. William H. Whyte, *The Social Life of Small Urban Spaces* (Washington, DC: Conservation Foundation, 1980).

5. William H. Whyte, *City: Rediscovering the Center* (New York: Doubleday, 1988), 130–131.

6. Joan Busquets, *Barcelona: The Urban Evolution of a Compact City* (Cambridge, MA: Harvard University Graduate School of Design, 2005), 110–112.

7. Vincent Scully, *American Architecture and Urbanism* (New York: Henry Holt, 1988), 203; Edmund N. Bacon, *Design of Cities* (New York: Viking Press, 1967), 70–71; Andrés Duany, "The Garden City: A General Theory of Urbanism," lecture, MIT Center for Advanced Urbanism, March 10, 2014.

8. Bacon, *Design of Cities.*

9. Ibid., 73.

10. London has many such mundane streets, thoroughfares that scholar Donald Olsen called "invariably ugly [and] undistinguished." Olsen found urban design or "good planning" more in the city's parks, squares, and residential districts than in its streets. Donald J. Olsen, *Town Planning in London: The Eighteenth and Nineteenth Centuries* (New Haven: Yale University Press, 1982), 5.

11. Allan B. Jacobs, *Great Streets* (Cambridge, MA: MIT Press, 1993), 9, 11.

12. Joan Busquets and Felipe Correa, eds., *Cities, X Lines: A New Lens for the Urbanistic Project* (Cambridge, MA: Harvard University Graduate School of Design, 2006).

13. Manuel de Solà-Morales i Rubió, *Ten Lessons on Barcelona: Urbanistic Episodes that Have Made the Modern City* (Barcelona: Colegio de Arquitectos de Cataluña, 2008); Manuel de Solà-Morales i Rubió et al., *Cerdà/Ensanche* (Barcelona: Escola Tècnica Superior d'Arquitectura de Barcelona, 2010); Busquets, *Barcelona*; Joan Busquets and Miquel Corominas, *Cerdà and the Barcelona of the Future: Reality versus Project* (Barcelona: Diputació Barcelona, 2009).

14. Of course many complete city street patterns, such Philadelphia (1683), Washington (1803), or Saint Petersburg (1711), were created before the twentieth century, but their designers did not attempt, nor were they empowered, to design the buildings within those street patterns. Only in the twentieth century did the concept of an entire city as a single design, with streets, buildings, and parks integrally considered, come to be, such as Burnham and Bennett's *Plan of Chicago* (1909/1993) or Le Corbusier's Ville Radieuse (1924).

15. Brazil was not alone in constructing a new federal capital. After decolonization, many countries, from Pakistan to Nigeria to tiny Belize, engaged in such exercises, but these other capital cities were less distinctive in their design and were completed to a much lower standard of quality.

16. Farès El-Dahdah, *Lucio Costa, Brasilia's Superquadra* (New York: Prestel, 2005).

17. Patrick Abercrombie, *Greater London Plan 1944* (London: H.M. Stationery Office, 1945); Peter Hall, Harry Gracey, Roy Drewett, and Ray Thomas, *The Containment of Urban England* (London: Allen and Unwin for PEP, 1973).

18. Ibid., 457.

19. Press Association, "Green Belt Housing 'Doubles in a Year,'" *Guardian,* August 25, 2013, https://www.theguardian.com/society/2013/aug/25/green-belt-housing-doubles-claim; Colin Wiles, "Build on the Green Belt to Solve London's Housing Crisis," *Guardian,* October 25, 2013, https://www.theguardian.com/housing-network/2013/oct/25/green-belt-london-boris-johnson.

20. See, for example, Spiro Kostof, *The City Shaped: Urban Patterns and Meaning through History* (Boston: Little, Brown, 1991); Leonardo Benevolo, *The History of the City* (Cambridge, MA: MIT Press, 1980); Anthony E. J. Morris, *History of Urban Form: Before the Industrial Revolutions* (New York: Wiley, 1994); Kevin Lynch, *A Theory of Good City Form* (Cambridge, MA: MIT Press, 1981); David Gosling and Maria-Cristina Gosling, *The Evolution of American Urban Design: A Chronological Anthology* (London: Wiley, 2003).

21. Alexander Cuthbert, "Whose Urban Design," *Journal of Urban Design* 15 (2010): 443–448.

22. Gosling and Gosling, *The Evolution of American Urban Design*.

23. Colin Rowe and Fred Koetter, *Collage City* (Cambridge, MA: MIT Press, 1978), 102–105.

24. Sharon Zukin, *Naked City: The Death and Life of Authentic Urban Places* (New York: Oxford University Press, 2010), 101.

25. Ibid., 103–115.

26. Jane Jacobs, *The Death and Life of Great American Cities* (New York: Random House, 1961), 244–260.

27. Thomas de Monchaux, "This Is the Time when Beautiful Girls … ," in Timothy Mennel, Jo Steffens, and Christopher Klemek, eds., *Block by Block: Jane Jacobs and the Future of New York* (New York: Princeton Architectural Press, 2007), 19–21.

28. Jane Jacobs, *The Economy of Cities* (New York: Random House, 1969).

29. Jacobs, *The Death and Life of Great American Cities*, 291–317.

30. Kevin Lynch, *What Time Is This Place?* (Cambridge, MA: MIT Press, 1972).

31. Brent D. Ryan, *Design after Decline: How America Rebuilds Shrinking Cities* (Philadelphia: University of Pennsylvania Press, 2012).

32. Allan B. Jacobs, *Looking at Cities* (Cambridge, MA: Harvard University Press, 1985), 31–39.

33. Gilles Ragot, "Le Corbusier's Cité Frugès in Pessac: A Paradoxical Appropriation," in Mary Corbin Sies and Robert Freestone, eds., *Iconic Planned Communities* (Philadelphia: University of Pennsylvania Press, 2015).

34. Peter Hall, *Cities of Tomorrow: An Intellectual History of Urban Planning and Design in the Twentieth Century*, 3rd ed. (Oxford: Blackwell, 2002), 229.

35. The inability of monumental architecture to adapt to inevitable change and architects' lack of interest in exploring time as an element of architectural design were pilloried by futurist Stewart Brand following his residency in MIT's notoriously inflexible Media Lab building designed by I. M. Pei.

36. Examples of demolished urban design ensembles in just a few American cities include Scollay Square in Boston, demolished in the late 1950s, the long-gone St. John's Square in Tribeca, lower Manhattan, and the World Trade Center, destroyed in 2001. Of course, the power required to remove urban design is greater than that required to demolish architecture. Each of the above three examples was expensive to remove. Scollay Square's obliteration required the substantial government capital and legal powers of urban renewal; the removal of St. John's Square needed the great power of the New York Central Railroad, one of the largest corporations of its time; and the World Trade Center fell in the catastrophe of September 11, 2001, with redevelopment requiring substantial amounts of public capital following the terrorist attack.

37. Busquets, *Barcelona*, 127.

38. Karl Baedeker, *Spain and Portugal: Handbook for Travelers* (Leipzig: Baedeker, 1898).

39. Marcel Smets, "Insights I Gained from Manuel," in *The Vision of Manuel de Solà-Morales: Roots for a Twenty First Century Urbanism*, conference pamphlet, Harvard University, Graduate School of Design, Cambridge, MA, October 10, 2013, 19–26.

40. Ibid., 19.

41. Manuel de Solà-Morales i Rubió et al., *A Matter of Things* (Rotterdam: NAi Publishers, 2008).

42. John William Reps, *Cities of the American West: A History of Frontier Urban Planning* (Princeton: Princeton University Press, 1979).

43. Ibid., 637.

44. Bill Hubbard, *American Boundaries: The Nation, the States, the Rectangular Survey* (Chicago: University of Chicago Press, 2009).

45. Reps, *Cities of the American West*, 638.

46. Scully, *American Architecture and Urbanism*, 29–35.

47. Thomas Wilson and Patrick Shay, "Oglethorpe and Savannah," *Planning Magazine*, March 2014.

48. Alexis de Tocqueville, *Democracy in America*, trans. and ed. Harvey C. Mansfield and Delba Winthrop (Chicago: University of Chicago Press, 2000), 35.

49. Ibid., 228.

50. Ibid., 444.

51. Reps, *Cities of the American West*, 646.

52. Ibid., 649.

53. A setting of thousands of fiercely protected small parcels bound to be deeply conservative: the *Kelo v. City of New London* anti–property condemnation case brought before the United States Supreme Court in 2005, relates directly to what Tocqueville called the "conservatism of democracy."

54. Tocqueville, *Democracy in America*, 608.

55. Astolphe de Custine, *Letters from Russia*, ed. Anka Muhstein (New York: New York Review Books, 2002), 643.

56. Custine, *Letters from Russia*, 336.

57. Ibid., 130.

58. Ibid., 124–125.

59. Ibid., 114–115.

60. Timothy Colton, *Moscow: Governing the Socialist Metropolis* (Cambridge, MA: Belknap Press of Harvard University Press, 1995).

61. Ibid., 211.

62. Ibid., 324.

63. Ibid., 277.

64. Ibid., 285–291.

65. Hall, *Cities of Tomorrow*, 215–217; Holger Christmann, "Als Moskau New York sein wollte," *Weltkunst* 80, no. 1–3 (2010): 142–146.

66. Colton, *Moscow*, 278.

67. Vladimir Putin, "Meeting on Expanding Moscow's Border," Kremlin, Official Internet Resources of the President of Russia, Novo-Ogaryovo, Moscow Region, August 14, 2012), http://en.kremlin.ru/news/4296.

68. Nikolai Volovich and Evgeniya Nikitina, "The Conflicts between the Systems of Public and Private Land Law in Russia," in Erwin Hepperle, Robert Dixon-Gough, Vida Maliene, Reinfried Mansberger, Jenny Paulsson, and Andrea Pödör, eds., *Land Management: Potential, Problems and Stumbling Blocks* (Zurich: VDF, 2013), 195–209.

69. Colton, *Moscow*, 323.

70. "City Block of Disagreement" is a more precise, if less sonorous, translation of the Spanish "La Manzana de la Discordia" ("Illa de la Discòrdia" in Catalan). As the Spanish word *manzana* means both "city block" and "apple," the term "Manzana de la Discordia" is a play on the disagreement among the gods that precipitated the Trojan War.

71. Plato, *Laws* 779b, quoted in Ferdinando Castagnoli, *Orthogonal Town Planning in Antiquity* (Cambridge, MA: MIT Press, 1971), 56–57.

72. Gordon Cullen, *Townscape* (New York: Reinhold, 1961).

73. Jacobs, *Great Streets*.

74. Andrés Duany and Elizabeth Plater-Zyberk, *Towns and Town-Making Principles* (New York: Rizzoli, 2006).

75. Michael Southworth and Eran Ben-Joseph, *Streets and the Shaping of Towns and Cities* (Washington, DC: Island Press, 2003).

76. Urban Design Council of the City of New York, *Housing Quality Guidelines: Housing Quality, a Program for Zoning Reform* (New York: Urban Design Council of City of New York, 1975), 7.

77. Richard Hedman and Andrew Jaszewski, *The Fundamentals of Urban Design* (Washington, DC: APA Planners Press, 1984), 1.

78. Ibid.

79. Peter Blake, *God's Own Junkyard: The Planned Deterioration of America's Landscape* (New York: Holt, 1964).

80. Ian Nairn, *The American Landscape: A Critical View* (New York: Random House, 1965).

81. Daniela Fabricius, "Resisting Representation: The Informal Geographies of Rio de Janeiro," *Harvard Design Magazine* 28 (Spring/Summer 2008).

82. Adriana Navarro Sertich, "Medellín: 'Social Urbanism,'" *FAVELissues* (blog), February 1, 2010, https://favelissues.com/2010/02/01/medellin-%E2%80%9Csocial-urbanism%E2%80%9D/.

83. Blake, *God's Own Junkyard*, 23.

84. Robert Venturi, Denise Scott Brown, and Steven Izenour, *Learning from Las Vegas: The Forgotten Symbolism of Architectural Form*, rev. ed. (Cambridge, MA: MIT Press, 1977).

85. Robert Venturi, *Complexity and Contradiction in Architecture* (New York: Museum of Modern Art, 1966).

86. Venturi, Scott Brown, and Izenour, *Learning from Las Vegas*, 8.

87. Ibid., 40.

88. Denise Scott Brown, *Urban Concepts* (New York: St. Martin's Press, 1990), 51.

89. Venturi, *Complexity and Contradiction in Architecture*, 104.

90. Rem Koolhaas, "Bigness, or the Problem of Large," in Rem Koolhaas and Bruce Mau, *S,M,L,XL*, ed. Jennifer Sigler (New York: Monacelli Press, 1995), 509–516.

91. Rem Koolhaas, "What Ever Happened to Urbanism?," in Koolhaas and Mau, *S,M,L,XL*, 958–971.

92. Rem Koolhaas, "Junkspace," *October* 100 (Spring 2003): 175–190.

93. Rem Koolhaas, "The Generic City," in Koolhaas and Mau, *S,M,L,XL*, 1239–1264.

94. Venturi, Scott Brown, and Izenour, *Learning from Las Vegas*, 13.

95. Koolhaas, "Cronocaos," *Log* 21 (Winter 2011): 119–123.

96. Rem Koolhaas et al., *Mutations* (Barcelona: ACTAR, 2000), 652.

97. Ibid.

98. Matthew Gandy, "Learning from Lagos," *New Left Review* 33 (May–June 2005); Jean-Loup Amselle, Noal Mellott, and Julie van Dam, "Primitivism and Postcolonialism in the Arts," *MLN* 118, no. 4

(2003): 974–988; Joseph Godlewski, "Alien and Distant: Rem Koolhaas on Film in Lagos, Nigeria," *Traditional Dwellings and Settlements Review* 21, no. 2 (2010): 7–19.

99. Tunde Agbola, *The Architecture of Fear: Urban Design and Construction Response to Urban Violence in Lagos, Nigeria* (Ibadan, Nigeria: IFRA ABB, 1997).

100. Sonja Luthi and Marc Schwarz, *De Drager / A Film about Architect John Habraken*, Vimeo video, 47:35, posted by "schwarzpictures.com," March 9, 2013, https://vimeo.com/61410893.

101. N. J. Habraken, *The Structure of the Ordinary: The Form and Control of the Built Environment* (Cambridge, MA: MIT Press, 1998), 67.

102. Luthi and Schwarz, *De Drager*, 4:47.

103. Luthi and Schwarz, *De Drager*, 14:30.

104. Venturi, *Complexity and Contradiction in Architecture*.

105. Koolhaas, "Bigness."

106. N. J. Habraken, *Supports: An Alternative to Mass Housing* (Amsterdam: Scheltema & Holkema, 1961; New York: Praeger, 1972).

107. Battery Park City Authority, *Battery Park City: Battery Place Residential Area Design Guidelines,* prepared by Cooper, Eckstut Associates in association with Battery Park City Authority, 1989.

108. Donald J. Olsen, *The City as a Work of Art* (New Haven: Yale University Press, 1988).

109. Rem Koolhaas, *Delirious New York: A Retroactive Manifesto for Manhattan* (New York: Monacelli Press, 1994), 294.

110. Ibid., 297–299.

111. Steen Eiler Rasmussen, *London: The Unique City* (Cambridge, MA: MIT Press, 1988), 198–199.

112. Paul E. Sprague, *Guide to Frank Lloyd Wright and Prairie School Architecture in Oak Park* (Oak Park, IL: Oak Park Bicentennial Commission of the American Revolution, 1976).

113. Wright's urban design visions, when they came to pass, had little to do with existing cities. Wright's Broadacre City of the 1930s was a unitary environment that seemed almost rural, a place with widely scattered houses where each and every structure together with their intervening spaces was designed by Wright.

114. Fumihiko Maki, *Investigations in Collective Form* (unpublished manuscript, School of Architecture, Washington University, 1964).

115. Florian Hertweck and Sébastien Marot, eds, *The City in the City: Berlin, a Green Archipelago*, critical ed. (Zurich: Lars Müller, 2013).

116. Reyner Banham, *Megastructure: Urban Futures of the Recent Past* (New York: Harper and Row, 1976), 8–10.

117. Maki, *Investigations in Collective Form*, 5.

118. Ibid., 6.

119. Ibid., 11–12.

120. Ibid., 14–23.

121. Fumihiko Maki, "Maki's Hillside Terrace," *Architecture Week*, April 6, 2011, http://www.architectureweek .com/2011/0406/culture_1-1.html.

122. Banham, *Megastructure*, 10.

123. Kees Christiaanse and KCAP Architects, *Situation KCAP* (Berlin: Birkhäuser, 2005); Pier Vittorio Aureli, *The Possibility of an Absolute Architecture* (Cambridge, MA: MIT Press, 2011); Hertweck and Marot, *The City in the City*.

124. Koolhaas, *Delirious New York*, 222.

125. Hertweck and Marot, *The City in the City*, 35–43.

126. Ibid., 17.

127. Ibid., 100.

128. Oswald Mathias Ungers and Stefan Vieths, *Oswald Mathias Ungers: The Dialectic City,* ed. Luca Molinari, trans. Francisca Garvie (Milan: Skira, 1997), 22.

129. Ibid.

130. Hertweck and Marot, *The City in the City*, 108.

Chapter 3: Three Pluralist Projects

1. Marcel Monmarche, *Les Guides Bleus: Roumanie, Bulgarie, Turquie* (Paris: Librarie Hachette, 1933), 70.

2. Radu Varia, *Brancusi* (New York: Rizzoli International, 1986), 11.

3. Alexandra Parigoris, "Brancusi and His Return to Romania," in Ernest Beck, ed., *Brancusi's Endless Column Ensemble: Targu Jiu, Romania* (London: Scala, 2007), 23.

4. Varia, *Brancusi*, 11.

5. Anna C. Chave, *Constantin Brancusi: Shifting the Bases of Art* (New Haven: Yale University Press, 1993); Friedrich Teja Bach, Margit Rowell, and Ann Temkin, *Constantin Brancusi: 1876–1957* (Cambridge, MA: MIT Press, 1995); Carmen Gimenez and Matthew Gale, *Constantin Brancusi: The Essence of Things* (London: Tate, 2004).

6. Sidney Geist, *Brancusi/The Kiss* (New York: Harper and Row, 1978), 52.

7. Ibid., 51.

8. William Tucker, "The Legacy of Târgu Jiu," in Beck, *Brancusi's Endless Column Ensemble*, 70.

9. Ibid.

10. Richard Newton, "Reclaiming Sacred Space," in Beck, *Brancusi's Endless Column Ensemble*, 54.

11. Sandra Miller, *Constantin Brancusi: A Survey of His Work* (Oxford: Clarendon Press, 1995), 201.

12. Parigoris, "Brancusi and His Return to Romania," 22.

13. Ibid., 27.

14. Ibid., 29.

15. Varia, *Brancusi*, 257, 265.

16. Tucker, "The Legacy of Târgu Jiu," 77.

17. Miller, *Constantin Brancusi*, 208.

18. Varia, *Brancusi*, 259–263.

19. Parigoris, "Brancusi and His Return to Romania," 26–27.

20. Miller, *Constantin Brancusi*, 212.

21. Varia, *Brancusi*, 268.

22. Tucker, "The Legacy of Târgu Jiu," 73.

23. Ibid., 74.

24. Varia, *Brancusi*, 254.

25. Miller, *Constantin Brancusi*, 197.

26. Newton, "Reclaiming Sacred Space," 54.

27. Ibid., 61.

28. Ibid., 63.

29. Ibid.

30. Mihai Radu, "Urban Redevelopment and a Visionary New Visitor Center," in Beck, *Brancusi's Endless Column Ensemble*, 64.

31. Ibid., 68.

32. Map data: Google Earth, DigitalGlobe, July 2012.

33. Radu, "Urban Redevelopment," 64.

34. Ibid.

35. Varia, *Brancusi*, 257.

36. Frédéric Chaubin, *CCCP: Cosmic Communist Constructions Photographed* (Cologne: Taschen, 2011).

37. Parigoris, "Brancusi and His Return to Romania," 23.

38. Radu, "Urban Redevelopment."

39. Robert A. Caro, *The Power Broker: Robert Moses and the Fall of New York* (New York: Knopf, 1974), 850–894.

40. Mariana Mogilevich, "Designing the Urban: Space and Politics in Lindsay's New York" (PhD diss., Harvard University, 2012), ProQuest (3514389); Juliette Spertus and Susanne Schindler, "A Few Days in the Bronx: From Co-op City to Twin Parks," *Urban Omnibus*, July 25, 2012, http://urbanomnibus.net/2012/07/a-few-days-in-the-bronx-from-co-op-city-to-twin-parks/#; Juliette Spertus and Susanne Schindler, "The Landscape of Housing: Twin Parks Northwest 40 Years On," *Urban Omnibus*, November 6, 2013, http://urbanomnibus.net/2013/11/the-landscape-of-housing-twin-parks-northwest-40-years-on/.

41. Clayton Knowles, "Governor Speaks on Bronx Housing," *New York Times*, October 1, 1970.

42. Jonathan Barnett, *Urban Design as Public Policy: Practical Methods for Improving Cities* (New York: Architectural Record Books, 1974), 89–105.

43. Mogilevich, "Designing the Urban," 137–145.

44. Ashley A. Foard and Hilbert Fefferman, "Federal Urban Renewal Legislation," in James Q. Wilson, ed., *Urban Renewal: The Record and Controversy* (Cambridge, MA: MIT Press, 1966), 75–79.

45. Mogilevich, "Designing the Urban," 138.

46. Lee E. Cooper, "Uprooted Thousands Starting Trek from Site for Stuyvesant Town," *New York Times*, March 3, 1945.

47. New York City Housing Authority, "NYCHA Housing Developments: Morrisania Air Rights," https://www1.nyc.gov/assets/planning/download/pdf/plans-studies/sustainable-communities/bmn/bronx_metro_report/full_report.pdf; "City View on Bronx Housing Plan Explained," *New York Times*, February 12, 1977.

48. Mayor John Lindsay was elected in 1965 in part for his commitment to provide citizens more of a voice in shaping city policies, a position that pragmatically accommodated what was anyway an increasing reality: urban renewal was getting harder for urban neighborhoods to accept, and increasing public participation in the process of neighborhood rebuilding was becoming the norm.

49. Barnett, *Urban Design as Public Policy*, 94.

50. Peter G. Rowe, *Modernity and Housing* (Cambridge, MA: MIT Press, 1993), 264–267.

51. Brent D. Ryan, *Design after Decline: How America Rebuilds Shrinking Cities* (Philadelphia: University of Pennsylvania Press, 2012), 14.

52. Le Corbusier died in 1965. Both Walter Gropius and Mies van der Rohe died in 1969.

53. Barnett, *Urban Design as Public Policy*, 98.

54. By the early 1990s Meier had been awarded the Pritzker Architecture Prize and had designed museums and civic buildings for Atlanta, Barcelona, Ulm, and The Hague. His most monumental commission, however, was in Los Angeles, where the Getty Foundation commissioned him to construct an art museum complex on a hilltop overlooking the city.

55. Richard Meier, *Richard Meier: Architect* (New York: Rizzoli, 1984), 121.

56. Richard Meier, *Building the Getty* (New York: Knopf, 1997), 15–16.

57. Richard Severo, "Bronx Buildings Novel in Design," *New York Times*, August 8, 1971; Paul Goldberger, "Twin Parks, an Effort to Alter the Pattern," *New York Times*, December 27, 1973; Vincent Scully, "Preface," in Alessandra Latour, *Pasanella + Klein: Public and Private Interventions in the Residential Field* (Rome: Edizioni Kappa, 1983), 7–8; Ada Louise Huxtable, "Architecture: 6 Designs Win Bard Merit Awards," *New York Times*, June 14, 1973; Norval White and Elliot Willensky, *AIA Guide to New York City* (New York: Collier Books, 1978).

58. Robert A. M. Stern, Thomas Mellins, and David Fishman, *New York 1960: Architecture and Urbanism between the Second World War and the Bicentennial* (New York: Monacelli Press, 1995), 956–961; Spertus and Schindler, "A Few Days in the Bronx."

59. Yonah Freemark, "The Entrepreneurial State: New York's Urban Development Corporation, an Experiment to Take Charge of Affordable Housing Production, 1968–1975" (master's thesis, MIT, 2013), 135–136, DSpace@MIT, http://dspace.mit.edu/handle/1721.1/79198.

60. Ibid., 146–148.

61. Mogilevich, "Designing the Urban," 156–172.

62. Spertus and Schindler, "A Few Days in the Bronx"; Spertus and Schindler, "The Landscape of Housing."

63. New York City Housing and Development Administration, "Twin Parks West [I], Twin Parks East [I A&B] Community Development Plan," in Mogilevich, "Designing the Urban," 142–143.

64. Mogilevich, "Designing the Urban," 143; Spertus and Schindler, "The Landscape of Housing."

65. Spertus and Schindler, "A Few Days in the Bronx."

66. Twin Parks was not the first scattered site housing development, however. This concept, initially called "vest pocket" housing, seems to have appeared as early as 1960 in a city policy report on housing ("Excerpts from Panuch Report to Wagner on Need for New Housing Board," *New York Times*, March 10, 1960, 34).

67. George W. Bromley, "Atlas of the Borough of the Bronx" (New York: G. W. Bromley, 1912), 172, 186, 187.

68. Barnett, *Urban Design as Public Policy*, 94–95.

69. D. Bradford Hunt, *Blueprint for Disaster: The Unraveling of Chicago Public Housing* (Chicago: University of Chicago Press, 2009), 44–47.

70. The term "skip-stop" refers to elevators that stop on every other floor in a multistory residential building, permitting a greater percentage of floor space to be dedicated to residential units, and typically permitting "floor-through" residential units. This idea was pioneered by Le Corbusier in his Unité d'Habitation.

71. Spertus and Schindler, "A Few Days in the Bronx."

72. Freemark, "The Entrepreneurial State," 287–306.

73. Barnett, *Urban Design as Public Policy*.

74. In fact, even the *New York Times* confused Slovenia for a Baltic country instead of the Adriatic nation that it actually is. See Thomas Fuller, "Confusion with Slovakia Prompts New Flag: Slovenia's Identity Crisis," *New York Times*, April 17, 2004.

75. Colm Tóibín, *The Sign of the Cross: Travels in Catholic Europe* (New York: Pantheon Press, 1994), 179–180.

76. Rachel B. Doyle, "36 Hours in Ljubljana, Slovenia," *New York Times,* November 15, 2012.

77. United Nations Human Development Programme, "Human Development Data (1980–2015)," Human Development Reports, http://hdr.undp.org/en/statistics/.

78. Lawrence Vale, *Architecture, Power, and National Identity* (New Haven: Yale University Press, 1992); Peter G. Rowe, *Civic Realism* (Cambridge, MA: MIT Press, 1997).

79. Ibid., 163–167.

80. Damjan Prelovšek, *Jože Plečnik, 1872–1952: Architecturea Perennis* (New Haven: Yale University Press, 1997); Rowe, *Civic Realism*; Peter Krečič, *Plečnik, the Complete Works* (New York: Whitney Library of Design, 1993); François Burkhardt, Claude Eveno, and Boris Podrecca, eds., *Jože Plečnik, Architect, 1872–1957*, trans. Carol Volk (Cambridge, MA: MIT Press, 1989).

81. Krečič, *Plečnik, the Complete Works*, 7–11.

82. Ibid., 171–191.

83. Dimitra Bablis, ed., *Chronocity: The Scale of Sustainable Change: Heritage Value and Future Opportunities and Challenges* (Florence: Alnea International, 2008), 106.

84. Ibid., 106–112.

85. Prelovšek, *Jože Plečnik*, 123–124.

86. Krečič, *Plečnik, the Complete Works*, 69.

87. Vladimir Slapeta, "Jože Plečnik and Prague," in Burkhardt, Eveno, and Podrecca, *Joze Plečnik, Architect*, 82–92.

88. Prelovšek, *Jože Plečnik*, 154.

89. Slapeta, "Jože Plečnik and Prague"; Krečič, *Plečnik, the Complete Works*; Prelovšek, *Jože Plečnik*, 154.

90. Krečič, *Plečnik, the Complete Works*; Burkhardt, Eveno, and Podrecca, *Jože Plečnik, Architect*.

91. Krečič, *Plečnik, the Complete Works*.

92. Lucius Burckhardt and Linde Burkhardt, "A City Promenade," in Burkhardt, Eveno, and Podrecca, *Jože Plečnik, Architect*, 186–196; Prelovšek, *Jože Plečnik*, 274.

93. Ljubljana Office of Tourism, *Plečnik Ljubljana* [map] (Ljubljana: CGP Delo, 1986).

94. Ibid.

95. Plečnik designed the Triple Bridge with two paths for pedestrians and one for cars; all three branches of the bridge are pedestrianized today (2016).

96. Burkhardt, Eveno, and Podrecca, *Jože Plečnik, Architect*.

97. Ibid.

98. Prelovšek, *Jože Plečnik,* 268.

Chapter 4: Three Plural Urbanists

1. Harvard University Graduate School of Design, "The Origins and Evolution of 'Urban Design,' 1956–2006," special issue, *Harvard Design Magazine* 24 (Spring/Summer 2006), and Harvard University Graduate School of Design, "Urban Design Now," *Harvard Design Magazine* 25 (Fall/Winter 2007); Alex Krieger and William S. Saunders, eds., *Urban Design* (Minneapolis: University of Minnesota Press, 2009).

2. Denise Scott Brown, "Urban Design at Fifty: A Personal View," in Krieger and Saunders, *Urban Design*, 72.

3. Denise Scott Brown, *Urban Concepts* (New York: St. Martin's Press, 1990), 12.

4. Rima M. Girnius and Emily T. Cooperman, "Crane, David A. (1927–2005)," American Architects and Buildings, https://www.philadelphiabuildings.org/pab/app/ar_display.cfm/19001.

5. David A. Crane, "The Dynamic City," *Architectural Design* 30, no. 4 (1960): 162.

6. David A. Crane, "Chandigarh Reconsidered," *Journal of the American Institute of Architects* 33 (May 1960): 36.

7. Ibid., 33.

8. David A. Crane, "The City Symbolic," *Journal of the American Institute of Planners* 26, no. 4 (1960): 282.

9. Ibid.

10. Ibid.

11. Department of City Planning, City of New York, *Zoning Handbook, 2011 Edition* (New York: Department of City Planning), 2.

12. Crane, "The City Symbolic," 280.

13. Crane, "Chandigarh Reconsidered," 36.

14. Ibid.

15. Crane, "The Dynamic City."

16. Crane, "Chandigarh Reconsidered" and "The Dynamic City."

17. Crane, "Chandigarh Reconsidered," 39.

18. Crane, "The Dynamic City," 162.

19. Ibid.

20. Crane, "Chandigarh Reconsidered," 38.

21. As I noted during a visit to informal settlements in Medellín, Colombia (January 2015).

22. Crane, "Chandigarh Reconsidered," 38.

23. Ibid., 39.

24. Ibid.

25. David A. Crane, "The Public Art of City Building," *Annals of the American Academy of Political and Social Science* 352 (March 1964): 88.

26. Crane, "The City Symbolic," 285.

27. Burnham's principal Chicago recommendations, and successes, had been in just this area of "capital design": major spaces such as Michigan Avenue, Grant Park, and Wacker Drive reflected urban design's potential to shape state-owned land, just as the plan's failed proposals for united railroad terminals and boulevards on valuable private land reflected Burnham's difficulties in corralling the thousand designers. Other City Beautiful plans, also by Burnham, similarly relied on capital design, for example San Francisco's City Hall Plaza and Cleveland's Mall, as did later modernist projects such as Boston's City Hall Plaza.

28. Crane, "The City Symbolic," 286.

29. Ibid.

30. Ibid.

31. Tunney Lee, "Remarks on David Crane at Crane's Death, 2005" (unpublished manuscript in the author's possession, provided to author by Tunney Lee, 2015).

32. Ibid. The BRA was created in 1957 to provide an organized agency structure to plan and implement "urban renewal" activities in the city.

33. Kevin Lynch, *The Image of the City* (Cambridge, MA: Technology Press, 1960), 16–25.

34. Yonah Freemark, "The Entrepreneurial State: New York's Urban Development Corporation, an Experiment to Take Charge of Affordable Housing Production, 1968–1975" (master's thesis, MIT, 2013), 96, DSpace@MIT, http://dspace.mit.edu/handle/1721.1/79198.

35. David A. Crane Associates, Lysander New Community drawings (uncatalogued) in Architectural Archive, University of Pennsylvania.

36. Brent D. Ryan, *Design after Decline: How America Rebuilds Shrinking Cities* (Philadelphia: University of Pennsylvania Press, 2012), 1–36.

37. Denise Scott Brown remains Crane's greatest admirer (see her *Urban Concepts* and "Urban Design at Fifty"), and he is also mentioned by Eugénie L. Birch, "From CIAM to CNU: The Roots and Thinkers of Modern Urban Design," in Tridib Banerjee and Anastasia Loukaitou-Sideris, eds., *Companion to Urban Design* (New York: Routledge, 2011), among others.

38. David B. Brownlee and David G. De Long, *Louis I. Kahn: In the Realm of Architecture* (New York: Rizzoli, 1991).

39. Nathaniel Kahn, *My Architect: A Son's Journey* (Louis Kahn Project, Inc.; Mediaworks, 2003), 44:23–44:50.

40. There is no comprehensive history of Philadelphia during the late twentieth century, but I comment on the city's post-1970 planning era in *Design after Decline*, 82–83, 128–132.

41. Hilary Ballon and Kenneth T. Jackson, *Robert Moses and the Modern City: The Transformation of New York* (New York: Norton, 2008).

42. For example Harris Steinberg, "Philadelphia in the Year 2059," in Scott Gabriel Knowles, ed., *Imagining Philadelphia: Edmund Bacon and the Future of the City* (Philadelphia: University of Pennsylvania Press, 2009), 112–144.

43. Rear cover copy for Knowles, *Imagining Philadelphia*.

44. Scott Larson, *Building Like Moses with Jacobs in Mind* (Philadelphia: Temple University Press, 2013).

45. Edmund N. Bacon, *Design of Cities* (New York: Viking Press, 1967), 23, 39, 46–47.

46. Ibid., 23.

47. Ibid., 23.

48. Bacon was hardly alone in his advocacy of movement as a vector for design thought. Both Gordon Cullen and Kevin Lynch had advocated much the same in *Townscape* (1961) and *The View from the Road* (1964), though Cullen was inspired by pedestrian movement and Lynch by the automobile. A full etiology of motion as motive for urban design is not our aim here, but Bacon effectively disowned his own authorship of the idea by situating motion as a formative element of urban design as early in history as classical Greece.

49. Bacon, *Design of Cities*, 130–161.

50. Edmund N. Bacon, *Rome: The Impact of an Idea* (Urban Productions, 1984), 27:00.

51. During that time, Sixtus V not only set the course for the future completion of St. Peter's Basilica, achieved in 1662, but established his greatest vision, and one of the most sweeping in the history of urban thought, with his spatial reorganization and reorientation of the city around a combination of classical obelisks, votive churches, and processional roads (Bacon, *Design of Cities*, 117).

52. Bacon, *Design of Cities*, 130–161.

53. Bacon, *Rome*, 11:55 ff.

54. Bacon, *Design of Cities*, 139.

55. Ibid., 298–299.

56. Kevin Lynch, *City Sense and City Design: Writings and Projects of Kevin Lynch*, ed. Tridib Banerjee and Michael Southworth (Cambridge, MA: MIT Press, 1990), 23.

57. Lynch, *The Image of the City*.

58. See for example Jacobs's *Economy of Cities* and *Cities and the Wealth of Nations*.

59. Kevin Lynch, *What Time Is This Place?* (Cambridge, MA: MIT Press, 1972).

60. Kevin Lynch, *A Theory of Good City Form* (Cambridge, MA: MIT Press, 1981). The title was subsequently shortened to *Good City Form* in 1984.

61. Lynch, *City Sense and City Design*; Kevin Lynch, *Wasting Away*, ed. Michael Southworth (San Francisco: Sierra Club Books, 1990).

62. Robert Goodman, *After the Planners* (New York: Simon and Schuster, 1972); Susan S. Fainstein, et al., *Restructuring the City: The Political Economy of Urban Redevelopment* (New York: Longman, 1983).

63. Kevin Lynch, *Visual Analysis: Community Renewal Program* (Brookline, MA: Brookline Board of Selectmen, 1965); Kevin Lynch with Sasaki, Dawson & Demay Associates, *Looking at the Vineyard: A Visual Study for a Changing Island* (West Tisbury, MA: Vineyard Open Land Foundation, 1973); Kevin Lynch and Donald Appleyard, *Temporary Paradise? A Look at the Special Landscape of the San Diego Region* (San Diego: San Diego City Planning Department, 1974).

64. Carr, Lynch Associates, *Anacostia Conserved* (Washington, DC: Department of Housing and Community Development, 1979); Carr, Lynch Associates, *A Comprehensive Arts Facilities Plan for Dallas* (Dallas: City of Dallas, 1977).

65. Michael Sorkin, "The End(s) of Urban Design," in Krieger and Saunders, *Urban Design*, 160.

66. Lynch, *City Sense and City Design*.

67. Kevin Lynch, "City Design and City Appearance" (1968), "The Immature Arts of City Design" (1984), and "City Design: What It Is and How It Might Be Taught" (1980), all republished in *City Sense and City Design*.

68. Lynch, *Good City Form*, 291.

69. Peter Hall, *Cities of Tomorrow: An Intellectual History of Urban Planning and Design in the Twentieth Century*, 3rd ed. (Oxford: Blackwell, 2002), 352–377.

70. *Dædalus* 90, no. 1, "The Future Metropolis" (1961).

71. Kevin Lynch, "The Pattern of the Metropolis," *Dædalus* 90, no. 1 (1961): 79–98.

72. Ibid.

73. Kevin Lynch, *Managing the Sense of a Region* (Cambridge, MA: MIT Press, 1976).

74. Lynch, *Good City Form*, 293–317.

75. Ibid., 314.

76. Ibid., 316.

77. Kevin Lynch, "City Design and City Appearance," in *City Sense and City Design*, 465.

78. Ibid., 485.

79. Lynch, *The Image of the City*, 25–32.

80. Lynch, "City Design and City Appearance," 487.

81. Some examples are *The Visual Environment of Los Angeles* (1971); *Visual Form of Dallas* (ca. 1974); and *Visual Survey of Portland* (1971).

82. Lynch, "The Immature Arts of City Design," in *City Sense and City Design*.

83. Donald Appleyard, Kevin Lynch, and John R. Myer, *The View from the Road* (Cambridge, MA: MIT Press, 1964).

84. Lynch, *Visual Analysis*.

85. Kevin Lynch, "Reconsidering the Image of the City," in *City Sense and City Design*, 247–256.

86. Lynch et al., *Looking at the Vineyard.*

87. Ian L. McHarg, *Design with Nature* (Garden City, NY: Natural History Press, 1969).

88. Lynch, "The Immature Arts of City Design," 504–507.

89. Lynch clearly considered Alexander's work in his own thinking; discussion of *A Pattern Language* (1977) occupies much of "City Models and City Design," chapter 16 of *Good City Form.*

90. Lynch, *Managing the Sense of a Region*, 86–87.

Chapter 5: Designing Pluralist Urbanism

1. Kevin Lynch, *A Theory of Good City Form* (Cambridge, MA: MIT Press, 1981), 293. The title was subsequently shortened to *Good City Form* in 1984.

2. Kevin Lynch, "The Pattern of the Metropolis," *Dædalus* 90, no. 1 (1961): 79–98.

3. David Crane, "Chandigarh Reconsidered," *Journal of the American Institute of Architects* 33 (May 1960): 38.

4. Edmund N. Bacon, *Design of Cities* (New York: Viking Press, 1967).

5. Ibid., 243–265.

6. John W. Reps, *The Making of Urban America* (Princeton: Princeton University Press, 1965), 185–192.

7. Robert A. Caro, *The Power Broker: Robert Moses and the Fall of New York* (New York: Knopf, 1974), 509–512.

8. Kevin Lynch, *The Image of the City* (Cambridge, MA: MIT Press, 1960).

9. Bacon, *Design of Cities*, 116–147.

10. David Crane, "The Dynamic City," *Architectural Design* 30, no. 4 (1960): 162.

11. Crane, "Chandigarh Reconsidered," 36.

12. Crane, "The Dynamic City," 162.

13. Crane, "Chandigarh Reconsidered," 37.

14. N. J. Habraken, *Supports: An Alternative to Mass Housing* (Amsterdam: Scheltema & Holkema, 1961; New York: Praeger, 1972).

15. Peter Hall, *Cities of Tomorrow: An Intellectual History of Urban Planning and Design in the Twentieth Century*, 3rd ed. (Oxford: Blackwell, 2002), 189–217.

Chapter 6: Principles and Potentials of Plural Urbanism

1. Daniel H. Burnham and Edward H. Bennett, *Plan of Chicago*, ed. Charles Moore (Chicago: Commercial Club, 1909; New York: Princeton Architectural Press, 1993), 99–118.

2. See Stewart Brand, *How Buildings Learn: What Happens after They're Built* (New York: Viking Press, 1994); Mohsen Mostafavi and David Leatherbarrow, *On Weathering: The Life of Buildings in Time* (Cambridge, MA: MIT Press, 1993).

3. Brent D. Ryan, "The Restructuring of Detroit: City Block Form Change in a Shrinking City, 1900–2000," *Urban Design International* 13, no. 3 (2008): 156–168.

4. Corey Kilgannon, "Change Blurs Memories in a Famous Suburb," *New York Times,* October 13, 2007.

5. Ford Fessenden, Tom Giratikanon, Josh Keller, Archie Tse, Tim Wallace, Derek Watkins, Jeremy White, and Karen Yourish, "The Bloomberg Years: Reshaping New York," *New York Times,* August 18, 2013.

6. Rem Koolhaas, "Cronocaos," *Log* 21 (Winter 2011), 119–123.

7. Edward L. Glaeser, "Preservation Follies," *City Journal*, Spring 2010, http://www.city-journal.org/html/preservation-follies-13279.html.

8. Kevin Lynch, *What Time Is This Place?* (Cambridge, MA: MIT Press, 1972), 24–28.

9. Michelangelo Antonio, *Chung Kuo, China* (Radiotelevisione Italiana, 1972).

10. Norval White, Elliot Willensky, and Fran Leadon, *AIA Guide to New York City* (Oxford: Oxford University Press, 2010), 408.

11. August Heckscher and Phyllis Robinson, *Open Spaces: The Life of American Cities* (New York: Harper and Row, 1977).

12. Jonathan Roughgarden, Robert M. May, and Simon A. Levin, eds., *Perspectives in Ecological Theory* (Princeton: Princeton University Press, 1989).

13. Kevin Lynch, "Controlling the Flow of Rebuilding and Replanning in Residential Areas" (undergraduate thesis, MIT, 1947), DSpace@MIT, http://hdl.handle.net/1721.1/12525.

14. François Loyer, *Paris Nineteenth Century: Architecture and Urbanism* (New York: Abbeville Press, 1988).

15. Joseph P. Schweiterman, Alan P. Mammoser, and John A. Schuter, *Beyond Burnham: An Illustrated History of Planning for the Chicago Region* (Lake Forest, IL: Lake Forest College Press, 2009), 79–95.

16. Tim Catchpole, *London Skylines: A Study of High Buildings and Views*, Review and Studies Series 33 (London: London Research Centre, 1987).

17. Kevin Lynch, *A Theory of Good City Form* (Cambridge, MA: MIT Press, 1981), 293–317. The title was subsequently shortened to *Good City Form* in 1984.

18. Lynch, *What Time Is This Place?*

19. Brand, *How Buildings Learn.*

20. Anne Vernez Moudon, *Built for Change: Neighborhood Architecture in San Francisco* (Cambridge, MA: MIT Press, 1986).

21. Brent D. Ryan, "Incomplete and Incremental Plan Implementation in Downtown Providence, Rhode Island, 1960–2000," *Journal of Planning History* 5, no. 1 (2006): 35–64.

22. City of Providence Department of Planning and Development, "Parcel and Zoning Map," http://gis.providenceplanning.org/PVD_Parcel_ZoningMap.

23. Farès El-Dahdah, *Lucio Costa, Brasilia's Superquadra* (New York: Prestel, 2005), 86.

24. Alain Bertaud, "Brasília Spatial Structure: Between the Cult of Design and Markets," revised version of a paper presented at Brasília Metropolitana 2050: Preservação e Desinvolvimento, Brasília, August 2010, 13.

25. The design travails of capital cities were well articulated by Lawrence Vale in *Architecture, Power, and National Identity* (New Haven: Yale University Press, 1991).

26. Ibid., 56.

27. Dennis McClendon, *The Plan of Chicago: A Regional Legacy* (Chicago: Burnham Plan Centennial Committee and Chicago Metropolis 2020, 2008).

28. Harvard University, Graduate School of Design, "The Vision of Manuel de Solà-Morales: Roots for a Twenty First Century Urbanism," conference pamphlet, Harvard University, Graduate School of Design, October 10, 2013, 19–26.

29. Seth Mydans, "Getty Center's Design Is Unveiled." *New York Times*, October 10, 1991.

30. "The City of Culture / Eisenman Architects," *Archdaily*, June 8, 2011, http://www.archdaily.com/141238/the-city-of-culture-eisenman-architects.

31. Rem Koolhaas, "Bigness, or the Problem of Large," in Rem Koolhaas and Bruce Mau, *S,M,L,XL*, ed. Jennifer Sigler (New York: Monacelli Press, 1995), 494–516.

32. Adolphe Joanne, *Le Guide "Parisien"* (Paris: Librarie L. Hachette, 1863).

33. David H. Pickney, *Napoleon III and the Rebuilding of Paris* (Princeton: Princeton University Press, 1958), 25–27.

34. Jean Des Cars and Pierre Pinon, *Paris Haussmann: Un nouvelle géométrie pour la ville* (Paris: Editions Picard, 1991), 81.

35. Michael Sorkin, "The End(s) of Urban Design," in Alex Krieger, ed., *Urban Design* (Minneapolis: University of Minnesota Press, 2009), 155–182.

36. Paul Rudolph, personal communication, July 1994.

37. Richard Weston, *Villa Mairea, Alvar Aalto* (London: Phaidon, 1992), unnumbered page, ca. 11.

38. Ernest Beck, ed., *Brancusi's Endless Column Ensemble: Târgu Jiu, Romania* (London: Scala, 2007).

39. Yonah Freemark, "The Entrepreneurial State: New York's Urban Development Corporation, an Experiment to Take Charge of Affordable Housing Production, 1968–1975" (master's thesis, MIT, 2013), 135–136, DSpace@MIT, http://dspace.mit.edu/handle/1721.1/79198.

40. David Crane, "Chandigarh Reconsidered," *Journal of the American Institute of Architects* 33 (May 1960): 37.

41. Lynch, "Controlling the Flow of Rebuilding and Replanning."

42. Kevin Lynch, *A Theory of Good City Form*, 301.

43. Kevin Lynch, "The Immature Arts of City Design," in *City Sense and City Design: Writings and Projects of Kevin Lynch*, ed. Tridib Banerjee and Michael Southworth (Cambridge, MA: MIT Press, 1990), 498–510.

Bibliography

Abercrombie, Patrick. *Greater London Plan 1944*. London: H. M. Stationery Office, 1945.

Agbola, Tunde. *The Architecture of Fear: Urban Design and Construction Response to Urban Violence in Lagos, Nigeria*. Ibadan, Nigeria: IFRA ABB, 1997.

Alexander, Christopher, Sara Ishikawa, Murray Silverstein, Max Jacobson, Ingrid Fiksdahl-King, and Shlomo Angel. *A Pattern Language: Towns, Buildings, Construction*. New York: Oxford University Press, 1977.

Amselle, Jean-Loup, Noal Mellott, and Julie van Dam. "Primitivism and Postcolonialism in the Arts." *MLN* 118, no. 4 (2003): 974–988.

Antonioni, Michelangelo. *Chung Kuo, China*. Radiotelevisione Italiana, 1972.

Appleyard, Donald, Kevin Lynch, and John R. Myer. *The View from the Road*. Cambridge, MA: MIT Press, 1964.

Architectural Association. "Projective Cities." Architectural Association Graduate School, 2014. http://projectivecities.aaschool.ac.uk/.

Aureli, Pier Vittorio. *The Possibility of an Absolute Architecture*. Cambridge, MA: MIT Press, 2011.

Bablis, Dimitra, ed. *Chronocity: The Scale of Sustainable Change: Heritage Value and Future Opportunities and Challenges*. Florence: Alnea International, 2008.

Bach, Friedrich Teja, Margit Rowell, and Ann Temkin. *Constantin Brancusi: 1876–1957*. Cambridge, MA: MIT Press, 1995.

Bacon, Edmund N. *Design of Cities*. New York: Viking Press, 1967.

Bacon, Edmund N. *Rome: The Impact of an Idea*. Urban Productions, 1984.

Baedeker, Karl. *Spain and Portugal: Handbook for Travelers*. Leipzig: Baedeker, 1898.

Bailey, Brian J. *The Luddite Rebellion*. New York: New York University Press, 1999.

Ballon, Hilary, and Kenneth T. Jackson. *Robert Moses and the Modern City: The Transformation of New York*. New York: Norton, 2008.

Banham, Reyner. *Megastructure: Urban Futures of the Recent Past*. New York: Harper and Row, 1976.

Barnett, Jonathan. *Urban Design as Public Policy: Practical Methods for Improving Cities*. New York: Architectural Record Books, 1974.

Battery Park City Authority. *Battery Park City: Battery Place Residential Area Design Guidelines*. Prepared by Cooper, Eckstut Associates in association with Battery Park City Authority, 1989.

Beck, Ernest, ed. *Brancusi's Endless Column Ensemble: Târgu Jiu, Romania*. London: Scala, 2007.

Benevolo, Leonardo. *The History of the City*. Cambridge, MA: MIT Press, 1980.

Ben-Joseph, Eran. *The Code of the City: Standards and the Hidden Language of Place Making*. Cambridge, MA: MIT Press, 2005.

Bertaud, Alain. "Brasília Spatial Structure: Between the Cult of Design and Markets." Revised version of a paper presented at Brasília Metropolitana 2050: Preservação e Desinvolvimento, Brasília, August 2010.

Blake, Peter. *God's Own Junkyard: The Planned Deterioration of America's Landscape*. New York: Holt, 1964.

Brand, Stewart. *How Buildings Learn: What Happens after They're Built*. New York: Viking Press, 1994.

Bromley, George W. *Atlas of the Borough of the Bronx*. New York: G. W. Bromley, 1912.

Brownlee, David B., and David G. De Long. *Louis I. Kahn: In the Realm of Architecture*. New York: Rizzoli, 1991.

Burckhardt, Lucius, and Linde Burkhardt. "A City Promenade." In François Burkhardt et al., *Jože Plečnik, Architect, 1872–1957*, trans. Carol Volk, 186–196. Cambridge, MA: MIT Press, 1989.

Burkhardt, François, Claude Eveno, and Boris Podrecca, eds. *Jože Plečnik, Architect, 1872–1957*. Trans. Carol Volk. Cambridge, MA: MIT Press, 1989.

Burnham, Daniel H., and Edward H. Bennett. *Plan of Chicago*. Ed. Charles Moore. Chicago: Commercial Club, 1909; New York: Princeton Architectural Press, 1993.

Busquets, Joan. *Barcelona: The Urban Evolution of a Compact City*. Cambridge, MA: Harvard Graduate School of Design, 2014.

Busquets, Joan, and Felipe Correa, eds. *Cities, X Lines: A New Lens for the Urbanistic Project*. Cambridge, MA: Harvard University, Graduate School of Design, 2006.

Busquets, Joan, and Miquel Corominas. *Cerdà and the Barcelona of the Future: Reality versus Project*. Barcelona: Diputació Barcelona, 2009.

Caro, Robert A. *The Power Broker: Robert Moses and the Fall of New York*. New York: Knopf, 1974.

Carr, Lynch Associates. *Anacostia Conserved*. Washington, DC: Department of Housing and Community Development, 1979.

Carr, Lynch Associates. *A Comprehensive Arts Facilities Plan for Dallas*. Dallas: City of Dallas, 1977.

Castagnoli, Ferdinando. 1971. *Orthogonal Town Planning in Antiquity.*, 56–57. Cambridge, MA: MIT Press.

Catchpole, Tim. *London Skylines: A Study of High Buildings and Views.* Review and Studies Series 33. London: London Research Centre, 1987.

Chaubin, Frédéric. *CCCP: Cosmic Communist Constructions Photographed.* Cologne: Taschen, 2011.

Chave, Anna C. *Constantin Brancusi: Shifting the Bases of Art.* New Haven: Yale University Press, 1993.

Christiaanse, Kees, and KCAP Architects. *Situation KCAP.* Berlin: Birkhäuser, 2005.

Christmann, Holger. "Als Moskau New York sein wollte." *Weltkunst* 80, no. 1–3 (2010): 142–146.

"The City of Culture / Eisenman Architects." *Archdaily*, June 8, 2011. http://www.archdaily.com/141238/the-city-of-culture-eisenman-architects.

Colton, Timothy. *Moscow: Governing the Socialist Metropolis.* Cambridge, MA: Belknap Press of Harvard University Press, 1995.

Cooper, Lee E. "Uprooted Thousands Starting Trek from Site for Stuyvesant Town." *New York Times*, March 3, 1945.

Crane, David A. "Chandigarh Reconsidered." *Journal of the American Institute of Architects* 33 (May 1960): 32–39.

Crane, David A. "The City Symbolic." *Journal of the American Institute of Planners* 26, no. 4 (1960): 280–292.

Crane, David A. "The Dynamic City." *Architectural Design* 30, no. 4 (1960): 158–162.

Crane, David A. "The Public Art of City Building." *Annals of the American Academy of Political and Social Science 352* (March 1964): 84–94.

Cullen, Gordon. *Townscape.* New York: Reinhold, 1961.

Custine, Astolphe de. *Letters from Russia.* Ed. Anka Muhstein. New York: New York Review Books, 2002.

Cuthbert, Alexander. "Whose Urban Design?" *Journal of Urban Design* 15 (2010): 443–448.

Dallas, City of, Department of Urban Planning. *Visual Form of Dallas.* Dallas: City of Dallas Department of City Planning, ca. 1974.

David A. Crane Associates. Lysander New Community drawings (uncatalogued). Architectural Archive, University of Pennsylvania.

De Monchaux, Thomas. "This Is the Time when Beautiful Girls . . . ." In Timothy Mennel, Jo Steffens, and Christopher Klemek, eds., *Block by Block: Jane Jacobs and the Future of New York*, 19–21. New York: Princeton Architectural Press, 2007.

Des Cars, Jean, and Pierre Pinon. *Paris Haussmann: Une nouvelle géométrie pour la ville.* Paris: Editions Picard, 1991.

Doyle, Rachel B. "36 Hours in Ljubljana, Slovenia." *New York Times,* November 15, 2012.

Duany, Andrés. "The Garden City: A General Theory of Urbanism." Lecture, MIT Center for Advanced Urbanism, Cambridge, MA, March 10, 2014.

Duany, Andrés, and Elizabeth Plater-Zyberk. *Towns and Town-Making Principles.* New York: Rizzoli, 2006.

Duffy, Stella. "Celebrating Joan Littlewood: It's Time to Build Her Fun Palaces." *Guardian,* September 18, 2013.

El-Dahdah, Farès. *Lucio Costa, Brasilia's Superquadra*. New York: Prestel, 2005.

Etherington, Rose. "Le Corbusier's Cabanon—the Interior 1:1." *Dezeen,* March 6, 2009. http://www .dezeen.com/2009/03/06/le-corbusier%E2%80%99s-cabanon-the-interior-11/.

Fabricius, Daniela. "Resisting Representation: The Informal Geographies of Rio de Janeiro," *Harvard Design Magazine* 28 (Spring/Summer 2008).

Fainstein, Susan S., et al. *Restructuring the City: The Political Economy of Urban Redevelopment*. New York: Longman, 1986.

Ferrier, Jean-Louis. *Art of Our Century: The Chronicle of Western Art, 1900 to the Present*. New York: Prentice-Hall, 1988.

Fessenden, Ford, Tom Giratikanon, Josh Keller, Archie Tse, Tim Wallace, Derek Watkins, Jeremy White, and Karen Yourish. "The Bloomberg Years: Reshaping New York." *New York Times*, August 18, 2013.

Foard, Ashley A., and Hilbert Fefferman. "Federal Urban Renewal Legislation." In *Urban Renewal: The Record and Controversy*, ed. James Q. Wilson. Cambridge, MA: MIT Press, 1966.

Freemark, Yonah. "The Entrepreneurial State: New York's Urban Development Corporation, an Experiment to Take Charge of Affordable Housing Production, 1968–1975." Master's thesis, MIT, 2013. DSpace@MIT. http://dspace.mit.edu/handle/1721.1/79198.

Fuller, Thomas. "Confusion with Slovakia Prompts New Flag: Slovenia's Identity Crisis." *New York Times*, April 17, 2004.

Gandy, Matthew. "Learning from Lagos." *New Left Review* 33 (May–June 2005): 37–52.

Geist, Sidney. *Brancusi/The Kiss*. New York: Harper and Row, 1978.

Gimenez, Carmen, and Matthew Gale. *Constantin Brancusi: The Essence of Things*. London: Tate, 2004.

Girnius, Rima M., and Emily T. Cooperman. "Crane, David A. (1927–2005)." American Architects and Buildings. http://www.philadelphiabuildings.org/pab/app/ar_display.cfm/19001.

Glaeser, Edward L. "Preservation Follies." *City Journal*, Spring 2010. http://www.city-journal.org/2010/20_2_preservation-follies.html.

Godlewski, Joseph. "Alien and Distant: Rem Koolhaas on Film in Lagos, Nigeria." *Traditional Dwellings and Settlements Review* 21, no. 2 (2010): 7–19.

Goldberger, Paul. "Twin Parks, an Effort to Alter the Pattern." *New York Times*, December 27, 1973.

Goldsmith, S. A., and L. Elizabeth, eds. *What We See: Advancing the Observations of Jane Jacobs*. New York: New Village Press, 2010.

Goodman, Robert. *After the Planners*. New York: Simon and Schuster, 1972.

Gosling, David, and Maria-Cristina Gosling. *The Evolution of American Urban Design: A Chronological Anthology*. London: Wiley, 2003.

Gosling, David, and Barry Maitland. *Concepts of Urban Design*. New York: St. Martin's Press, 1984.

Habraken, N. J. *The Structure of the Ordinary: The Form and Control of the Built Environment*. Cambridge, MA: MIT Press, 1998.

Habraken, N. J. *Supports: An Alternative to Mass Housing*. New York: Praeger, 1972.

Hall, Peter. *Cities of Tomorrow: An Intellectual History of Urban Planning and Design in the Twentieth Century.* 3rd ed. Oxford: Blackwell, 2002.

Hall, Peter, Harry Gracey, Roy Drewett, and Ray Thomas. *The Containment of Urban England.* London: Allen and Unwin for PEP, 1973.

Harvard University, Graduate School of Design. "The Origins and Evolution of 'Urban Design,' 1956–2006." Special issue, *Harvard Design Magazine* 24 (Spring/Summer 2006).

Harvard University, Graduate School of Design. "Urban Design Now." *Harvard Design Magazine* 25 (Fall 2006/Winter 2007).

Harvard University, Graduate School of Design. "The Vision of Manuel de Solà-Morales: Roots for a Twenty First Century Urbanism." Conference pamphlet, Harvard University, Graduate School of Design, October 10, 2013.

Heckscher, August, and Phyllis Robinson. *Open Spaces: The Life of American Cities.* New York: Harper and Row, 1977.

Hedman, Richard, and Andrew Jaszewski. *The Fundamentals of Urban Design.* Washington, DC: APA Planners Press, 1984.

Hertweck, Florian, and Sébastien Marot, eds. *The City in the City: Berlin, a Green Archipelago.* Critical ed. Zurich: Lars Müller, 2013.

Hilberseimer, Ludwig. *Metropolisarchitecture and Selected Essays.* Trans. and ed. Richard Anderson. New York: GSAPP Books, 2012.

Hilberseimer, Ludwig. *The Nature of Cities.* Chicago: P. Theobald, 1965.

Hirt, Sonia, and Diane Zahm, eds. *The Urban Wisdom of Jane Jacobs.* New York: Routledge, 2012.

Howard, Ebenezer. *Garden Cities of To-Morrow.* London: Faber and Faber, 1946.

Hubbard, Bill. *American Boundaries: The Nation, the States, the Rectangular Survey.* Chicago: University of Chicago Press, 2009.

Hunt, D. Bradford. *Blueprint for Disaster: The Unraveling of Chicago Public Housing.* Chicago: University of Chicago Press, 2009.

Huxtable, Ada Louise. "Architecture: 6 Designs Win Bard Merit Awards." *New York Times,* June 14, 1973.

Jacobs, Allan B. *Great Streets.* Cambridge, MA: MIT Press, 1993.

Jacobs, Allan B. *Looking at Cities.* Cambridge, MA: Harvard University Press, 1985.

Jacobs, Jane. *Cities and the Wealth of Nations.* New York: Random House, 1984.

Jacobs, Jane. *The Death and Life of Great American Cities.* New York: Random House, 1961.

Jacobs, Jane. *The Economy of Cities.* New York: Random House, 1969.

Joanne, Adolphe. *Le guide "parisien."* Paris: Librairie L. Hachette, 1863.

Kahn, Nathaniel. *My Architect: A Son's Journey. Louis Kahn Project, Inc.* Mediaworks, 2003.

Kelbaugh, D., and R. Mehrotra, eds. *Post-Urbanism: Michigan Debates on Urbanism.* Ann Arbor: University of Michigan, 2006.

Kilgannon, Corey. "Change Blurs Memories in a Famous Suburb." *New York Times,* October 13, 2007.

King, Bart. *An Architectural Guidebook to Portland*. Salt Lake City: Gibbs-Smith Publisher, 2001.

Kinkead, Eugene. *Central Park 1857–1995: The Birth, Decline, and Renewal of a National Treasure*. New York: Norton, 1990.

Knowles, Clayton. "Governor Speaks on Bronx Housing." *New York Times*, October 1, 1970.

Knowles, S. G., ed. *Imagining Philadelphia*. Philadelphia: University of Pennsylvania Press, 2009.

Koolhaas, Rem. "Bigness, or the Problem of Large." In Rem Koolhaas and Bruce Mau, *S,M,L,XL,* ed. Jennifer Sigler, 509–516. New York: Monacelli Press, 1995.

Koolhaas, Rem. "Cronocaos." *Log* 21 (Winter 2011): 119–123.

Koolhaas, Rem. *Delirious New York: A Retroactive Manifesto for Manhattan*. New York: Oxford University Press, 1978.

Koolhaas, Rem. "The Generic City." In Rem Koolhaas and Bruce Mau, *S,M,L,XL,* ed. Jennifer Sigler, 1239–1264. New York: Monacelli Press, 1995.

Koolhaas, Rem. "Junkspace." *October* 100 (Spring 2003): 175–190.

Koolhaas, Rem. "What Ever Happened to Urbanism?" In Rem Koolhaas and Bruce Mau, *S,M,L,XL,* ed. Jennifer Sigler, 958–971. New York: Monacelli Press, 1995.

Koolhaas, Rem, et al. *Mutations*. Barcelona: ACTAR, 2000.

Koolhaas, Rem, and Bruce Mau. *S,M,L,XL*. Ed. Jennifer Sigler. New York: Monacelli Press, 1998.

Kostov, Spiro. *The City Shaped: Urban Patterns and Meaning through History*. Boston: Little, Brown, 1991.

Krečič, Peter. *Plečnik, the Complete Works*. New York: Whitney Library of Design, 1993.

Krieger, Alex, and William S. Saunders, eds. *Urban Design*. Minneapolis: University of Minnesota Press, 2009.

Lambert, Phyllis, ed. *Mies in America*. Montreal: Canadian Centre for Architecture, 2001.

Larson, Scott. *Building Like Moses with Jacobs in Mind*. Philadelphia: Temple University Press, 2013.

Lee, Tunney. "Remarks on David Crane at Crane's Death, 2005." Unpublished manuscript in the author's possession, provided to author by Tunney Lee, 2015.

Ljubljana Office of Tourism. *Plečnik Ljubljana* [Map]. Ljubljana: CGP Delo, 1986.

Los Angeles Department of City Planning. *The Visual Environment of Los Angeles*. Los Angeles: Department of City Planning, 1971.

Loyer, François. *Paris Nineteenth Century: Architecture and Urbanism*. New York: Abbeville Press, 1988.

Luthi, Sonja, and Marc Schwarz. *De Drager / A Film about Architect John Habraken*. Vimeo video, 1:00:44. Posted by "schwarzpictures.com," March 9, 2013. https://vimeo.com/61410893.

Lynch, Kevin. "City Design and City Appearance." In *City Sense and City Design: Writings and Projects of Kevin Lynch*, ed. Tridib Banerjee and Michael Southworth, 465–497. Cambridge, MA: MIT Press, 1990.

Lynch, Kevin. "City Design: What It Is and How It Might Be Taught." In *City Sense and City Design: Writings and Projects of Kevin Lynch*, ed. Tridib Banerjee and Michael Southworth, 652–660. Cambridge, MA: MIT Press, 1990.

Lynch, Kevin. *City Sense and City Design: Writings and Projects of Kevin Lynch*. Ed. Tridib Banerjee and Michael Southworth. Cambridge, MA: MIT Press, 1990.

Lynch, Kevin. "Controlling the Flow of Rebuilding and Replanning in Residential Areas." Undergraduate thesis, MIT, 1947. DSpace@MIT. http://hdl.handle.net/1721.1/12525.

Lynch, Kevin. *A Theory of Good City Form*. Cambridge, MA: MIT Press, 1981.

Lynch, Kevin. *The Image of the City*. Cambridge, MA: MIT Press, 1960.

Lynch, Kevin. "The Immature Arts of City Design." In *City Sense and City Design: Writings and Projects of Kevin Lynch*, ed. Tridib Banerjee and Michael Southworth, 498–510. Cambridge, MA: MIT Press, 1990.

Lynch, Kevin. *Managing the Sense of a Region*. Cambridge, MA: MIT Press, 1976.

Lynch, Kevin. "The Pattern of the Metropolis." *Dædalus* 90, no. 1 (1961): 79–98.

Lynch, Kevin. "Reconsidering the Image of the City." In *City Sense and City Design: Writings and Projects of Kevin Lynch*, ed. Tridib Banerjee and Michael Southworth, 247–256. Cambridge, MA: MIT Press, 1990.

Lynch, Kevin. *Visual Analysis: Community Renewal Program*. Brookline, MA: Brookline Board of Selectmen, 1965.

Lynch, Kevin. *Wasting Away*. Ed. Michael Southworth. San Francisco: Sierra Club Books, 1990.

Lynch, Kevin. *What Time Is This Place?* Cambridge, MA: MIT Press, 1972.

Lynch, Kevin, and Donald Appleyard. *Temporary Paradise? A Look at the Special Landscape of the San Diego Region*. San Diego: San Diego City Planning Department, 1974.

Lynch, Kevin, with Sasaki, Dawson & Demay Associates. *Looking at the Vineyard: A Visual Study for a Changing Island*. West Tisbury, MA: Vineyard Open Land Foundation, 1973.

Maki, Fumihiko. "Investigations in Collective Form." Unpublished manuscript, School of Architecture, Washington University, 1964.

Maki, Fumihiko. "Maki's Hillside Terrace," *Architecture Week*, April 6, 2011. http://www.architectureweek.com/2011/0406/culture_1-1.html.

Dennis McClendon, *The Plan of Chicago: A Regional Legacy*. Chicago: Burnham Plan Centennial Committee and Chicago Metropolis 2020, 2008.

McHarg, Ian L. *Design with Nature*. Garden City, NY: Natural History Press, 1969.

Meier, Richard. *Building the Getty*. New York: Knopf, 1997.

Meier, Richard. *Richard Meier: Architect*. New York: Rizzoli, 1984.

Miller, Sandra. *Constantin Brancusi: A Survey of His Work*. Oxford: Clarendon Press, 1995.

Mogilevich, Mariana. "Designing the Urban: Space and Politics in Lindsay's New York." PhD diss., Harvard University, 2012. ProQuest (3514389).

Monmarche, Marcel. *Les Guides Bleus: Roumanie, Bulgarie, Turquie*. Paris: Librairie Hachette, 1933.

Morris, Anthony E. J. *History of Urban Form: Before the Industrial Revolutions*. New York: Wiley, 1994.

Mostafavi, Mohsen, and David Leatherbarrow. *On Weathering: The Life of Buildings in Time*. Cambridge, MA: MIT Press, 1993.

Moudon, Anne Vernez. *Built for Change: Neighborhood Architecture in San Francisco*. Cambridge, MA: MIT Press, 1986.

Mumford, Lewis. "The Sky Line: Mother Jacobs' Home Remedies." *New Yorker*, December 1, 1962, 148–179.

Mydans, Seth. "Getty Center's Design Is Unveiled." *New York Times*, October 10, 1991.

Nairn, Ian. *The American Landscape: A Critical View*. New York: Random House Press, 1965.

Newton, Richard. "Reclaiming Sacred Space." In Ernest Beck, ed., *Brancusi's Endless Column Ensemble: Târgu Jiu, Romania*, 54–63. London: Scala, 2007.

New York, City of, Department of City Planning. *Zoning Handbook,* 2011 *Edition*. New York: Department of City Planning, 2011.

New York City Housing and Development Administration. "Twin Parks West [I], Twin Parks East [I A&B] Community Development Plan." In "Designing the Urban: Space and Politics in Lindsay's New York," by Mariana Mogilevich, PhD diss., Harvard University, 2012. ProQuest (3514389).

New York City Housing Authority. "NYCHA Housing Developments: Morrisania Air Rights." https://www1.nyc.gov/assets/planning/download/pdf/plans-studies/sustainable-communities/bmn/bronx_metro_report/full_report.pdf

New York Times. "City View on Bronx Housing Plan Explained." February 12, 1977.

New York Times. "Excerpts from Panuch Report to Wagner on Need for New Housing Board." March 10, 1960.

Olsen, Donald J. *The City as a Work of Art*. New Haven: Yale University Press, 1988.

Olsen, Donald J. *Town Planning in London: The Eighteenth and Nineteenth Centuries*. New Haven: Yale University Press, 1982.

Parigoris, Alexandra. "Brancusi and His Return to Romania." In Ernest Beck, ed., *Brancusi's Endless Column Ensemble: Târgu Jiu, Romania*. London: Scala Publishers, 2007.

Pickney, David H. *Napoleon III and the Rebuilding of Paris*. Princeton: Princeton University Press, 1958.

Portland, City of. Urban Design Guidelines. https://www.portlandoregon.gov/bps/34250.

Portland Chapter, American Institute of Architects. *Visual Survey of Portland*. Portland, OR: Portland Chapter, 1971.

Prelovšek, Damjan. *Jože Plečnik, 1872–1952: Architecturea Perennis*. New Haven: Yale University Press, 1997.

Press Association. "Green Belt Housing 'Doubles in a Year.'" *Guardian,* August 25, 2013. http://www.theguardian.com/society/2013/aug/25/green-belt-housing-doubles-claim.

Providence, City of, Department of Planning and Development. "Parcel and Zoning Map." http://gis.providenceplanning.org/PVD_Parcel_ZoningMap.

Putin, Vladimir. "Meeting on Expanding Moscow's Border." Kremlin, Official Internet Resources oAf the President of Russia. Novo-Ogaryovo, Moscow Region, August 14, 2012. http://en.kremlin.ru/news/4296.

Radu, Mihai. "Urban Redevelopment and a Visionary New Visitor Center." In Ernest Beck, ed., *Brancusi's Endless Column Ensemble: Târgu Jiu, Romania*. London: Scala Publishers, 2007.

Ragot, Gilles. "Le Corbusier's Cité Frugès in Pessac: A Paradoxical Appropriation." In Mary Corbin Sies and Robert Freestone, eds., *Iconic Planned Communities*. Philadelphia: University of Pennsylvania Press, 2015.

Rasmussen, Steen Eiler. *London: The Unique City*. Cambridge, MA: MIT Press, 1988.

Reps, John William. *Cities of the American West: A History of Frontier Urban Planning*. Princeton: Princeton University Press, 1979.

Reps, John William. *The Making of Urban America: A History of City Planning in the United States*. Princeton: Princeton University Press, 1965.

Rosenzweig, Roy, and Elizabeth Blackmar. *The Park and the People: A History of Central Park*. Ithaca: Cornell University Press, 1998.

Roughgarden, Jonathan, Robert M. May, and Simon A. Levin, eds. *Perspectives in Ecological Theory*. Princeton: Princeton University Press, 1989.

Rowe, Colin, and Fred Koetter. *Collage City*. Cambridge, MA: MIT Press, 1978.

Rowe, Peter G. *Civic Realism*. Cambridge, MA: MIT Press, 1997.

Rowe, Peter G. *Modernity and Housing*. Cambridge, MA: MIT Press, 1993.

Ryan, Brent D. *Design after Decline: How America Rebuilds Shrinking Cities*. Philadelphia: University of Pennsylvania Press, 2012.

Ryan, Brent D. "Incomplete and Incremental Plan Implementation in Downtown Providence, Rhode Island, 1960–2000." *Journal of Planning History* 5, no. 1 (2006): 35–64.

Ryan, Brent D. "The Restructuring of Detroit: City Block Form Change in a Shrinking City, 1900–2000." *Urban Design International* 13, no. 3 (2008): 156–168.

Schulze, Franz, and Edward Windhorst. *Mies van der Rohe: A Critical Biography*, rev. ed. Chicago: University of Chicago Press, 2012.

Schweiterman, Joseph P., Alan P. Mammoser, and John A. Schuter. *Beyond Burnham: An Illustrated History of Planning for the Chicago Region*. Lake Forest, IL: Lake Forest College Press, 2009.

Scott Brown, Denise. *Urban Concepts*. New York: St. Martin's Press, 1990.

Scott Brown, Denise. "Urban Design at Fifty: A Personal View." In Alex Krieger and William S. Saunders, eds., *Urban Design*, 61–87. Minneapolis: University of Minnesota Press, 2009.

Scully, Vincent, *American Architecture and Urbanism*. New York: Henry Holt, 1988.

Scully, Vincent, "Preface." In *Pasanella + Klein: Public and Private Interventions in the Residential Field,* by Alessandra Latour. Rome: Edizioni Kappa, 1983.

Sennott, R. Stephen, ed. *Encyclopedia of Twentieth Century Architecture*. New York: Taylor & Francis, 2004.

Sertich, Adriana Navarro. "Medellín: 'Social Urbanism,'" *FAVELissues* (blog), February 1, 2010. http://favelissues.com/2010/02/01/medellin-%E2%80%9Csocial-urbanism%E2%80%9D/.

Severo, Richard. "Bronx Buildings Novel in Design." *New York Times*, August 8, 1971.

Slapeta, Vladimir. "Jože Plečnik and Prague." In François Burkhardt, Claude Eveno, and Boris Podrecca, eds., *Jože Plečnik, Architect, 1872–1957*, trans. Carol Volk, 82–92. Cambridge, MA: MIT Press, 1989.

Smets, Marcel. "Insights I Gained from Manuel." In "The Vision of Manuel de Solà-Morales: Roots for a Twenty First Century Urbanism." Conference pamphlet, Harvard University, Graduate School of Design, Cambridge, MA, October 10, 2013.

Smets, Marcel. *Melding Town and Track: The Railway Area Project at Leuven*. Ghent, Belgium: Ludion, 2002.

Solà-Morales i Rubió, Manuel de. *Ten Lessons on Barcelona: Urbanistic Episodes that Have Made the Modern City*. Barcelona: Colegio de Arquitectos de Cataluña, 2008.

Solà-Morales i Rubió, Manuel de, et al. *Cerdà/Ensanche*. Barcelona: Escola Tècnica Superior d'Arquitectura de Barcelona, 2010.

Solà-Morales i Rubió, Manuel de, et al. *A Matter of Things*. Rotterdam: NAi, 2008.

Sorkin, Michael. "The End(s) of Urban Design." In Alex Krieger and William S. Saunders, eds., *Urban Design*, 155–182. Minneapolis: University of Minnesota Press, 2009.

Southworth, Michael, and Eran Ben-Joseph. *Streets and the Shaping of Towns and Cities*. Washington, DC: Island Press, 2003.

Spertus, Juliette, and Susanne Schindler. "A Few Days in the Bronx: From Co-op City to Twin Parks." *Urban Omnibus*, July 25, 2012. http://urbanomnibus.net/2012/07/a-few-days-in-the-bronx-from-co-op-city-to-twin-parks.

Spertus, Juliette, and Susanne Schindler. "The Landscape of Housing: Twin Parks Northwest 40 Years On." *Urban Omnibus*, November 6, 2013. http://urbanomnibus.net/2013/11/the-landscape-of-housing-twin-parks-northwest-40-years-on/.

Sprague, Paul E. *Guide to Frank Lloyd Wright and Prairie School Architecture in Oak Park*. Oak Park, IL: Oak Park Bicentennial Commission of the American Revolution, 1976.

Spreiregen, Paul D. *Urban Design: The Architecture of Towns and Cities*. New York: McGraw-Hill, 1965.

Steinberg, Harris. "Philadelphia in the Year 2059." In Scott Gabriel Knowles, ed., *Imagining Philadelphia: Edmund Bacon and the Future of the City*, 112–144. Philadelphia: University of Pennsylvania Press, 2009.

Stern, Robert A. M., David Fishman, and Jacob Tilove. *Paradise Planned: The Garden Suburb and the Modern City*. New York: Monacelli Press, 2013.

Stern, Robert A. M., Thomas Mellins, and David Fishman. *New York 1960: Architecture and Urbanism between the Second World War and the Bicentennial*. New York: Monacelli Press, 1995.

Strickland, R., ed. *Post Urbanism and Reurbanism: Peter Eisenman vs. Barbara Littenberg and Steven Peterson, Designs for Ground Zero. Michigan Debates on Urbanism 3*. Ann Arbor: University of Michigan, 2006.

Tocqueville, Alexis de. *Democracy in America*. Trans. and ed. Harvey C. Mansfield and Delba Winthrop. Chicago: University of Chicago Press, 2000.

Tóibín, Colm. *The Sign of the Cross: Travels in Catholic Europe*. New York: Pantheon Press, 1994.

Toronto, City of. Urban Design Guidelines. http://www1.toronto.ca/wps/portal/contentonly?vgnextoid=3e6652cc66061410VgnVCM10000071d60f89RCRD.

Tucker, William. "The Legacy of Târgu Jiu." In Ernest Beck, ed., *Brancusi's Endless Column Ensemble: Târgu Jiu, Romania*. London: Scala Publishers, 2007.

Ungers, Oswald Mathias, and Stefan Vieths. *Oswald Mathias Ungers: The Dialectic City*. Trans. Francisca Garvie, ed. Luca Molinari. Milan: Skira, 1997.

United Nations Human Development Programme. "Human Development Data (1980–2015)." Human Development Reports. http://hdr.undp.org/en/statistics/.

Urban Design Associates. *The Urban Design Handbook: Techniques and Working Methods*. Ed. Karen Levine. New York: Norton, 2003.

Urban Design Council of the City of New York. *Housing Quality Guidelines: Housing Quality, a Program for Zoning Reform*. New York: Urban Design Council of City of New York, 1975.

Vale, Lawrence. *Architecture, Power, and National Identity*. New Haven: Yale University Press, 1992.

Vancouver, City of. Urban Design Guidelines. http://vancouver.ca/home-property-development/land-use-and-development-policies-and-guidelines.aspx.

Varia, Radu. *Brancusi*. New York: Rizzoli International, 1986.

Venturi, Robert. *Complexity and Contradiction in Architecture*. New York: Museum of Modern Art, 1966.

Venturi, Robert, Denise Scott Brown, and Steven Izenour. *Learning from Las Vegas: The Forgotten Symbolism of Architectural Form*. Rev. ed. Cambridge, MA: MIT Press, 1977.

Volovich, Nikolai, and Evgeniya Nikitina. "The Conflicts between the Systems of Public and Private Land Law in Russia." In Erwin Hepperle, Robert Dixon-Gough, Vida Maliene, Reinfried Mansberger, Jenny Paulsson, and Andrea Pödör, eds., *Land Management: Potential, Problems and Stumbling Blocks*, 195–209. Zurich: VDF, 2013.

Weston, Richard. *Villa Mairea, Alvar Aalto*. London: Phaidon, 1992.

White, Norval, and Elliot Willensky. *AIA Guide to New York City*. New York: Collier Books, 1978.

White, Norval, Elliot Willensky, and Fran Leadon. *AIA Guide to New York City*. Oxford: Oxford University Press, 2010.

Whyte, William H. *City: Rediscovering the Center*. New York: Doubleday, 1988.

Whyte, William H. *The Social Life of Small Urban Spaces*. Washington, DC: Conservation Foundation, 1980.

Wiebenson, Dora. *Tony Garnier: The Cité Industrielle*. New York: George Braziller, 1969.

Wiles, Colin. "Build on the Green Belt to Solve London's Housing Crisis." *Guardian*, October 25, 2013. http://www.theguardian.com/housing-network/2013/oct/25/green-belt-london-boris-johnson.

Wilson, Thomas, and Patrick Shay. "Oglethorpe and Savannah." *Planning Magazine*, March 2014.

Zukin, Sharon. *Naked City: The Death and Life of Authentic Urban Places*. New York: Oxford University Press, 2010.

Illustration Credits

1.1 *Plan de la ville de 6 million d'Habitants*, Le Corbusier. © FLC/ARS, 2016.

1.2 *Peabody Terrace Apartments—Harvard University, Cambridge, Massachusetts, USA* by Daderot/ CC0 1.0.

1.3 *The "Corbusierhaus" in Berlin (Unité d'Habitation, type Berlin). Built for an International exhibition (Interbau) in 1957. Architect: Le Corbusier.* By Manfred Bruckels/ CC-BY-SA 3.0.

1.4 *Mrs. Jane Jacobs, chairman of the Comm. to save the West Village holds up documentary evidence at press conference at Lions Head Restaurant at Hudson & Charles Sts* / World Telegram & Sun photo by Phil Stanziola. 1961 November 28. New York Telegram and the Sun Newspaper Photograph Collection, Library of Congress.

1.5 *Visions of Seaside: Foundation, Evolution, Imagination, Built & Unbuilt Architecture* by Dhiru A. Thadani (Rizzoli, 2013). Courtesy of Dhiru A. Thadani.

1.6 Elia Zenghelis, Zoe Zenghelis, *Hotel Sphinx Project, New York, New York, Axonometric.* 1975–76. Collection of the Museum of Modern Art.

1.7 *Construction view. China Central Television Headquarters, Beijing, China.* Harvard University Visual Information Access.

1.8 Photograph by author.

1.9 Photograph by author.

1.10 Photograph of Medellín, Colombia by Lorena Bello Gomez, 2015. Courtesy of Lorena Bello Gomez.

1.11 Cedric Price, *The Fun Palace at Lea River site.* Photomontage, 1961. Centre Canadien d'Architecture/ Canadian Centre for Architecture.

3.5 Originally published in *Brancusi: A Survey of His Work*, by Sandra Miller (Oxford: Oxford University Press, 1995).

3.6 Originally published in *Brancusi: A Survey of His Work*, by Sandra Miller (Oxford: Oxford University Press, 1995).

3.7 Originally published in *Brancusi*, by Radu Varia (New York: Rizzoli, 1986). Any copyright holder should contact publisher.

3.8 Courtesy of Mihai Radu Architects.

3.9 *Architectural Record.*

3.10 *Twin Parks Study*, Urban Design Group, City of New York, 1967.

3.11 *Architectural Record.*

3.12 Courtesy of University of Pennsylvania School of Design.

3.13 Courtesy Richard Meier & Partners Architects.

3.14 Ennead.

3.15 Photo courtesy of PKSB Architects.

3.16 Photo courtesy of PKSB Architects.

3.17 © Richard Langendorf/ CC BY-NC 3.0.

3.18 Courtesy of Damjan Prelovšek.

3.19 Photograph by Daniel Campo, 2015. Courtesy of Daniel Campo.

3.20 Courtesy of Damjan Prelovšek.

3.21 Photographs by author, 1998.

3.22 Courtesy of Plečnik House.

3.23 Courtesy of Plečnik House.

3.24 Courtesy of Plečnik House.

4.1 Architectural Archives, School of Design, University of Pennsylvania.

4.2 Courtesy of University of Pennsylvania School of Design.

4.3 Courtesy of University of Pennsylvania School of Design.

4.4 Courtesy of University of Pennsylvania School of Design.

4.5 1965/75 General Plan for the City of Boston.

4.6 Boston Redevelopment Authority.

4.7 Architectural Archives, School of Design, University of Pennsylvania.

4.8 Architectural Archives, School of Design, University of Pennsylvania.

4.9 Architectural Archives, School of Design, University of Pennsylvania.

4.10 Architectural Archives, School of Design, University of Pennsylvania.

4.11 Zentrum Paul Klee, Bern.

4.12 Courtesy of the Bacon family.

4.13 Courtesy of the Bacon family.

4.14 Courtesy of the Bacon family.

4.15 Citizens Council on City Planning, *Philadelphia Old and New, Annual Report 1959–1960*.

4.16 Citizens Council on City Planning, *Philadelphia Old and New, Annual Report 1959–1960*.

4.17 *Society Hill*. Photograph by G. E. Kidder Smith. © Massachusetts Institute of Technology.

4.18 Courtesy of the Bacon family.

4.19 Courtesy of David Lynch and the Lynch family.

4.20 Photograph by Mark B. Sluder. Courtesy of David Lynch and the Lynch family.

4.21 Kevin Lynch, *The Image of the City* (Cambridge, MA: MIT Press, 1960).

4.22 Kevin Lynch, "The Pattern of the Metropolis," *Daedalus* 90:1 (Winter 1961), pp.79–98. © American Academy of Arts and Sciences, published by the MIT Press.

4.23 Dallas Department of Urban Planning, *Visual Form of Dallas* (City of Dallas, n.d., c. 1975).

4.24 Kevin Lynch, *Visual Analysis, Community Renewal Program, Brookline, MA* (Town of Brookline, 1965).

4.25 Vineyard Open Land Foundation, *Looking at the Vineyard* (Edgartown, 1974).

4.26 Donald Appleyard and Kevin Lynch for the City of San Diego, *Temporary Paradise?* (City of San Diego, 1974).

5.1–5.17 Illustrations by the author and Allison Hu, 2016.

6.1 Frederic Edwin Church, *Niagara Falls, from the American Side*, 1867.

6.2 *Chicago. Bird's-eye view, showing the location of the city on the shores of Lake Michigan, together with the smaller surrounding towns connected with Chicago by radiating arteries*. Painted for the Commercial Club by Jules Guerin. From *Plan of Chicago*, by Daniel H. Burnham and Edward D. Bennett, 1909.

6.3 *Chicago. Plan of the Proposed Group of Municipal Buildings or Civic Center, at the Intersection of Congress and Halsted Streets*. From *Plan of Chicago*, by Daniel H. Burnham and Edward D. Bennett, 1909.

6.4 *Instant City Visits Bournemouth*, by Peter Cook. Archigram Archive.

6.5 Photograph courtesy of Marcel Smets.

6.6 Photograph courtesy of Marcel Smets.

6.7 *Levittown, New York*. Julie Campoli, author, and Alex MacLean, photographer, ca. 2007. Harvard University Visual Information Access.

6.8 *Tour Montparnasse seen from Arc de Triomphe*, by Vlasenko. CC-BY-SA 3.0.

6.9 Originally published in *Open Space: The Life of American Cities*, by August Heckscher, Phyllis Robinson, and Dick Fledderus (New York: Harper and Row, 1977).

6.10 Tim Catchpole, *London Skylines: A Study of High Buildings and Views* (London: London Research Centre, Reviews and Studies Series number 33, 1987).

6.11 Illustration by the author and Allison Hu, 2016.

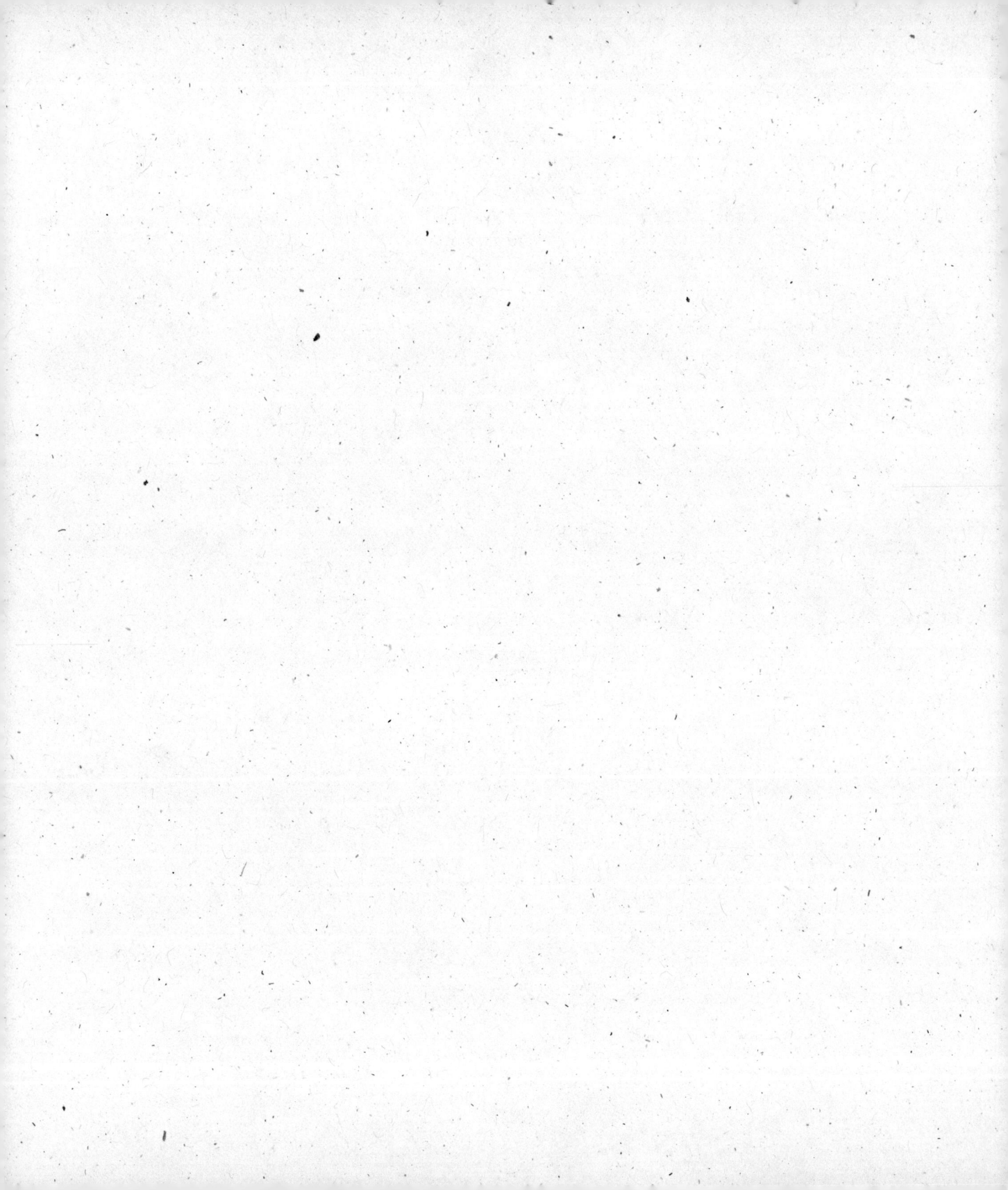